LOCAL ATTACHMENTS

LOCAL ATTACHMENTS

THE PROVINCE OF POETRY

FIONA STAFFORD

OXFORD
UNIVERSITY PRESS

OXFORD
UNIVERSITY PRESS

Great Clarendon Street, Oxford OX2 6DP

Oxford University Press is a department of the University of Oxford.
It furthers the University's objective of excellence in research, scholarship,
and education by publishing worldwide in

Oxford   New York

Auckland Cape Town Dar es Salaam Hong Kong Karachi
Kuala Lumpur Madrid Melbourne Mexico City Nairobi
New Delhi Shanghai Taipei Toronto

With offices in

Argentina Austria Brazil Chile Czech Republic France Greece
Guatemala Hungary Italy Japan Poland Portugal Singapore
South Korea Switzerland Thailand Turkey Ukraine Vietnam

Oxford is a registered trade mark of Oxford University Press
in the UK and in certain other countries

Published in the United States
by Oxford University Press Inc., New York

© Fiona Stafford 2010

The moral rights of the author have been asserted
Database right Oxford University Press (maker)

First published 2010

British Library Cataloguing in Publication Data
Data available
Library of Congress Cataloging in Publication Data
Data available

Typeset by SPI Publisher Services, Pondicherry, India
Printed in Great Britain
on acid-free paper by
MPG Biddles, Bodmin and King's Lynn

ISBN 978-0-19-955816-2

1 3 5 7 9 10 8 6 4 2

Acknowledgements

Small sections of this book have already appeared in other publications. Parts of Chapter 1 were included in 'Local Attachments', *Archipelago*, 2 (2008); a section of Chapter 4 was published as 'Writing on the Borders', in Claire Lamont and Michael Rossington (eds.), *Romanticism's Debatable Lands* (Basingstoke, 2005). Thanks are due, accordingly, to Andrew McNeillie of Clutag Press, to Claire Lamont and Michael Rossington. Material from chapter 4 is reproduced with permission from Palgrave Macmillan.

I would also like to thank the following friends and colleagues for various kinds of help and encouragement in connection with this book: Ben Brice, Gerard Carruthers, Jeff Cowton, Robert Crawford, David Duff, Mina Gorji, Stephen Gill, Richard Gravil, Catherine Jones, John Kirk, Kirsteen McCue, Liam McIlvanney, Lucy Newlyn, Andrew Noble, Meiko O'Halloran, Murray Pittock, George Watson. My family has been, as ever, a constant support. To Andrew McNeillie, Jacqueline Baker, Ariane Petit, and all those at Oxford University Press who contributed to the publication of this book, I am also deeply indebted.

The staff at the following libraries have also been unfailingly helpful: the British Library; the Bodleian Library; the Burns Cottage Museum, Alloway; the English Faculty Library, Oxford; the Jerwood Centre at the Wordsworth Trust, Grasmere; Somerville College Library. I am grateful, too, to the English Faculty in Oxford and to Somerville College for their support for various trips made in connection with the research for this book.

Contents

Introduction

Part I: The Place of Poetry

The place of poetry was eloquently addressed by Seamus Heaney, when he accepted the Nobel Prize for Literature in 1995. For Heaney, the question of poetry's role in the modern world is inseparable from its origins in a particular culture and environment. To consider the place of poetry, it is therefore necessary to understand the poetry of place. This does not mean that the only worthwhile poetry deals with landscape or adopts a pastoral mode, but rather that true poetry is conditioned by its original location, wherever that may be. 'Crediting Poetry', the Nobel Lecture that he included in his own volume of collected poems, *Opened Ground*, makes very bracing claims for the vital importance of cultural traditions to the maintenance of a healthy political state. As he connected poetry to politics, Heaney was also paying a personal tribute as an Irish poet to his predecessor, W. B. Yeats, who had won the Nobel Prize in 1923, just after the Irish Civil War. At the heart of his lecture is a summary of Yeats's purpose, seventy years before: 'He came to Sweden to tell the world that the local work of poets and dramatists had been as important to the transformation of his native place and time as the ambushes of guerrilla armies.'[1] It is an astonishing claim for the role of poetry in the real world—not as an art reflecting the things that matter, but as an active power every bit as vital to a country as political or military forces.

If Heaney's tribute to Yeats seems to suggest a validation of poetry through nationalism, however, his argument is, in fact, more subtle and inclusive altogether. His admiration for local poetry arises not from any claims it might seem to be making for the superiority of Ireland, but rather from its perceived capacity to travel across the divisions of politics. Far from endorsing nationalism, true poetry can sometimes moderate its more dangerous tendencies and act as a redemptive force in societies whose need is especially great.

Though dealing with very ambitious cultural questions, the published lecture also conjures up a speaker acutely conscious of his immediate audience and surroundings. Heaney presented himself, not as an authoritative voice uttering transcendent truths, but, in more Wordsworthian style, as 'a man speaking to men'. The invitation to the Swedish capital had prompted personal recollections, and so the Nobel laureate began by inviting his audience to share his own early memories of sitting on the family sofa in the Derry farmhouse during the Second World War, listening to the wireless and making out the name 'Stockholm' on the dial.[2] For a poet whose own work has always drawn heavily on childhood experience, the anecdotal opening is both natural and appropriate; it is also characteristic of Heaney in its capacity to carry more meaning than may be immediately apparent. The image of the evening at home recalls a host of poems and prose pieces deriving from family memories, while the powerful chiaroscuro that highlights an intimate domestic scene against a dark background is recurrent in his writing. Central to the scene is the wireless, symbolizing the way in which language can travel and connect people in distant countries and cultures. At the same time, the child beside it, straining to pick up words from far beyond the family sitting room, suggests the process of literary development, which begins in a loving, familiar environment and yet responds with excitement to the unknown and newly discovered. By the end of the lecture, the effort to distinguish between the bewildering sounds of the wireless has also become an image for the way in which certain poems emerge from the vast mass of existing speech and writing by embodying truths recognizable from their special cadence and form. These are the redemptive poems, whose place in the world is self-evident, if not always immediately understood, and sometimes wilfully obscured.

At the heart of Heaney's lecture is a celebration of local truth. And, although it may seem surprising that he should choose the significance of local work as his theme for such an international audience, he is really demonstrating the paradoxical power of creative work to be both local and universal. As he told a 'story out of

Ireland'—that of St Kevin, who knelt for days with his hands outstretched while the blackbirds hatched eggs, nursed their nestlings, and eventually flew away—he presented an image of writing that was at once 'equal to *and* true'.³ St Kevin's story was local not in the sense of having its meaning restricted to those familiar with Glendalough, but rather because it embodied an utterly convincing truth to life. It was rooted in something recognizable.

In his own poem on the story, Heaney describes the life-affirming effect on Kevin of feeling a bird in his hands: 'finding himself linked | Into the network of eternal life', the saint is 'moved to pity' and must

> hold his hand
> Like a branch out in the sun and rain for weeks
> Until the young are hatched.⁴

In an instant, the isolated man in his cell is revealed to be an integral part of the larger, organic unity of the world, connected by his feelings—emotional, physical, spiritual. It is as if the bird's arrival makes him complete in himself and therefore able to participate in a greater wholeness. Like the Ancient Mariner, surprised into blessing by the unexpected beauty of the water snakes, Kevin is moved by something outside himself, which alights by accident and releases his dormant love and regenerative powers. Suddenly he sees that his hand is 'like a branch'.

The larger truth embodied in the local detail enables the story to move in the same way that the blackbird does, startling solitary readers into recognizing the possibility of connection. The poem avoids sentimentality by acknowledging Kevin's physical hardship, forcing readers to imagine the extreme cold of his motionless vigil, the frightening paralysis of his limbs. Although the lyric conveys the experience of divine revelation, it remains firmly in touch with the world that we can all recognize: this is a real man, suffering the same pains as any other. As the numbness spreads through his body, however, it also becomes a metaphor for the way in which any individual labour may gradually transcend its original circumstances. For, in the process of reaching out to others, which his outspread arms symbolize so emphatically, 'he has forgotten self, forgotten bird, | And on the riverbank forgotten the river's name'.

Heaney's admiration for St Kevin is not just that of a writer for a legend that works perfectly on its own terms, nor a reflection of partisan pride in County Wicklow. St Kevin is a local hero whose story is very well made, but he also stands as a symbol of hope for the entire human race. The courageous and yet tender truth embodied in the image of St Kevin has the power to speak to people who have never been to Ireland, know nothing of the Catholic faith, and would not be able to identify a blackbird. Anyone can be moved by the thought of the humble man, 'Alone and mirrored clear in love's deep river', but the story's persuasiveness is dependent partly on its specifics—the particular Irish setting, the words chosen to embody the truth, the order and rhythm of their arrangement. To underline the point, Heaney described his own emotion during a recent visit to Sparta on seeing an ancient Greek carving of Orpheus and a bird, both enchanted by music, and labelled centuries later as a 'Votive panel possibly set up to Orpheus by local poet. Local work of the Hellenistic period.'[5] For Heaney, the modestly described artefact was a kind of clear mirror in which he could see his own life's work. Though its origins lay far from County Wicklow, it represented the same faith in the network of eternal life and in each creative artist's essential contribution. The quality of conviction was assured by both its unassuming character and its connection to a particular place, or, as Heaney put it more succinctly, 'its trustworthiness and its travel-worthiness have to do with its local setting'.[6]

The anecdotal account of his accidental discovery and the subsequent revelation of its larger meaning is itself a confirmation of Heaney's point. The unexpected corroboration of home truths in a Greek museum demonstrates both the visitor's pleasure in finding connections and the power of a local creation to speak to those from elsewhere. If work deemed 'local' might be greeted by condescension or neglect in some quarters, it emerges here triumphantly as the very kernel of aesthetic value. The assumptions that underpin the terms 'local news' or 'local radio', implying a somewhat limited audience or a lower standard of journalism, are effectively being overturned by a poet who not only celebrates local connection, but makes it central to the existence of true poetry. Unlike Matthew Arnold, who criticized the 'provincial spirit' because of its tendency to exaggerate 'the value of its ideas for want of a high standard at

hand by which to try them', Heaney was elevating the idea of the
'local' as the touchstone for the best kind of art.[7]

Heaney's attitude to the local, though expressed with greater
humility, is indebted to Patrick Kavanagh, whose poetry, when
encountered during his time as a student at Queen's, had brought the
younger writer's 'arts-degreed generation' back to their roots— and
their senses.[8] Kavanagh's poems, and his clearly articulated distinc-
tion between the 'provincial' and the 'parochial', offered a welcome
justification to the modern writer who found inspiration close to
home.[9] For, while the 'provincial' outlook might suggest a sense of
underlying inferiority to somewhere widely regarded as the cultural
'centre', the 'parochial' mentality was in no doubt about the impor-
tance of its own sphere, and the centrality of the writer within. His
very definition, however, reflects an awareness of metropolitan
prejudices, of Beckettian discomfort with rural Irishness, and ulti-
mately of Arnoldian contempt for the provincial mentality with its lack
of 'urbanity', 'lucidity', and graciousness', in contrast to the civilized
qualities possessed by the 'large and centrally placed intelligence'.[10]

In his well-known sonnet, wittily entitled 'Epic', Kavanagh
explored the conflicting imaginative attractions of local and interna-
tional convulsions. The poem explicitly poses the question: 'Which
was more important?'—the dispute between the Duffys and the
McCabes, or 'the Munich bother'?[11] But, just as public events appear
to be winning, Homer's ghost makes a timely appearance: 'I made
the Iliad from such | A local row. Gods make their own importance.'
Heaney found corroboration for his lyric poetry in the Spartan
museum, and, so too, Kavanagh's understanding of the 'parochial
mentality' was as indebted to Ancient Greece as to Ballyrush and
Gortin. His poem, as Heaney observed, is 'more in praise of Kavan-
agh's idea of Homer than in praise of Kavanagh's home'.[12] Affirma-
tion of local work depends, paradoxically, on encounters that take
place far from home, as writers find themselves in the clear mirror of
other people's art. Confidence in the long familiar is very often a
reward for the returning traveller or the comfort of one far from
home; it is when a place has become part of the internal landscape
that it provides the richest foundation for art.

The struggle against metropolitan prejudices is not exclusive to
Irish poets of the twentieth century, of course. Thomas Hardy was
emphatic in his opposition to Arnold: 'A certain provincialism of

feeling is invaluable,' he observed, when reflecting on his own achievements; 'it is of the essence of individuality, and is largely made up of that crude enthusiasm without which no great thoughts are thought, no great deeds done'.[13] When he defended his Wessex novels against charges of provincial limitation, Hardy too turned to classical Greece to argue that the greatest dramatists had found room enough for their remarkable action in an area 'not much larger than the half-dozen counties' that formed his own artistic stage.[14] The decision to place characters within a specific region of south-west England was nothing to do with ignorance of the wider world, but represented a considered choice, based on the belief that confined space made human action all the more powerful. In *The Woodlanders*, he made explicit the connection between small, isolated communities and explosive emotions, as he introduced the sequestered village of Little Hintock, 'where, from time to time, dramas of a grandeur and unity truly Sophoclean are enacted in the real, by virtue of the concentrated passions and closely-knit interdependence of the lives therein'.[15]

Arnold's disdain for the provincial writer's tendency to work on the blood and passions rather than the spirit and intellect seemed decidedly unhelpful where the aim was to recreate the profound emotions of Greek tragedy. Hardy was convinced that human passions had 'throbbed in Wessex nooks with as much intensity as in the palaces of Europe' and accordingly grappled with the modern novel in order to develop a form suitable for such powerful local dramas.[16] As he was at pains to explain, his rural characters 'were meant to be typically and essentially those of any and every place...beings in whose hearts and minds that which is apparently local should be really universal'.[17] It was only by being faithful to the world he knew so well, however, that he could create work of such ambition: like Kavanagh and Heaney, Hardy knew that local truth was the way to reach audiences distant in time and space. For, just as Kavanagh and Heaney were to turn to Ancient Greece to understand their own creative endeavours, so Hardy saw in his Wessex novels affinities with the work of classical dramatists. The notion of classical models representing local work was, however, entirely at odds with Arnold's influential ideas about what constituted Hellenism, and strikingly different from the neoclassical conceptions of earlier critics, for whom the very idea of 'local detail' suggested transitoriness and limitation.[18] Hardy's view that the local should really be universal was nevertheless drawing on earlier models, as we shall see, and paving the way for later twentieth-century writers.

For Heaney's Nobel Lecture is concerned with both the intrinsic value and the reach of creative work. The place of poetry has as much to do with its varied destinations as with its nesting grounds. If the test of good writing is that it should be 'equal to *and* true', however, the conditions of the twentieth century have proved especially challenging for art. The likelihood of creating any art equal to a world in which the instruments of power are tanks and machine guns must at times seem doubtful. 'Crediting Poetry' refers explicitly to the menaces of Nazism, Stalinism, and sectarianism, but still insists that local traditions strong enough to remain unshaken even by the most terrifying inducements to ideological conformity are vital resources of survival. Heaney's apparently modest local theme rapidly turns into a most ambitious claim for the redemptive power of literature and its essential contribution to the future of civilization. As the argument develops, the simple Irish folk tale emerges as a carrier of 'cultural values' and 'psychological resistances' sufficiently powerful to withstand even a totalitarian regime. If Ancient Greece can provide a reassuring parallel for the modern writer, the real place of his work is thrown into relief by urgent contemporary threats.

Political upheavals often accentuate the value of cultural continuity and provoke a countering reverence for things that seem to offer hope through their own quiet stability. The well-documented appeal of Jane Austen's novels to wartime readers and the widely felt sense that they offer some 'new hope' of better times to come is an obvious testament to this aspect of her work.[19] One of her earliest admirers was her younger brother Charles, who read *Emma* three times during his slow voyage home from a disastrous mission in which the ship he commanded had been wrecked in the eastern Mediterranean.[20] Austen's brothers had to face the prospect of violent death on an almost daily basis for long periods of their naval careers, but their sister's response to a lifetime of international turbulence was to focus intensely on crafting perfectly formed works of art. As Paul Fussell observed in his thoughtful consideration of the persistence of pastoral during trench warfare, 'if the opposite of war is peace, the opposite of experiencing moments of war is proposing moments of pastoral'.[21] The experience of violence often seems to intensify appreciation of the vulnerable, as Paul Nash found when he returned home to draw English landscapes after active service in France: 'I see so much more now; everywhere I see form and beauty in a thousand, thousand diversities.'[22]

Heaney's own awareness of form and beauty, like his faith in the staying power of local work, has been fostered similarly through the Troubles and deepened by the threat of destruction. His admiration for writers such as Osip Mandelstam, who was almost silenced by direct experience of political oppression and yet continued to create things of beauty, has also helped to cement a belief in the power of poetry even when its place seems most doubtful. Heaney is only too aware of the personal benefits of writing poetry in the midst of violent disruption, as his powerful account of Wordsworth's 'symbolic resolution of a lived conflict' in *The Prelude* demonstrates, but his concern is wider than that of the individual well-being of the poet.[23] In the face of civil unrest or imminent invasion, thoughts of any creative endeavour that has continued successfully in spite of the dire circumstances are heartening to all those afflicted by fear and uncertainty.

Heaney's long-standing admiration for the Greek poet George Seferis, for example, was founded on the realization that, for Seferis, poetry was 'an adequate response to conditions in the world at a moment when the world was in crisis and Greece *in extremis*'.[24] Through the inspiring example of Seferis and other writers working in times of crisis, Heaney found corroboration for his own faith that poetry could be 'an answer'.[25] The works of art that emerge in spite of tyranny embody a spirit of resistance and inner clarity, even when their own form seems most fragile.

Recognition of local value finds passionate expression in Simone Weil's book *The Need for Roots*, which was written during the Second World War, when she worked for the Free French Government in exile in London. Her personal discovery of the 'reality' of France was a direct result of the Nazi occupation and the ensuing atmosphere of 'anguish, solitude, confusion, uprootedness', in which the traditions of different regions suddenly seemed 'worth preserving, like treasures of infinite value and rarity, worth tending like the most delicate plants'.[26] For Weil, the very survival of her people seemed dependent on local loyalties, which lived on in the art, poetry, and distinct cultural traditions. It is a kind of startled patriotism, revealed by the threat of annihilation, which 'bears a close resemblance to the feelings which his young children, his aged parents, or a beloved wife inspire in a man'.[27] Her very emphasis on the 'purity' of such patriotic emotion, however, is the corollary of an acute awareness of the less admirable aspects of national feeling, and the danger of local culture being harnessed in disastrous ways.

The catastrophic effects of excessive nationalism have never been more apparent than in 1940, and register indirectly in every line of *The Need for Roots*. As she celebrated French traditions, Weil distinguished carefully between two different kinds of patriotic feeling: one involving ideas of international triumph; the other giving rise to tenderness for 'some beautiful, precious, fragile and perishable object'.[28] The patriot had a choice between admiring France for her glorious role in world history and loving her as 'something, which being earthly, can be destroyed, and is all the more precious on that account'. Love of the kind displayed by St Kevin when he cradled the blackbirds was, for Weil, the only appropriate feeling, and so her essay is a call for compassion. Like Heaney, she also saw that any local feeling sufficient to counter political oppression would never be confined to the original locale: 'this same compassion is able, without hindrance, to cross frontiers, extend itself over all countries in misfortune, over all countries without exception, for all peoples are subjected to the wretchedness of our human condition.'[29] The compassion that transfigures suffering might be the basis for local attachment, but it was also resistant to national boundaries and capable of forming lasting connections.

The vulnerability that elicited this compassionate patriotism, however, was a direct consequence of the other, more aggressive manifestation. Ideally, reverence for the local leads to a protective loving kindness, but it is only too easy to recall examples of native tradition being pressed into the cause of exclusion or persecution. Love of the familiar can go hand in hand with contempt for the unknown, while unfamiliar traditions provoke alarm or disdain. The less positive aspects of local pride can easily be manipulated by power-hungry leaders, the symbols of cultural distinction can be the targets of aggressive regimes. Even nationalisms that begin in a spirit of self-preservation and proper defensiveness against oppression can turn into a new exclusiveness or even xenophobia. If the indigenous becomes the goal rather than a starting point, local art is in danger of seeming divisive or oppressive, and one man's patriotism becomes another's tyranny.

The dangers associated with turning local work into some sort of membership badge are only too evident to Heaney, with his background in a community deeply divided and highly attuned to the signals of difference. His poetry is alert to both the menacing sound of 'Orange Drums' ('like giant tumours') and the bands of 'hard-mouthed Ribbonmen'.[30] In 'Crediting Poetry', he acknowledges the proper fear of 'elevating the cultural forms and conservatisms of any nation into normative and exclusivist systems', a warning reminiscent of Richard Kearney's observations on the power of local myths to incarcerate as well as to emancipate.[31] The same local traditions that prompt feelings of protectiveness may in some circumstances provide communities 'with a straight-jacket of fixed identity', so that their preservation tends to extinguish rather than facilitate dialogue with others.[32] In places where even Christian names function as sectarian labels, local culture can provide the means to exclude those perceived to have a different history, religion, or political purpose. George Watson has written thoughtfully of his own complicated experience of growing up in a Catholic family in the predominantly Protestant town of Portadown in Northern Ireland, where his name 'signaled sure-fire Prod, or if not, somebody whose blood did not flow the pure green, white, gold of the Republic'.[33] For Watson, cultural protectionism, with its divisive codes, was dangerous, not just because it polarized neighbours into hostile camps, but also because of its tendency to limit the potential fullness of an individual or an entire community to a single, reductive label.

Ireland offers numerous examples of communal traditions stirring feelings that prove ultimately neither tender nor compassionate, of local history that leads to hostility. In his study of the role played by the Gaelic past in nineteenth-century Ireland, Joep Leerssen wrote of the 'ringing patriotism' of the late eighteenth century, but added ominously: 'nationalism had not yet arrived on the scene, like an occupying army to commandeer those bells, and recast them into cannons.'[34] The line between tender patriotism and aggressive nationalism can be a thin one, and so reluctance to celebrate local culture may sometimes reflect fear of its potential power rather than scepticism over its wider relevance.

Such anxieties, though understandable, can nevertheless bring dangers of their own, by denying the more positive aspects of local attachments. It is partly in answer to this kind of 'ancestral dread' and the fear of nationalism's tendency towards ideological extremes that Heaney makes his eloquent plea for local culture.[35] The Nobel lecture urges faith in 'the possibility of a world where respect for the validity of every tradition will issue in the creation and maintenance of a salubrious political space'.[36] Far from being reclusive or exclusive, the poet who writes from his own home is a figure of international significance, contributing to the foundation of a better future. Though writing in a different context from Weil, Heaney shares her horror of regimes that restrict free thought and creative independence. Stalinist repression of local traditions is as threatening to individual freedom as the fascist elevation of national culture, because both demand the imposition of an ideology from above. The life-giving work of local artists, on the other hand, grows unshowily from the ground, quiet, unobtrusive, but ultimately strong enough to resist the distortions of an invasive regime, and sufficiently mobile to reach out to those who can respond sympathetically. The very continuity of local work can seem the embodiment of freedom and truth, and is thus able to provide a symbol of hope for people everywhere. The poetry of inner freedom, so admired by Heaney, is not a poetry of retreat or exclusion, but rather a kind of art most capable of reaching out to audiences at home and abroad.

Heaney's ideal for poetry is premised on a belief that the best art is travel-worthy, but this does not imply that art is the same throughout the world. His very recognition of the value of the local, the particular, and the distinct may have been heightened by a growing awareness of globalization, which has facilitated both easy international communication and the growth of a somewhat homogenized consumer culture. The World Wide Web opens up far greater possibilities to children in the twenty-first century than the radio at Mossbawn offered to the young Heaney, but, in the face of so much potential communication, there is perhaps an even greater need for memorable, sustaining forms through which distinctive, truthful voices can be heard.

Adequate Poetry

When Heaney insisted on the redemptive qualities of poetry, he was not just referring to its subject matter or imagery. The meaning of a poem, and its attendant power to affect an audience, is embodied in its form and cadences—'the energy released by linguistic fission and fusion'.[37] The language was carefully chosen for the Nobel audience, and was part of Heaney's affirmation of literature's centrality in the modern world, alongside science, politics, and peace. Indeed, the claims made for his art are of a kind rarely encountered since the Romantic period, when Wordsworth could announce without qualification that 'Poetry is the breath and finer spirit of all knowledge'.[38] Wordsworth's faith in the poet as 'the rock of defence of human nature; an upholder and preserver, carrying every where with him relationship and love', is very similar to the idea of poetry credited by Heaney in his lecture. Wordsworth, too, famously emphasized the importance of local inspiration and recognized that poetry's ability to carry 'relationship and love' depended on embodying a truthful response to the world as it is. These are the qualities that also mark the poetry of Wordsworth, who stands as 'proof that poetry can be equal to *and* true at the same time'.[39] In Heaney's eyes, Wordsworth, Yeats, and Mandelstam were all kindred spirits, because they succeeded in producing 'completely adequate poetry' at corresponding moments of 'historical crisis and personal dismay'.[40]

The 'adequacy' of poetry may owe something to Arnold's emphasis on the necessary union between 'a great epoch and a great literature', which led him to questions over the greatness of Lucretius ('Yes, Lucretius is modern, but is he adequate?') or to reservations about Heine ('not an adequate interpreter of the modern world').[41] Where Arnold envisaged cultural excellence within the peaceful stability of a great civilization, however, Heaney regards adequate poetry as an achievement of those caught in more turbulent times. Truly adequate poetry, for Heaney, must be strong enough to measure up to periods of violent struggle, to have a self-delighting quality that cannot be cowed by contemporary destruction. It is a way of understanding poetry that has grown through years of experiencing, not only the Troubles of his native Ireland, but also the demand by his contemporary critics for an 'adequate response' to the situation.[42] The very act of writing poetry at a time when others are being shot is sometimes subject to charges of political evasion or irresponsibility, as evident in some of the more anxious, soul-searching of Heaney's early volumes. As his work developed, however, so did his mature ideas about poetry, which are at once gentle and quietly combative.

In a lecture delivered in Grasmere in 1984 at the invitation of the Wordsworth Trust, Heaney explicitly rejected the separation of poems from politics, observing that 'poetry may be exercising in its inaudible way a fierce disdain of the activist's message, or a distressed sympathy with it'.[43] In the following decade, the defiant character of pure art became fundamental to his conviction that true poetry had a vital role to play in the world, especially at times of crisis. Adequate poetry offers the promise of survival through its own intricate structure of careful stresses and consoling sounds: the very delicacy of poetic form is the secret of its strength.

Heaney's definition of the 'adequacy' of poetry combines lyrical satisfaction with clear-sighted understanding of a world in which pain and suffering *almost* predominate. Although he refers explicitly to Mandelstam's resilient faith in 'the steadfastness of speech articulation', his language in 'Crediting Poetry' continues to evoke Wordsworth, who had himself written of the poet's 'adequate notion of the dignity of his art'.[44] Mandelstam's own emphasis on the connection between the revival of hope and the 'steadfastness' of language is strongly reminiscent of Wordsworth's writings, but it is Heaney's allusive admiration for 'the resolution and independence which the entirely realized poem sponsors' that specifically calls Wordsworth to mind. For 'Resolution and Independence' not only traces the paralysing progress of self-doubt, but also answers these anxieties resoundingly. The hardship endured so calmly by Wordsworth's Leech Gatherer is reminiscent of St Kevin's long vigil, while his cheerfulness and perseverance in the face of dwindling success display a similar faith in the greater order of things. In answer to the young man's misplaced despondency—'the fear that kills; | The hope that is unwilling to be fed;'—the older figure emerges

> like a Man from some far region sent;
> To give me human strength, and strong admonishment.[45]

He is an image of complete adequacy, and his significance is immortalized in the beautifully paced longer line that closes the stanza.

Wordsworth's poem is local work, in the sense that its inspiration came from a real encounter with an old man, a few hundred yards from Dove Cottage, and from recollections of a real walk 'over Barton Fell from Mr Clarkson's at the foot of Ullswater, towards Askam'.[46] It is as rooted in the Lake District as St Kevin's prayer is in

Glendalough, and has just the same capacity to transfigure closely observed human experience into a tale of universal significance. Like Kevin, too, the Leech Gatherer roaming from pond to pond seems vitally connected to his surroundings, but, as he enters the consciousness of the poem, local detail partakes of an elemental quality, accessible to readers everywhere. He is described successively as like 'a huge Stone', a 'Sea-beast', a 'Cloud', and someone from a 'Dream': his wandering not only connects the different parts of the landscape, but also dissolves the barriers between self and other, and between the inner mind and the external world. His impact on the speaker is described directly, but his diligent pursuit also evokes the larger suffering of a world in which sickness and death are all around. Leeches are not the most obvious subject for poetry, but Wordsworth's poem overturns conventional attitudes, rebuking readers as well as the speaker, and reminding us of the primary meaning of 'leech'—a healer. By the end of the poem, the Leech Gatherer has emerged as a symbol of patience, humility, and hope, labouring for the good of others irrespective of personal reward. Though physically vulnerable, he is in fact possessed of the firmest mind.

Poetry, too, may seem fragile in the face of a hostile world, but it has similar resilience and durability. The figure of the Leech Gatherer recalls the ideal presented in the expanded preface to *Lyrical Ballads*, which Wordsworth wrote within months of 'Resolution and Independence'. He is an 'upholder and preserver, carrying everywhere with him relationship and love', and his work is thus oddly akin to the creation of poetry. Like the poet, his success depends, not on self-aggrandising thoughts of the Mighty Dead, but rather on attentive observation of what might be hidden under his very eyes. The salutary distinction between love of glory and true compassion is as pertinent for the poet as it is for the patriot. But the extra challenge for the poet, of course, is that of measuring up to the ideal through the creation of verse. How to make a poem that is completely 'adequate', in Heaney's terms—that recognizes the world as it is, but still responds with the promise of something better?

Heaney's focus on Yeats's 'Meditation in Time of Civil War', with its lyrical invitation to the honeybees, 'Come build in the empty house of the stare', demonstrates the power of poetry to acknowledge brutal destruction and yet affirm hope in new life. The invitation to 'build' is striking, not just because it dares to confront violence with something as delicate as a bird's nest, however, but because of the perfect rhythm of the line, and its insistent repetition through four distressing stanzas on the Civil War. If the poem offers the possibility that there is 'More substance in our enmities | Than in our love', it also answers these darker thoughts with a refrain built from cadences far more powerful. What makes Yeats's lyric such a fine example of the 'necessary poetry' that Heaney is attempting to define is 'the sheer in-placeness of the whole poem as a given form within language'.[47] The work of the honeybees and the starlings provides the natural counterpart of the poem, representing, not just sustenance and care, but also structural beauty. The circle of the woven nest, the hexagonal chambers of the honeycomb, all recall the beauty of eternal forms and thus offer their defiance of destruction simply through being. It is the adequacy of a form at once self-sufficient and yet designed to nurture and sustain—and hence the invitation to further creative endeavour—'Come build in the empty house of the stare'.

For the place of poetry is not just a question of literature's importance to the world at large, nor of its original truth, but is secured, primarily, by its own special form. The capacity to awaken sympathetic feelings in a reader may depend on a writer's response to certain circumstances, but, unless the acoustics ring true, the poem will fail to convince.[48] Local work does not derive power simply from an artist's first-hand knowledge of a particular landscape. As Heaney observed many years ago, 'I began as a poet when my roots crossed with my reading'.[49] In order to create work that will respond adequately to the challenge of their own place and moment, writers and artists need models and practice, to perfect their individual skills. The poet and artist David Jones, whose admiration for his own countryside was, like many of his generation, heightened by the experience of the First World War, still emphasized the paramount importance of artistic form and tradition. Though deeply moved by a particular part of Wales, he was quite clear that 'a feeling for some especially beloved *patria*—this hill, that sea-coast or whatever it may be, will not, in *itself*, be of avail to the artist *qua* artist'.[50] Unless he had the expertise to re-create feeling in a form that could speak to others, then the emotional response to the local, however powerful, would not result in art that mattered. Indeed, the primary response to 'this hill, that sea-coast, or whatever' is itself conditioned by earlier writers and artists, whose work has opened up ways of seeing and expressing the best response.

When Wordsworth reflected on his own purpose in life in *The Prelude*, he admitted to hoping that a work of his might prove 'Enduring and creative, might become | A power like one of Nature's'.[51] The idea that his verse should possess lasting value, and even be equal to the creative processes of the natural world, suggests the same kind of aspiration as that voiced by Heaney in 'Crediting Poetry' and the same faith in the redemptive power of art. Like Heaney, Wordsworth also acknowledged his grateful sense of participation in both the eternal network of life, and in the reassuring fellowship of poets, 'Each with each | Connected in a mighty scheme of truth' (*The Prelude*, xiii. 301–2). Although stressing that each poet has his own individual power, 'By which he is enabled to perceive | Something unseen before', Wordsworth's long poem to his friend Coleridge demonstrates that his poetic self-belief was confirmed by the recognition of like minds and exemplary creative work. Wordsworth expressed deep gratitude for the nurturing qualities of the surrounding landscape, but his ability to build 'a work that should endure' (xiii. 278) was dependent on the corroboration of other writers, past and present. His grateful sense of local attachment emerged in tandem with a recognition of literary attachments. The vital connections between an individual and a particular place could find permanent form only through the poet's connection with other poets.

Even when Wordsworth celebrated the pleasure of unmediated interactions with the natural world most passionately, the very expression of powerful, physical experience was still indebted to earlier writing. In 'Lines Written a Few Miles above Tintern Abbey', he described his attachment to the natural world:

> Therefore am I still
> A lover of the meadows and the woods,
> And mountains; and of all that we behold
> From this green earth; of all the mighty world
> Of eye and ear, both what they half-create,
> And what perceive; well pleased to recognize
> In nature and the language of the sense,
> The anchor of my purest thoughts, the nurse,

The guide, the guardian of my heart, and soul
Of all my moral being.   (ll. 103–12).

As he re-created his vivid personal response to the landscape, his choice of blank verse and allusive language was recalling Coleridge's 'Frost at Midnight', Cowper's *The Task*, Young's *Night Thoughts*, and Milton's *Paradise Lost*.[52] The 'language' of the sense could be exalted only because of Wordsworth's familiarity with a congenial literary tradition: poems are just as much a part of the 'mighty world | Of eye and ear', and the individual poet will always be a half-creator and perceiver, an heir as much as a benefactor.

Heaney has written movingly on the psychological recovery experienced by Mandelstam, when he visited Armenia after years of creative paralysis in Soviet Russia:

All of his old trust in the resources of language, his identification with the clarity and classical aura of the Mediterranean, his rejoicing in the Hellenic nature of the Russian inheritance, the ebullient philological certitude of his essay 'On the Nature of the Word'—all this was revived by his physical encounter with the Armenian language and landscape.[53]

What Heaney marvels at is the reviving powers of language and landscape—and the ensuing restoration of hope and creativity. In his account, poetry's redemptive capacity in a brutal world is dependent both on particular places and on the continuity of their cultural traditions. New work gains strength from earlier poems and from their truth to a recognizable world, but, as it comes into being, it creates its own independent place. In an earlier essay on Mandelstam, Heaney drew attention to the absolute quality of his poetry, writing with obvious sympathy that 'Everything—the Russian earth, the European literary tradition, the Stalin terror—had to cohere in an act of the poetic voice'.[54] In 'Tintern Abbey', Wordsworth is similarly concerned with the spiritual revival that attends the return to a familiar place, but when he refers to nature as 'the anchor' of his thoughts, 'the nurse, the guide, the guardian' of his heart, he is also talking about literature. Without poetry, he could neither articulate his own gratitude, nor present it as a guide and guardian to others. The place was a vital catalyst to creation, but the poem also possessed its own 'in-placeness'.

Years later, he looked back on the period of creative renewal celebrated in 'Tintern Abbey' and acknowledged his personal debts to

Burns and Cowper, whose work had rescued him from damaging influences at a key moment of his personal development. The 'simplicity', 'truth', and 'vigour' of Burns and the 'sympathies of Cowper' were dwelt on with gratitude, as the mature poet reflected on the way in which his own natural tendencies had been endangered by the 'dazzling manner of Darwin' and the 'extravagance' of contemporary German writers.[55] Wordsworth's reflections were presented as 'a warning to youthful Poets, who are in danger of being carried away by the inundation of foreign Literature', and revealed his long-standing commitment to a kind of poetry that is equal to and true. Local work—or what Wordsworth might term 'native poetry'—was as necessary as nature for anchoring the poet in the real world. The writer who understood this had a responsibility to pass on his discovery and thus ensure the healthy continuity of adequate poetic traditions.

When Heaney described poetic form in 'Crediting Poetry' as 'both the ship and the anchor', he was surely recalling 'Tintern Abbey', where nature is described as an 'anchor' for the young poet, and 'Michael', where the same Christian symbol of hope is offered as a vital source of stability to the potentially wayward youth.[56] But he may also have had John Keats in mind, for, when Keats was searching for proper poetic form and personal direction in the disorienting expanses of the Scottish mountains, he too recalled the reassuring Wordsworthian anchor:

> No, no that horror cannot be, for at the cable's length
> Man feels the gentle anchor pull and gladdens in its strength.[57]

If Wordsworth had felt himself saved by Burns, Keats was in turn rescued by memories of Wordsworth. The anchor is a symbol of hope and connection, keeping the poet attached to the ground, and to other poets. This is why Heaney, a poet so concerned with the earth, takes it as a metaphor for poetic form, and why it figures so memorably in his own work.

In his 1991 collection *Seeing Things*, Heaney retold another story out of Ireland, which describes the medieval monks at prayer in Clonmacnoise, when suddenly 'a ship appeared above them in the air'. As the anchor caught on their altar, one of the men climbed down to untangle it and had to be helped by the monks before he drowned. At once, the ship sailed on,

And the man climbed back
Out of the marvellous as he had known it.[58]

Heaney's anchor is not only a sign of hope and connection, a link between the mundane and the spiritual; it also conveys the surprise of poetry. For what appears calamitous from one perspective turns out to be marvellous. The tug of the anchor is not just a means of connecting to the like-minded, but also a way to discovering unexpected new truths, of prompting wonder. Its very action reminds us of buoyancy as well as security, and of the free, self-sufficiency of the lyric form. This is the 'mood of buoyancy' that Heaney admired in Kavanagh's later poetry, and has also identified as crucial to the transfiguration of local work into the universal: the 'liberated moment, when the lyric discovers its buoyant completion'.[59] The anchor is a vital image of connection, but also enables the thrill of release—as the 'freed ship' sails away.

Heaney's poem demands a reassessment of conventional assumptions about the world, but is still reliant on its local detail, tight form, and unelevated language. The old story is recounted simply, in four unrhymed triplets, which convey complete conviction. This is how it was. Through its clear form, the short poem succeeds in matching up to Heaney's own definition of necessary poetry—it touches 'the base of our sympathetic nature while taking in at the same time the unsympathetic reality of the world to which that nature is constantly exposed'.[60] The stranger from the ship is in danger of drowning, but he does not because the monks are moved by a predicament that speaks directly to their own experience. His anchor disrupts their customary behaviour, and they are surprised into compassion. In freeing him, they are freeing themselves by finding their own fears misplaced and their familiar surroundings transfigured. For both the stranger from the flying ship, and the monks at prayer, the moment is an encounter with the marvellous, and, since Heaney's skills with language and rhythm are so accomplished, the poem offers a similar experience of wonder to its readers. Like 'Resolution and Independence', the poem startles readers into sympathy and proves as travel-worthy as it is trustworthy.

The 'anchor' of poetry offers stability to the individual poet, not through the reassuring longevity of lyric form alone, nor merely through attachment to a recognizable world. Its hope also resides in the capacity to make surprising connections, and to reveal common bonds in unlikely places. Rather than fixing a poet in a cultural tradition that might eventually prove constricting, the anchor of poetry catches at the unexpected, and enables art to reveal its surprising affinities in ways that expand imaginative horizons. Poetry, possessing its own energy and sense of direction, has the ability to right itself and float independently of more conventional modes of understanding. Like the freed ship, with its anchor on board, lyric poetry has the power to cross established boundaries of space and time, and to link sympathetic writers in very different periods and places.

Part II: The Discovery of Local Truth

The resilient and resistant qualities of 'local work', which Heaney celebrated in 'Crediting Poetry', first became fully apparent to writers during the Romantic period. The phenomenal success of Robert Burns demonstrated that poems rooted firmly in an identifiable region might present an invigorating challenge to neoclassical assumptions about the nature and purpose of literature. For Wordsworth, intense celebration of a particular area of Britain was part of a complicated psychological, religious, and political response to a period of international crisis. At the same time, the development from the first edition of *Lyrical Ballads* of 1798 to the larger, 1800 collection, with its series of carefully located 'Poems on the Naming of the Places' and Lake District pastorals, was also symptomatic of a wide-scale, collective shift towards a new understanding of the importance of local work. In the same year that the newly grounded collection of *Lyrical Ballads* appeared, Maria Edgeworth published *Castle Rackrent*, an unassuming text that nevertheless established the fiction of 'particular locality' as an important form for the nineteenth century.[61] Suddenly, parallel claims were being made for 'a plain unvarnished tale' about 'Irish squires' and for the 'ungarnish'd' story of a Grasmere shepherd—both insistently local and both being presented for the benefit of audiences far from the places to which the tales belonged.[62] The tone of 'Michael' could hardly be more different from Edgeworth's satirical mock-memoir, but both texts are indicative of a new willingness to enter imaginatively into the lives of those whose homes were remote from the contemporary centres of power.

Wordsworth's new compositions were neither formal, loco-descriptive poems of the kind made fashionable in the early eighteenth century by Denham's *Cooper's Hill* and Pope's *Windsor Forest*, nor picturesque scenes set off by carefully grouped peasants in accordance with the later landscape theories of William Gilpin. Instead, Wordsworth was exploring the personal, emotional charge of particular places, attempting to understand the deep, hidden narratives associated with habitual experience of an area and developing a kind of adequate poetry that was at once equal to this task *and* to readers elsewhere. The poems created by Burns and Wordsworth were not 'local' in the sense of having meaning only for those living in the areas where they were set, but represented a kind of art whose truthfulness was universally recognizable. As Heaney has emphasized, and this book attempts to demonstrate, the vital significance of local attachment for art arises from truth's need for strong foundations, not with any restriction of scope or audience. His very emphasis on local truth is, however, indebted to the eighteenth-century transformation of aesthetic and moral attitudes, which paved the way to the poetry of the Romantic period.

In his great *Life of Johnson*, published in 1791, four years after the Kilmarnock edition of Burns's *Poems, Chiefly in the Scottish Dialect*, James Boswell recorded Johnson's observation that 'the value of every story depends on its being true'.[63] Johnson went on to add that a story 'is a picture either of an individual or of human nature in general: if it be false, it is a picture of nothing'. Never mind the traditional emphasis on the power of literature to delight and to teach: what mattered was an intrinsic truthfulness. As Leo Damrosch has pointed out in a penetrating essay on the 'great cultural shift from ontology to epistemology' during the eighteenth century, literary judgements of this kind reflected new, post-Lockean empiricist attitudes to the arts.[64] The preoccupation with literary truth was part of the far-reaching psychological readjustment demanded by new philosophical doubts over whether any truth could be apprehended by any human being with any degree of certainty. Once Descartes had begun to question his own existence, nothing could ever be taken for granted again—especially in Britain, where philosophical doubts were intensified by the convulsions of the Civil War. Where seventeenth-century aesthetic values, inherited from the Renaissance, had largely been based on classical notions of ideal forms and universal categories, writers in the early eighteenth century had to accommodate a completely different approach to truth, arising from Locke's argument for the derivation of all human knowledge from the senses. Since all sensory experience was, by definition, an individual matter and its interpretation, inevitably, subjective, it followed that neoclassical assumptions concerning ideal forms had to be radically reconsidered. If there were no innate ideas, but only mental images and ideas abstracted from individual perceptions, there could be no unchanging, universal patterns for the artist to emulate. Instead, truth was to be found in the immediate world of the senses and, once discovered by an individual, could be tested only through comparison with the experience of others. Texts that seemed to embody the feelings and experiences of other men and women provided a source of corroboration for personal experience in a new psychological universe where everyone was unique—and, therefore, isolated. Locke's empirical epistemology made each individual reliant on personal reflection and first-hand physical experience—but such extreme subjectivity also prompted a desire for connection and the sympathetic reassurance of the like-minded.

The notion of the mind being blank at birth, rather than inherently flawed, meant that even traditional Christian ideas about Original Sin began to be reconsidered, while the earth, in turn, ceased to be viewed as a ruin.[65] Newton's astonishing revelation of the workings of the solar system helped to reaffirm the idea of divine craftsmanship, which man's small part could hardly destroy.[66] At the same time, the scientific emphasis on observation of the physical universe dovetailed neatly with post-Reformation ideas on individual religious communion, leading to a new interest in reading God's ways in his works.[67] Education was increasingly concerned not just with controlling the child's sinful nature but with ensuring good influences in the formative years, which began to seem crucial to individual character. The behaviour of adults could, conversely, be understood through gaining greater knowledge of their backgrounds and experience, as the new appetite for memoirs demonstrates. For eighteenth-century authors and thinkers, the pursuit of both human nature and the Book of Nature became an overriding concern, for social, religious, scientific, and moral reasons.

When John Toland published his *Life of Milton* in 1698, he presented it as neither satire, nor panegyric, but rather as a 'True History of his Actions, Works and Opinions'.[68] Writing about real people was no longer a matter of producing exemplary patterns, nor satirizing vice, but rather of representing the true character of an individual—a trend mimicked in the burgeoning genre of prose fiction. And a key element in the empirical pursuit of truth was the effect of particular places on the people who lived there. It is as evident from *Robinson Crusoe* as from Joseph Spence's *A Full and Authentick Account of Stephen Duck*, the Wiltshire Thresher poet, that, by the early decades of the eighteenth century, human beings were being closely identified with their own peculiar environments, while character was increasingly understood as the product of the individual's peculiar experience. Even the great classical authors became subject to retrospective empirical investigation, as evident in Thomas Blackwell's influential *Enquiry into the Life and Writings of Homer*, of 1735, with its speculation on where Homer derived his formidable knowledge of human nature. Suddenly, the lives of poets began to seem essential to a full understanding of their poetry. Toland's *Milton* and Spence's *Duck* were early manifestations of a new biographical approach to reading that became fully established with Johnson's monumental *Lives of the English Poets*, commissioned in the 1770s by a group of London publishers to enhance their edition of the poetry.[69] Understanding poetry had, by the end of the eighteenth century, become a question of understanding place, and, when James Currie published the first major edition of *The Works of Robert Burns* in 1800, it was prefaced not only by a biography of the poet but also by 'Observations on the Character and Manners of the Scottish Peasantry'.

The physical nature of Locke's account of the human mind led his followers to assume that human minds were actually imprinted with images of the external world, which made the connection between an individual and his home environment fundamental to his entire understanding of the world. It also stimulated investigations into those who, like Duck, demonstrated great talent in apparently uncongenial circumstances—how could this happen?[70] At the same time, a mass of new information about different counties, countries, and continents revealed to British readers that their own distinctive experiences and familiar communities were often very different from those of other peoples.[71] Comparative studies of societies separated by geography or history were a major part of the Enlightenment, and, since many of the prominent thinkers were working in Scotland, their research often reflected a sense of immediate cultural distinction from neighbouring regions as well as the more theoretical global analysis. Philosophers became concerned with the influence of climate and scenery on residents of mountainous, fertile, or seabound regions, and, although the discourses often assumed a rather general tone, these new approaches to understanding society encouraged the burgeoning interest in the lives and circumstances of poets and artists. When James Beattie, the Aberdeen Moral Philosopher, composed his *Essays on Poetry and Music*, for example, he dwelled at some length on the psychological effects of bleak Highland scenery on 'persons of a lively imagination', while his own, very popular poem, *The Minstrel, or the Progress of Genius*, traced the growth of a young poet among the Scottish hills, roaming 'the lonely mountain's head' or 'the precipice o'erhung with pine'.[72] As art became more firmly associated with the circumstances of its composition and with the unique mind of its creator, then traces of its origins no longer seemed irrelevant blemishes and came to be seen rather as reassuring signs of inherent truthfulness.

As the sheer scale of cultural differences became apparent, however, the struggle to establish reliable principles from the analysis of numerous examples became more and more daunting. Johnson's ideal of surveying mankind 'from China to Peru' retained a certain rhetorical appeal, but was increasingly difficult to reconcile with the dawning realization that the Chinese and Peruvians were as individually various as the English, Scots, Welsh, or Irish.[73] Abstracting general truths from a mass of particular information was fraught with difficulty, but, for imaginative artists, it might still be possible to apprehend larger significances within a tiny fragment of the world. Blake's desire to see eternity in a grain of sand was, in many ways, an honest response to the realization that abstract truths might not be truths at all. Small details, on the other hand, could embody or symbolize great truths. Even if they did not, they were still more amenable to artistic recreation than abstract generalizations and as such provided appropriate material for a kind of art that instantly reassured audiences of its truthfulness to life.

The cultural shifts of the eighteenth century extended far beyond aesthetic debate and were impelled by numerous developments— political, religious, social, and technological. Nevertheless, concerns with truth were fundamentally philosophical. Once truth began to be pursued from the basis of individual experience rather than being understood to originate in an ideal world of universal, unchanging forms, new kinds of art were bound to emerge. In Plato's account, art was a representation of things that were merely inferior copies of a great ideal and was, therefore, inevitably concerned with surfaces and descriptions rather than with reality. In the eighteenth century, however, poets began to respond to the external world, not merely as something to be copied, but as a vital source of truth. And, once the ordinary world could be seen to furnish artists with the materials for truthful creation, then the scope of great art widened immeasurably. It was not that the quality of literature or the visual arts was fundamentally different, but the range of possible subjects increased and so did the number of people who tried their hand at artistic and literary expression. The effects of empiricism were enormously egalitarian, because knowledge ceased to be understood as received wisdom, accessible only to those privileged to enjoy the best education (even if Locke's own *Some Thoughts on Education* was directed primarily at the sons of gentlemen). True knowledge now depended, not on books and masters alone, but also on the intelligent consideration of first-hand experience—on perception, on memory, on conversation and activity. Personal knowledge could provide the means to arrive at profound truths, which meant that anyone could achieve authority, irrespective of his or her position in the social hierarchy. Even the poorest agricultural worker could attain deep knowledge of his own world, so that, when he saw a wren, his perception differed entirely from that of the passing traveller, who might not even see the tiny bird. As Wordsworth pointed out gently in the opening lines of 'Michael', the story is connected with an unassuming heap of straggling stones that a stranger to the area 'might see, and notice not'.

One of the great gifts of poets in the later eighteenth and early nineteenth centuries was their courageous creation of works that drew unapologetically and sympathetically on the tiniest features of their immediate surroundings. Burns's 'To a Mouse' or Wordsworth's 'To a Small Celandine' or John Clare's 'The Swallow' all testified to the significance of the small and unassuming and, in the process, demonstrated the extraordinary potential of the apparently ordinary. Their work delighted readers at every level of society, but offered special inspiration to those who had been conditioned to think of themselves as ignorant and therefore powerless. Poems on birds, flowers, insects, even vermin, that treated their subjects with seriousness and technical brilliance helped to reveal the possibilities that were open to anyone who perceived the world attentively and sympathetically. Everyone knew something, and most people knew quite a lot, but not everyone recognized the importance of what they took for granted, until their eyes were opened by poets who viewed the world with wonder and felt driven to share the revelation with their fellow men and women. This was Wordsworth's great gift to society, as Coleridge emphasized when describing his ability to direct the mind 'to the loveliness and the wonders of the world before us; an inexhaustible treasure, but for which, in consequence of the film of familiarity and selfish solicitude, we have eyes, yet see not, ears that hear not, and hearts that neither feel nor understand'.[74]

Wordsworth's poetry was compelled by a desire to show others that paradise could be glimpsed in the light of the common day, if only people noticed what was all around. Nor was he restricting his discoveries to those lucky enough to live amidst stunning scenery, for he knew only too well that it was the personal, human relationship with the world that created its full meaning, not the external forms of beauty. By the time Wordsworth began to publish poetry, the empirical emphasis on first-hand experience of the external world had begun to seem limiting rather than entirely liberating, as William Blake's image of Newton bent double over his compasses, designing a circumscribed world, suggests. For Blake, the mind at birth was not a blank tablet but a fully planted garden, bursting with the potential for imaginative growth, irrespective of outward circumstances. He knew that 'Every body does not see alike' and that a tree 'which moves some to tears of joy is in the Eyes of others only a Green thing that stands in the way'.[75] Seeing was determined not by the physical facts of the external world, but by the imaginative action of the individual mind.

For the great poets of the Romantic period, as M. H. Abrams emphasized in his seminal work on the subject, the mind was a lamp, not a mirror: a creative agent, rather than a merely passive recipient of external impressions. The individual human imagination was part of a great active universe, while its own capacity to work with its surroundings in a creative act of perception gave it a quasi-divine quality. Wordsworth imagined the dawning consciousness of a baby, nourished by the 'beloved presence' of its mother, whose early experience was akin to that of the great Creator of all things:

> No outcast he, bewilder'd and depress'd;
> Along his infant veins are interfus'd
> The gravitation and the filial bond
> Of nature, that connect him with the world.
> Emphatically such a Being lives,
> An inmate of this *active* universe;
> From nature largely he receives; nor so
> Is satisfied, but largely gives again,
> For feeling has to him imparted strength,
> And powerful in all sentiments of grief,
> Of exultation, fear, and joy, his mind,
> Even as an agent of the one great mind,
> Creates, creator and receiver both,
> Working but in alliance with the works
> Which it beholds.   (*The Prelude*, ii. 261–75)

Far from presenting the child's apprehension of the world as a purely rational process, Wordsworth's emphasis was on feeling—and, in particular, on love. Although the exultant passage goes on to acknowledge that the early creative spirit was often 'abated or suppressed', the idea that everyone was imaginative by nature and primed to engage actively and positively with a world created by God was a vital counter to the potentially alienating effects of Lockean thought. Wordsworth's image of man was not of the 'outcast...bewildered and depressed', but of a being intimately connected with a great network of divine life. That something of God's image might still be discovered in the minds of ordinary men and women was radically uplifting to those given to considering themselves very far from godlike—people socially disempowered by rank, religion, or gender. If everyone possessed creative potential as well as a wealth of knowledge, the personal possibilities were immense.

The growing realization that knowledge was being acquired from birth onwards meant that poetry now had different sources on which to draw. Rather than requiring a decent attainment in Latin and Greek, a poet could learn from cultural traditions familiar from childhood as well as from personal experiences. The first challenge was to recognize that such resources provided genuine material from which to create, the second, to develop forms and styles adequate to the task. As poets drew increasingly on material that seemed part of their very being, they also began to create a kind of poetry that aspired to substance rather than surface, to things rather than appearances. Burns's conscious projection of himself as a ploughman actually enhanced the reality of his poems, which seemed to have been made by the strong hands of someone used to hard, physical work. Not only were his poems braced with strong rhythms and unforced rhymes, but they also possessed the intricacy of natural forms. Behind Burns's lyrics was the touch of a farmer, pausing from strenuous labour to create something tiny, beautiful, and ultimately more durable than the produce of his land.[76] Wordsworth's emphasis on the intimate relationship between the natural features of his Lake District boyhood and those of his internal landscape seemed similarly reflected in the fluid movement and cumulative momentum of his blank verse. His lyrics, too, possessed the resilient rhythms and unadorned language that seemed the perfect counterpart of the northern rocks and trees he had known since childhood. These were poems that seemed to resist the Platonic view of art as mere representation, seeking rather the power to 'endure', like permanent natural features, entering the hearts and minds of those open to their transformative influence.

It was not that earlier poets had failed to create work of similar substance and depth, but rather that, by the Romantic period, poets were more conscious of the need to emulate the strength of the external world and to develop forms that might really *embody* truth. Burns's sense of his poems as real, physical objects is as evident in his language as in his carefully crafted verse forms, as he presents the poet 'stringing blethers up in rhyme', or seeing the 'words come skelpan, rank an file'.[77] While Burns treated the reality of his creations with a certain self-mocking playfulness, however, Wordsworth presented the nature of language with deep reverence, arguing that, 'if words be not . . . an incarnation of the thought but only a clothing for it, then surely will they prove an ill gift'.[78] The serious tone and religious language was appropriate to the context—an 'Essay upon Epitaphs'—but Wordsworth's profound concern with what constituted 'real language' is evident throughout his work. In the preface to *Lyrical Ballads*, he declared his aim to compose poems in the 'real language of men', and, while he was referring in part to recognizable speech, there was also a sense in which the proper language of poetry must, in itself, be 'real'.[79] His fascination with epitaphs, with words graven in stone, has a strongly physical as well as aesthetic dimension. It was in the third 'Essay upon Epitaphs' that Wordsworth articulated the problem that he had grappled with for years most plainly: 'Language, if it do not uphold, and feed, and leave in quiet, like the power of gravitation or the air we breathe, is a counter-spirit, unremittingly and noiselessly at work to derange, to subvert, to lay waste, to vitiate, and to dissolve.'[80] Language was like the force of gravity, like air, like food, in other words, as essential to the well-being of mankind as any physical requirement. The responsibilities of the writer were, therefore, immense.

For poets to create work that might 'uphold, and feed' their readers, they needed to apprehend truths that were not only certain but also recognizable to others. Wordsworth addressed the issue directly when he presented *The Excursion* to the public in 1814, explaining his decision to retire to his native mountains in the hope of creating 'a literary Work that might live'.[81] Reality was no longer something beyond human apprehension, but might be perceived in the everyday world. As Wordsworth announced in the preface, 'Beauty, a living Presence of the earth', surpassed the 'most fair ideal Forms | Which craft of delicate spirits hath composed from earth's materials'.[82] Man's handiwork could never be *more* beautiful than the world in which he lived, but recognizing the truths inherent in his surroundings was an essential step towards an art that might aspire to godlike creation. It was an astonishing vision of possibility, because, in Wordsworth's view, 'Minds, Once wedded to this outward frame of things | In love' could recover Paradise—in 'the growth of common day'.[83] Regaining paradise in this life was not a question of inheriting myths, money, or titles, but of possessing personal vision. Like the awakening consciousness of the infant babe, the adult's re-entry into paradise depended on love.

For the poet, the task was not just one of loving devotion and grateful perception, however. To create verse that would 'live...to chear | Mankind in times to come', the poet had to distinguish 'Inherent things from casual, what is fixed | From fleeting'.[84] Personal experience offered a vital source of truth, but, from the mass of experience drunk in through thirsty senses, the poet had a responsibility to select the things that really mattered—the matter that was real. Tiny things were not necessarily trivial—they could be the secret entrances to emotional narratives or apocalyptic moments. Modern man was only too aware of his minute stature in the vast cosmos, so a new approach to reaffirming his almost forgotten resemblance to God was much needed, especially in the period of prolonged warfare and general confusion that followed the French Revolution in 1789. The idea that the very act of observing the world with admiration and love might be redemptive was cheering, to say the least. For the poet, too, re-creation in adequate language of a personal response to a tiny fragment of the overwhelmingly large universe seemed just about possible. And, rather than view such an ideal as the low pursuit of a minor artist, Romantic poets saw their activity as being directed towards the highest goal and the greatest benefit to mankind. Little things, if properly understood, were signs of greater and might even be understood as miniature imitations of the original, divine act of creation.[85] No matter that poems were so often conveyed on the most fragile paper, their own powerful shapes could be impressed on the minds of readers, carried internally, and passed on to future generations. Poems, if well made and truthful, could achieve a new kind of reality in the world, even aspiring to live as long as there were readers to respond to their special truths.

The period now known as 'Romantic' constitutes a defining moment in literary history, when local detail ceased to be regarded as transient, irrelevant, or restrictive, and began to seem essential to art with any aspiration to permanence. The debates of this revolutionary age also prompted passionate justifications of poetry's vital role in modern society, which in turn transformed the work of the local poet into a task of national and universal proportions. This book is an attempt to explore the dawning realization that the place of poetry matters and to trace some of the routes laid down by the poetic pioneers of the Romantic period. Kavanagh's immensely liberating insight into Homer's creation of the *Iliad* from 'a local row' was a response in part to Ancient Greek epic and in part to the goings-on of his own parish, but it was also profoundly, if less consciously, indebted to the radical reassessment of what poetry could and should do, which took place at the beginning of the previous century. When Heaney paid tribute to Wordsworth in his Nobel Lecture, his gratitude was not for a body of well-made lyrics alone, but for an entire way of thinking about poetry and its vital role in society.

I

In the First Place

The idea of 'local work' articulated in 'Crediting Poetry' was not a new one, though Heaney had never before expressed it with quite such clarity. Much of the writing for which he was now receiving international recognition already embodied the ideal he was presenting in Stockholm, and so, when he isolated this guiding principle for poetry, he was also commenting on his own creative development. An award for lifetime achievement inevitably prompts reassessment, but, throughout Heaney's writing career, the return to roots and associated gratitude for personal growth have been vital to his creativity. Like Wordsworth two centuries before, Heaney's energies have drawn power from memories of youthful experience in a particular region, a parallel acknowledged explicitly in the 'Singing School' sequence of *North*, with its opening quotation from *The Prelude*, 'Fair seedtime had my soul, and I grew up | Fostered alike by beauty and by fear' (i. 305–6). More recently, Heaney has published substantial volumes of selected prose and poetry, as well as giving extensive autobiographical interviews, which all reaffirm his origins as a writer and reveal his affinities with Romantic predecessors.[1] Although in his Nobel Lecture and elsewhere Heaney has been at pains to signal the changes in his creative attitudes over the years, the underlying structures remain unmoved. The crossing of his roots and his reading is apparent throughout, even when the re-creation of first-hand experience of a real place is most compelling.

Heaney's substantial volume of prose, *Finders Keepers*, opens with a return to childhood. The family farm is 'the first place', and the essay bearing its name, 'Mossbawn', begins with the word 'omphalos', the navel, centre of the body, centre of the world, and also the sound made by the pump in the backyard. The essay is the prose equivalent of 'Digging', which is placed on the first page of *Opened Ground* to remind readers of Heaney's beginnings as a poet and as a person. At the centre of his own ever-increasing circles of experience is Mossbawn—a specific place, whose memories continue to supply the adult poet and his readers, just as it provided for the surrounding families in his youth. Heaney's retrospective arrangements reveal the same aesthetic assumptions as those informing his Nobel Lecture. They demonstrate that his poetry should be understood as local work and that his development as a poet is rooted in an identifiable area. Any aspiration to reach an international audience has depended on the discovery of a voice and form adequate to the truths he began to understand as a boy.

Even as he emphasized the personal dimension of certain facts about the world in 'Mossbawn', Heaney was revealing attitudes shared with, and partially inherited from, Wordsworth. To begin with 'Mossbawn' is to acknowledge that the child is father of the man, even though the allusion to Wordsworth's 'Immortality Ode' is not spelled out. Once recognized, however, Heaney's evocations of childhood take us back not just to Ireland in the mid-twentieth century, but also to Cumbria in the late eighteenth, raising questions about the possible connections between his own growth as a poet and Wordsworth's. As Heaney explained in 'Crediting Poetry', true poetry has the vital capacity to cross divisions and to reveal affinities in surprising places. Though his own faith in local work was realized through personal experience in Ireland, its foundations also lie in Romanticism, an international movement that was also intensely local. In a lecture on the poet's feeling for place, delivered at the Ulster Museum in 1977, Heaney made the telling remark that 'Wordsworth was perhaps the first man to articulate the nurture that becomes available to the feelings through dwelling in one dear, perpetual place'.[2] When Heaney draws on the memories of his boyhood in Derry, he is demonstrating the influence of revolutionary developments in late-eighteenth-century European culture, whose effects were so permanent that they have come to seem the natural way of thinking about the world.

'Mossbawn' begins with the voice of the educated adult, but rapidly slips into the re-created consciousness of a child, vulnerable and yet subject to constant reassurances: 'lost in the pea-drills in a field behind the house', he is wrapped in a 'green web, a caul of veined light, a tangle of rods and pods, stalks and tendrils, full of assuaging earth and leaf smell, a sunlit lair'.[3] The boy's fears are acknowledged, but answered by the comfort of earth and sunlight, transforming bewilderment into gratitude. He seems very much like a 'Foster-Child' of nature, asleep in a green cradle, safe from harm and at one with the earth.[4] Though intensely personal, Heaney's memory, like Wordsworth's, gestures towards the universal. The observation that 'All children want to crouch in their secret nests' magnifies a specific, individual moment into an all-embracing truth, and thus the nourishing memory of Mossbawn can be shared by anyone reading the essay.[5] The little boy half-asleep in the pea-green field awakens the reader's dormant dens, and, for a moment, each is safely cocooned in a sunlit lair. 'Mossbawn' suggests that heaven *might* lie about us in our infancy and, if not heaven, then something very like it.

If the intimations of 'Mossbawn' are reminiscent of Wordsworth, however, Heaney is careful to avoid the elevated language and philosophy of the great Ode. His nests may be soft and secret, but they are also sharply drawn in colloquial tones: 'I loved the fork of a beech tree at the head of our lane, the close thicket of a boxwood hedge in the front corner of the house, the soft, collapsing pile of hay in a back corner of the byre; but especially I spent time in the throat of an old willow tree at the end of the farmyard' (pp. 3–4). The recollection is vivid because it is specific—these are not just 'trees', but 'beech', 'boxwood', and 'willow'. The rhetoric is in the detail: every inch of Mossbawn was known to the young Heaney, and its subsequent existence in distant minds depends on that original, deep intimacy. In less skilled hands, the farmyard might have blurred into sentimental cliché, but the clear prose and sinuous sentences bring it sharply before the reader's eyes. There is no need to consult a map of Derry to believe that what he is saying is true. The documentary detail is instantly trustworthy and therefore travel-worthy.

As in 'Mossbawn', 'Digging' shifts rapidly from the adult poet at his writing desk to the boy on the farm, whose selves are linked by the familiar rhythm of his father's spade. Again the language is uncompromising in its detail, with references to chopping the tall tops of potato plants and the glimpse of his grandfather, cutting turf on Toner's bog. The speaker's mind is rooted in the muddy fields, and so his readers can feel the 'cold smell of potato mould, the squelch and slap | Of soggy peat'.[6] Although the poem is emphasizing the gap between the adult and the child—the 'two consciousnesses', as Wordsworth put it in *The Prelude* (ii. 33)—it is also celebrating the connective powers of memory, imagination, and poetry. Heaney's recollections reveal the layers of natural resources that accumulate over years of vivid experience. His fascination with bogs, moss, ponds, and rivers is part of a persistent desire to delve below the surface, and become immersed in what lies hidden from view. Old pumps and wells were, as he described in 'Personal Helicon', a source of constant inspiration:

> A shallow one under a dry stone ditch
> Fructified like any aquarium.
> When you dragged out long roots from the soft mulch,
> A white face hovered over the bottom.[7]

Heaney's discoveries of the marvels hidden in wells is similar to Wordsworth's description of seeking in still water 'weeds, fishes, flowers, | Grots, pebbles, roots of trees', but seeing also with such 'beauteous sights' the reflection of his own face and the mountains and the clouds above.[8] Wordsworth's complicated re-creation of looking down to the bottom through his own face is an image of memory, and a comment on the adult mind, 'incumbent o'er the surface of past time'. It conveys both the excitement of recovering vivid, early experience, and a sense of its elusiveness, with a quiet ambivalence similar to that of Heaney's 'white face' hovering over the bottom of the well.

The idea of the disused pump becoming fruitful, with the lifting of roots revealing a ghostly self-image, is strongly reminiscent of Wordsworth's view that the imagination discovers its creative powers through memory and draws especially on 'spots of time, | Which with distinct pre-eminence retain | A fructifying virtue'.[9] Although the metaphors are not identical, the underlying ideas of the recovery of forgotten experience leading to both an affirmation of the self and a release of creative energy are remarkably similar. Heaney's pithy 'I rhyme | To see myself' is a very concise version of Wordsworth's detailed internal probing, which had resulted at last in renewed faith in his own ability to build 'a work that should endure'.[10] Whether what emerged from the mud was a natural phenomenon, a buried narrative, or a personal memory, discovery is often a corroboration of something already known, but perhaps not seen properly. As Heaney suggested in a later poem from *Seeing Things*, 'what's come upon is manifest | Only in the light of what has been gone through'.[11] 'Going through' is exactly what his father and grandfather are doing in 'Digging', and thus their familiar activity provided a lasting model for the poet with his pen.[12] As a writer, the natural layers are personal, historical, and literary, and so his creative work of thirty years represents *Opened Ground*.[13]

In the warm reflections of 'Mossbawn', the attractions of both water and earth are apparent at once, with the description of the boy digging black soil, and the celebration of the pump in the yard. Like those in 'Personal Helicon', the Mossbawn pump is a site of revelation. When it was installed, the workmen dug down through the hard surface, exposing seams of golden sand and bronze gravel beneath the unpromising black crust, and inadvertently providing a vivid metaphor for the hidden riches accessible to the poet who digs in his own backyard. If the descent into earth revealed unexpected wonders, however, its memory also reminded the adult poet of his need for something much less yielding than collapsing pea rods and piles of hay. A firm grounding in the earth was vital to his future growth, for the creative imagination had to be 'centred and staked' as well as fed and watered.[14] The reassuring repetitions of everyday experience furnished the child with utterly unquestioned truths, which in turn provided a saving anchor in later life. The Mossbawn pump figures in Heaney's mind as a vital source of replenishment, revelation, and stability, not unlike Wordsworth's idea of nature as a nurse, guide, and guardian.

Admiration for firm foundations is often, however, a sign of attendant anxiety. In a later poem that begins by echoing the 'sand' and 'gravel' of 'Mossbawn', Heaney observes that 'The places I go back to have not failed | But will not last'.[15] Memory itself, 'everything accumulated ever', is fraught with fear. Heaney's explicit articulation of the unsettling nature of memory places again recalls similar passages of *The Prelude*, where Wordsworth reflects on the instability of his mental resources:

> The days gone by
> Come back upon me from the dawn almost
> Of life: the hiding-places of my power

> Seem open; I approach and then they close;
> I see by glimpses now; when age comes on,
> May scarcely see at all.   (xi. 334–9)

Celebration of childhood memory is the corollary of an acute aware-
ness of the passage of time. The sense of perpetual change that
prompts identification of early mental landmarks also drives the poet
to record their significance. What has been uncovered requires
preservation—and hence Wordsworth's compulsion to 'give | A
substance and a life to what I feel' (*The Prelude*, xi. 341–2). If the crea-
tive being is anchored psychologically by familiar sights, the internal
landscape is itself saved by the power of language and the transfor-
mation into poetry. Once turned into well-chosen words, personal
memories can be passed on and might in time become part of
another's creative resources, but the initial impulse to make the
momentary permanent is riven by uncertainty.

Heaney's anxiety about memory is not just a consequence of his
daily travel further from childhood perception, however, for
throughout 'Mossbawn' the sense of remembered fear is palpable.
The young Heaney was subject not only to the normal hazards of a
farm, but also to the larger threats of its particular historical situa-
tion. The 'omphalos' is fixed firmly in County Derry in the early
1940s, with the immediate sound of the pump offset by the sounds of
American aircraft overhead. The sense of domestic security is inten-
sified from the beginning of the essay by the boy's alertness to the
alien, articulated at first through references to the Second World
War, but later in the signs of more local conflict. The 'melancholy
strain of hymn-singing from a gospel hall' and the 'rattle of Orange
drums from Aughrim Hill' are as much part of the internal acoustic
as the reassuring rhythms of the backyard. Heaney's remembered
rural community is not a timeless idyll, but a 'realm of division',
where natural patterns seem inseparable from human conflict: 'Like
the rabbit pads that loop across grazing, and tunnel the soft growths
under ripening corn, the lines of sectarian antagonism and affiliation
followed the boundaries of the land.'[16] The local names for each field
and farm are symbols of contested territory, making the mental map
of home 'some script indelibly written into the nervous system'. This
is partly an image for the memory as something written permanently
into the mind, but it also carries the sense of a dramatic text, whose

characters can be understood as prompts to action. The landscape is marked by human history, the mindscape characterized accordingly by a place already steeped in meaning. Words are again a way of preserving the past, but can also cause rather than combat fear. Shades of the prison house begin to appear very quickly in the consciousness of this growing boy.

Although Heaney was emphasizing the specific historical coordinates of his imaginative ground plan, his essay reveals a similar impulse to connect with the outside world as that displayed in the later Nobel Lecture. Even as he runs through the list of resonant local names, 'Broagh, The Long Rigs, Bell's Hill; Brian's Field, the Round Meadow, the Demesne', he insists that repeating them has a distancing effect, and 'turns them into what Wordsworth once called a prospect of the mind'.[17] It is only as Heaney confronts the history of sectarian division at home that his allusion to Wordsworth in 'Mossbawn' becomes explicit. At this point, he aligns himself with a great poet of another time and place, as if to suggest the possibility of different loyalties and influences. As the local memory presses most strongly, it is made bearable by thoughts of someone else's local memory, already transformed into art. Wordsworth may not have had to contend with sectarian disputes, but his courageous confrontation of psychological and international crises and demonstrable ability to turn turmoil into truly 'adequate' poetry offer an enduring model for the later writer.

The line quoted by Heaney is from a passage in *The Prelude*, where Wordsworth, recalling his rural childhood, described the feeling inspired by a morning walk:

> How shall I trace the history, where seek
> The origin of what I then have felt?
> Oft in those moments such a holy calm
> Did overspread my soul, that I forgot
> That I had bodily eyes, and what I saw
> Appear'd like something in myself, a dream,
> A prospect in my mind.   (ii. 365–71)

Recollection of Wordsworth's lines helped to contain the Derry landscape, because they encourage internal exploration, convey a sense of overwhelming calmness, and affirm the human mind's extraordinary powers. Wordsworth's exploration of the creative psyche was so deep and extensive that his legacy to future poets is immense. His admiration for the all-absorbing imagination of the child, whose mind is filled with 'prospects', offered Heaney both a way to comprehend his own independent experience *and* a resonant phrase with which to control unsettling facts. Once the surrounding history of violent conquest and dispute had become a 'prospect of the mind', its presence was workable and could, therefore, be properly acknowledged.

'Prospect' implies both distance and future possibility. When understood as the contrary to 'refuge', as Jay Appleton has suggested, it also implies an active assessment of the capacities of a landscape, rather than a retreat into a lair, sunlit or otherwise.[18] Although Heaney has been criticized for political evasiveness, for which he took himself to task in *Station Island*, where his murdered cousin rises to accuse him of confusing 'evasion with artistic tact', the evocation of childhood memory has never been an escape from an unmanageable present.[19] Wordsworth has similarly attracted charges of displacing politics in personal and picturesque poems that erase the historical moment.[20] Neither poet retreated into the past, however, any more than they retreated into the pastoral. Their representations of earlier states of being have always been framed by consciousness of the present and draw energy from the contrasting perspectives: re-creations of familiar places are at once vividly present and yet enhanced by the more distanced understanding of their distinct relation to other times and situations. In the case of each poet, recognition of his place in a world not entirely satisfactory made the desire to contribute to its improvement all the stronger, however unlikely the odds might sometimes have seemed. The inner journey was not a rejection of active participation in the real world, but actually reflected and fortified the poet's deep sense of duty to a contemporary society in crisis—and hence Heaney's persistent recourse to Wordsworth.

Why Wordsworth?

Wordsworth was the earliest writer to understand fully the necessary connections between the poet and his 'first place'. He recognized the vital legacy of a child's largely unconscious enjoyment of a particular environment, whose contours provided such a strong mental land-scape for the adult poet. Knowing the volatility of the mind, he also understood the importance of a firm imaginative grounding. In *The Prelude* he described the inner commotions of the sensitive artist:

> The Poet, gentle creature as he is,
> Hath, like the Lover, his unruly times;
> His fits when he is neither sick nor well,
> Though no distress be near him but his own
> Unmanageable thoughts.   (i. 145–9)

Acknowledgement of such internal 'goadings' prompted further exploration of both his rebellious creative impulses and the stabi-lizing influence of familiar surroundings: the 'ceaseless music' of the Derwent, which tempers 'human waywardness', or the 'calm | Which Nature breathes among the hills and groves' (i. 279–83). Although, in 'Mossbawn', Heaney recalled a moment of tranquillity, much of *The Prelude* deals with mental turbulence. Nor is Wordsworth's represen-tation of childhood especially concerned with peace and quiet. The 'secret nests' are made, not by the infant poet, but by the birds whose eggs he plundered. The boy depicted in the early books is more inclined to plunge into streams, hang from crags, gallop over sands, strike his oars into a darkened lake, or hiss across the ice than he is to crouch secretively. This is the inspirational figure recalled by Heaney in a recent lyric, 'on frozen Windermere | As he flashed from the clutch of earth along its curve | And left it scored'.[21]

In *The Prelude*, Wordsworth makes no attempt to brush over the destructive aspects of childhood. The happiness he conveys so skil-fully is not unalloyed by memories of predatory behaviour and acts of stealth. Stealing ravens' eggs and snaring woodcock is as vividly recalled in the opening books of *The Prelude* as the dawn shoots and drowning kittens of Heaney's *Death of a Naturalist*. Such childhood memories seem a far cry from the motionless care of St Kevin and the blackbirds, or from the patient perseverance of the Leech Gath-erer. Nevertheless, it is Wordsworth's refusal to obscure the violent energies of the past that makes his poetry so convincing. Snared birds or French city squares 'Heaped up with dead and dying' are Wordsworth's equivalent of 'That dead young soldier in his blood', which Yeats recognized as part of what happens in the world, and thus made integral to his mature poetry.[22] Since Wordsworth acknowledged the destructive power in himself, his tender regard for human suffering and overwhelming emphasis on sympathy is all the more persuasive.

The Prelude explores the same movement as that traced in 'Tintern Abbey', from the 'glad animal movements' of thoughtless youth to the voice of the reflective speaker, but makes plainer that the energies needing to be chastened and subdued are essentially creative. The intense physical activity of the early books is closely related to the strong emotions that make the mind so receptive to new experience. The same connection between the early passions and the creative power of the adult poet is suggested in 'Home at Grasmere', where Wordsworth reflects on the powerful emotions that 'enflamed' his 'infant heart', and realizes that they survive in the adult 'though changed their office'.[23] The Prelude is, in part, an attempt to analyse the process of change and to show how potentially dangerous energies could be harnessed for the greater good of man.

As Wordsworth recalled the unruly passions of his youth, he recognized that such experiences had somehow intertwined with enduring features of the landscape, forming deep, if hitherto unnoticed, attachments that were ultimately 'purifying' and 'sanctifying'.[24] It was as if the best of his childhood—the intense joy and spontaneous energy—had been purged of unthinking selfishness by the special surroundings that nurtured the child and provided an internal guide for the man. The 'giddy bliss' might have faded, but passionate feelings left indelible traces, imaged in the memories of places where the boy had splashed and chased:

> The scenes which were a witness of that joy
> Remained, in their substantial lineaments
> Depicted on the brain, and to the eye
> Were visible, a daily sight.   (The Prelude, i. 627–30)

So intense was the joy experienced by the young lad that his mental landscape was formed by the emotional residue. Repeated experience in the same settings meant that they gradually became part of the mental landscape, deepening from momentary excitement to abiding affection:

> By the impressive discipline of fear,
> By pleasure and repeated happiness,
> So frequently repeated, and by force

Of obscure feelings representative
Of joys that were forgotten, these same scenes
So beauteous and majestic in themselves,
Though yet the day was distant, did at length
Become habitually dear, and all
Their hues and forms were by invisible links
Allied to the affections.   (*The Prelude*, i. 631–40)

The repetition is re-enacted in the verse, with its linked line-openings, 'By…By…So…Of…Of…So', leading to something 'habitu*all*y dear', in which 'all' is 'allied'. Over the years, the familiar landscape had become not only a comforting memory but an essential part of the imaginative and emotional landscape. The formation of mental alliances may have gone unnoticed at the time, but their enduring strength was unmistakeable to the reflective, and thankful, adult.

As well as proving 'invigorating' to the adult poet, then, thoughts of former years were also capable of fixing 'the wavering balance' of the mind.[25] When Heaney admitted that his imagination was 'centred and staked' by the pump at Mossbawn, he was thus revealing an additional and less explicitly acknowledged debt to Wordsworth, who had been similarly grounded by the Lake District. The discipline required to create poetry and avoid fruitless meanderings (as Heaney instructs the poet: 'Don't waver | Into language. Do not waver in it'[26]) was not learned from early experience of familiar places alone, but also from the work of exemplary figures. By making the growth of the poet's mind the subject of his greatest work, Wordsworth had prepared the ground for future writers to understand the importance of their own early experiences, and to make them a proper subject for poetry. The 'first place' is not simply the earliest.

Wordsworth's Place

Although Wordsworth analysed the early workings of his mind with such care, the clarity achieved in *The Prelude* in 1805 was the culmination of more recent experience. In 'Tintern Abbey', composed in July 1798 at the age of 28, he had registered the creative impact of revisiting a particular landscape, and recognized that such

experience was startlingly self-revelatory. During his visit to
Germany the following winter with his sister Dorothy, he began to
make imaginative returns to childhood, seeking in memories of the
Lake District the sources of both his creative power and his sense of
self.[27] As Dorothy observed in a letter to Coleridge: 'A race with
William upon his native lakes would leave to the heart and imagina-
tion something much more Dear and valuable than the gay sight of
Ladies and Countesses whirling along the lake of Ratzeburg.'[28] The
sight of German aristocrats enjoying winter sports seems to have
awoken in Wordsworth a deep longing for home and prompted some
of his most vivid lines of recollected pleasure:

> All shod with steel,
> We hiss'd along the polished ice, in games
> Confederate, imitative of the chace,
> And woodland pleasures, the resounding horn,
> The Pack, loud bellowing, and the hunted hare.
> So through the darkness and the cold we flew,
> And not a voice was idle: with the din,
> Meanwhile, the precipices rang aloud,
> The leafless trees, and every icy crag
> Tinkled like iron, while the distant hills
> Into the tumult sent an alien sound
> Of melancholy, not unnoticed, while the stars,
> Eastward, were sparkling clear, and in the west
> The orange sky of evening died away.[29]

Bitterly cold weather in a strange country brought back childhood
memories so powerfully that Wordsworth almost seemed to be
re-enacting his early years. And yet, the adult experience is present,
too, in the 'far distant hills', which sent their 'alien sound | Of melan-
choly', as if to provide the bass against which youthful voices sound
out even more clearly. As Wordsworth laboured to master a foreign
culture, the siren voices of home began to call insistently, reminding
him of what he had left behind.

The Wordsworths' decision to go back and rediscover the land-
scape where they had grown up, after an absence of ten very full and
unsettling years, was at once logical and momentous, the imagina-
tive outpouring that followed, immense. In 'Home at Grasmere', the
poem written when he returned to Cumbria in 1800, Wordsworth

tried to articulate the unique feeling belonging to the valley where he was now able to settle:

> The one sensation that is here; 'tis here,
> Here as it found its way into my heart
> In childhood, here as it abides by day,
> By night, here only; or in chosen minds
> That take it with them hence, where'er they go.[30]

The astounding quality of the place resounds in the word 'here', repeated five times in as many lines, almost like quiet cheering. What begins as a simple indicative rapidly gathers force until it seems to convey something too remarkable for ordinary language:

> 'Tis (but I cannot name it) 'tis the sense
> Of majesty, and beauty, and repose,
> A blended holiness of earth and sky,
> Something that makes this individual Spot,
> This small abiding-place of many men,
> A termination and a last retreat,
> A Centre, come from wheresoe'er you will,
> A Whole without dependence or defect,
> Made for itself and happy in itself,
> Perfect Contentment, Unity entire.   (ll. 161–70)

In Grasmere, Wordsworth found a kind of completeness that was at once a revelation and a recovery. His destination was also a starting point and centre: its special quality united the poet's different selves and made him one. What had entered his heart in childhood had been there all the time, but could now be properly identified, because of experiences elsewhere—'manifest | Only in the light of what's been gone through'. In 'Home at Grasmere', Wordsworth avoided recounting the traumatic events of his life and the time spent in Cambridge, London, or Revolutionary France, all of which contributed so much to *The Prelude*. The horror of being 'tossed about in whirlwinds' and ravaged by the 'unnatural strife' experienced during the period of Revolution and war would eventually be recorded with great power in *The Prelude*, but had no place in the celebratory poem of homecoming.[31] A barely articulated sense of less happy times is nevertheless crucial to the reverential tone of this verse. 'Home at Grasmere' is a hymn of praise for paradise regained, but the force of its gratitude derives from the knowledge of what had been lost.

The Grasmere of Wordsworth's poem was not an uninhabited Eden of the kind ironically imagined by Marvell in 'The Garden', however, but a 'small abiding-place of many men'. For Wordsworth, the familiar landscape was valuable, not just for its peaceful beauty, nor for the powerful personal emotions invested in its well-remembered contours, nor for its promise of permanence, though all of these were essential to his creative well being. The immediate countryside was like a living being, its ancient countenance creased with the memories of collective human experience. Despite the sense that Grasmere was the 'last retreat' after long and arduous travels, it was not the seclusion that was being celebrated, but rather the layers of human significance:

> Look where we will, some human heart has been
> Before us with its offering, not a tree
> Sprinkles these little pastures, but the same
> Hath furnished matter for a thought; perchance
> To some one is as a familiar friend.
> Joy spreads and sorrow spreads; and this whole Vale,
> Home of untutored Shepherds as it is,
> Swarms with sensation, as with gleams of sunshine,
> Shadows or breezes, scents or sounds.
>
> ('Home at Grasmere', ll. 659–67)

The local hillside was rich in hidden feelings, its features a generous legacy from those who had loved it in the past, or were living there still. The emotions were essentially shared—both joy and sorrow spread. From his standpoint 'here', the poet signals towards 'Yon Cottage', 'That Ridge', and 'yonder grey-stone that stands alone'. Since each had a tale to tell, Wordsworth's poem was providing the landscape with a voice. As he recounted successive stories of an unfaithful husband whose guilt drove him to desperation, or the widower whose grief was countered by the lively company of his six daughters, or the couple whose fir grove continued to thrive even after the husband's death had left his wife 'withering in her loneliness', the entire vale seemed alive. The swarm of sensation may be likened to the physical effects of wind and sunshine, but the poem shows that it arose from the sympathetic discovery of human presences. The paradise entered by the poet was a place already loved by others, and their personal narratives offered guidance and inspiration.

When Heaney wrote of his formative attachment to Mossbawn, he had the dual influences of his family and his reading; the example provided by Wordsworth was itself nurtured by the local traditions and human narratives he learned to understand when he returned to the Lake District. During his journey to Grasmere late in 1799, for example, he passed Hart-Leap Well, near Richmond in Yorkshire, named after a 'remarkable chace', centuries before, which still lived on in local memory.[32] In his poem on the subject, Wordsworth described a conversation between a traveller and a shepherd, who relates the tale of the hart's death and meditates on its love for the well:

> This water was perhaps the first he drank
> When he wandered from his mother's side.   (ll. 147–8)

Although the simple language of the poem does not seem to invite a complicated response, it is not difficult to read additional meanings into the image of the lonely hart, desperate to return to the place where he first drew refreshment from a natural spring.[33] The poem is not concerned solely with returns, however. As the speaker congratulates the shepherd, 'thou hast spoken well' (l. 161), he is suggesting both that words have been given to the Well *and* that the shepherd's deep understanding of the place reveals a natural sympathy in which every imaginative being can participate. As the history of thoughtless human cruelty, the creature's suffering, and its place in the larger order of things is shared by the two men, any superficial differences between the horseback traveller and the shepherd dissolve in common humanity. Hart-Leap Well was a kind of personal Helicon, through which Wordsworth could begin to see the connection between different parts of himself and to recognize his place in a greater, interconnected whole.

In the series of 'Poems on the Naming of Places', composed soon after 'Home at Grasmere', Wordsworth continued to explore the ways in which human emotion interacted with the landscape. Each poem was a verbal monument to particular rocks, lakesides, or clearings where 'little Incidents will have occurred, or feelings been experienced, which will have given to such places a private and peculiar Interest'.[34] What appears to have stemmed from a private impulse, however, was also a contribution to the life of a community inseparable from its surroundings. The poems described places

invested with feelings associated with beloved family and friends—
Emma's Dell, Joanna's Rock, Point-Rash-Judgment, Mary's
nook—but they also created a domestic counterpart to the local
meanings that already deepened the Vale of Grasmere. The newly
named places contributed to the swarm of sensation that Words-
worth had learned to feel by attending to the 'untutored Shepherds'.
    Collective experience and habits of memory-sharing provided a
strong sense of connection, which in turn inspired and offered justifi-
cation for the poet's response to the region. Naming local landmarks
after personal incidents might have seemed rather self-indulgent were
it not for the parallel practices of those who had always lived there.
The shared records of the mountain communities spoke directly to
the poet's own preoccupation with mortality and memorials; his desire
to be remembered in the 'lonesome Peak', just as other local figures
were associated with natural features, is embodied in verse that aspired
to the same permanence.[35] Wordsworth's account of chiselling out
'rude characters...upon the living stone' in 'Joanna's Rock' reflects a
deep desire to immortalize the best feelings in language as strong as
the 'brotherhood of ancient mountains'.[36] As he sought the words and
forms necessary to build a work that would endure, Wordsworth
found inspiration in both the unchanging features of the landscape
and the human histories that enriched the hills. When the speaker of
'Home at Grasmere' addresses his female companion, saying

> we are not alone, we do not stand,
> My Emma, here misplaced and desolate,
> Loving what no one cares for but ourselves,   (ll. 646–8)[37]

he is testifying to the reassurance of being part of a community, in
which personal meaning is confirmed by perceived correspondence
with others. Far from presenting Grasmere as a retreat from society,
Wordsworth made plain that he had found his true place among men
at last:

> Society is here:
> The true community, the noblest Frame
> Of many into one incorporate;
> That must be looked for here.   (ll. 818–21)

In such a place, every inhabitant made a vital contribution to main-
tain the healthy fabric of the whole; as Wordsworth pointed out, 'we

do not tend a lamp | Whose lustre we alone participate' (ll. 656–7). The poet's light, like those of his neighbours, was not hidden under a bushel, but shining brightly through his verse.

As Wordsworth attended to the special character of the Lake District, marked out in the different cottages, rocks, or clumps of trees, he recognized the way in which particular places could continue to cradle feelings long after individual events had occurred. To someone who knew the area, even the least assuming field might be a site of extraordinary emotion. Although Wordsworth did not suggest the kind of parallels with Sophoclean tragedy that Hardy would later claim for his Wessex characters, his sensitive accounts of what lay within the local landscape demonstrated extremes of feeling every bit as memorable. In 'The Brothers', he retold a story that he had heard in Ennerdale about a man who had fallen to his death from a crag while sleepwalking, leaving his staff stuck halfway down the mountainside until it eventually rotted.[38] In Wordsworth's imagination, the tale developed into a more complicated narrative of fraternal love, separation, and despair; as it did so, other local memories were drawn in to suggest different ways in which the natural and human worlds might be understood to interact. The image of the crag with the trapped stick was an obvious visual reminder of a particular fall, the staff's steady decay a reminder of passing time and the fate of its owner. However, Wordsworth also included reference to a phenomenon observed near Haweswater, when Kidstow Pike was struck by lightning so powerful that one of its 'fountains disappeared, while the other continued to flow as before'.[39] Though unrelated to the original source of inspiration, the remarkable natural event was made to serve as a prologue to the story of James's death, and linked by the imaginative description of the two springs as 'Companions to each other' and 'brother fountains' (ll. 140–1). Even as the central narrative dwelt on separation and crass casualty, the poem was quietly pointing to the possibility of connection and meaning. Neither of the speakers in the poem comments on the symbolic dimension of the stopped fountain, but any reader would recognize the way in which the natural and human worlds were mirroring each other, as if in sympathy.

'The Brothers' is presented through an imaginary dialogue between the local minister and James's surviving brother, Leonard, who returns home unrecognizable after years at sea. Through this

structure, Wordsworth was able to show how the details of the land-
scape had profound human meaning for those who lived there, as
well as for people returning after travelling abroad. For the Priest,
the moving story is just one of numerous tales that fill his parish,
while James is one of many now dead and lying in the graveyard
where the encounter is taking place. For Leonard, however, the news
is personally devastating, and, as he departs from his native country-
side for a second time, readers are left to imagine the full significance
of what has been related. As Leonard learns the horror of his own
story, he stands as a figure for the magnitude of what might be
revealed through returning to a familiar landscape and reopening
the self to what had been left behind. The re-encounter with a once-
loved place uncovered profound truths, but the depths of emotion
stirred by such revelations could be almost overwhelming.

The Priest's perspective is essential to the equilibrium of 'The
Brothers', because it helps to contain individual tragedy within a
larger, loving framework. Even as he describes James's decline after
Leonard's departure, he also recalls the kindness of everyone around,
'we took him to us. | He was the child of all the dale... and wanted
neither food, nor clothes, nor love' (ll. 338–41). The same sense of
community is evident in the Priest's attitude to local events and the
way in which all his parishioners keep 'a pair of diaries, one
serving... | For the whole dale, and one for each fire-side' (ll. 161–2).
Their closeness to the land is confirmed by the kinds of events that
'chronicle' the vale—a field ploughed, a wood felled, a late snow
storm that kills twenty sheep—and show that the individual and
communal diaries, like the surrounding rocks and hills, are also part
of 'the great book of the world', made by God (l. 261). In such a
community, the records are oral rather than written, so momentous
events are passed on through the living medium of the human voice.
In the graveyard the Priest explains that they 'have no need of names
and epitaphs', because those who have died are never forgotten: 'We
talk about the dead by our fire-sides' (ll. 175–6). It was a kind of
immortality that Wordsworth found especially heartening, as his
note on the poem makes clear:

There is not any thing more worthy of remark in the manners of the inhab-
itants of these mountains, than the tranquillity, I might say indifference,
with which they think and talk upon the subject of death. Some of the

country church-yards, as here described, do not contain a single tombstone, and most of them have a very small number.[40]

In such mountain communities, each individual was recognized and cherished, but his or her significance was also confirmed through participation in a larger network of connection. The idea of possessing two diaries, neither of which extended beyond the events of the dale, might in other contexts suggest a slightly comic view of provincial limitation. In 'The Brothers', however, it rapidly becomes apparent that the Priest's outlook has relevance for those living well beyond his congregation, even if he remains focused on the immediate. Details of Lakeland tradition that may not make sense initially are shown to be the fruit of a collective wisdom, as beneficial to Wordsworth's remote readers as to those in the poem. Leonard's appearance as a stranger enables him to stand in for the reader, benefiting from the inside knowledge being shared by the resident of the dale. The Priest's observation in relation to the absence of tombstones makes clear that his familiar community is in possession of eternal truths not always grasped by those who might deem themselves superior,

> *we* want
> No symbols, Sir, to tell us that plain tale:
> The thought of death sits easy on the man
> Who has been born and dies among the mountains.   (ll. 178–80)

The choice of a dialogue between the local Priest and a perceived stranger allowed Wordsworth to offer not only a deeply moving human tale but also clues to its interpretation, through the perspective of a man who had lived in the same parish for many years and had much to teach those from elsewhere. Although the language of 'the homely Priest of Ennerdale' initially seems offhand and conversational, the plain-speaking tone has the power to surprise both the listener in the poem and the audience of readers. The comic opening, with the Priest's exasperation over 'These Tourists, Heaven preserve us!' gradually comes to be seen as an integral part of the deeper concerns of the entire poem, with the image of the visitors flitting about like butterflies, 'Long as their summer lasted' (l. 5), carefully chosen to contrast with the ideas of permanence and immortality associated with the people of the dales. In the poem, as in his own mind, Wordsworth had created connections that could be fully understood only on revisiting. By encouraging his readers to re-examine what might initially seem unimportant, he enabled them to discover deeper meanings beneath the surface of his poetry, just as his own mental prospects were yielding untold riches. Even a relatively short poem could reinforce the imaginative importance of returns and reconsiderations, making readers active participants in the process.

Wordsworth's interest in the 'pair of diaries' can be seen in the poems he composed in 1800, which were engaged with memories both personal and collective. As suggested in 'The Brothers', he seems to have found his own experiences clarified and made fruitful by the discovery of a larger community of remembered stories. In an environment where people continued for many years in the same homes as those of their parents and grandparents, memories were passed on, accumulating resonances as they went. As a child, Wordsworth had absorbed numerous tales about the people who lived in the Lake District, which now re-emerged as he re-encountered the landscape and language of his earliest years. After his mother's death in 1778, Wordsworth had been sent to school in Hawkshead and boarded with Ann Tyson, who provided him with not only food and clothes and love, but also a fund of stories about the local area. Wordsworth was, as Robert Woof observed, 'a poet who listened'.[41] One of the stories told by Ann Tyson was a poem about an old Grasmere shepherd who, many years ago, had tended his sheep at Greenhead Gill. Now that Wordworth was living in the Vale of Grasmere, the story that had lain quietly in the depths of his memory for so many years re-emerged to inspire one of his greatest poems: 'Michael'. Wordsworth presented the tale accordingly, as part of a communal heritage, known since his childhood:

> It was the first,
> The earliest of those Tales that spake to me
> Of Shepherds, dwellers in the Vallies, men
> Whom I already lov'd, not verily
> For their own sakes, but for the fields and hills
> Where was their occupation and abode.　(ll. 21–6)

This was not a fiction created by the poet, but rather a tale belonging to the place and familiar to the speaker for as long as he could remember. In an apparently casual recollection of his source,

Wordsworth pointed to an extraordinarily well-integrated circuit of connections—he loved the tale for the men who lived in the vale, which was itself the source of the tale. It was not the shepherds who related the story, but the story that spoke of the shepherds. The profound connection between the landscape, the people, and their personal stories, which Wordsworth would analyse in far greater depth in *The Prelude*, was presented in 'Michael' as an unquestioned given. As the poem briefly recalls the poet's childhood, this story stands out as the prompt to awakening sympathies and profounder thoughts:

> And hence this Tale, while I was yet a boy
> Careless of books, yet having felt the power
> Of Nature, by the gentle agency
> Of natural objects led me on to feel
> For passions that were not my own, and think
> At random and imperfectly indeed
> On man, the heart of man, and human life. (ll. 27–33)

When Wordsworth returned to Grasmere and re-experienced the landscape of his youth, he recognized the complicated ways in which he had been influenced by the Lakes. Though love of outdoor life had made the sedentary pursuit of books seem insufficiently satisfying to the energetic child, Wordsworth was nevertheless deeply affected by the stories of local people. Michael's tale, especially, which described a shepherd who felt the fields and hills to be 'his living Being, even more |Than his own Blood', had special resonance for such a boy. The delight over human presences in the local landscape evident in 'Home at Grasmere' is being traced back to earlier years in 'Michael', making the adult perception more akin to recovery than discovery.

The narrator in the poem is able to act as a mediator between the mountain community and his anonymous readers because he can claim lifelong familiarity with the hidden valley, while still possessing the voice of a more educated, well-travelled man. As in 'Home at Grasmere' and 'The Brothers', the special value of the place is understood because of experiences elsewhere. Here, the poet again derives his confident tone from the dual perspective, and his opening address is accordingly direct and welcoming: 'If from the public way you turn your steps.' Through attentive recreation of local detail, Wordsworth leads readers convincingly 'Up the tumultuous brook of Green-head Gill' until they arrive at a 'straggling Heap of unhewn stones' (l. 17). The doubly sighted poet is aware that, in such a beautiful valley, this unremarkable feature is unlikely to catch the attention of outsiders; but he also knows that it is nevertheless the focal point of the whole landscape, because 'to that place a Story appertains' (l. 18). As in 'Home at Grasmere' and 'Hart-Leap Well', Wordsworth demonstrates the investment of human emotion in physical detail, and the transformative effect of memory on the landscape. His poem may be a retelling of an old story, but its insistent address to the present underlines the continuing importance of things that we 'Might see and notice not'. If the unfinished sheepfold is a relic from a largely forgotten era, it is also a starting point for fresh imaginative endeavour.[42] The modest 'Heap' at the beginning of the poem is gradually magnified by the revelation of a hidden, unexpected narrative, until it assumes monumental significance for those capable of seeing properly.

Crucial to the quiet power of the tale are the specificity of its setting and the matter-of-fact tone:

> Their Cottage on a plot of rising ground
> Stood single, with large prospect North and South,
> High into Easedale, up to Dunmal-Raise,
> And Westward to the Village near the Lake.   (ll. 139–42)

Those now reading Wordsworth's poem could, it suggests, go and see for themselves the hillside that has meant so much. Like all the best local work, 'Michael' carries its meaning through well-crafted language to people who may know nothing of Grasmere or its fells and valleys. When the poem first appeared in the new edition of *Lyrical Ballads*, in 1800, Wordsworth added notes on any details that might puzzle more distant readers, explaining that 'Clipping is the word used in the North of England for shearing' and identifying the 'Chapel, floored with Marble' as Ings Chapel, 'on the right hand side of the road leading from Kendal to Ambleside'.[43] The poem's careful foundations possess the kind of documentary adequacy that convinces readers in other times and places of its unquestionable truth. Michael himself is already a legendary figure when the poet hears his story as a boy, but the shared landscape enables him to respond imaginatively to the old man's experience and, in adulthood, to re-create the tale for his contemporaries.

Although Michael is described as 'a Shepherd', his exemplary character is apparent at once, for he is a man of 'unusual strength', 'prompt | And watchful more than ordinary men' and apt to understand the changes in the weather 'When others heeded not'. He is, in fact, not dissimilar to the ideal poet described by Wordsworth in the Preface to *Lyrical Ballads*, who was

> endued with more lively sensibility, more enthusiasm and tenderness, who has a greater knowledge of human nature, and a more comprehensive soul than are supposed to be common among mankind; a man pleased with his own passions and volitions, and who rejoices more than other men in the spirit of life that is in him; delighting to contemplate similar volitions and passions as manifested in the goings-on of the Universe.[44]

Even more striking than this exceptional sensitivity to his surroundings, though, is Michael's stalwart character, which takes him into the hills to care for his flock irrespective of bad weather or more daunting adversity. In his steady adherence to the way of life allotted to him, in his duty to his family and sheep, Michael again resembles Wordsworth's ideal, 'the rock of defence of human nature; an upholder and preserver, carrying every where with him relationship and love'.[45] Wordsworth acknowledged the important lessons learned from Lakeland shepherds more explicitly in the eighth book of *The Prelude*, but in 'Michael' he paid tribute to the old man in terms that indicate a poetic aspiration as much moral and social as aesthetic. Throughout 'Michael', points of resemblance emerge between the shepherd and the poet, but they remain understated, and visible largely on reflection. Michael's deep attachment to the land, for example, demonstrates a special relationship similar to those already celebrated by Wordsworth in 'Home at Grasmere':

> the hills, which he so oft
> Had climb'd with vigorous steps; which had impressed
> So many incidents upon his mind
> Of hardship, skill or courage, joy or fear;
> Which like a book preserv'd the memory
> Of the dumb animals, whom he had sav'd,
> Had fed or shelter'd   ('Michael', ll. 66–72)

Michael's hills, 'like a book', resemble the Priest of Ennerdale's 'diaries' and provide a similar record of the memorable incidents that had taken place there. Later in the poem, when Michael takes Luke to lay the cornerstone of the sheepfold, he does it in the same faith that the bonds between the land and those who live there are enduring. An event so momentous as Luke's departure from the family farm has to be written permanently into the hillside: Michael's creative materials are the rocks that lie around him.

Although the narrative relates Luke's departure and subsequent decline with distressing rapidity, Michael's attitude is never mocked or shown to be misguided.[46] The sheepfold remains as an anchor and shield, not just for the animals that shelter there, but as a symbol of the lasting ties between father and son, farmer and land, man and the universe. The sheepfold is emblematic of the life his fathers lived, just as Michael is, as he carries on regardless of his crippling sorrow:

> Among the rocks
> He went, and still look'd up upon the sun,
> And listen'd to the wind, and as before
> Perform'd all kinds of labour for his Sheep,
> And for the land.   (ll. 464–8)

Despite his devastating loss, Michael continues to care for his sheep, a model of selfless perseverance, sustained by duty, faith, and love. By the end of the poem, the sheepfold stands for Michael too, matching his last years in both its steadiness and incompleteness.

When Michael began his building, it was the idea of the sheepfold rather than the physical object that was offered to Luke as an anchor and shield. Michael knew only too well that Luke would neither be tending sheep nor following the ways of his fathers in any literal way, but he nevertheless declared his faith in the power of memory to provide stability for a young man far from home. If the narrative suggests that the anchor fails to keep Luke safe, it balances this individual misfortune with a larger sense of Michael's courageous faith and its enduring power to affect others. Biblical resonances run throughout the poem, with old Michael evoking at different moments the patriarchs of the Old Testament, the Good Shepherd of the New, and, in his suffering, Job. He is presented as a figure from whom future generations can learn, irrespective of their situations and callings. Michael's sheepfold is intended to be an emblem, something to exist as a permanent feature in the prospect of the mind. The poem acknowledges human failings and distress, but still suggests that Michael and his work can live in the mind of readers anywhere, just as vividly as in that of the young poet who first heard the story in childhood.

The story is related for 'a few natural hearts' and 'for the sake of youthful Poets'—in other words, for those blessed with sympathetic understanding and for those who were most likely to benefit and to share their discoveries with others. A story that spoke to Wordsworth when he was young should be passed on—and the image of Michael's lamp corresponds closely to the poet's lamp in 'Home at Grasmere', whose lustre is not exclusive to the poet (ll. 656–7). In the earlier poem, the speaker reflects on the nature of a light not shared with others, and pronounces it 'Mortal though bright, a dying, dying flame' (l. 658). Michael is not given to analysing the meaning of his lamp, but the poet underlines the significance of the 'Surviving Comrade of uncounted Hours' whose constant presence furnishes the old couple 'with objects and with hopes' ('Michael', ll. 120–3). Crucially, the light extends beyond the immediate household, as the narrator is at pains to point out:

> Not with a waste of words, but for the sake
> Of pleasure, which I know that I shall give
> To many living now, I of this Lamp
> Speak thus minutely: for there are no few
> Whose memories will bear witness to my Tale.
> The Light was famous in its neighbourhood,
> And was a Public Symbol of the life,
> The thrifty Pair had liv'd.   (ll. 131–8)

Michael's lamp turns out to be a model for that of the poet in 'Home at Grasmere', since both are indebted to the Sermon on the Mount: 'let your light so shine forth among men that they may see your good works and glorify your father which is in heaven'[47]. Though different in kind from the work of the Good Shepherd, for Wordsworth poetry should be similarly inspired by the love of others and directed towards their benefit. Like Heaney's definition of 'local work', found serendipitously in the Greek museum, it was a kind of 'votive offering' as well as a contribution to the immediate community and the wider world of mankind.

As Wordsworth concluded his great programme for future work in 'Home at Grasmere', he prayed that his verse 'may live, and be | Even as a light hung up in heaven to chear | Mankind in times to come!' (ll. 1032–3). When he had worked with radical thinkers in the 1790s, Wordsworth planned to publish a magazine that would 'put into each man's hand a lantern to guide him', in the hope of making a personal contribution to the steady universal enlightenment envisaged by political philosophers such as William Godwin.[48] By 1800, he saw the source and nature of the lamp rather differently, but still maintained his commitment to the spiritual salvation of mankind. In order to accomplish this high purpose, he now realized that he—and others—had much to learn from those in largely neglected and undervalued sectors of society. Rather than putting lanterns in the hands of the lower orders, Wordsworth now saw that he might gain from seeing his own work in the light that they had been shedding unself-consciously for years.[49] 'Michael' offers both a profound exploration of the truths to be discovered in an unassuming corner of the Lake District and an affirmation of their far-reaching benefits for humanity. Far from representing a refuge from modern society, the attraction of Grasmere for Wordsworth was its potential for facilitating the recovery of vital human knowledge that seemed to have disappeared from the political centre.

Wordsworth's own belief in the value of Michael's example is evident, not only in the poem's quiet conviction, but also in a letter sent by the poet to one of the most prominent politicians of his day, the great Whig leader Charles James Fox. Wordsworth despatched a copy of *Lyrical Ballads* to Fox in January 1801, with a covering note saying that he was sending it 'solely on account of two poems in the second volume, the one entitled "The Brothers", and the other "Michael"'.[50] These poems, he explained, were meant to embody an ideal of domestic affection through their faithful representation of the lives and relationships of independent smallholders, who worked land inherited from their ancestors. The letter describing the ties between such men and their small properties echoed 'Michael' directly, with the land being presented as 'a kind of permanent rallying point for their domestic feelings, as a tablet upon which they are written which makes them objects of memory in a thousand instances when they would otherwise be forgotten'.[51] The idea of the hills as diaries or books, which record the human experience of those who have lived there, now assumed the even more substantial form of a tablet, which in turn imbued local memories with the resonance of Commandments. The memory of human actions and responsibilities, which are permanently written into the strong features of inherited land, serve as an essential guide to the heirs in their choice of life. Not only was the land a 'rallying point' and a 'tablet', however, but also 'a fountain fitted to the nature of social man from which supplies of affection, as pure as his heart was intended for, are daily drawn'. The small, inherited estates described in the two poems are valuable not just for their moral inspiration, but also because they provide daily replenishment of those profound human feelings that Wordsworth regarded as crucial to the health of the nation at large.

The letter to Fox was written in response to an urgent anxiety about the condition of modern Europe, and especially Britain. Wordsworth's concern about the suffering of those with limited means was spelled out with great clarity, as he listed the various contributing factors, including low wages, high prices on essential items, heavy taxes, the spread of factories and workhouses, and then condemned their cumulative and 'most calamitous' effect on the natural bonds of feeling among the poor. In a country afflicted with numerous evils, not least prolonged warfare and an oppressive government, Wordsworth singled out the new social systems that resulted in families being torn apart and ejected from the places where they had lived for generations as among the most pressing concerns for the liberal statesman. By publishing poems that might 'excite profitable sympathies in many kind and good hearts', Wordsworth was aspiring to the same faith in human nature and hope in the face of apparently overwhelming odds that Michael, 'proverb in the vale', lived by.

'Michael' and 'The Brothers' were not intended merely to elicit sympathy for the suffering poor, however. The poems, far more radically, dared to present such figures as an example to the whole of modern Britain. The deep familial attachments fostered by a shared landscape and the related way of life, which both poems convey so powerfully, offered an alternative model to what seemed to Wordsworth the current, lamentable state of affairs. As he observed in terms that anticipated the admonishments of 'Resolution and Independence', the poems show that 'men who do not wear fine cloaths can feel deeply' and that the best qualities of human nature 'are possessed by men whom we are too apt to consider, not with reference to the points in which they resemble us, but to those in which they manifestly differ from us'.[52] Through the creation of poems,

Wordsworth was able to pay tribute to those who had provided the life-saving influences of his own childhood, and to pass on their exemplary significance to those entirely ignorant of their existence. Men like Michael were independent individuals—their suffering demanded not only sympathy, but also admiration. They were not 'the poor', whose experience in general was at best pitied, and all too often entirely ignored. Instead, Wordsworth presented figures from a community whose ways reflected values and attitudes largely lost to modern, commercial society, but whose memory might still offer some hope of salvation.

In his remarkable letter, Wordsworth praised Fox for the political efforts he had made towards 'the preservation of this class of man', and clearly saw his own task as a poet in a similar light. Though he might not have the power to pass legislation effecting social changes, his imaginative sympathy, perceptive insight and capacity to create a moving narrative in memorable lines of verse could do much towards preserving what was most important and alerting others to its true value. Hence Wordsworth's subsequent claim for the poet as 'the rock of defence of human nature; an upholder and preserver'—if he could develop a form of verse sufficiently powerful to match the mountains that were at once diaries, books, tablets, and fountains, his own poetry would provide a permanent rallying point for the affections of individuals united, not by blood or property, but by sympathetic understanding.

Wordsworth's concern with preservation is part of an acute awareness of the changes affecting a landscape that might once have seemed immutable, and his own efforts were directed towards rendering permanent its potentially fragile human dimensions. Both 'Michael' and 'The Brothers' are set firmly among the enduring mountains of Cumbria, but each relates a tale of dispossession and irreversible change. The Ewbank brothers were separated after their grandfather's death, because the family's land, house, and sheep had to be sold off, leaving the boys destitute, while Michael loses his son as a result of an old obligation to his kinsman, who falls suddenly into financial difficulty. Participation in the landscape, though so valuable to the inner well-being of the residents, also brought its own dangers and distresses. Wordsworth was especially alert to the rapid transformations in the countryside he remembered from his youth and knew that Michael's story, told to him as a boy, was prophetic of the experience of numerous freeholders and independent sheep-farmers in the later eighteenth century.[33]

The poet's sense of responsibility was deepened by the threat of destruction, and his work, like the sheepfold, was a monument to a disappearing way of life. Disappearance did not, however, erase the enduring value of those preserved in 'Michael', and its invitation to understand the meaning of something that might otherwise be seen and noticed not serves as an opening to the poem and to the hearts of readers far removed from eighteenth-century Grasmere. It is a poem that fully acknowledges the staggering misfortunes of life, and yet remains premised on hope.

Although 'Michael', like 'The Brothers', seems to be a poem of loss and rupture, its more pessimistic tendencies are checked by an understated, and yet ultimately far more powerful, framework of love and hope. Luke's disgrace and disappearance are followed immediately by the most memorable statement in the poem: 'There is a comfort in the strength of love' ('Michael', l. 456). The calm balance of the line and emphasis on the internal rhymes—there/strength, is a/in the, comfort/love—answers the preceding narrative sequence with quiet dignity. There is no equivocation, and Michael seems to find comfort as surely as he finds lost sheep. Just as Yeats would answer the disruptions of the Civil War with his bracing refrain, 'Come build in the empty house of the stare', so Wordsworth created a poem that recognized affliction and failure, but still sought to uncover the best in human nature. As he explained in the preface to *Lyrical Ballads*, part of the pleasure in poetic metre derives from 'the sense of difficulty overcome'; in 'Michael' the narrative corresponds exactly to the poem's rhythmic satisfactions. It is just the kind of fully 'adequate' poetry celebrated by Heaney, which faces even the most dire crisis with a reminder of the possibility of something better.

Wordsworth's Legacy to Youthful Poets

Wordsworth presented his poems to Fox in response to a moment of national crisis, but they were also explicitly directed to those with 'natural hearts' and to 'youthful poets'. He could not have envisaged Seamus Heaney reading his work in a different place and a different century, but would undoubtedly have been pleased by the sympathetic

understanding of the young Irish poet. When Heaney confronted the
troubled history of his own surrounding landscape with Wordswor-
thian notions of mental prospects, he may have been imagining a
peaceful alternative to the community he knew so well. The Lake
District evoked in some of the most appealing passages of *The Prelude*
seems comfortingly free of sectarian conflict, while 'Home at Gras-
mere' and the poems in *Lyrical Ballads* offer a model of communal
participation rather than rivalry. However, the very metaphors that
seemed to come so naturally to Heaney as he wrote about Mossbawn
were the same as those in Wordsworth's poems. The pump in the
backyard has much in common with Wordsworth's explanation to
Fox that the little tract of inherited land in Lake District communities
was 'a fountain' (a spring) supplying daily draughts of affection to
those who live there. The neighbouring fields that formed 'a script,
indelibly written' into Heaney's nervous system are close relatives of
the natural features that provided the diaries, books, and tablets of
Wordsworth's landscape, while the language of internal writing
echoes *The Prelude*'s recurrent imagery of printing, which is used to
emphasize the permanent impressions left on both the poet's mind and
his surroundings.

Wordsworth's very notion of reading the human history of the
land was prompted, not just by familiarity, however, but also by fear.
The threat to the mountain community depicted in his poetry was
already being realized when he returned to the landscape of his
youth in 1800 and did much to provoke the passionate response that
inspired so much of his best poetry. Although the Lakes had provided
a psychological anchor for the young Wordsworth during his own
travels, he saw when he came back that even such an enduring land-
scape was liable to destruction because of its vital—but therefore
vulnerable—human dimension. Although, when Heaney was
growing up, the nature of the surrounding menace was very different
in kind, his own attachment to the family farm was clearly intensi-
fied by his awareness of its potentially precarious situation. What
Wordsworth's poetry offered was not a temporary escape into an
idyll of unchanging tranquillity, but rather a fully adequate response
to a recognizable world. In *The Prelude*, the poet acknowledged both
the destructive tendencies of even the most creative individuals, and
the cataclysmic effects of larger, collective energies in conflict, while
in *Lyrical Ballads* the most admirable figures are shown to be afflicted

by appalling personal losses and subject to forces beyond their control.

When Wordsworth wrote his pastoral poems, Britain was enduring not only the alarms and hardships associated with prolonged warfare, but also the related threats to free speech and human rights, as the government clamped down on the possibility of internal sedition. The suspension of habeas corpus between 1795 and 1801 meant that anyone could be arrested and imprisoned on suspicion rather than criminal evidence, a situation that contributed much to Wordsworth's perception of contemporary British society as living 'in these times of fear'.[54] For the young radical who had embraced the early days of the French Revolution as the dawn of a new age of freedom and equality, the course of the 1790s had felt like a dismaying slide into a 'melancholy waste of hopes o'erthrown'.[55] In spite of this oppressive atmosphere and the larger social changes outlined to Fox, his poetry quietly continued to observe the best in human nature, to assert its hope for a better world, and to reaffirm the beauty of the one we have. Such verse had strong appeal for a poet whose formative years were spent in Derry, who lived in Belfast during the onset of the Troubles, and who witnessed brutal violence and the severe measures taken in response to civil unrest: 'There was the baton charge in Duke Street in Derry in October 1968 and the surge of protest marches after that. Then the pogroms into the Falls. The arrival of the British army. Internment. Bombings like the Abercorn restaurant. Shootings like the linen workers in Armagh. The shootings in the Pentacostal church at Darkley.'[56]

Wordsworth's alertness to the beauty to be found in things that might generally go unnoticed offers a powerful source of hope in situations that may otherwise seem desperate. It is not just the capacity to delve within the self and unearth wonders from the mud that has proved inspirational to Heaney, but also his sympathy for others—for Michael, for the Leech Gatherer, for all those figures whose age and suffering might make them seem unlikely subjects for admiration. Wordsworth's poetry has an eye-opening quality that is really an expansion of the heart. By gaining a more informed way of looking at things, the reader's experience is suddenly enlarged. This is part of his great legacy to subsequent generations, which Heaney has received, developed, and passed on. Heaney's 'Field of Vision', for example, describes an old woman who would sit for hours in her wheelchair, staring out of the same window at

> The stunted agitated hawthorn bush,
> The same small calves with their backs to wind and rain,
> The same acre of ragwort, the same mountain.[57]

The depressing nature of old age and invalidity is palpable in the poem, and yet, in its very emphasis on sameness and immobility, the scene is alive with feeling and movement. Rather than eliciting pity, the speaker comments that being 'Face to face with her was an education'. The immobilized woman offers a startling lesson, for through her

> you could see
> Deeper into the country than you expected
> And discovered that the field behind the hedge
> Grew more distinctly strange.

The Wordsworthian truths are beautifully transferred to the old woman's home in the late twentieth century. Immediate surroundings, however dull and familiar, can, when properly understood, reveal something extraordinary; seeing properly is a matter of feeling; and the mundane is potentially the marvellous. Wordsworth's poetry showed that paradise was still attainable by anyone, anywhere, provided that he or she was prepared to seek it in 'the very world which is the world | Of all of us, the place in which, in the end, | We find our happiness, or not at all.'[58] He also emphasized that those who may seem the least fortunate or engaging can possess a rare wisdom and a redemptive quality from which the more formally educated might learn much, if they thought to look. The poet who discovers not only the visionary in the unassuming, but also the right language and form through which to share his revelation, offers an enormous gift to those who respond imaginatively to his work.

   Wordsworth's admiration for the men and women of the Lakes, though a reflection of immediate experience, was by no means a simple matter of local pride. In the preface to *Lyrical Ballads*, he made very clear that, although many of his poems focused on 'low and rustic life', his choice arose from a desire to re-create in verse the essential qualities of human nature and thus to produce a kind of art that would have permanent value to society. His faithful depictions of Lakeland figures were therefore not restricted to an audience in the north-west of England. Like Hardy many years later, the local for Wordsworth was really universal, and hence the power of his verse to affect those in other places and times. When he revised the preface in 1802, Wordsworth clarified these aims:

> In spite of difference of soil and climate, of language and manners, of laws and customs, in spite of things silently gone out of mind and things violently destroyed, the Poet binds together by passion and knowledge the vast empire of human society, as it is spread over the whole earth, and over all time.[59]

This is a foundational statement of poetry's place in the world and has close affinities to Heaney's views on 'local' poetry and its capacity to reach out to sympathetic audiences everywhere. Wordsworth understood the need for poetry to represent the world truthfully: to reflect the immediate in order to create something of transcendent power. He recognized, too, that the task must often be undertaken in the least auspicious circumstances—in spite of things gone out of mind and things violently destroyed. His own facility for language, his imaginative sympathy, and his ear for the most satisfactory cadences also meant that his best work achieved the kind of proper 'in-placeness' that rendered his high ideals a practical possibility.

But what Wordsworth also provided for subsequent writers was a kind of poetry that, in responding to such ideals, entailed struggling with distractions, frustrations, and even defeat. The exemplary figures in his work are often those being observed, but the speakers who encounter them and learn wisdom in unlikely places are also heartening models. The uncertainties of the youthful poet as portrayed in 'Resolution and Independence' or *The Prelude* are every bit as engaging to a sympathetic reader as the admirable figures who are upheld as guides. The admonished speakers of Wordsworth's poetry provided important forerunners for Heaney in his own soul-searching and self-rebuking moments, as he cast himself successively as the 'artful voyeur' of 'Punishment', or as mad Sweeney, escaping from the battlefield, or as the penitent pilgrim of 'Station Island', or even the reluctant visionary of *Seeing Things*, who had taken 'so long for air to brighten, | Time to be dazzled and the heart to lighten'.[60] Poetry that admits to doubt may lack the marching certainties of more emphatic verse, but has a resilient strength of its own, and an openness to many different kinds of reader.

In his dual perspectives, Wordsworth was mediating between his neighbours and a wider audience, but at the same time he was also inviting different kinds of response. Many readers would identify more readily with the travelling observer than with the men who drew their strength from being rooted in patrimonial acres and hence Wordsworth's invitation to those who do not feel securely bound to any particular spot. Since his own admiration for the mountain communities of the Lake District had grown through his experience of other places, the poetry reflecting his feelings had strong appeal to those who felt a sense of displacement, whether actual or imminent. Wordsworth's own experience of other places was crucial to the persuasiveness of his verse. His admiration for shepherds carries conviction because it comes from a voice informed by knowledge of different places, societies, and values. The poetry also acknowledges that certain kinds of life had largely disappeared from modern Britain, and recognizes the power of the forces that had demolished Michael's home, or sent Leonard Ewbank away to sea. These might represent a set of circumstances specific to late-eighteenth-century Cumbria, but their human effects can be imagined by readers in very different situations. The question of what poetry could do to help was central to Wordsworth's creative endeavour, as it has been to Heaney's. For both writers, however, the possibility that ultimately art might not persuade the sceptics—might not quite measure up to the challenges of the world as it is—was a very real one.

2

Lakes or Oceans?

Heaney's admiration for Wordsworth is of a kind inspired by a poet whose standing in literary history is beyond question. Wordsworth had indeed created 'work that might live', and his words are still capable of touching hearts and fortifying minds two centuries after their first appearance. In the opening decades of the nineteenth century, when he was formulating his ambitious ideas about poetry, however, a warm reception by 'second selves' was by no means assured. The best known of the rising generation of poets, Lord Byron, responded to Wordsworth's celebration of humble life and natural poetry with witty disdain:

> There is a narrowness in such a notion,
> Which makes me wish you'd change your lakes for ocean.[1]

Wordsworth's views of contemporary society, though welcomed by some readers, were greeted with varying degrees of amusement, annoyance, and astonishment by others.[2] What now seems a natural association between Wordsworth's poetry and the English Lakes emerged very rapidly, after the publication of the enlarged collection of *Lyrical Ballads*, with its deliberately polemical preface.

Not long after the appearance of the 1802 edition of *Lyrical Ballads*, with its expanded title ('with Pastoral and other Poems') and even larger preface, Francis Jeffrey turned his formidable pen on the small, but vocal, circle of poets who had opted, unaccountably, to live in the Lake District. Keen to attract readers for the new *Edinburgh Review*, Jeffrey launched the first of his memorably scathing attacks on Wordsworth by condemning *Lyrical Ballads* in a review of Southey's *Thalaba* and accusing both poets of a 'splenetic and idle discontent with the existing institutions of society'.[3] Jeffrey's irritation bristled beneath his carefully chosen language, which echoed the accusations of the preface in order to turn them against Wordsworth, pointing out that he was a malcontent, with sufficient leisure to be penning idle verses and promoting disaffection.

As a trained lawyer, Jeffrey was well equipped to bring charges against Southey, and, by drawing Wordsworth and Coleridge into the same review, he was able to hint at an undesirable brotherhood of poets, who reinforced each other's oddities through their distance from the cultural mainstream. Since Jeffrey's own publication was partly launched in order to provide a voice for Whig opinion at a time when the prospect of liberal reforms seemed bleak, the decision of intelligent, radical poets to retreat into rustic self-indulgence was especially vexing.[4] When *Poems, in Two Volumes* was published in 1807, Jeffrey continued his offensive, by coining the term 'Lake School' to underline Wordsworth's eccentricity and potentially dangerous influence, a point later rammed home in his review of *The Excursion*, which attacked Wordsworth for his retreat into rural seclusion and argued that 'all the greater poets lived…in the full current of society'.[5] Rather than pointing the public towards more admirable literature and morality, Wordsworth's successive volumes of poetry, with their explicit endorsements of a better way of life, were received in some quarters as little more than a stick for beating the author. In particular, the very landscape that Wordsworth had found such a source of creative recovery and reaffirmation had now been reduced to a pejorative adjective among the influential, city-centred reviewing circles of the age.

During the following two decades, even those most likely to be sympathetic to Wordsworth's radical purposes seemed to reject his ideas and to resist his influence publically. Byron's objections to his older contemporaries were clearly stated in *Don Juan*: 'You gentlemen,' he remarked, 'by dint of long seclusion | From better company, have kept your own at Keswick'.[6] Such anti-social and apparently reactionary behaviour deserved a well-rhymed rebuke: the 'continued fusion', and implicit mental confusion, of Wordsworth and Coleridge had led to the unhappy 'conclusion' that only their own poetry really mattered. By the time Byron wrote the Dedication to *Don Juan* in 1818, Wordsworth had been living in the Grasmere area for eighteen years, publishing substantial volumes of poetry and becoming firmly established in the public mind as the 'Sage of Rydal'. Robert Southey, who had become Poet Laureate in 1813, had also lived in the nearby town of Keswick since 1800, while Coleridge, though much less settled than his fellow poets and based in London from 1815 onwards, had stayed with both the Wordsworths and the Southeys for considerable periods. The result in each case of this strange preference for the Lake District was, according to Lord Byron, a misplaced self-importance and wilful ignorance of the wider world. Far from being redemptive, the Lakes and the local were not even regarded as positive ideas by Byron. Unlike the author of *Don Juan*, whose foreign travels had apparently provided a far superior knowledge of human nature, Wordsworth was culpably inclined to stay at home. With an ocean of knowledge and experience spread out before him, Wordsworth seemed to have retreated to the comforts of the tiny, familiar lakes of his childhood.

Wordsworth's attachment to the north-western corner of England, when not understood according to his own principles, was frequently scorned as narrow, provincial, or peculiar, his enjoyment of solitary walks in the Cumbrian hills a sign of chronic self-absorption. In the eyes of a satirist such as Thomas Love Peacock, Wordsworth and Coleridge spent whole days going up and down hill, congratulating themselves: 'Poetical genius is the finest of all things, and we feel that we have more of it than anyone ever had.'[7] Presented thus, it hardly seemed a fail-safe route to higher truths, public influence, or literary excellence. Wordsworth's admiration for the Lake District, obvious to readers since the publication of the enlarged edition of *Lyrical Ballads* in 1800 and confirmed by his subsequent collections, was easy to caricature. He was routinely mocked for choosing local sources and humble narrators: the retired merchant seaman of 'The Thorn' was pilloried in Byron's draft preface to *Don Juan*, the 'old women and sextons' from whom he 'picked up stories' brought forward by Peacock as evidence that the modern poet did nothing but wallow 'in the rubbish of departed ignorance'.[8]

Peacock's attack was as much on Wordsworth's philosophy as on his poetry, but again his residence in the northern hills provided an easy satirical target: 'Poetical impressions can be received only among natural scenes: for all that is artificial is anti-poetical. Society is artificial, therefore we will live out of society. The mountains are natural, therefore we will live in the mountains.'[9] If Wordsworth's

insistence on the human dimensions of exemplary mountain communities were ignored and his exploration of the role of the poet
dismissed as self-obsession, then the criticisms of modern society and
personal decision to live in a remote rural area could be viewed as
misanthropy. The very accusations Wordsworth had attempted to
pre-empt with his 'Lines Left upon a Seat in a Yew-tree', with its
cautionary portrait of the disappointed visionary, and that he
continued to rebut in the debates over solitude in *The Excursion*,
were now being levelled at the poet who dared to proclaim his love
of nature so emphatically. The bold condemnation of the accumulation of men in cities had not, perhaps, been a line of argument especially appealing to critics in London or Edinburgh. Their retaliation,
unsurprisingly, tended to concentrate on Wordsworth's choice of
abode and the easy equation between rural seclusion and unsociability. Local work, in Heaney's redemptive sense, might have been
pioneered by Wordsworth, but his contemporaries were not necessarily amenable to his calls to salvation.

In *The Four Ages of Poetry*, Peacock extracted a great deal of comedy
from Wordsworth's anguish over the state of the contemporary
world, but his essay also exposed the very real threats to creative
writing that the preface to *Lyrical Ballads* had not even begun to
analyse. For even more damaging to modern poetry than the multitude of causes currently eroding the contemporary quality of life
were the attitudes outlined so clearly by Peacock: many intelligent
members of society were apparently content to dismiss creative
writing altogether. Poets of the modern 'age of brass' were, according
to Peacock's witty polemic, worrying among themselves about
virtue, nature, and new poetic principles, while the more rational
majority of the educated population were getting on with the practical business of life. What could poetry do to improve society? In
Peacock's essay, the 'light' that was dispersing the darkness of ignorance was that of progressive reason, from which contemporary
poets refused to benefit. As he warmed to his theme, Peacock adopted
Wordsworth's favourite images for the purposes of ridicule,
presenting the modern poet, not as a lamp hung up in heaven, but in
retreat from the light of reason and burrowing, 'like a mole, to throw
up the barren hillocks'.[10]

Throughout the *Four Ages*, Peacock played on the idea of place, with
its various connotations of physical location, order, and importance,

mischievously echoing Wordsworth's language in order to expose his limitations:

The philosophic mental tranquillity which looks round with an equal eye on all external things, collects a store of ideas, discriminates their relative value, assigns to all their proper place, and from the materials of useful knowledge thus collected, appreciated, and arranged, forms new combinations that impress the stamp of their power and utility on the real business of life, is diametrically the reverse of that frame of mind which poetry inspires, or from which poetry can emanate.[11]

As Peacock pursued the opposition between the philosophic eye and the poetic (in an obvious retort to Wordsworth's 'Immortality Ode', with its resounding consolations about the years that bring the philosophic mind), he was building up to the remarkable extended sentence that concluded his essay by assigning 'to all their proper place'. The jibes about Wordsworth's retreat into the mountains culminated at last in a striking image that condemned poetry to ever-diminishing significance in the real world, for the closing paragraph presented a modern 'pyramid' of useful knowledge, built by 'mathematicians, astronomers, chemists, moralists, metaphysicians, historians, politicians, and political economists' and contrasted this enormous construction with the tiny 'modern Parnassus far beneath'.[12] All those who reached the summit of the pyramid of modern knowledge could look down on poetry to see 'how small a place it occupies in the comprehensiveness of their prospect'. Far from being an image of enduring magnitude, the Wordsworthian mountain was reduced in Peacock's hands to little more than a molehill.

Wordsworth had hoped to convince readers of 1800 that poetry had a vital place in modern society, because it was grounded in the world of real men and women. Despite the personal discoveries that inspired so much of Wordsworth's finest poetry when he returned to settle in Grasmere, many eloquent readers seemed persuaded neither by his admiration for nature and shepherding communities, nor by his development of a new kind of cadence that responded to the world with truth and hope. Even Coleridge expressed disappointment over The Excursion, because of its narrow focus and failure to include what he considered essential to any extensive philosophical meditation on human life: 'the different ages of the world, and in the different states—Savage—Barbarous— Civilized—the lonely Cot,

or Borderer's Wigwam—the Village—the Manufacturing Town—
Sea-Port—City—Universities.'[13] Coleridge's baffled response reveals
the same Enlightenment assumptions about the development of
human society as those influencing Peacock, Jeffrey, Byron, and a
host of other educated readers. In the same letter, Coleridge described
the work of the true poet as 'representative, generic', and soon after-
wards made the distance between his own aesthetic ideas and those
of his old friend public, by denouncing Wordsworth's adherence to
'low and rustic life', even as he explained that the volume had initially
been their joint project.[14] The man who had once been most sympa-
thetic to Wordsworth's ideas seemed at last to be turning away and
joining in the public rejection. Despite his failure to win universal
approval or even the support of some of his closest friends, however,
Wordsworth's commitment to the deep resources of his local envi-
ronment remained unshaken.

When Peacock's *Four Ages* appeared in 1820, Wordsworth's faith in
the importance of poetry as 'local work' was being reaffirmed by the
publication of *The River Duddon*, a new volume of poetry, which
included extensive notes on the people who lived in the remote
Cumbrian valley, as well as his own 'Guide to the Lakes'. As Stephen
Gill has observed, 'local specificity, local pride, loving attention to
the unsung and the little known are the keynotes' of the collection.[15]
Contemporary reviewers saw at once that the sonnet sequence had
been suggested by 'the river which flows from Wrynose Fell, at first
through a mountain district, and thence through a more cultivated
tract, for twenty-five miles, and enters the Irish Sea'.[16] The poems
could hardly have been more specifically located, nor the location
more obscure and, yet, the reception was surprisingly positive. Even
those who remained baffled by Wordsworth's perverse choice of
subject still had to bestow some begrudging praise—'when we see
the beautiful verses Mr Wordsworth has written on this insignificant
river, with its barbarous name, we may exclaim,—what would he
not have written had the majestic Thames employed his muse'.[17]
Though many still failed fully to grasp Wordsworth's promotion of
the local, the new readiness to acknowledge the value of his poetry
is indicative of a dawning acceptance of local truth. By 1820, even
reviewers based in Edinburgh were referring to Wordsworth as 'the
great poet of the Lakes' and finding in the *Duddon* volume 'the true
inspiration of the Grecian lyre'.[18]

When *The River Duddon* appeared, the *British Review* evoked Samuel Johnson's well-known critical definition of 'local poetry' in order to underline the originality of Wordsworth's volume, in which particular landscapes were described in such a way that the picturesque actually enters 'into the heart, and annexes an interior feeling'.[19] The anonymous reviewer had no doubt about Wordsworth's transformation of a genre familiar since the early eighteenth century, but, unlike Jeffrey, Peacock, or Byron, he responded warmly to the way in which the contemplative modern poet had 'philosophized, and spiritualized, and raised into commerce with the soul' the most unlikely rural objects, and stretches of scenery, 'general, local and domestic'. Wordsworth's 'local poetry' was a new kind of verse that recognized the importance of man's relationship, personal and traditional, with the world around him, and saw the potential for spiritual elevation in the most familiar places. That Wordsworth's treatment of the local should be so much closer to twentieth-century views than to Dr Johnson's, however, highlights, not only his originality, but also the massive obstacles that deterred so many of his less receptive contemporaries from understanding his innovations. Wordsworth demonstrated again and again the fundamental importance of the humble and local to the creation of art that mattered, but the task of persuading those brought up on neoclassical aesthetics was a hard one.

'Local Poetry'

When Byron announced that Wordsworth and Coleridge should change 'their Lakes for Ocean', he was, after all, articulating what had oft been thought, if never so pithily expressed. That great literature should not be narrowly confined was a well-established critical axiom. More than half a century earlier, the influential voice of Samuel Johnson had urged readers of 'The Vanity of Human Wishes' to obtain the most extensive possible view of human behaviour, by surveying mankind 'from China to Peru'. Though equally driven by the pursuit of truth, Johnson's advice could hardly have been further removed from Wordsworth's belief that the best subjects for the poet and moralist were men in the lower ranks of rural society, where 'the sameness and narrow circle of their intercourse' gave rise to a simpler

and 'far more philosophical language'.[20] It was a fundamental differ-
ence about the way to discover human nature, for, while Johnson
had suggested that universal meanings might be reached by ranging
widely over numerous individual examples, Wordsworth was
convinced that the best method was to spend long periods of time
with those confined to 'cottages and fields', thus avoiding the 'sad
mistake' made by so many 'of supposing that human nature and the
persons they associate with are one and the same thing'.[21] If Johnson
advocated a steady ascent to truth over the vast mass of particulars,
for Wordsworth it was more a matter of descending sympathetically
into the depths of the human heart. For a generation brought up on
Johnson's resounding lines and influential critical views, Words-
worth's approach to the great question of truth was going to take
some time to accept.

Despite his own interest in biographical detail, the idea of finding
the kinds of truths amenable to the creation of great poetry in a
familiar environment was not one that Johnson was keen to promote,
as his account of John Denham demonstrates. For, while Denham's
significance as the pioneer of a new genre of 'local poetry' was
acknowledged, the somewhat caustic references to his followers
implies that it was hardly an enviable claim to fame: 'little will be
gained by an enumeration of smaller poets, that have left scarce a
corner of the island not dignified either by rhyme, or blank verse.'[22]
By the middle of the eighteenth century, the impulse to record
immediate locations was becoming widespread, but clearly such
poems could not measure up to Johnson's ideals of higher literature,
which must convey universal truths about the human condition.

'Local poetry', as defined by Johnson, was identified by its content
rather than by form or character—'the fundamental subject is some
particular landscape, to be poetically described, with the addition of
such embellishments as may be supplied by historical retrospection,
or incidental meditation'.[23] Cooper's Hill, for example, was real
enough, but Denham's poetic description of the distant views of
London, Windsor, Chertsey, and Runnymede provided an opportu-
nity for public meditation on English history, kingship, commerce,
and political power. Published in 1642, Cooper's Hill was a Civil War
poem, just as Windsor Forest, by Denham's most distinguished
successor, was an ambitious conception of the Royal Park as a site of
national, international, and even cosmic importance:

> Thy Forests, *Windsor*! And thy green Retreats,
> At once the Monarch's and the Muse's Seats.[24]

In this 'local poem', Pope was paying tribute to his queen and his country, as well as to his patron, his classical education, his poetic predecessors, and his God. The tone was public, the approach, philosophical. Despite the specific location, the generalized references to 'Hills and Vales, the Woodland and the Plain' served as prompts to historical and mythological narrative, and to visions of future national prosperity. The royal oaks were grand symbols of the monarchy and the nation, with the material advantage of supplying timber to the Navy and thus extending British power across the globe: 'Earth's distant Ends our Glory shall behold' (l. 401). A local scene, in Pope's fertile imagination, could expand with remarkable energy into one of global domination. It was just the kind of expansive patriotism that Simone Weil would criticize in *The Need for Roots* and place in direct opposition to the tender, protective attachment of an individual to his home. The formal, topographical poetry of the earlier eighteenth century could hardly have been more different from the kind of 'local work' celebrated by Heaney or Kavanagh, but nor was it remotely similar to Wordsworth's evocation of special places, whose significance depended on the investment of personal feeling. Although Windsor Forest had some meaning for every British citizen, it was not the kind of deep personal significance that Wordsworth considered foundational to the individual and to his art.

Johnson's views on the presence of the local in art were by no means unusual in the middle decades of the eighteenth century. In 1770, for example, his friend Joshua Reynolds was warning students at the newly established Royal Academy to 'disregard all local and temporary ornaments, and look only on those general habits which are everywhere and always the same'.[25] In Reynolds's eyes, accurate representation of an 'individual spot' often led to painting that was 'very faithful', but with such fidelity came the risk of becoming 'very confined'.[26] Like Imlac telling Rasselas that the business of the poet was 'to examine, not the individual, but the species; to remark general properties and large appearances' and to 'neglect the minuter discriminations', Reynolds instilled in his students an ambition to transcend the realistic and particular, in pursuit of general—and therefore higher—truths.[27]

Reynolds's lectures ranged over various kinds of painting to illustrate the point, with the Dutch School's adherence to 'local principles' upheld as an example of how art might be accomplished and distinctive, but still fail in the higher pursuit of general history or allegory. The very kind of art that would later be celebrated by George Eliot as the model for any writer bent on achieving truthful depictions of the world was roundly dismissed by Reynolds as irredeemably minor. In her early novels, Eliot developed a more realistic style of fiction by presenting detailed descriptions of 'commonplace people' in ordinary places, while in her critical writing she argued that 'the most crapulous boors that Teniers ever painted' were preferable to any idealized image of human life, because of their uncompromising truthfulness.[28] Far from representing a technical curiosity, the Dutch masters were upheld as an inspiration for modern novelists and, despite Arnold's denunciations of provincialism, Eliot offered her greatest work, *Middlemarch*, without apology, as 'A Study of Provincial Life'.[29] Just as many nineteenth-century painters turned against the neoclassical ideals of historical and heroic painting to find new subjects in the fresh air of first-hand observation, so novelists began to draw on the rich resources of their immediate surroundings. For many influential aestheticians of the mid eighteenth century, however, particular places, whether represented in art or literature, were a sign of narrowness, restricted interest, and impermanence.

In the eighteenth century, assumptions about truth often depended on comparisons. General ideas about human society were derived from the study of different languages and manners, while numerous accounts of ancient civilizations, modern nations, and newly discovered peoples in a 'primitive' condition were carefully juxtaposed to produce a larger understanding of mankind. Montesquieu's magisterial study *De l'Esprits de Lois*, for example, gathered material from across the globe and throughout human history for its analysis of different kinds of government and comparative study of climatic and cultural influences on political systems. Adam Smith would range in a matter of sentences from the Tartars and Arabians to the North American Indians, while Lord Kames amassed details from the authors of Ancient Greece and Rome, from contemporary travel writers and from recent European history to establish the grounds for his *Sketches of the History of Man*.[30] This was the intellectual context

in which Johnson suggested ranging from China to Peru and studded
his own poem with such confident couplets as this:

> All times their scenes of pompous wealth afford,
> From Persia's tyrant to Bavaria's lord.   (ll. 223–4)

The wider the survey, the more authoritative the argument. It was
the very outlook that informed Coleridge's response to *The Excur-
sion*, when he admitted that his idea of a philosophical poem would
include every aspect of human society, from the savage to the civi-
lized, from the wigwam to the palace.

As philosophers worked tirelessly on analyses of civil society (and,
especially, on its 'progress'), attitudes to the arts were inevitably
coloured by the period's wider intellectual ambition. Since the
evidence for continuing improvement in art and literature was some-
what less assured than that of the various sciences, there was consid-
erable pressure on creative writers and aestheticians to demonstrate
their contribution to the collective effort. When Hugh Blair, the
first Professor of Rhetoric and Belles Lettres, lectured to students in
Edinburgh, he attempted to account for the rise and progress of
language and to assess the function of poetry from the earliest stages
of society to the most civilized, while urging his audiences to polish
their own prose style.[31] James Thomson's highly successful poem *The
Seasons* demonstrated its philosophical credentials by ranging from
the 'Nubian rocks' to the 'wintry Baltic', from Cato to Newton,
from pineapples to constellations; but among the vast sweeps of time
and space were stumbling blocks of uncertainty over the contempo-
rary arts—'But who can paint like Nature?…Ah, what shall
language do?'[32] The creative artist had a strong sense of duty to God
and to society, but the possibility of matching the rapid advances of
the scientists and philosophic historians was rather daunting.

Both Johnson and Reynolds, in offering guidance on the best kind
of writing and painting, were attempting to fulfil their own respon-
sibilities to civic society and to participate in the wider progress of
their age. Inevitably, their aesthetic values were shaped by the empir-
ical and expansive outlook of the contemporary intellectual milieu.
It is not surprising, therefore, to find Reynolds announcing in the
Royal Academy that, if great art were to aspire to the universal, and
to the 'eternal, invariable idea of nature', the artist must enlarge his
mental horizons through acquaintance with many minds and

cultures, and through studying the best models of all time.[33] In eighteenth-century Britain, where ambitions to rival the acknowl-edged classical and European Masters were becoming increasingly insistent, many artists felt compelled to travel to the Continent to learn from the finest works of antiquity, while the wealthier Grand Tourists returned with sculptures and paintings to adorn their grand houses and to provide inspiration for native artists and writers.[34] Reynolds himself spent three years in Italy, studying Greek sculpture and Renaissance paintings, which furnished him with ideas for his own art and ambitions for the general elevation of British culture.[35] At the end of such a century of aspiration, expansion, and improve-ment, Wordsworth's decision to compose poetry that focused so intensively on small parts of England was bound to strike some contemporaries as oddly self-limiting and constricted. For Byron, educated at Aberdeen, Harrow, and Cambridge, where he learned from both classical authors and modern philosophers, as well as imbibing the fashionable desire to see as much of the world as he could manage, Wordsworth's stories about Lakeland shepherds were hardly providing the most congenial model.

Not everyone shared Byron's taste for the Ocean, however. Cosmo-politanism was really possible only for those fortunate enough to inherit the means and motivation to travel, and a well-stocked library to enable extensive mental exploration. Talented artists might obtain financial support from wealthy patrons whose social standing demanded an impressive gallery of family portraits and neoclassical scenes, but for much of the population, the idea of going abroad, either physically or mentally, was out of the question. During periods of warfare with France, especially, travel to Europe was difficult except for those whose military or diplomatic missions took them there. In 1809, when Byron secured his trip to the eastern Mediterranean, he had to sail south via the Bay of Biscay and the Iberian Peninsula rather than following the traditional Grand Tourist routes across the Alps. Although Wordsworth had succeeded in walking across much of France and Switzerland before the outbreak of hostilities, he was then confined to Britain until after the defeat of Napoleon, except for a visit to Calais, during the brief Peace of 1802. For many women, continental Europe was attainable only through conversation, reading, and prints, while for anyone lower down the social ladder, unless they were soldiers or sailors, emigrants or convicts, the world beyond these islands was largely a closed book. Many members of eighteenth-century British society were more likely to be busy struggling to feed their families than dreaming of becoming Citizens of the World. Though Byron's aristocratic protagonists seemed free to roam the Mediterranean, their destinations remained well beyond the reach of most of the population. Not everyone was able to scoff at Wordsworth's references to Greece in *The Excursion* with the same first-hand confidence that Byron could display.[36]

In contrast to Byron, writers who chose British characters and settings were speaking much more directly to the first-hand experience of their audiences. To suggest, as Wordsworth did so emphatically when he published *The Excursion*, that paradise was 'the growth of common day' and regaining it, more a question of looking properly than travelling widely, was to offer imaginative liberation to a host of readers whose circumstances might constrain both their physical and political freedom. Although some were slow to respond to his insights, others welcomed his work as the entrance to a new world. What Wordsworth tried to show a generation of readers shaken by years of warfare and social upheaval was that everyone had something remarkable to discover, if only they thought to look.

Wordsworth's far-reaching insights, however, were not reached in isolation. Though the satirists delighted in casting him as a cranky recluse because so much of his literary philosophy ran counter to established ideas, Wordsworth's powerful response to the cultural crisis of his age can be better understood as part of a larger movement. In his emphasis on the vital role of poetry in modern society, Wordsworth was fostering the traditions of Chaucer, Shakespeare, Milton, and the old British bards and minstrels, whose various poems were now being recognized as irrefutable evidence of native genius.[37] In his emphasis on the essential connection between writing and places, however, he was drawing on a much more piecemeal, but nevertheless growing, sense of regional distinction and its cultural importance. In the 1770s, Johnson had commented ruefully on the new loco-descriptive poems that dignified every corner of the country, but Denham's legacy was only part of a much larger phenomenon. Wordsworth brought an unprecedented depth and assurance to what had once seemed a minor genre and, as the reviews of *The River Duddon* demonstrate, his work eventually changed perceptions of what was possible in serious art.

The title of Wordsworth's 'Lines Written a Few Miles above Tintern Abbey' may have led its original readers to expect a loco-descriptive poem on a particular site already deemed picturesque by Gilpin and a host of contemporary tourists, but, instead of describing the tourist trail up the Wye, he had composed a passionate meditation on a place whose significance was primarily personal. Rather than offer his readers Popean couplets celebrating kingship or commerce, in 'Tintern Abbey' Wordsworth presented the moment in which a landscape's power to touch the heart is revealed in all its power. Unlike the many preceding topographical poems, in 'Tintern Abbey' the history that mattered was that of the visiting speaker's psychological development and of the memory place occupied by the scene now being revisited. Once Wordsworth returned to the landscape of his childhood, he not only revived personal memories but recovered those belonging to people whose powerful local attachments seemed to offer a very different example to society from those of public life and British history. If Wordsworth's response to the Lakes was nourished and corroborated by the stories of those who lived there, however, his poetry also participated in a widespread, if not always fully articulated, contemporary fascination with the relationship between people and places. The transformation of 'local poetry' was part of an extraordinary contemporary movement that inspired writers—and readers—in every region.

Regional Writing

Part of the new interest in places arose, as ever, from practicalities. Continental Europe remained out of reach for many, but during the eighteenth century a new network of improved roads circulated like a bloodstream through England, Wales, Scotland, and Ireland. Much of the traffic was commercial or professional and in some areas, such as the Scottish Highlands, military. The very fact of roads and inns, however, meant that those with the time, the means, or the need had greater opportunities to travel than ever before, while those without were more aware of the existence of distant places. Even where circumstances made personal journeys impossible, the arrival of travellers, news, letters, books, and periodicals opened mental horizons everywhere. Nor was the expansion simply a matter of

information and ideas emanating from London and being received
by the rest of Britain and Ireland. Booksellers, quick to recognize a
new market, began to publish tours, travel guides, landscape prints,
local histories, and topographical verse collections, in which the
focus was on anywhere but the metropolis.

For writers, regional differences offered not only fresh material
for expanding markets, but also new models for interpreting contem-
porary society. London, seat of the monarch, Parliament, the Law
Courts, the Bank of England, and the Royal Exchange, still domi-
nated eighteenth-century Britain and Ireland, but the growing read-
iness to find value in smaller communities represented a significant
redress of traditional assumptions.[38] If the court literature of the
Restoration had tended to evoke 'the country' as the rather dull
source of remote estates and brides less experienced in the ways of
the world, comic writers a century later were representing rural areas
as intrinsically interesting, full of memorable characters, and, increas-
ingly, as the sites of alternative moral codes. Wordsworth's revival of
the pastoral as a vital counter to the more worrying signs of the times
was building on an ancient opposition between the virtuous coun-
tryside and corrupt city, which had experienced a major resurgence
during the eighteenth century because of growing anxieties over the
possible influence of both 'luxury' and London.[39]

The developing genre of the novel, always in creative dialogue
with other kinds of writing, began to embrace the tour, the national
tale, and the regional history, as authors saw the comic and political
potential in transporting characters around the islands. In *The Expe-
dition of Humphry Clinker*, published in 1771, Tobias Smollett created
a robust vehicle for satirical observation on men and manners by
taking a motley collection of passengers from an estate in the Welsh
Marches through the spa towns and cities of England and Scotland
to the Highlands, and back again. Smollett's fictional journey around
Britain offered no 'centre', and London was just one of the many
stages on the way. Nor was it the highlight of the tour as far as the
central character, Matthew Bramble, was concerned. Through
Bramble's horrified descriptions of Londoners, 'rambling, riding,
rolling, rushing, jostling, mixing, bouncing, cracking, and crashing
in one vile ferment of stupidity and corruption', Smollett was able to
present a damning portrait of the metropolis, in strong contrast to
more flattering images of other places.[40] Though other characters,

such as Bramble's niece, Lydia, were delighted by London's splendour and variety, Smollett's novel contained the capital city by placing it firmly in the context of a larger whole and recognizing the competing claims of Cardiff, Bath, Edinburgh, or Newcastle. London was an important part of the expedition, but it was neither the point of departure, nor the goal, nor even the structural centre.

Tour novels, describing real rather than fictional places, offered tremendous scope to writers from Scotland and Ireland to present different perspectives on contemporary society. The popular epistolary form meant that satire could also be directed towards the tourist rather than the destination, by exposing the limitations of the fictional visitor/writer whose observations formed the text. Smollett had underlined the subjectivity of his characters' views through the deliberate contrast in their successive accounts of the same place, thus alerting the reader to the conditioning effects of personality, class, and gender. In *The Wild Irish Girl*, Sydney Owenson was able to undermine the apparent domination of the English male visitor's gaze by afflicting him with a number of mishaps and obvious misconceptions.[41] As writers living in regions remote from London became aware of a potentially wider interest in their homes, they began to engage in fictional performances—or, in Joep Leerssen's words, 'auto-exoticisim'—for the benefit of distant readers.[42] In *Castle Rackrent*, for example, Maria Edgeworth surrounded the first-person narrative of Thady Quirk with copious notes and a glossary for the '*ignorant* English reader', neatly reversing metropolitan assumptions by pointing out that it was those furthest from rural Ireland who needed the most help in understanding the text.[43] Presentation of the familiar to those far away also empowered the author, who took on the role of guide and cultural translator.

What was remarkable about the new regional novel was its relish for everyday detail and for the distinctive features of places unknown to fame. These were the very works that enabled Walter Scott to recognize the power of fiction as a mediator between different regions, and inspired him to celebrate the special characteristics of his own beloved Borders.[44] By the early nineteenth century, even local anecdotes seemed worthy of a reading public, as James Hogg realized when submitting his short stories to Edinburgh journals, or arranging them into substantial volumes such as *Winter Evening Tales, collected among the Cottagers in the South of Scotland*. His own persona,

the Ettrick Shepherd, was as much a collector and storyteller as a
creator, and thus offered an unsettling challenge to the ideas of
ownership that underpinned most contemporary notions of the
'author'. Hogg's popularity depended on his ability to represent his
native country, the Scottish Borders, authentically, but his work
grew from a common store of local memories and tales that belonged
to the people not the copyright. Though less inclined than Words-
worth to meditate on the larger significance of local tradition, Hogg,
like Owenson and Edgeworth, was tapping into familiar resources in
order to create a new kind of literature that might initially seem
minor and marginal but was, in fact, a vital force of resistance to
prevailing literary values.

If Johnson had thought that everywhere had found its muse
by 1779, he would have been startled by the preponderance and
variety of 'local' poetry in the following decades. While some writers
merely followed Denham and Pope in memorializing a nearby land-
scape in rhyming couplets, others were clearly participating in the
larger realization of regional value, expressing more personal trib-
utes in blank verse, grounding religious devotion in familiar places,
sending verse epistles to local bards, or adapting traditional ballads
and songs. 'Local poetry' was overwhelming Johnson's orderly defi-
nition, as the poetic variety hidden beneath even a small selection of
contemporary titles makes plain: *The Olney Hymns*; 'To the River
Itchin'; *Beachy Head*; *Poems, Chiefly in the Scottish Dialect*; *Minstrelsy of
the Scottish Border*; *Beaumaris Bay*; *The Tour of the Dove*; *Irish Melodies*;
Welsh Melodies; 'Lines Written a Few Miles above Tintern Abbey'.
Particular regions inspired not only the most talented poets of the
Romantic period, but also numerous men and women whose names
are now less familiar, such as Richard Llwyd, the 'Bard of Snowdon',
or Robert Anderson, 'Author of Cumberland Ballads'.

Many poets emphasized both home and work on their title-pages,
as when Thomas Bakewell published *The Moorland Bard* in 1807, with
the subtitle 'Poetical Recollections of a Weaver, in the Moorlands of
Staffordshire'. Ever since John Taylor, the Thames bargeman, had
risen to fame as the 'King's Water Poet' in the seventeenth century,
poets from the lower sectors of society had often been linked to their
places of origin. The success of Stephen Duck, 'the Wiltshire Thresher
Poet', had rapidly prompted John Banckes, 'the Spittlefield Weaver',
into poetry, so their work was inevitably received with thoughts of

their specific origins in mind.[45] In the Romantic period, such identifications became an essential part of many poets' self-presentation, while also enhancing their market value. Ann Yearsley's *Poems upon Several Occasions*, for example, appeared with a frontispiece of Lactilla, the Milkwoman from Bristol, while Janet Little was similarly labelled as 'the Scotch Milkmaid' when her poems were published a few years later in Ayr.[46] In 1820, John Clare's first collection was published under the title *Poems, Descriptive of Rural Life and Scenery*, and under the authorship of 'A Northamptonshire Peasant'. Regional naming was a way of placing people socially as well as geographically, and was thus often a double-edged attribute, as Keats found to his cost when he saw his early works mocked by Scottish reviewers as the misguided outpourings of a Cockney poet.[47]

When Jeffrey started referring to Wordsworth, Coleridge, and Southey as the 'Lake School', he was responding, not only to their place of residence, but also to the larger movement that was only too easy to deride, given the rather uneven quality of modern 'local poetry'. For, although many were prompted to produce verse that could be described as 'local work', not all were capable of achieving 'fully adequate poetry'. Nevertheless, the very existence of so much poetry in so many places demonstrated a new urge towards individual and communal self-expression, which did not conform readily to existing critical rules and standards. Some of the poets were interested primarily in seeing their work in print and, better still, in earning money for their literary labours; collectively, their work demonstrated a new confidence in the intrinsic merits of places far from the centres of political, social, and cultural power. To publish a poem about the local community was a way of saying 'We matter', and 'We have a voice'. What's more, it was an expression of faith that new voices were worth hearing, that the aspiring country Miltons need no longer remain mute.

Wordsworth may have acted as a mediator for those whose lives might not otherwise have found a permanent record, but his poetry was responding to a rich, self-authenticating culture that had operated for years independently of metropolitan judgements and was suddenly becoming visible through the new technology of print and circulation. For many writers of the period, the new willingness to publish poetry from all classes and all areas was immensely liberating. Throughout Britain, small presses began printing books for regional audiences, often through local subscriptions, which opened up opportunities for writers and readers who had never been to London or Edinburgh or Dublin.[48] Not only were people keen to read books about familiar places; they wanted to write them as well. Well-educated reviewers might pour scorn on footmen and governesses, or offer patronizing praise to heaven-sent ploughmen, but their own powers were somewhat circumscribed by the existence of circles of writers, readers, and publishers who could manage quite well without their opinions. As Burns observed memorably, in his own debut collection, published in Kilmarnock:

> Your Critic-folk may cock their nose,
> And say, 'How can you e'er propose,
> 'You wha ken hardly *verse* frae *prose*,
>   'To mak a *sang?*'
> But by your leaves, my learned foes,
>   Ye're maybe wrang.[49]

The poem was addressed to John Lapraik, 'an old Scotch Bard', and, like the other verse epistles in the Kilmarnock edition, helped to create an image of a vibrant, but largely self-sufficient circle of Ayrshire poets who worked quite independently of the metropolitan centres of the age. A poet who focused on his immediate surroundings, rather than offering more sweeping representations of the world at large, might risk being dismissed by the critics because of his limited education or opportunities, but the sudden ubiquity of insistently local writing suggests something remarkable and deep-seated. Indeed, the title of Jeffrey's own influential *Edinburgh Review* is indicative of the very desire to associate words with particular places that he attacked in the work of the Lake School.

When Robert Crawford analysed the development of modern Scottish literature since the eighteenth century, he argued that it was essential to consider 'matters of local origin', because otherwise the literary critic might be guilty of a 'naïve cultural imperialism, acting as if books grew not out of particular conditions in Nottingham, Dublin, St Lucia, or Salem Massachusetts, but out of the bland uniformity of airport departure lounges'.[50] The telling contrast between the particular place and the airport departure lounge is a late-twentieth-century version of the kinds of anxieties that began to trouble people in the Romantic period, when the possibility of words becoming detached from any identifiable context was being realized through the new print culture and the associated drive to standardize grammar and remove regional variations in speech. To label a text as the *Edinburgh Review*, or *The Olney Hymns*, was to make plain its connection with a real place and its people, even if the uniformity of the modern English language and standard typography meant that the text itself circulated in neutral tones, offering few clues to its origins.

Crawford's attack on cultural imperialism was launched during the 1990s in a book dedicated 'To Scotland', but the deep feelings associated with the idea of a United Kingdom had been stirred up just as strongly in 1800, after the Act of Union with Ireland. Since the Treaty of Union in 1707, people in England and Scotland had, in theory, begun to see themselves as members of Great Britain, but the new awareness of being part of an even larger United Kingdom, accentuated by continuing fears of a French invasion, also provoked strong expressions of identification with small, long-familiar, and clearly defined areas.[51] Scottish publishers and writers, such as James Watson and Allan Ramsay, had been alerted to the distinctive traditions of their nation by the Union debates of the early eighteenth century, but it was several decades before their impulse to ensure the survival of cultural differences really gathered force, strengthened by social, economic, and political developments.[52] The convulsions of the Jacobite uprising and defeat during the 1740s forced Scottish Highlanders to recognize the distinctive character of their own culture, as laws were passed preventing their traditional choice of dress, music, and weaponry. It was largely in response to this sense of cultural erasure that Alexander MacDonald published the first book of Gaelic poetry, *Ais-Eiridh na Sean-Chanoin Albannaich*, in Edinburgh in 1751 and that James Macpherson created his translations of the Ancient Celtic bard, Ossian, a decade later. Often the impulse to commit the familiar to print stemmed from fears of its disappearance or from the desire to protect it from an external threat. Everyone had always known that their village or town was different from those on the other side of the river, the hill, the county, or the national border, but in the later eighteenth century the need to preserve the familiar stories became acute—and conscious.

By the end of the eighteenth century, the move to standardize language and establish grammatical norms for the entire country was in full flow, so any emphasis on the distinctive regional origin of a piece of writing required a decision to go against the prevailing tide. The growth of dialect poetry, and writing in every region, is one of the most significant aspects of Romantic culture and shows that Wordsworth's desire to withstand the forces threatening to suppress creative individuality was part of a larger, collective response. Paradoxically, the need to assert personal connection to a larger, living community seems to have stemmed in part from the desire to resist an imposed uniformity, even though the very means to self-expression—print culture—was integral to the problem. If the standardization of language provoked resistance in some areas, however, it was as nothing to the widespread fears of foreign invasion that gripped British hearts at the end of the eighteenth century.

During the revolutionary 1790s, the long war with France intensi-fied feelings of local attachment, because the sense of imminent invasion was strong. To see the late-eighteenth-century emphasis on local feeling purely in terms of Burkean ideals of patriotism is, however, to overlook its complexity and scale. When Burke argued that love of country was nurtured by the human tendency to 'love the little platoon we belong to in society', he was addressing a sector of society for whom the inheritance of large estates seemed part of the natural order of things.[53] For Burke, 'the country' was an organic entity, to which everyone naturally belonged and to which change happened gradually over the course of many years, 'a permanent body composed of transitory parts'.[54] Michael Baron has pointed out, however, that, during the war with France, even though small areas were valued by many as the nurseries of native strength, producing men ready to stand shoulder to shoulder with other Britons against Napoleon, they were also seen from within as distinct communities operating in their own independent ways. Small local centres were dynamic points sustained by centrifugal as well as centripetal forces, their internal resources often remaining resistant to the larger influ-ences from without.[55] External influence could, however, mean London just as much as Paris.

Celebration of the regional was often connected to patriotic impulses, but, as Baron has argued, it could reflect an urge rather more radical and recalcitrant than the desire for harmonious unification: 'towards decentralisation, resisting the centripetal pull towards London values, whether political or aesthetic.'[56] In the 1790s, the continuing success of Macpherson's *Ossian*, the newer interest in Iolo Morganwy, the revival of the Robin Hood ballads and the enormous popularity of Scottish songs all testify to a contemporary need for regional challenges to metropolitan influence. Poetry that originated in an identifiable region seemed especially able to speak for individual distinction and to assert the importance of every member of society whatever their background—a development that owed as much to the radical, egalitarian impulses of the revolutionary decade as it did to the Burkean patriotism.

The resistant character of poetry that dared to use dialect is obvious enough, but any literature that celebrated communities operating independently of London shared something of the same impulse. Writers as different as Wordsworth and Austen both chose to represent small societies in recognizable parts of England that were subjected to the introduction of metropolitan values, and yet proved able to erect internal defences and repair any damage sustained. Neither writer rejected the linguistic standards of the day, but each depicted individuals living and working according to their own consciences and the peculiar customs of their small, but self-sufficient communities. The appeal of such creations has sometimes struck later readers as escapism or nostalgia, but it is also possible to see the realistic depiction of an English village as part of the same 'decentralisation' that has been seen in the dialect and lower-class writings of the period. It is really a question of *re-centralizing*, since the writer who depicts a small, familiar society as if it were the whole world is challenging conventional ideas about the centre of power by placing London, Edinburgh, or Paris in the margins. This is perhaps one of the reasons why Walter Scott responded so warmly to *Emma*, since Austen's example demonstrated that any spot and any individual, if properly represented, could assume immense proportions in the mind of readers. As Austen's favourite poet, William Cowper, had pointed out, even an 'atom' was 'an ample field', if properly understood and imagined.[57]

Deserted Villages and Recovered Parishes

The turmoil of the 1790s compounded attitudes already well established in numerous writings of the later eighteenth century. Wordsworth's account of the contemporary malaise in the preface to *Lyrical*

Ballads wisely focused on effects rather than causes, but his identi-
fication of increasing urbanization as a distinguishing feature of
modern British society was astute. The accumulation of men in cities
reflected a major, and irreversible, shift from a predominantly agri-
cultural to an industrial and manufacturing economy, with the
attendant changes in land ownership, demography, and relationships
between social classes. During the second half of the eighteenth
century, new mills, mines, and factories began to draw workers from
rural areas, a process consolidated by the replacement of traditional
farming methods and common lands by modern crop rotation and
stock breeding in large, enclosed fields. Contemporary writers,
though benefiting from the new technology of print and publishing
markets, were not unreserved in their enthusiasm for national
economic prosperity.

As early as 1771, Goldsmith touched a sensitive and widely felt
area, when he lamented the state of a land 'where wealth accumu-
lates, and men decay', judging by the runaway success of 'The
Deserted Village'.[58] Whether readers were responding to the plight
of the people fleeing the land (an image that had special resonance
for the Anglo-Irish poet), however, or to the more personal distress
of the poem's speaker, whose long-cherished wish to return home
has been destroyed by the changes in his village, is open to question.
For 'The Deserted Village' combines both social comment on rural
hardship and a rather different psychological focus on the dislocated
poet, whose feelings stand in for those of the silent dispossessed. The
sympathy for the 'wretched matron, forced, in age, for bread, | To
strip the brook with mantling cresses spread' (ll. 131–2) is genuine
enough, but lacks the specificity that might allow readers to enter
imaginatively into the situation of the hungry woman. Much of the
poem's feeling swells from the speaker's personal distress over trans-
formations that have destroyed memory's consolations and turned
'the past to pain' (l. 82). Goldsmith's poem deals with thwarted
desire—the speaker longs to return home but he knows that home is
no longer there. The elegant couplets, which appear to run so effort-
lessly through the rural features—'the sheltered cot, the cultivated
farm, | The never-failing brook, the busy mill'—only underline the
sense of dislocation, the knowledge that even the brook has ceased to
flow: and hence, perhaps, the determination of later readers to attach
the poem firmly to Lissoy or Nuneham Courtenay.[59] Goldsmith's

haunting poem is a lament for a home, irretrievably lost, and thus captures a grief that might be experienced by people at every level of society.

The work of historical geographers has helped us to understand the development of modern society in terms of a shifting balance between man and the environment, which accelerated rapidly in the eighteenth century. Instead of remaining active participants, people were gradually becoming observers, distanced from the land by changing social structures and economic, demographic, and employment patterns, together with advances in science, philosophy, technology, and agriculture. Modern man, increasingly cut off from his biological origins, was no longer an insider connected to the greater whole, while the external world became both an object to view, chart, and quantify and an asset on which to capitalize.[60] Advances in science encouraged the observation of the earth and all its hidden wonders, as well as promoting the new perception of its place as a small part in the vast, divinely constructed, universe.[61] At the same time, philosophical investigation into the human mind led to profound, and often disturbing, questions regarding the relationship between the interior consciousness and the external world. As the earth became an idea and an object, rather than an essential part of instinctive, lived experience, the implications for the arts were immense. Denis Cosgrove has pointed out that 'landscape is not merely the world we see, it is a construction', an observation with resonances for not only visual artists, but also the landowners, agriculturalists, landscape gardeners, tourists, and empirical scientists of the eighteenth century.[62] The idea of landscape as a 'form of control' is helpful for interpreting the great prospect poems and the picturesque, but it can also shed light on the work of writers in very different circumstances, whose well-justified fears of disempowerment and displacement provoked a strong desire to take control of their immediate surroundings.

Traditional assumptions about the place of an individual in the world had been rocked by the change to structures of power, which had taken place in the preceding century. Unquestioning faith in a single Church and its religious doctrines had not existed since the Reformation, and, although the rise of Protestantism has often been identified as a powerful unifying force within Britain, the history of civil dispute and bloody suppression of insurrection, together with growing congregations in Dissenting orders and increasing demand for more just conditions for the Catholic majority in Ireland, meant that, by the end of the eighteenth century, it was much more difficult for any individual to feel unconsciously secure in relationship to an immediate religious community that was part of a larger, sacred body.[63] The experience of the Civil War and the passing of the Act of Settlement also affected older ideas about social hierarchy as both natural and divinely ordained, with obvious far-reaching consequences for the individual's sense of being born into a particular level on the social ladder. With the complicated rise of individualism, people were free to move up or down, but with their new liberty came a growing uncertainty about their relationship with the world at large.

The new sense of national consciousness that many historians have discerned in west European countries in the eighteenth century has often been related to the decline of older 'cultural conceptions', as people felt the need to reassert their connection to those around and understand their own place in the world; in Benedict Anderson's well-known formulation, 'the search was on...for a new way of linking fraternity, power and time meaningfully together'.[64] The importance of print culture to the re-creation of a new sense of national connection is well established—though, as we have seen, it also stimulated some resistance to ideas of union. It is also possible to relate the development of landscape painting and poetry to the larger impulse to link individuals to new, collective identities through the construction of common points of connection. In seventeenth-century Holland, for example, the absence of traditional symbols of social unity encouraged painters and their patrons to invest in careful re-creations of the land itself. As Ann Jensen Adams has argued persuasively, 'the political, economic, and religious shifts that together convulsed seventeenth-century Holland gave new meaning to the local, the prosaic, and recognizable features of land'.[65] Dutch painting registered the success of the new commercial nation, but in its detailed observation of particular places there was also, perhaps, a desire to confirm the stability of a landscape that was startlingly prone to alteration—and inundation. Though Britain was not subject to the same natural threats as Holland, it is possible to see cultural parallels in the creation of local landscapes at a time of rapid social change. Painting a familiar landscape, complete with tiny windmills and church towers, was a way of suggesting a reassuring continuity and a sense of community. The growth of local poetry in Britain shared something of the same impulse, but, in addition to descriptions of harmonious fields and villages, literature offered the additional dimension of local history. Through retelling local stories and capturing local characters, the writer reminded readers of essential, shared links to the past. Human narratives made the past real, and in poetry, especially, powerful feelings could be caught and made permanent. Such vital links between individuals and between generations helped to counter the pains of displacement by securing a meaningful past, which helps to account for the survival of traditional ballads, songs, and stories among people who have emigrated, whether willingly or otherwise, to another country. Even in more personal reflections on the landscape of home, the memory of a place familiar since childhood worked as an anchor to the free, but potentially alienated adult. Local poetry was not necessarily contributing to the creation of a new sense of a single nation, but it was playing an important psychological role in emphasizing possible connections to a body whose existence extended beyond that of the individual.

Friedrich Schiller's essay 'On the Naïve and Sentimental' is often cited as an expression of civilized man's nostalgia 'for the nature we have lost'.[66] His account of the modern condition, which describes man eternally separated from nature and looking back on it with painful longing from 'the distant exile of art', was the result of his own philosophical analysis of contemporary society, but the metaphors and embodied feelings were very similar to those employed by Goldsmith and a host of contemporary English writers.[67] According to Schiller, all those capable of reading his essay were in the same situation as Goldsmith's speaker, remembering the parental home from which they had rushed, and painfully aware that return was impossible. The 'Deserted Village' was, in this sense, another name for the modern condition, a state of self-conscious division and inner conflict, which could strive to recover an ideal unity only through culture.

Schiller urged his philosophical readers onwards, but the powerful imagery of home and childhood spoke of a natural unity now destroyed, and a future direction far from certain.[68] Not everyone suffered the painful eviction referred to in 'The Deserted Village', but a fear of psychological deracination was only too common. Whether it was the factory worker, longing for the fields of his rural youth, or the intellectual, paralysed by self-consciousness and cut off from primary experience by his habits of reflection, the troubled sense of distance from the earth was profound; and, though the physical experiences were very different, the mental anguish might be just as distressing. Desire for attachment was a corollary of the experience of *detachment*, which seems to have gripped the imaginations of people at all levels of society. The very fascination with the external world, which so marked eighteenth-century culture, was largely a consequence of a dim but pervasive sense of its inaccessibility. And, while it might seem helpful, in retrospect, to attribute the new uncertainty to Cartesian dualism, Lockean epistemology, or the Newtonian discovery of space, most people were probably affected just as much by the more obvious social, political, religious, and economic changes that had a direct, discernible impact on their lives. When Burns imagined a destitute old age in his 'Epistle to Davie', for example, he was articulating the very real fear of homelessness that haunted numerous agricultural workers in rural Scotland.

The fear of disconnection nevertheless affected people at every level of eighteenth-century society. In *The Seasons*, Thomson attempted to 'join every living soul | Beneath the spacious temple of the sky',[69] in a reassuring vision that seemed to reaffirm man's place in the divine creation, but his very emphasis on finding God's meaning through observation of the natural world showed that his readers were assumed to be viewers rather than participants. *The Seasons* may have prompted first-hand encounters with 'Nature' and, as Joseph Warton commented, 'been very instrumental in diffusing a general taste for the beauties of *nature* and *landscape*,[70] but it also contributed to the sense of separation on which observation depended. The discovery of 'Nature' was also the realization of distance. Books such as Gilpin's *Observations on the Picturesque* turned much of Britain into a kind of picture gallery, to be viewed by intrepid tourists who stood with their backs to the scenery, composing an ideal landscape in their Claude glasses. No wonder Schiller regarded the return to nature as doomed from the start.

The new sense of loss, however, also acted as a powerful catalyst to creative activity and regional assertion. Traditional connections might be under threat or even obsolete, but this only made the desire to reaffirm them more intense. Goldsmith disguised his own origins with the invention of 'Sweet Auburn', which could have been the loveliest village of any plain, but writers of the next generation were keen to affirm the special importance of their own areas, whether or not their readers had heard of them. The disappearance of Michael's cottage was part of the same full-scale transformation of the British countryside that Goldsmith lamented, but there is a great difference between Wordsworth's invitation to readers to walk up the tumultuous brook of Greenhead Gill, and Goldsmith's generalized recollections. Although Wordsworth could speak for the modern outsider, cut off from his natural environment by his education, he also recovered the understanding of the insider, participating in the culture of his region and demonstrating his right to do so by the detailed knowledge of the landscape. Michael may have lost control of his hills, but, in writing the poem, Wordsworth was not only restoring possession to the rightful owner but also renewing connections between the alienated reader and the nurturing communities of earlier days.

Wordsworth understood the true value of the humble man living peacefully in his native hills and had the poetic skills necessary to make such a figure meaningful to those whose sense of certainty was far less secure. Though as conscious as Goldsmith of the extensive transformation of modern Britain and Ireland, Wordsworth realized that the deepest attachments could be embodied in words that then had the power to unite readers in shared experiences. If a poet could create a work that lived like one of nature's, readers everywhere might then respond to its strong form and to the reality of its rhythms. Through his poetry, Wordsworth was attempting to restore modern man to the instinctive feeling of being an inmate of this active universe, irrespective of his changing circumstances or way of life. Reading seemed to offer the possibility of recovering a connection to the great network of life, especially if the words were grounded by undeniable local truths.

One of the perennial best-sellers of the Romantic period is *The Natural History of Selborne*, a detailed record written by the local clergyman, Gilbert White, of a tiny village in Hampshire. With his Oxford education and relatively leisurely existence as a country curate, White was hardly an embodiment of 'low and rustic life', but, like Wordsworth, he knew the value of habitual experience in a confined area. As he remarked to his principal correspondent, Thomas Pennant, 'my little intelligence is confined to the narrow sphere of my own observations at home'.[71] Within this narrow sphere, however, White had discovered an entire world. There was nothing apologetic about the excited and minute attention given to the various birds, plants, and animals he had studied on a daily basis. Instead, White's local knowledge was the foundation of his own confidence and his generosity to other living beings. Like Heaney's poetry, White's was local work, and resulted from roots crossing with reading to create a votive offering that revealed connections between writer, subject, and the living universe. His tone may have been more scientific than Heaney's or Wordsworth's, but the sense of grateful participation was just as strong.

White presented his idea of 'parochial history' as a work inclusive of 'natural productions as well as antiquities', but it is also parochial in Kavanagh's sense. When Kavanagh distinguished the 'parochial' from the 'provincial', he was not referring to a small country parish, but rather to an attitude of mind: 'In recent times we have had two great Irish parishioners—James Joyce and George Moore. They explained nothing. The public had either to come to them or stay in the dark.'[72] White was a very different kind of writer from Joyce or Moore, but it is evident from every page of *The Natural History of Selborne* that, like them, he had no doubt about the intrinsic value of his parish. What White demonstrated was the kind of authority attainable even by those in the humble backwaters of rural England. It is the authority of the certain knowledge that arises from habitual experience in a confined area. White's was the irrefutable truth of careful, personal observation, and every page of his *Natural History* possesses the same quiet conviction. His familiarity with his neighbourhood gave him the confidence to question the conclusions of even the most distinguished contemporary scientists:

I suspect much there may be two species of water-rats. Ray says, and Linnaeus after him, that the water-rat is web-footed behind. Now, I have discovered a rat on the banks of our little stream that is not web-footed, and yet it is an excellent swimmer and diver: it answers exactly to the *mus amphibious* of Linnaeus.[73]

Even the most widely accepted systems could be challenged by White's living and lived environment. All over England, Scotland, Ireland, and Wales, a similar wealth of natural and human history could be found on the doorstep in every parish—the Romantic literature of local attachment revealed that immediate truths were often more remarkable and reliable than those learned from more widely recognized authorities.

In the preface to his *Natural History*, White offered no apology for his intense focus on the few square miles around Selborne, but he did reflect on the intrinsic value of his work. His history was an authentic record of his parish, but it was also a means to awaken in his readers a sense of the wonders of God's world, 'too frequently overlooked as common occurrences'. Like Wordsworth, White knew that paradise was the growth of common day, and part of his duty as a clergyman was to open his readers' eyes to the glories all around. His work revealed not only his participation in a vital, long-lasting, environment, but also the consequent 'health and cheerfulness of spirits'. This emphasis on the satisfactions of being engaged, body and mind, with his immediate surroundings anticipates Wordsworth's description of the infant babe, blessed by being an 'inmate of this *active* universe... creator and receiver, both' (*Prelude*, ii. 266–73). Both writers offered profound gratitude for their own discovery of what it meant to be part of an eternal network of life and thereby encouraged others to become thankful participants rather than isolated spectators.

What the great writer feels in the blood and along the heart can be felt by sympathetic readers. Wordsworth's poetry could do nothing to halt industrial expansion, military invasion, or an unjust social system, but the capacity to transform his intense experiences into affecting, beautiful works of art has made a vital, permanent contribution to society. In a characteristic description of walking alone in the Cumbrian hills, Wordsworth expressed his own instinctive response to the unexpected discovery of local work:

> If looking round I have perchance perceiv'd
> Some vestiges of human hands, some steps
> Of human passion, they to me have been
> As light at day-break, or the sudden sound
> Of music to a blind man's ear who sits
> Alone and silent in the summer shade.
> They are as a creation in my heart.[74]

In the same way, his own lines, warm to the efforts of an unknown, unnamed local craftsman, can become a creation in the heart of any sympathetic reader, irrespective of first-hand knowledge of what the poet himself has actually seen. There has never been a need to visit Grasmere or Ennerdale in order to be moved by 'Michael' or to share the emotions conveyed in 'The Brothers'. Since the early nineteenth century, many readers who have never been to Cumbria have still learned to love its imagined mountains and communities, sharing the sense of connectedness created by writing, because poetry invites readers to participate in its local truth.

One of Wordsworth's early American readers, Peter Bryant, was deeply affected by his encounter with the poems: 'a thousand springs seemed to gush up at once in his heart, and the face of nature, of a sudden, to change into a strange freshness and life.'[75] Byron, Peacock, and Jeffrey might have berated Wordsworth for his narrow preference for the Lakes, but his verse was rapidly travelling thousands of miles across the ocean to teach people how to feel. Countless readers have seen the world change before their eyes, as they experienced and emulated Wordsworth's 'creations of the heart'. When John Stuart Mill buckled beneath severe depression, it was not his father's utilitarian reliance on fact, reason, and practical improvement that saved him, but Wordsworth's poetry. Mill realized in the early 1820s that an education based exclusively on factual learning and analysis, with no 'natural tie', could never bring about the social improvement envisaged by those who were constructing the great pyramid of modern knowledge.[76] It was not Wordsworth's descriptions of natural scenery that helped Mill, but his ability to share powerful, life-affirming emotions: 'What made Wordsworth's poems a medicine for my state of mind, was that they expressed, not mere outward beauty, but states of feeling, and of thought coloured by that feeling, under the excitement of beauty.'[77] Mill, for whom the rewards of reason and analysis had been empty, was restored to creative life by discovering the 'culture of feelings' in Wordsworth's poetry: 'I seemed to draw from a source of inward joy, of sympathetic and imaginative pleasure, which could be shared in by all human beings.' The modern Parnassus might be small, but, if it had the power to heal a sick society, it was offering something ultimately far more valuable.

3

Local Attachment and Adequate Poetry

With hindsight, it is easy to see that the various expressions of regional distinction which appeared in later eighteenth-century Britain and Ireland were part of a widespread movement. Paradoxically, whenever a writer in Wiltshire or County Antrim or Inverness-shire asserted the individuality of a local story or historical monument, he was inadvertently contributing to a collective sense of the importance of particular places. The growing awareness of local culture does not, however, fully explain the seriousness with which Wordsworth began to treat insistently localized subjects from 1800 onwards, nor his recognition of local attachment as the foundation for fully adequate poetry. Though Wordsworth, like the rest of his contemporaries, was affected by the broader historical, philosophical, and social changes of the eighteenth century, the tone of his extraordinary preface to *Lyrical Ballads* suggests an urgent response to national crisis. Not many poets would think to offer their latest collection to an eminent statesman in order to alert him to the problems of the day, but when Wordsworth sent *Lyrical Ballads* to Charles James Fox he was expressing his personal alarm at the state of the nation and offering his poems as a counter to damage that seemed almost irreversible.

This chapter considers Wordsworth's perception of a country in crisis, his sense of a poet's responsibilities to society, and his admiration for the kind of poetry that seemed strong enough to help. Wordsworth found corroboration for his own deep attachment to the Lake District, not just in exemplary rural figures such as Michael, but also through his reading—in the poetry of Robert Burns and the work of Walter Scott. In the collections published by both of these prominent Scottish poets, local attachment was a defining feature, and so Wordsworth was able to find support in their work for his own growing admiration for Grasmere. Neither example was unproblematic, however, as the following chapters will demonstrate. In order to achieve a poetry of 'resolved crisis', as admired by Seamus Heaney, Wordsworth had to grapple with the personal as well as the public responsibilities attendant on the desire to be 'a Poet'. Before we can understand Wordsworth's attraction to his Scottish contemporaries and his renewed faith in the power of poetry to fortify an ailing society, however, it is important to recognize the depth of his disillusionment with the condition of England in the late 1790s.

The steady transformation of rural Britain, with the advantages and anxieties attendant on increasing urbanization, mechanization, and mobility, had been taking place since the middle of the eighteenth century. Wordsworth's profound concern over the state of the nation, however, reflected a heightened awareness of change that accompanied the political turbulence of the closing decade. Crucial to his capacity to articulate complicated feelings about his country was the close friendship with Coleridge that developed after Wordsworth's return from revolutionary France and subsequent period of internal conflict. As the two men talked and worked together in Somerset and Dorset, Coleridge's deep admiration for the surrounding landscape helped Wordsworth to see the value of his own childhood. The threat of an imminent invasion by French forces seemed to accentuate the beauty of the gentle hills and fields, as is most obvious in Coleridge's heartfelt tribute to the nurturing powers of the English landscape, 'Fears in Solitude, written in April 1798, during the alarm of an invasion':

> But, O dear Britain! O my Mother Isle!
> Needs must thou prove a name most dear and holy
> To me, a son, a brother, and a friend,
> A husband, and a father! Who revere
> All bonds of natural love, and find them all
> Within the limits of thy rocky shores.
> O native Britain! O my Mother Isle!
> How shouldst thou prove aught else but dear and holy
> To me, who from thy lakes and mountain-hills,
> Thy clouds, thy quiet dales, thy rocks and seas,

> Have drunk in all my intellectual life,
> All sweet sensations, all ennobling thoughts,
> All adoration of the God in nature,
> Whatever makes this mortal spirit feel
> The joy and greatness of its future being?
> There lives nor form nor feeling in my soul
> Unborrowed from my country![1]

Deep gratitude to the great 'Mother Isle' from whom he had 'drunk' his entire intellectual, emotional, and spiritual being arose partly from Coleridge's own feelings of displacement. His verse letter 'To the Rev. George Coleridge of Ottery St Mary, Devon' explicitly contrasted his elder brother's stability in the family home with his own sense of exile: 'from the spot where I first sprang to light | Too soon transplanted'.[2] In 'Frost at Midnight', which was published in the same pamphlet as 'Fears in Solitude', Coleridge's anxieties about having been 'reared | In the great city, pent mid cloisters dim' prompted the wish that his baby son, Hartley, would have a much better childhood, wandering 'like the breeze'.[3] As Wordsworth listened to Coleridge, it is easy to see why he would begin to appreciate his own experience of being brought up in rural Cumbria, free to feel the wind on his face and becoming unconsciously familiar with the shapes of the local fells.

For Coleridge, wistful images of loving family and natural surroundings went hand in hand with profound feelings of isolation. Despite his sensitivity to the natural world, the underlying fear of disconnection is frequently apparent in his poems, letters, and notebooks. In a letter to John Thelwall, written a few months before 'Fears in Solitude', he had vented his frustration over finding the entire universe nothing more than 'an immense heap of *little* things' and expressed a passionate desire for some overwhelming sense of connection: 'My mind feels as if it ached to behold & know something *great*—something *one & indivisible* and it is only in the faith of this that rocks or waterfalls, mountains or caverns give me the sense of sublimity or majesty!'[4] Coleridge's craving for emotional reassurance was religious and psychological, his preoccupation with the physical universe part of a larger spiritual quest. If God was in nature, as 'Fears in Solitude' and other poems of the period suggest, then a sense of real connection to the earth was essential to the spiritual well-being of the individual. Fears of the dark consequences that might attend an early uprooting were bound up with an acute sense of distance from the divine.

For Coleridge, the concerns observed by Schiller about the gulf dividing the modern intellectual from nature had a profoundly religious dimension, but during the later 1790s the rapidly shifting political climate rendered a vague, collective problem acute—and personal. In 1798, when the threat of a French invasion was at a height, personal connection to the world in which we live was beginning to seem the basis of spiritual health, not only for the individual, but also for the whole of society. During the long war with France, attachment to things associated with home inevitably intensified. For those who had initially been passionate supporters of the overthrow of an unjust regime in France, the realization that less than ten years had turned the revolutionary forces into potential oppressors of Britain was especially difficult to accept. Both Coleridge and Wordsworth had welcomed the Fall of the Bastille and the early days of the French Revolution as the dawning of a new era in Europe, in which age-old institutions would be replaced by a better society, inspired by ideals of equality, liberty, and fraternity. As events in France became more violent, however, and war was declared on Britain, hopes of a peaceful revolution evaporated. Instead of increased liberty, radical circles in Britain and Ireland found themselves muzzled by new laws passed hurriedly by a wartime government determined to silence any potential enemies within. At the same time, news of the increasingly aggressive expansion of French forces in Europe meant that the great modern model for radical hope seemed increasingly tarnished. Deep, protective feelings began to erupt powerfully as Britain came increasingly under threat, though for radical writers such as Wordsworth and Coleridge, the very idea of natural bonds had to be treated with great care because of the fierce political debates of recent years.

During the 1790s, questions of identity, loyalty, and continuity, which had exercised people ever since the Civil War, especially at critical moments of internal tension or international conflict, were once again at the forefront of public consciousness. Passionate and polarized responses to the French Revolution, which followed hard on the foundation of a modern, independent, American Republic, led many people in England, Scotland, Ireland, and Wales to reconsider their places within the existing social and national structures.

With the rising of the United Irishmen in 1798, it became abundantly clear that the ties between the four nations were neither secure nor universally acceptable—and could not, therefore, be deemed 'natural' by anyone who gave the matter serious thought. 'Love of country' became a highly contested issue, exercising the most prominent political writers of the day and demanding the attention of every British citizen. But what 'love of country' actually meant was becoming less and less clear. The dissenting minister Richard Price, for example, whose radical sermon in November 1789 triggered the pamphlet war over the French Revolution, argued that 'country' had nothing to do with 'the soil or the spot of earth on which we happen to have been born' and everything to do with membership of a community.[5] Though entirely persuasive to many who heard or read his sermon in the months following the Fall of the Bastille, Price struck others as alarmingly unpatriotic. Edmund Burke was so troubled by the idea of 'love of country' being separate from ideas of home and family that his own magisterial *Reflections on the Revolution in France* made the question central to his conception of a stable state. Burke was emphatic that the love of country was nurtured by a natural, early tendency 'to love the little platoon we belong to in society', but his related insistence that society itself depended on hereditary property offered little scope to those who had not inherited large estates.[6] As people struggled to determine the nature of a 'country' and their own places within it, questions of origin and local attachment became issues of political and patriotic affiliation.

For radical writers, the private feelings of local loyalty startled into consciousness by the invasion scare thus demanded a justification as well as an outlet. When Coleridge composed his affectionate tribute to the Revd George, who was now raising a family in the very house where they had lived as children, he also had to consider the political implications of his instinctive sympathy with the kind of continuity represented by his elder brother. He had no desire to endorse an aristocratic system of ownership as cherished by Burke, but was rather attempting to promote a more egalitarian idea of community in which love of society grew from domestic attachments at every level. Coleridge's celebration of home and family in fact shared some of Burke's insight into the psychological importance of the 'little platoon', but, as a committed radical, he was keen to distance himself from the hierarchical assumptions of the *Reflections*. In the political lectures he delivered in Bristol during 1795, for example, he had promoted the idea of national feeling developing directly from family affection: 'Love of Friends, parents, and neighbours leads us to the love of our Country to the love of all Mankind. The intensity of private attachment encourages, not prevents, universal philanthropy.'[7] Where Burke had envisaged men of consequence and property, Coleridge invoked the example of Jesus, who was at once a 'Son', a 'Friend', and a boy reared in the home of a carpenter. This was a love of country open to all members of society, irrespective of rank and very similar to the ideal of 'domestic affections' Wordsworth described to Charles James Fox, when he sent him *Lyrical Ballads*. Acknowledgement of local attachment as 'an obvious fact of human nature' was also an explicit rejection of the recent revival among 'professed friends of civil freedom', such as the radical philosopher William Godwin, of 'the Stoical Morality which disclaims all the duties of Gratitude and domestic Affection'.[8] In other words, Coleridge's lecture propounded views very similar to those embodied in 'Michael'—that civil liberty was founded on the kind of local attachments felt more powerfully by carpenters and shepherds than by any landed gentleman.

Wordsworth and Coleridge were strongly attracted by the radical principles of the early Revolutionary debate, but gradually realized that any absolute separation of 'love of country' from the 'spot of earth on which we happen to have been born' was somewhat problematic. Wordsworth increasingly came to see the radical ideals for society alive in the Cumbrian hills in the unassuming 'Republic of Shepherds and Agriculturalists, among whom the plough of each man was confined to the maintenance of his own family', as described in his *Guide to the Lakes*;[9] and he knew that a sense of deep local attachment was fundamental to their entire way of life. When he attempted to trace the conflicted feelings that had gripped him during the French Revolution in *The Prelude*, the inner confusion caused by the separation between his political sympathies and his familiar world gave rise to a memorable passage:

> Now had I other business, for I felt
> The ravage of this most unnatural strife
> In my own heart; there lay it like a weight
> At enmity with all the tenderest springs
> Of my enjoyments. I, who with the breeze

> Had play'd, a green leaf on the blessed tree
> Of my beloved Country, nor had wish'd
> For happier fortune than to wither there—
> Now from my pleasant station was cut off
> And toss'd about in whirlwinds.   (x. 249–59)

The painful sense of distance from home expressed in this passage is far more immediate than the general wistfulness of 'The Deserted Village'—this is not the normal separation of an adult from his childhood, of urban man from his rural past, or even of the psychologically exiled son who has left home and made good. It is an account of sudden painful cutting-off and the tumultuous consequences.

Wordsworth's use of natural imagery here is also very different from that of the earlier books of *The Prelude*, where it seems the most appropriate language for recollections of a boyhood spent running in the hills and streams. 'The blessed Tree of my beloved Country' has no reference to a particular oak or ash, but stands as a political metaphor quite different in kind from Wordsworth's characteristic use of language. The simple image of the tree is nevertheless perfect for the state of confusion that is being recalled, since organic metaphors had been central to the political debates over the French Revolution, and commandeered by both radical and reactionary writers. Nature had been evoked by Burke in his argument for the ideal development of the national constitution, gradually evolving 'after the pattern of nature'.[10] For Thomas Paine and the United Irishmen, however, nature furnished the powerful image of the Tree of Liberty, springing up in America and France to replace the rotten wood.[11] Wordsworth could not have chosen a more resonant image to convey his own sense of being cut off from familiar certainties—his very language demonstrated the way in which competing political claims destroyed habitual associations and left him reeling from the massive internal dislocation. The passage continues with a remarkable confession of the feelings inspired by his continuing support for the Revolution:

> I rejoiced,
> Yea, afterwards, truth painful to record!
> Exulted in the triumph of my soul
> When Englishmen by thousands were o'erthrown,
> Left without glory on the Field, or driven,
> Brave hearts, to shameful flight. It was a grief,
> Grief call it not, 'twas anything but that,

> A conflict of sensations without name,
> Of which he only who may love the sight
> Of a Village Steeple as I do can judge,
> When in the Congregation, bending all
> To their great Father, prayers were offer'd up
> Or praises for our Country's Victories,
> And mid the simple worshippers, perchance,
> I only, like an uninvited Guest
> Whom no one owned, sate silent, shall I add,
> Fed on the day of vengeance yet to come?
>
> (*The Prelude*, x. 249–75)

The need to grapple honestly with feelings that had come to seem deeply disloyal shows that Wordsworth still understood both his early passionate support for the Revolution and the personal difficulties it entailed. There is a kind of horror in his reflection on the 'uninvited Guest', sitting in a rural congregation and relishing the thought of eventual French victory, and he seems more isolated here, surrounded by people, than at any other point in the poem. For Wordsworth to find himself so entirely at odds with the 'simple worshippers' in a rural community was a moment of internal alienation that posed the most searching challenge to the revolutionary principles he had espoused with such enthusiasm. The difficulty of reconciling the rational defence of the oppressed French people with his own counter-attachment to the ordinary folk at home was apparently impossible. It is not surprising, at such a juncture, to find Wordsworth struggling to find words adequate to the truth: 'it was a grief, | Grief call it not, 'twas anything but that'. At times like this, words seemed unable to accommodate the overwhelming confusion. The fact that he included the passage at all, however, also reveals the importance of shocking dislocation to his growth as a poet—a truth more evident by 1805, when he composed these lines, than in 1793, when in the midst of the experience. Looking back, Wordsworth realized, as Heaney reading the passage nearly two centuries later saw at once, that he had been 'displaced from his own affections by a vision of the good located elsewhere' and, as a result, felt 'like a traitor among those he knows and loves'.[12] Recovery from such shocking internal displacement had depended on the reaffirmation of loving relationships with his sister, friends, and familiar places.

In 1798, when Coleridge offered his profound thanks to his Mother Isle, he was working closely with Wordsworth and sharing in the gradual recovery from the post-revolutionary psychological chaos, which is so vividly recorded in *The Prelude*. By this time, both poets had come to recognize that 'love of country' could draw strength from love of a particular part of 'the country' and that, for many, this was a normal element of their emotional well-being. Although this new understanding was partly responsible for Coleridge's anxieties about early deracination, it provided Wordsworth with an enormous boost of self-confidence and renewed hope. The larger context visible in 'Fears in Solitude' helps to explain the revelatory tone of 'Tintern Abbey', in which the experience of returning to a landscape after an absence of five years provokes a similar outpouring of gratitude:

> well pleased to recognize
> In Nature and the language of the sense,
> The anchor of my purest thoughts, the nurse,
> The guide, the guardian of my heart, and soul
> Of all my moral being.   (ll. 108–12)

What Wordsworth records in 'Tintern Abbey' is a moment of glad recognition—that his mind, heart, and soul have a guide and guardian in the natural world, or, in other words, that the strength of his relationship with the active universe is the foundation of all his better endeavours. So momentous was Wordsworth's realization that the title records its place ('A few miles above Tintern Abbey') and date (13 July 1798), and in doing so demonstrates how local detail can act as a kind of witness to personal epiphanies. The importance of what seems an intensely personal experience is made public by the reference to a well-known place and particular time—just nine years after the Fall of the Bastille. Wordsworth's preoccupation with private emotion was criticized by some early readers (as it has been by more recent critics) for evading public concerns, but, when read in relation to the political and social anxieties spelled out in 'Fears and Solitude' and reiterated in the preface to *Lyrical Ballads*, the faith expressed in 'Tintern Abbey', 'that Nature never did betray the heart that loved her' (l. 123), seems as much an address to the nation at large as it is to the sister lovingly portrayed in the poem.[13]

'Tintern Abbey' presents the experience of a changed man—a traveller who, in a matter of five years, has lost the unreflecting energy of his youth, has witnessed suffering and unkindness, but whose return to a familiar scene produces the overwhelming conviction 'that all which we behold is full of blessings' (ll. 134–5). In his remarkable thanksgiving poem, Wordsworth's sense of universal interconnection expands through the series of simple, but entirely sufficient, nouns and adjectives, until the landscape, the speaker, and the reader are all part of the larger, living presence:

> And I have felt
> A presence that disturbs me with the joy
> Of elevated thoughts; a sense sublime
> Of something far more deeply interfused,
> Whose dwelling is the light of setting suns,
> And the round ocean, and the living air,
> And the blue sky, and in the mind of man,
> A motion and a spirit, that impels
> All thinking things, all objects of all thought,
> And rolls through all things.   (ll. 94–103)

What begins as private experience steadily opens to embrace the entire world.

Though the need to be connected to a larger, living entity was evidently intensified by the international conflict, it did not entail any necessary support for aggressive foreign policy. For Wordsworth, the individual who felt part of a familiar landscape stood fast at the heart of the nation, resistant to various threats, including foreign invasion, but he was not in himself threatening. The truths to which 'Tintern Abbey' stands witness are those of humanity at large, even though the moment of confirmation is so carefully located. Once Wordsworth had settled in Grasmere, his private affections were deepened by memories of his childhood, but the local celebrations of his verse were meant to be exemplary not exclusive. Wordsworth's renewed feeling for the Lakes was more like the tender and protective patriotism admired by Simone Weil and quite distinct from the aggressive national pride that seeks domination over other countries. Indeed, Jonathan Bate has suggested that Wordsworth 'sought the foundations of true patriotism and found them in localism', arguing that respect for local origins prevents patriotism from taking 'a Napoleonic, expansionist turn'.[14]

In the decade following the publication of 'Tintern Abbey', the war with France continued to take its toll and Wordsworth continued to reiterate his belief in the common man as a nation's fundamental source of strength: 'For he is, in his person attached, by stronger

roots, to the soil of which he is the growth.'[15] This was not a jingo-
istic rallying of Englishmen, however, but an expression of esteem
for a natural quality that nourished the heroic virtues of courage and
self-sacrifice and was just as apparent among the courageous men and
women who were attempting to defend the Iberian Peninsula as in
Britain. Selfless acts of courage were the attributes of figures such as
William Wallace or William Tell, whose examples could inspire
anyone in any nation. The organic connection between ordinary
people and their land made local traditions a common birthright,
and in *The Convention of Cintra* Wordsworth explicitly denounced
the kind of oppression that divided ordinary people from their
emotional pedigree: 'Perdition to the Tyrant who would wantonly
cut off an independent Nation from its inheritance in past ages.'[16]
Like Heaney, hoping for a world in which 'the validity of every
tradition' would command equal respect, Wordsworth was arguing
for the intrinsic value of any communal culture. His personal
experience of being 'cut off' from his roots made him deeply averse
to any force that might effect similar destruction. By 1809, when
Wordsworth turned his attention to the Peninsular War, he had
become deeply aware of the importance of local attachments, but
had also realized that personal connections were cumulative as well
as individual. Intense personal experience could be deepened by a
shared love of the same place: attachment to the landscape meant
attachment to those who dwelled there. Life in Grasmere had also
heightened Wordsworth's appreciation of the poetry, songs, and
stories that distinguished small, independent communities in other
regions and he knew that tyranny was not always exclusive to foreign
powers. Wordsworth's recognition of the life-sustaining, emotional
relationship between man and nature was celebrated as a kind of
epiphany in 'Tintern Abbey', but the larger idea of 'local attachment'
as fundamental to both poems and nations developed more slowly,
emerging through a series of explorations and poetic encounters.

The Struggle for Adequacy

The confident voice of 'Tintern Abbey' appeared in an anonymous
volume of *Lyrical Ballads* in 1798, but within two years Wordsworth
had redesigned the collection, adding the series of Lake District

pastorals and a substantial preface, whose remarkable claims seemed to suggest that the purpose of the poems might not be entirely self-evident. The eloquent statements that introduced *Lyrical Ballads* in 1800 were provoked by profound fears about a society afflicted by war, rapid urbanization, an expanding population, and the attendant problems of poverty and hunger. The very problems that led Thomas Malthus to publish his *Essay on the Principles of Population* in 1798, with its draconian solutions to the prospect of the national population outstripping the food supply, made Wordsworth think very hard about the role of the poet. Not only was he concerned about the suffering of those least able to find relief; he was also concerned about the apparently uncaring attitudes of the more educated, wealthy, and powerful sectors of society. The poet's duty must be to awaken others to a better understanding of the world, but how was this to be achieved?

In the current climate, only the strongest poetry could really provide much hope, but little help was on offer in the pages of the fashionable magazines or the books circulating in the new subscription libraries. Wordsworth's alarm about the state of English literature in 1800 is only too apparent in his preface, where he notes that 'the invaluable works of our elder Writers, I had almost said the works of Shakespear and Milton, are driven to neglect by frantic novels, sickly and stupid German tragedies, and deluges of idle and extravagant stories in verse'.[17] There was nothing very new about the fear of being invisible in the mass of new publications, but what distinguished Wordsworth's anxieties from those of earlier poets such as Pope and Swift were his passionate language and obvious concern for the whole of British society. The image that emerges from the preface to *Lyrical Ballads* is of a national disaster, calling not for humour or even bitter satire, but rather for the most earnest cry and prayer. The language verges on the apocalyptic, except that it is responding to a creeping obscurity rather than heralding a revelation. The flood of undistinguished books seemed to Wordsworth to threaten the nation with the very kind of malaise that radical thinkers had hoped to address—'sickly', 'stupid', 'idle', 'extravagant'. At the end of the decade, as the rain poured down and corn prices rocketed, as the Allies failed to liberate Switzerland and Napoleon returned from Egypt to seize power in Paris, radical optimism was sinking into 'the melancholy waste of hopes o'erthrown'.[18] There seemed a very real danger that literature, too, instead of bringing about the universal improvement of man's lot, was merely hastening the downward slide. Not only was there too much writing of the wrong kind, but its effect was to submerge the best poetry of the past as well as the present, preventing even the greatest writers from shedding their light on future generations. Given the seriousness of Wordsworth's own purpose and his reverence for the poetry of all ages, such unconscious vandalism was a matter of personal distress and public concern.

In the preface to *Lyrical Ballads*, Wordsworth made plain that the unhappy condition of the contemporary literary scene was part of a wider situation, especially alarming because of its unprecedented nature: 'a multitude of causes, unknown to former times, are now acting with combined force to blunt the discriminating powers of the mind.'[19] Wordsworth did not spell out the various social factors that he would soon identify in the letter to Fox, though he did single out for special mention the 'great national events which are daily taking place' and the 'accumulation of men in cities'. What he emphasized in the preface to *Lyrical Ballads* were not the causes behind the contemporary situation, which his writing could do little to alter, but rather their effects on individuals—the way in which recent social and political developments seemed to be reducing the minds of his fellow men 'to a state of almost savage torpor'.[20] This was the real danger—not hunger, not dispossession, not mechanized labour, not a French invasion—but rather the internal decay of the human spirit, which crept unnoticed but threatened ultimately to render resistance to anything impossible. The magnitude of the problem was such that Wordsworth confessed: 'I am almost ashamed to have spoken of the feeble effort with which I have endeavoured to counteract it.'[21] If the works of Shakespeare and Milton were being cast aside by an increasingly unthinking public, what hope was there that anyone would listen to the warnings of a young and virtually unknown poet?

When Wordsworth published the new edition of *Lyrical Ballads* two years later, he did not retract the warnings of 1800, but merely enlarged the preface with further thoughts on the nature of 'the Poet' and the malign effects of 'poetic diction'. It is only too apparent from the political sonnets he composed later in the same year that the condition of the English nation still seemed dire. As Wordsworth called on the memory of Milton to rouse those who seemed to be sinking in a 'fen | Of stagnant waters' and help them recover 'manners, virtue, freedom, power', he was emphasizing both the gravity of the national crisis and the seriousness of the poet's responsibility.[22] The faith in poetry's power to help was being challenged not only by the enormity of the national crisis, but also by an inner fear that modern poets might just not measure up. What form did the adequate poem take when the islands seemed to be sinking so alarmingly? And where did the modern poet turn for help when so many seemed to be abandoning hope—or their principles?

The long years of war had exacted a heavy human cost, while, more recently, the aggressive tactics of the French army under Napoleon had made it only too apparent in radical circles that the heady atmosphere of the early 1790s had proved something of a false dawn. The Treaty of Amiens, signed in March 1802, struck many as a political compromise, buying a brief interlude in the hostilities but providing no satisfactory resolution to the war. It nevertheless offered Wordsworth a chance to revisit France for the first time in ten years, to meet his daughter and her mother, Annette Vallon, and to reflect on the differences and distance between 1792 and 1802.[23] When he returned to England and began preparing for his marriage to Mary Hutchinson in October, complicated personal feelings undoubtedly added to the general anxiety that he expressed in the series of political sonnets. So much had changed in ten years, and yet the England that might have taken inspiration from the principles initially espoused by Revolutionary France was now even more deeply entrenched in social inequality than before, while the voices of those who had risen to proclaim the injustices had effectively been silenced. In June 1802, Wordsworth had attempted to explain to Sara Hutchinson his complicated response to the old leech-gatherer who had inspired a new poem, describing with reverence and indignation 'the survivor of a Wife and ten children, travelling alone among mountains and all lonely places, carrying with him his own fortitude, and the necessities which an unjust state of society had entailed upon him'.[24] The unjust state of society was obvious wherever Wordsworth looked, but the attempts of writers to redress the situation had been heavily curtailed by the wartime government's clampdown on anything deemed seditious. As honest men starved, the Prince of Wales and his friends indulged in lavish parties, but little could be done to expose such inequalities once the very idea of the 'rights of man' had become so readily associated with rebellion. What kind of poem was adequate to these circumstances?

Lyrical Ballads presented images of lives uncluttered by possessions but filled with deep emotion and humble devotion, whereas the new series of sonnets revealed a nation in which 'plain living and high thinking are no more'.[25] 'Written in London, September 1802' registered Wordsworth's dismay over the corrosion of natural pleasures by jaded tastes. Contemporary society seemed no longer capable of distinguishing either virtue or true achievement from the mere accumulation of riches:

> The wealthiest man among us is the best:
> No grandeur now in nature or in book
> Delights us. Rapine, avarice, expence,
> This is idolatry; and these we adore.   (ll. 7–10)

The powerful condemnation implied in the word 'Rapine' is a direct evocation of one of Wordsworth's favourite sonnets, 'On the Lord General Fairfax', in which Milton had praised Fairfax's 'firm, unshaken virtue' only to end gloomily,

> In vain doth valour bleed
> While avarice and rapine share the land.[26]

To conjure up the Civil War and, in particular, Milton's despair over corruption in high places was a bold strategy for Wordsworth to adopt, especially as he was suggesting collective responsibility through his use of the first-person plural—these *we* adore. The pessimistic assessment of modern, commercial society, in which everyone's better talents were forfeited—'getting and spending, we lay waste our powers'[27]—is the corollary of the depictions of small rural communities in *Lyrical Ballads*, where both plain living and high thinking were much in evidence. The possibility that Wordsworth's portrayals of a better life would go unnoticed in the world of getters and spenders was only too real, however, and, though some of his sonnets called on the memory of Milton and Shakespeare to stir up a proper response, he knew only too well that 'noble feelings' might just continue to 'fade, and participate in man's decline'.[28]

Equally depressing was the prospect of Republican France, Switzerland, and indeed much of Europe being pressed into the service of a leader who had already reintroduced slavery in the French colonies and proclaimed himself 'Consul for life'.[29] Wordsworth's dismay over Napoleon's rise and self-aggrandisement is evident from 'I grieved for Buonaparte', which he wrote rapidly in May 1802, but his feeling deepened when he visited Calais three months later and saw

> Lords, Lawyers, Statesmen, Squires of low degree,
> Men known, and men unknown, Sick, Lame, and Blind,
> Post forward all, like Creatures of one kind,
> With first-fruit offerings crowd to bend the knee
> In France, before the new-born Majesty.[30]

In what seemed a mockery of the Revolutionary hopes, the whole French nation now seemed eager to embrace a leader who had started to behave like an absolute monarch. Nor was such inconsistency peculiar to France, as the despairing line that follows the description of willing prostration suggests: "Tis ever thus.' England might still be free in the sense of having avoided succumbing to a French conquest so far, but whether she had any more reliable internal strength hardly seemed assured. With first-hand experience of French political movements over the past decade, Wordsworth's faith in a nation's ability to maintain its inner health and secure a proper future was badly shaken. Whether England could possibly retain her own proud reputation for liberty seemed decidedly doubtful. The political sonnets Wordsworth composed in 1802 reflected a deep disillusionment with the course of events in Europe, but perhaps an even greater anxiety about the decline of integrity in contemporary England. He sought inspiration from the great Republican thinkers of the seventeenth century, who had 'called Milton Friend', but the comfort of their memory was undermined by the realization that their days were long gone—'Great men have been among us'.

The very existence of these sonnets nevertheless embodies Wordsworth's fundamental belief in the necessity of poetry and its capacity to help in times of trouble. They reveal his instinctive recourse to Milton and Shakespeare for guidance and constitute an impassioned response to the sense of contemporary threat. Though he had settled in Grasmere with a huge sense of relief and gratitude, he had not abandoned the kind of humanitarian concerns that had led him, only ten years before, to join the radical movement in France, nor his

personal commitment to social justice. Wordsworth was attracted to
the Miltonic sonnet, not only because it had been the choice of a
great poet, but also because it was the form favoured by a great
Republican. By 1802, Wordsworth's admiration for Milton had also
been strengthened by his new understanding of local attachments:
the sonnets now seemed an embodiment of *native* strength.

As he explained in a letter of November 1802, Milton's sonnets
were 'manly and dignified compositions, distinguished by simplicity
and unity of object and aim, and undisfigured by false or vicious
ornaments'.[31] Although he admitted to their lack of polish and
tendency to be 'incorrect, sometimes uncouth in language, and,
perhaps, in some, inharmonious', the very capacity to break with
convention was essential to their power. Since the edition of *Lyrical
Ballads* published earlier in the year had included an appendix
deploring the peculiar perpetuation of an 'adulterated phraseology'
in English poetry, Wordsworth's commendation of Milton's sonnets
was especially significant. For, if poetic diction was becoming 'daily
more and more corrupt, thrusting out of sight the plain humanities
of nature by a motley masquerade of tricks, quaintnesses, hiero-
glyphics, and enigmas', then poems like Milton's, 'undisfigured by
false or vicious ornament', had an invaluable moral force as well as
aesthetic power.[32]

For a poet who saw avarice, luxury, and excess as the outward
signs of a nation in serious decline, the unornamented Miltonic
sonnet, with its clear purpose, dense matter, and disregard for tradi-
tional rules, seemed a form that might be equal to the task of
combating the prevailing trends. It had, in Wordsworth's eyes, 'an
energetic and varied flow of sound crowding into narrow room more
of the combined effect of rhyme and blank verse than can be done
by any other kind of verse'.[33] The sonnet's self-sufficient gravity
emphasized its meaning and allowed large topics to be condensed
into only a few lines. Its very narrowness offered a kind of 'solace',
as Wordsworth reflected in a sonnet written at about this time, in
which his work recalled nuns in 'their Convent's narrow room' or
'Hermits' who remain 'contented with their Cells'. The very language
of confinement nevertheless suggests that, despite his admiration for
the manly Milton, Wordsworth did not find the sonnet quite suffi-
cient for his larger purposes. It might possess a strong form, an 'ener-
getic and varied flow of sound' and the capacity to pack in both

rhyme and blank verse, but, ultimately, the fourteen, tightly rhymed lines were too limited for Wordsworth's exploratory instincts. For all its virtues, the Miltonic sonnet was also a conscious throwback to a vanished age. Its high moral tone and intricate form were not perhaps the most natural for a poet in his early thirties whose own life had been somewhat chequered and whose latest collection of poems had been presented as 'experiments'.

In *Lyrical Ballads*, Wordsworth had made great claims for the contribution of the poet to contemporary society, but the poems themselves are full of complexity, questioning, and self-rebuke. Although the sonnets offered a kind of formal resolution, they seemed to allow insufficient room for probing the inner feelings and failings of the poet, or for exploring fully the proper response of poetry to the world as it is. Honest confrontation of the difficulties presented by the contemporary world was vital to the inherent truth of a poem, but so was the acknowledgement of the poet's own uncertainties. Milton's moments of self-doubt were rare enough, but, in much of Wordsworth's best work, it is the speaker/poet who receives admonishment rather than those he might be addressing. Though he used the first person carefully in his sonnets to suggest his own collusion in the national collapse, it was hard to avoid a somewhat censorious tone in poems that were issuing such strong admonishments to most of modern Britain. In 'Simon Lee', 'Michael', or 'We are Seven', the persuasive power of the verse depended instead on the humility of the poet persona, which helped the reader's enjoyment through a sense of shared, sympathetic enlightenment.

By 1802, Wordsworth was well aware that the challenging nature of contemporary conditions demanded particular kinds of strength and skill. As he explained to John Wilson, who had written an enthusiastic letter about *Lyrical Ballads*, the only judge of poetry that mattered was 'human nature', and the 'best measure' of this was to be found within. Wordsworth's letter to his young Glasgow reader reveals much about his own perception of contemporary society and its problems, for it is possible to see beneath the contempt for the superficial layers of fashionable life, truths gained from his experiences in France and the human suffering witnessed then and since. Human nature, he stated unequivocally, could be discovered only 'by stripping our hearts naked, and by looking out of ourselves towards men who lead the simplest lives according to nature men who have never known false refinements, wayward and artificial desires, false criticisms, effeminate habits of thinking and feeling, or who, having known these things, have outgrown them'.[34] It is easy to see why Wordsworth was turning to poetic forms that he considered to be 'undisfigured by false and vicious ornament'. The letter to Wilson, however, also reveals that Wordsworth's poetic choices were inseparable from his emphasis on self-knowledge and the pursuit of truths fundamental to humanity. In the light of this letter and other work of the same year, it becomes evident that, though the sonnet provided a suitable form for railing against the state of the nation, its rooms were too narrow for the proper representation of human nature that was Wordsworth's measure of real poetry. Creation of an adequate poem required a profound understanding of human nature and therefore a structure flexible enough to carry conviction—and doubt.

That Wordsworth had already mastered blank verse was plain from 'Tintern Abbey', 'Michael', 'The Ruined Cottage', and 'Home at Grasmere', but his letter on Milton's sonnets reveals a continuing admiration for rhyme. Earlier in the year, he had composed four beautifully but variously rhyming stanzas of what later became known as 'Ode: Intimations of Immortality'. Although these were laid aside, unfinished, they suggest that, during 1802, Wordsworth was actively seeking serious alternatives to blank verse as part of his struggle to achieve a new kind of poetry fully adequate to the grave concerns of the day. The opening of the great Ode shows that, despite Milton's inspiring example (or perhaps because of it), the self-image projected in Wordsworth's poetry was often of one given to uncertainty:

> Turn where so e'er I may,
> By night or day,
> The things which I have seen I now can see no more.[35]

The speaker, though conscious of loss, does not even seem clear about what he had had in the first place.

In 'Resolution and Independence', which was composed in the early summer of 1802, Wordsworth presented the poet/speaker, not as a Miltonic star guiding a benighted people from on high, but as a rather aimless young man, prone to sudden mood swings and in need of admonishment himself. The poem is haunted by memories of Chatterton and Burns, who had died prematurely in poverty and despair, and acknowledges that, far from being a 'rock' or 'preserver' of human society, some of the best modern poets had been its victims.

Currie's four-volume edition of *The Works of Burns*, which had been published in 1800, just as Wordsworth and Coleridge were articulating their own ideas about poetry's place in modern society for *Lyrical Ballads*, presented a harrowing biographical account of the rapid rise and decline of a brilliant young poet. The preface to *Lyrical Ballads* still presented the reading public with a stirring ideal for the modern poet, but it was also issuing a daunting personal challenge, with which Wordsworth had to grapple. Even the most optimistic observer could hardly avoid moments of doubt about the power of the artist, when the mortal frames and mental stability of some of the best contemporary writers had proved so fragile. Some years later, Wordsworth recalled the 'acute sorrow' he felt when first reading Currie's description of 'a man of exquisite genius and confessedly of some high moral virtues, sunk into the lower depths of vice and misery'.[36] Especially troubling to Wordsworth were the gaps in the record, which meant that not even the most attentive reader could understand 'how a mind, so well established by knowledge, fell and continued to fall, without power to prevent or retard its own ruin'. The horror of such a sudden, inexplicable decline for a poet who had already suffered a severe psychological breakdown found expression in the haunting lines of 'Resolution and Independence':

> We Poets in our youth begin in gladness;
> But thereof comes in the end despondency and madness. (ll. 48–9)

The young poet in 'Resolution and Independence' sets off in high good humour, only to find himself engulfed in sudden gloom. It was a moment of deep personal resonance for Wordsworth, as he later admitted: 'A young Poet in the midst of the happiness of Nature is described as overwhelmed by the thought of the miserable reverses which have befallen the happiest of men, viz Poets—I think of this till I am so deeply impressed by it, that I consider the manner in which I was rescued from my dejection and despair almost as an interposition of Providence.'[37] Though Wordsworth was only too conscious of his own salvation from deep depression, the vast uncertainties that were gathering around made the possibility of another descent seem only too real.

The young poet's sudden loss of spirit was also a telling image for Wordsworth's own creative situation in 1802, as the confidence of *Lyrical Ballads* seemed to give way, while the truths expressed in 'Michael' and 'Home at Grasmere' offered no clear way forward. Earlier in the year, the beautifully experimental stanzas of his new Ode had been created to express deep anxieties about the inevitable decline of visionary experience, to which Coleridge had responded at once—but not with a robust refutation. Instead, Coleridge, too, had articulated an even more anguished lament for failing creative powers in the verse letter subsequently published as 'Dejection: An Ode'.[38] When he came to write 'Resolution and Independence', then, Wordsworth was only too aware that 'gladness' could turn very rapidly into 'despondency and madness', his use of rhyme under-lining the speed of the transformation.

Unlike the sonnet's narrow room, the new narrative form, with its unusual seven-line stanzas, allowed for shifting moods, action, and reflec-tion. The poem is long enough to create character, set the scene, and introduce a meeting that is at once humbling and uplifting. Both clear moral guidance and humility can coexist in the poem because of its dramatic dimension and opposing voices. The poem is strong enough to acknowledge the paralysing effects of self-doubt unflinchingly, while at the same time making careful use of the engaging qualities of a volatile speaker whose sense of direction seems so uncertain. The internal tensions produce a dynamic energy that propels the reader beyond the simple language and the confines of the stanzas, turning attention within even as it directs us outside the self. The opening lines set up an expecta-tion of Spenserian stanzas, but the verse then checks readers by stopping two short of the conventional nine lines, while simultaneously offering a longer finale. Each stanza builds momentum through five rhyming pentameters, before being halted by the final hexameter, which rhymes with the penultimate line, to form an uneven couplet. Though often impelled forward by repetitions between the closing line of one stanza and the opening of the next, the reader's progress is perpetually slowed by the longer lines, which demand a moment of reflection:

> I was a Traveller then upon the moor;
> I saw the Hare that rac'd about with joy;
> I heard the woods, and distant waters, roar;
> Or heard them not, as happy as a Boy:
> The pleasant season did my heart employ:

> My old remembrances went from me wholly;
> And all the ways of men, so vain and melancholy.   (ll. 15–21)

The entire poem is, indeed, poised between stasis and movement, as the two travellers come to a halt and remain held firmly in place by the steady rhymes and rhythmic stanzas, until the final lines, which send the young man on his way, and turn the leech-gatherer into a saving memory. It combines first-hand recollection of the old man Wordsworth had met a few hundred yards from Dove Cottage, whom he described to Sara Hutchinson and later to Isabella Fenwick, with memories of a different kind—of Thomas Chatterton's 'An Excelente Balade of Charitie' and Milton's 'Ode on the Morning of Christ's Nativity', both of which had employed the same, distinctive stanza form.[39]

Narrative progression is at once ordered and magnified by the dim presence of earlier poems, whose memories offered very different associations. Though the speaker in the poem recalls that his 'old remembrances went...wholly', the moment is deepened by competing remembrances. Like Heaney's acknowledgement that he became a poet when his roots crossed with his reading, so Wordsworth's poem is born from the fusion of local and internal experience. When Heaney spoke of the adequacy of poets such as Yeats and Wordsworth, he distinguished between a 'documentary adequacy' that confronted the immediate world, with its ugliness and beauty, and the adequacy of the lyric form, with its self-sufficient capacity to exist independently of the circumstances in which it was made. In 'Resolution and Independence', Wordsworth's documentary truthfulness was tempered by the different truth of lyric verse, which orders emotion and brings the collective authority of metre to bear on individual experience. The result is the creation of a completely adequate poem—strong enough to measure up to its own cultural moment and to carry on delighting readers of later generations and other societies.

For Heaney, the depth and wholeness of Wordsworth's best poetry represents the 'hard-earned reward of resolved crisis', a comment informed by his sympathy for the psychological and creative upheavals re-created in *The Prelude*.[40] It was 'Resolution and Independence', however, that he singled out in his own introduction to the poetry, as being characteristically 'Wordsworthian'.[41] The combination of democratic, philosophic, visionary, and self-analytical impulses, with complete mastery of the stanza form, made it an exemplary poem for Heaney—adequate to contemporary conditions and adequate in its form and language.[42] Wordsworth had seen an old man travelling alone, with little more than the 'necessities which an unjust state of society had entailed', but he had also recognized that he was 'carrying his own fortitude'.[43] As first-hand experience turned into art, Wordsworth developed a verse that possessed an internal strength corresponding to the old traveller, but also enough flexibility to express both waywardness and purpose, fear and resolution. It measures up fully to what Heaney has identified as 'the contradictory needs which consciousness experiences at times of extreme crisis' and by honestly acknowledging the coexistence of the contradictory, achieves a wholeness that is also an openness.[44]

For, if the power of the poem derived from a resolution of personal crisis, its fascination depends also on a sense of other possibilities. The reader is left, like the young poet, to think of the leech-gatherer on the lonely moor, but the poem encourages sympathetic engagement with the speaker, too—his changing mood, enlightenment, and recovery. 'Resolution' sustains the old man and relieves the younger traveller, whose anxieties are checked or resolved, but it also implies a sense of new purpose, which is not necessarily assured. The sudden melancholy that descends is dark with fears about the young man's own future, and, while the poem reveals that these are inappropriate, it refuses to offer any sense of subsequent direction. Although the leech-gatherer offers human strength and strong admonishment, everything about him still remains troubling to the poet. For Wordsworth, the reward of a resolved crisis was not calm inactivity, but rather a sense of urgent responsibility—hope was being renewed rather than rendered irrelevant. The fully adequate poem, too, was as much a prompt to continuing creative effort as it was a defence against apparently overwhelming odds. Courageous resistance, though invaluable, was still not enough, and hence the poem ends with an invitation to continue the journey, fortified and clarified by what has been revealed.

The meeting of two solitary figures in 'Resolution and Independence' produces a creative depth charge whose force is felt by every reader, if not fully understood. *Lyrical Ballads* had included several poems where memorable encounters surprise the speaker into fresh understanding, but the encounter with the leech-gatherer possesses an almost baffling momentousness and, with it, stern promise of new imaginative life. The feeling that the leech-gatherer has been 'from a far region *sent*' imbues him with a mysterious purpose, which arrests the aimless traveller and invites curiosity about the strange old man and his origins. His arrival seems as if 'by peculiar grace, | A leading from above, a something given', in other words, what seems a chance encounter also seems anything but. The poem inhabits a world between the realms of myth and reality, its supernatural or divine suggestions poised by realistic observation.

One of its many startling moments is the description of the old man's language, for the figure who appears to be so unelevated, socially, so lacking, materially, and so weak, physically, speaks with an authority firm enough to stop the traveller's unthinking questions:

> His words came feebly, from a feeble chest,
> But each in solemn order follow'd each,
> With something of a lofty utterance drest—
> Choice word, and measured phrase, above the reach
> Of ordinary men; a stately speech!
> Such as grave Livers do in Scotland use,
> Religious men, who give to God and man their dues.   (ll. 99–106)

Far from being lowly, the old man's speech is 'lofty', 'stately', 'above the reach | Of ordinary men'. His words, though not directly reported at this point, are strong enough to answer the poet and the situation. Wordsworth challenges his readers to imagine the 'lofty utterance', to create their own idea of an adequate language, while the old man himself remains elusive, beyond the reach of the ordinary.

At the same time, the strangeness is partially explained by the attribution of stately speech to that of 'grave Livers' in Scotland. There is nothing, after all, so amazing about the discovery of an old Scotsman in a northern county of England, close to the Scottish border, and Wordsworth secures the trustworthiness of his poem by offering just enough detail to allow his readers some foothold in the world of solid sense. We can accept the other-worldly quality of the leech-gatherer because something in his lofty utterance is local and particular—he can inhabit the borders between life and death, the internal and external worlds, the natural and supernatural, because he has also crossed a real border that was open to any of Wordsworth's readers.

He is a grave liver in the sense of being a serious person, as well as carrying suggestions of the revenant or wise man. In the leech-gatherer Wordsworth created a figure who could hold up a mirror to the poet, which revealed the self and the very nature of humanity, but its power was gathered from ordinary experience, from the world of all of us. 'Resolution and Independence' dramatizes a moment of admonishment, but it is also explicitly a moment of renewal—an expression of gratitude for the gift of 'human strength'. In his poem, Wordsworth was offering thanks for the hope that came unexpectedly, from common things, and thus providing an exemplary tale for his readers.

In the poetry of encounter, the meeting of reader and poem is just as vital as the represented dialogue, and 'Resolution and Independence' is opening the same kind of revelatory experience to its audience that the poet attempts to describe. Just as his own experience is informed by the memory of earlier writing, so he offers his poem as a mental resource for the future. Despite Wordsworth's recognition of the physical vulnerability of some young poets, 'Resolution and Independence' still demonstrates the saving power of poetry. Part of its admonishment is directed towards those who, like the young man on the moor, miss the truth by taking heed of less important things, or who mistakenly embrace despondency when redemption is within their grasp.

Key to the old Scottish leech-gatherer's admonishment is the memory of Burns, whose great importance was already being largely missed by a sympathetic, but misguided modern readership. In Wordsworth's poem, Burns's untimely death appears to be held up as an image of the fragility of the poet, but, in fact, the strong lines of 'Resolution and Independence' are braced throughout by allusions to Burns's poems. The figure of Burns is invoked directly, but his poetry is also echoed at every turn, from the obvious reference to 'The Mountain Daisy' and 'To a Mouse' in 'Him who walked in glory and in joy | Behind the plough, upon the mountainside', to the less easily visible recollections of 'Despondency', 'Man was Made to Mourn', and 'The Cotter's Saturday Night'. Key words in the poem—'despondency', 'recompense', 'admonishment'—recall each of these poems, while the hares have bounded in from 'Holy Fair'. The old man, with his solemn Scottish accent, seems to have come from the pages as much as from the land of Burns.

The real hare that Wordsworth later recalled having seen on the ridge of Barton Fell, on his way from Ullswater, was magnified by the hares he remembered from 'Holy Fair', just as the old leech-gatherer gained meaning from the old men in Burns's poetry and in *Lyrical Ballads*.[45] Poetry, which connected personal experience to earlier moments embodied in other poems, was a site of shared pleasure that also invited readers to seek fresh correspondences in their own lives. Though Burns had already been dead for nearly eight years, he lived on in his words, delighting readers and guiding younger poets to new creative action. He too was a 'grave liver' from Scotland, whose familiar lines could remain a presence in the new compositions they prompted. If Burns's life provoked melancholy thoughts, his work inspired fresh hope for the modern poet.

The distinction between the poet as a human being and the 'poet' as an ideal whose *work* might provide a rock for others is one of the underlying preoccupations of 'Resolution and Independence' and one that continued to drive Wordsworth's creative explorations. Wordsworth's sense of the poet's responsibility to contemporary society was after all nourished by his own love of stories, poems, and songs. In 'Hart-Leap Well', 'Home at Grasmere', 'Michael', and 'The Brothers', he had acknowledged his debts to the hidden narratives of the local area, as well as celebrating the unrefined, but admirable lives of those who constituted both subjects and storytellers. Often the tales passed through generations, with their authors' identities becoming submerged in the process, so that Wordsworth's gratitude was as much to a body of work as to individual storytellers. These were 'poets' of real humility, whose words had come to matter more than their names and whose work was given freely, with no thought of fame or fortune.

As Wordsworth dwelled on the virtues of the simple life, he began to recognize the generosity of the unknown creative talents who sustained their communities through songs and stories. In the preface to *Lyrical Ballads* he had addressed the question 'What is a Poet?', but he had not singled out any individual writer as the answer. Instead, Wordsworth had considered the characteristics of the poet—sensibility, enthusiasm, tenderness, sympathy for others, delight in the universe and imaginative power—but only to emphasize the faculties needed in order to arrive at the truth. The purpose of poetry, as Wordsworth stated emphatically in his new additions to the preface, was not to ensure the reputation of the poet, but to give pleasure to readers. In order to achieve the kind of truth Wordsworth sought, which was 'not individual and local, but general and operative; not standing upon external testimony, but carried alive into the heart by passion', it was necessary to look at the world 'in the spirit of love', paying homage to 'the native and naked dignity of man'.[46] In other words, the poet had to be more concerned with seeking the truths available to him in the world around than with his own distracting fears or vanities—more like the leech-gatherer than the young, self-styled, poet.

Though Wordsworth advocated the poet's complete immersion in the feelings of those he wanted to describe for no more than 'short spaces', the need to overcome self-absorption and personal ambition is plain enough. Nevertheless, the preface also emphasized that the poet was not only delighted by 'the goings-on of the universe', but also 'habitually impelled to create them where he does not find them'.[47] In other words, imaginative capacity was just as important to the creation of a great poem as sympathetic observation of other human beings. This is what he meant by emphasizing that the ideal truths of poetry were 'general and operative', rather than 'local and individual'—they were truths like those of Burns's poetry, which could speak to people everywhere in all times and were not 'local' in Johnson's restricted sense of 'local poetry'. Wordsworth's ideal truths derived from the immediate world, but only through the kind of sympathetic response that intuitively selected essential human significance from the mass of available detail, which was why a poet required tenderness as well as technical ability. True poetry at once depended on and embodied 'the spirit of love' and hence its power to connect individuals to each other and to the living universe. When Wordsworth celebrated 'domestic affections' and 'local attachment', it was the nouns that gave meaning to the adjectives.

Wordsworth was wrestling to reconcile an ideal of selflessness with a potentially competing understanding of special, personal creativity—the poet's 'genial spirits', which Coleridge had seen failing in himself. Where the acknowledgement of opposing ideals might risk seeming contradictory in a prose essay, however, they offered a dynamic opposition when dramatized within a narrative poem. 'Resolution and Independence' has the strength of a resolved crisis, not because it offers absolute answers but because it allows room for doubt and conviction, for the complexities to coexist without threatening to unbalance the whole poem. When Wordsworth came to write *The Prelude*, three years later, the beautiful blank verse that he had used for 'Tintern Abbey' and 'Home at Grasmere' had become an even more flexible form, as it deepened to embrace the tensions he had confronted in 'Resolution and Independence'.

The desire to reconcile the different conceptions of a poet as one endowed with special traits and one whose purpose is to serve others, evident in both the preface to *Lyrical Ballads* and 'Resolution and Independence', shows that the crisis with which Wordsworth was struggling in 1802 was personal as well as public. What is a poet? Is he a man or a body of work? Do poems belong to their author or their audiences? When a modern poet called on his greatest predecessors for inspiration, was he thinking of the benefits to his readers or of his own place in the literary pantheon? The question of what poetry could do in response to a national crisis was a question about the very nature and purpose of the individual poet, and hence, perhaps, Wordsworth's preoccupation with the idea of 'Burns'. James Currie's new edition of *The Works of Burns* presented not only the poems, letters, and songs, but also the life—as if to ensure that the former should be read only in the light of the latter. At the same time, his essay emphasized the astonishing global reach of Burns's songs, arguing that they were sung 'with equal or superior interest on the banks of the Ganges or the Mississippi, as on those of the Tay or Tweed'.[48] Burns's works already had a life of their own, independent of their creator, and owed much of their existence in the first place to the anonymous traditions that flourished in rural Scotland. Wordsworth's increasing admiration for those whose words survived even though their names did not, such as the writers of rural epitaphs or unknown ballad-makers or the old pedlars who passed on stories to younger audiences, deepened through his own encounters with Burns—who seemed at once to confirm the radical power of poetry while demonstrating the potential dangers of being 'a Poet'.

Wordsworth's Obligations to Burns

In 'Resolution and Independence', thoughts of Burns come with a sudden descent into despondency, but the stanza is held in check by the description of 'Him who walked in glory and in joy', with its echoes of Lycidas, lifted at last, by 'him that walked the waves'.[49] Wordsworth knew that his whole direction as a poet had been redeemed by Burns, though it was many years later, when working on a new collection of *Poems, Chiefly of Early and Later Years*, that Wordsworth took the opportunity to acknowledge publicly his 'obligations' to Burns. At a time when his 'taste and natural tendencies were under an injurious influence from the dazzling manner of Darwin, and the extravagance of the earlier Dramas of Schiller and that of other German Writers', the poems of Burns had helped to restore Wordsworth to his true poetic self.[50] Burns's work enabled his young admirer to recover tendencies that were 'natural'—true to his own nature as well as to the natural world and human nature. His ability to represent his immediate surroundings and to draw on Scottish poetic tradition showed that neither language nor forms needed to be borrowed from abroad. Even more striking, as Wordsworth recognized when he reread the poems he had known since his schooldays, Burns had the rare distinction of conveying genuine emotion: 'His Ode to Despondency I can never read without the deepest agitation.'[51] Wordsworth had understood Burns's poems from the start, not just because the language was familiar enough to readers in Cumberland and Westmoreland, but because he could 'feel them'.[52]

The contrast between the simple truths of Burns and the extravagance of German dramatists that Wordsworth underlined in 1842 also recalled his own crucial experiences in Germany during the winter of 1798–9, between the publication of the first and second editions of *Lyrical Ballads*. For it was then that he began to rediscover his youthful passion for the English Lakes and to compose the first passages of *The Prelude*. Wordsworth had made the trip across the North Sea in order to become proficient in the language of so many of the leading contemporary writers, but, as he battled to learn enough to appreciate the poetry that seemed to be entrancing English radical circles, he found his anchor in the Lakes and the memories of native British poetry tugging more insistently. Efforts to understand the appeal of Gottfried Bürger, whose poems had prompted an ecstatic response from Charles Lamb ('Have you read the ballad called "Leonora"...? If you have!!!!!!!!!!!!!!'), produced in Wordsworth only a deeper admiration for the work of Robert Burns.[53] For what Wordsworth, sick for home, found sadly lacking in Bürger's poems were 'manners connected with the permanent objects of nature and partaking in the simplicity of those objects'.[54] Bürger's poetry revealed none of the essential elements of human nature that Wordsworth would soon be recommending to John Wilson as the only test of true poetry and making fundamental to the new collection of *Lyrical Ballads*. In the work of Robert Burns, on the other hand, the reader was constantly in 'the presence of human life' as the poems struck home with 'the charm of recognitions'. For Wordsworth, this contrast between the German and Scottish poets was fundamental: 'Now I find no manners in Bürger, in Burns you have manners everywhere.'[55] In a strange country, surrounded by people speaking their own native language, Wordsworth had found deep pleasure in poems that could strike home 'with the charm of recognitions'.

Wordsworth's delight in the comforting familiarity of Burns was similar to Heaney's feeling of surprise at finding Burns getting straight 'into the kitchen life' of his affections, when he first encountered the poems in school. For Heaney, Burns's poetry has an 'emotional fidelity' that is guaranteed by perfectly fitted forms and language, but, while his initial, boyish attention was caught by local, non-standard, words, he later came to understand its linguistic and literary complexity.[56] Heaney's alertness to the 'drama' played out in Burns, as 'in every poet between the social self and the deeper self', helps to illuminate the special significance of Burns for Wordsworth in 1799, as he grappled with his own definition of the 'Poet' and his sense of social responsibility. Heaney admires the comic brilliance and 'documentary accuracy' of Burns's work, but he values even more highly the 'deep poetic self' that could touch 'the oldest survival-truths' of humankind and find fresh expression for 'immemorial utterances'.[57] These are qualities less easy to apprehend on a first reading of Burns, but ones that Heaney recognized when he returned to the work as a mature poet and that Wordsworth discovered on rereading Burns in Germany.

Wordsworth's encounter with fashionable, European literature intensified his sense of belonging to the north of Britain, while helping, inadvertently, to clarify his ideas about the kind of poetry that could touch the hearts of all people in all places. Going abroad meant the unexpected discovery of home truths. The appeal of Burns to an Englishman abroad demonstrated that, if poetry embodied

essential truths, it had both universal value and the staying power
that marked the greatest work. As Wordsworth realized, when
comparing Burns's work to both contemporary German poems and
those of the English writers most fashionable a century before, 'such
pictures must interest when the original shall cease to exist'.[58] This
discovery had been vital to the creation of a poem such as 'Michael',
because it meant that human stories did not become irrelevant even
when the situations in which they originally took place were super-
seded. Burns's poetry, whose truth was self-evident, had a lasting
quality that seemed resistant to literary fashions and fickle tastes.
These were poems with a power to speak to people far removed in
space or time, because they expressed powerful emotional responses
to the real world, in forms and language that rang true.

When Wordsworth defined pastorals in 1802 as poems, stripped
of later literary accretions and conveying the natural power of
'passion excited by real events', he could have been describing
Burns.[59] There was no place for the absurd nymphs and shepherds of
neoclassical pastoral in a volume that included such tender comic
masterpieces as the 'Lament for Mailie'. Mailie was a completely
convincing sheep, as Seamus Heaney recognized when re-examining
his own delight in Burns and praising 'the special mixture of inti-
macy and documentary accuracy' in the dying words of the 'Author's
only pet yowe'.[60] Although Wordsworth's Lake District pastorals
were generally imbued with more gravitas than Burns's elegies on
his favourite yowe, his own desire to restore modern pastoral to the
truthfulness of the ancient mode found a cheering counterpart in
Poems, Chiefly in the Scottish Dialect. In the preface to the Kilmar-
nock edition, Burns had distinguished his approach from that of
gentlemen-poets who liked to cite Virgil and Theocritus rather
than look at the real men and women who worked on the local
farms. Instead, he presented himself as writing not 'by rule', but
according to 'what he felt and saw in himself and his rustic compeers
around him, in his and their native language'.[61] Such a straightfor-
ward defence of native wit had been a salutary reminder to a poet,
marooned in Germany, and increasingly disenchanted with fashion-
able contemporary literature.

On his return to England, Wordsworth had also been able to
read Burns's 'Poem on Pastoral Poetry', published for the first time
in Currie's edition. Burns had paid tribute to Allan Ramsay in

the preface to the Kilmarnock edition, as well as in poems such as the 'Epistle to J. L****k', but here he hailed him as the modern Theocritus, rising to the challenge of the Ancient Greeks, just as 'Will Shakespeare' and 'Jock Milton' had done in tragedy and epic:

> Thou paints auld Nature to the nines,
> In thy sweet Caledonian lines;
> Nae gowdan stream thro' myrtles twines
>   Where Philomel,
> While nightly breezes sweep the vines,
>   Her griefs will tell![62]

Unlike most modern poets, whose idea of writing pastoral struck Burns as 'spates o' nonsense' swollen with 'bombast', Ramsay's work seemed 'Nature's sel''. Though part of his admiration for Ramsay stemmed from a desire to promote Scottish poetry as the equal of English, the sentiments regarding literary convention in Burns's poem were very similar to those expressed in Coleridge's 'The Nightingale' and Wordsworth's appendix on poetic diction. The self-confidence of the poem also offered a challenge to the literary convention that placed pastoral at the bottom of the poetic hierarchy. Burns's recuperation of pastoral was far-reaching enough to include political comment, just as Virgil, Spenser, and Milton had done when they experimented with the mode.[63] A poem such as 'The Twa Dogs' was pastoral in its use of dialogue and rural subject matter, but also in its critique of social injustices. Burns's pastoral thus had a multifaceted appeal for a poet angered by inequality, but limited by sedition laws, dismayed by contemporary literature, and searching for poetic adequacy.

Currie's edition of Burns, with the 'Poem on Pastoral' and many other hitherto unpublished pieces, had appeared in 1800, just as Wordsworth was preparing the new collection of *Lyrical Ballads* for the press. When Coleridge arrived in Keswick in July, he was fresh from Liverpool and conversations with James Currie, whose new *Life of Burns* he greatly admired for its philosophical approach.[64] Though Wordsworth was horrified by the biographical revelations, he must nevertheless have found much in Currie's work to reinforce ideas he was currently developing in relation to *Lyrical Ballads*.[65] By now, Wordsworth, living in Grasmere, was taking deep pleasure in every aspect of the surrounding landscape and its stock of stories.

To find a modern editor who regarded the local detail evident in Burns's poems as intrinsic to their power was heartening, to say the least.

Far from regarding Burns's humble background or his choices of subject and setting as obstacles to his wider success, Currie presented rural Scotland as the groundwork of his creative strength. The poems were full of specific reference to the Lugar and the Doon, to Mauchline and Alloway, but, in Currie's eyes, this was evidence of the beneficial formative influences of traditional songs. There was no suggestion in his essay that local detail rendered the work narrowly provincial. Instead, the focus on the particular rather than the general ('the distinguishing feature' of Scottish song) was the source of its emotional power. Central to Currie's account of Burns was a deep admiration for the capacity of lyric poetry to embody genuine feeling, an aesthetic underpinned by particularization. He dwelled upon the way in which Scottish songs described scenes where a tender encounter had taken place, arguing that the feelings gained conviction because the spot itself was 'particularised'. The songs of Burns were the living demonstration of a new aesthetic: that local truth was essential to the creation of poetry with proper emotive power. Since Wordsworth's own aim was to write poems whose truthful embodiment of human nature had the power to move readers profoundly, the new edition of Burns's wonderful work, with its editorial endorsement of local truth as the basis for genuinely emotive poetry, could not have been more welcome. Here was a volume that offered corroboration for his own bold decision to move to the Lakes and draw on their largely unplumbed depths.

Since Currie admired the way feeling was guaranteed by reference to particular places in the poetry, Burns's personal experience was crucial to his critical approach. Burns was shown, accordingly, wandering 'alone on the banks of the Ayr', listening to blackbirds on a summer Sunday, or working in the fields, 'humming the songs of his country, musing on the deeds of ancient valour, or rapt in the illusions of his fancy'.[66] Physical labour encouraged Burns's imagination to wander, while the hours were helped along by communal songs whose use of local place names made them seem so much part of the landscape. Scottish song was not the province of the gentleman at leisure, but part of the daily life of the ordinary people. For anyone sympathetic to radical principles of equality and fraternity, the idea of the common man as an accomplished poet had a strong appeal.

But, for one who was also troubled by the increasing marginalization of true poetry in contemporary Britain, the idea of a farmer for whom poetry was as essential as the earth from which he drew his living was a revelation. Furthermore, the image of the young Burns suggested a wholeness and balance of faculties that made a striking contrast to the sickliness and 'savage torpor' of so much of contemporary society.

The bard at the plough or wielding a scythe was a suitably manly counterpart to the heroes of the old songs, with their 'ancient valour', though it neatly avoided the more destructive aspects of early society that troubled Enlightenment primitivist critics such as Hugh Blair. As a farmer, Burns had the physical strength and masculinity that constituted so much of the appeal of heroic society to urban and sedentary readers, but his work was essentially peaceful and productive. He was an ideal antidote to the faintly ludicrous men who featured in the contemporary literature of sensibility, and so his work could be enjoyed by readers eager for emotional depth but somewhat queasy about namby-pamby poetry. Anxieties about manliness and effeminacy recur in Wordsworth's writings during the critical years that saw Napoleon's meteoric rise to power, for he was only too aware of the difficulty of creating affecting poetry that might be forceful rather than feeble. Burns's work was the poetry of the heart, not of the merely tearful.

The plough, like an anchor, also symbolized Burns's connection to the earth, which was as evident in his concrete verses as in his biography. For particularization was the literary equivalent of participation in the earth, drawing strength, Antaeus-like, from the real world of first-hand experience. Burns was not observing the landscape from a distance, but living and working within a known environment, and he re-created its fresh physical reality in his poems. He was grounded by his circumstances and by ties formed through the communal experience that had developed over centuries. In fact, as will become clear in Chapter 5, the close community of rural Ayrshire was not always the perfect, nurturing environment painted by Burns's editor, but Currie's account nevertheless did much to promote an idea of the poet as an integral part of his society. This provided an important counter to the kind of contemporary criticism that saw only extraordinary natural genius, bursting into spontaneous song, because it attempted to make sense of Burns's achievement and to acknowledge the traditional influences on his work. Currie's 'Observations on the Scottish Peasantry' included considerable information about the unusual quality of the education available to the common people of Scotland since the Reformation, for example, while his biography included a description of Burns's father encouraging his children's reading. According to Currie, Burns's gift was not 'heaven-sent', but rather the result of an imagination nurtured by first-hand experience, by a distinctive education, and by the inheritance of moving songs featuring the local landscape.[67]

Throughout the prefatory essay, Currie placed emphasis on the strong attachment that characterized the people of rural Scotland and identified their songs as the crucial factor: 'the scenery...the peculiar manners of its inhabitants, and the martial achievements of their ancestors, are embodied in national songs, and united to national music'.[68] This powerful combination, absorbed from infancy, helped to strengthen 'the ties that attach men to the land of their birth'. Life in a mountainous region, according to his analysis, fostered a particular kind of culture and community. Not only did the tough physical conditions breed a sturdy kind of independence among the inhabitants, but the small valleys where people naturally settled were 'situations well calculated to call forth and concentrate the social affections, amidst scenery that acts most powerfully on the sight, and makes a lasting impression on the memory'.[69] When Wordsworth read the essay soon after his own return to the Lakes, he must have been struck by the parallels.

Currie's account of the characteristics of those living in mountainous countries was a confirmation of Wordsworth's own feelings about the Lake District. Especially encouraging was the way in which the social role of poetry was presented as a fact rather than as an argument or ideal. As a medical man and well-known figure in the liberal intellectual circle of Liverpool, he presented his 'Observations on the Character and Condition of the Scottish Peasantry' in an objective, philosophical tone that seemed to result from careful scientific and historical research. The idea that strong local attachments were nurtured by both the countryside and the song culture thus possessed a kind of unquestionable logic. The Scottish people included their familiar landscape and language in their songs, which then strengthened their sense of connection to the land, the language, and fellow-countrymen each time they were sung. For a young poet

so horrified by the erosion of 'domestic affections' among the British
people that he wrote to Fox to urge appropriate political awareness,
Currie's essay was a very timely contribution. Far from acting as a
limitation, the local attachments embodied in certain kinds of poetry
were the guarantee of a healthy community in which people minded
about each other and felt part of a shared history and environment.
Such self-sustaining communities offered an alternative model to the
materialistic society berated in his political sonnets as well as
providing a secure base for those who had the privilege to grow up
there.

   Wordsworth's travels had helped him understand the need for
internal guides and anchors, which ideally seemed to be formed in
childhood, but he had no desire to restrict his discoveries to
poets and intellectuals. When he composed the 'Character of a
Happy Warrior', for example, his image of the man who 'does not
stoop, nor lie in wait | For wealth, or honors, or for worldly state',
emphasized the importance of an internal equilibrium, sustained by
memories of home:

> He who, though thus endued with a sense
> And faculty for storm and turbulence,
> Is yet a Soul whose master bias leans
> To home-felt pleasures and to gentle scenes;
> Sweet images! which wheresoe'er he be,
> Are at his heart; and such fidelity
> It is his darling passion to approve;
> More brave for this, that he hath much to love.   (ll. 57–64)

Though the warrior's way of life could hardly seem more different
from that of the leech-gatherer, the echo of 'Resolution and Inde-
pendence', with its image of the huge Stone as 'a thing endued with
sense', recalls the earlier embodiment of fortitude and endurance. In
his own note on the 'Happy Warrior', Wordsworth recalled his
brother's admiration for the young sailors he had known profession-
ally over the years, the best of whom 'came from Scotland: the next
to them from the north of England especially from Westmoreland &
Cumberland, where, thanks to the piety & local attachments of our
ancestors, endowed, or as they are commonly called, free, Schools
abound'.[70] The young men who travelled far from their northern
homes possessed the kind of inner resources most admired by Words-
worth, because of the special communities that had nursed them and

remained, internally, as a saving memory. Ideally, modern poetry, too, could act as an anchor, embodying such remembered truths and thus able to startle readers into a sense of their better selves. Through poetry, Wordsworth was attempting to liberate readers who, though perhaps richer materially, seemed caught in a spiritual poverty trap. By presenting as exemplary figures who might normally attract no attention at all, Wordsworth was overturning social and literary convention in an attempt to shake his contemporaries into hope.

In his political sonnets, Wordsworth called on the memory of Milton to rescue England from stagnation, but when he looked back on the period when his country had seemed most in danger of 'inundation', he recognized that he had been helped just as much by Burns. Indeed, when he reread *Paradise Lost*, he was struck by the passage in which Satan, 'on the brow of some high-climbing hill', was stunned by his first sight of Eden, commenting, 'how much of the real excellence of Imagination consists in the capacity of exploring the world really existing & thence selecting objects beautiful or great as the occasion may require'.[71] For Wordsworth, Milton's 'description of so familiar appearance' was far preferable to 'the preceding account of the sea of Jasper and liquid pearl, the palace gate embellished with diamond and with gold, or the golden stairs which were occasionally let down from heaven'.[72] Finding paradise in the real world and re-creating his discoveries in verse that might live were the goals Wordsworth had set for himself in 'Home at Grasmere'. Of all modern poets, it was Burns who seemed most to have prepared the way for Wordsworth's own independence and who continued to offer corroboration for his project.

Burns's poems possessed the 'charm of recognitions', and this was ultimately what Wordsworth also strove to achieve. He had also come to realize, partly through conversations with Coleridge, that observation of the real world was a creative activity and not a question of merely passive reflection. When Coleridge came to reconsider the distinctive qualities of Wordsworth's writing, he recognized that it shared, with Burns's poetry, a rare capacity 'to carry on the feelings of childhood into the powers of manhood; to combine the child's sense of wonder and novelty with appearances, which every day...had rendered familiar'.[73] The ability to see what others took for granted as things brimming with surprise and possible delight was a mark of poetic genius. Burns, like Wordsworth and Shakespeare, was able to awaken in others a 'kindred feeling' and 'freshness of sensation' by representing familiar objects in startling new lights: this was the rare power that just might arouse the getters and spenders of modern Britain from their 'savage torpor' and restore them to a proper sense of themselves and their place in the world.

The degree to which Wordsworth's ideas about local attachment and pastoral were directly indebted to Currie's *Burns* is hard to determine precisely, but he clearly found vital corroboration for his own poetry in the new edition of Burns's *Works*. Just as Heaney would turn to Mandelstam, to Yeats and to Wordsworth himself for corroboration of his own writing, so Wordsworth found reassurance in the congenial work of his contemporaries. The very virtues he had celebrated so thoughtfully in 'Michael' and 'The Brothers' were apparently prevalent among the country people north of the Border, who seemed to offer living evidence of his ideals. It is not surprising that the old man's speech in 'Resolution and Independence' should recall the people of Scotland, given the preoccupations of 1802, nor that Wordsworth should find his imagination increasingly drawn to Scotland and Scottish literature. The bracing independence of the leech-gatherer was a counterpart of the self-sustaining communities of the North where vital, lasting bonds were formed from infancy and renewed through song.

It is evident from Heaney's description of his deeply personal response to the image of Orpheus in the Spartan museum that a better understanding of his own artistic purpose could be stimulated by the discovery of 'local work' elsewhere. In a similar way, Wordsworth's realization of the wider importance of his feelings for the Lake District was helped and corroborated by the work of other writers and other places. The celebration of Grasmere that accompanied his return to the Lakes in 1800 was intensified by the long years of absence, in which he had lived in France and Germany, Cambridge, London, and the West Country, but his continuing gratitude for the nurturing creative influence of the Cumbrian hillsides was fostered by subsequent reading and touring. Scotland, in particular, offered vital inspiration for the kind of poetry Wordsworth was developing in Grasmere. The literary claims he made in the preface to *Lyrical Ballads* and the ambitious project of exploring man's true place in the world, which informed so much of his writing from 1800 onwards, drew strength from Scottish poetry, as well as from the land and the people that it celebrated. The work of so many Scottish writers seemed inseparable from their origins, while the names of Scottish rivers and mountains were widely familiar from their place in songs. As Wordsworth came to recognize his own deep attachment to the Lakes and the essential connections between his physical experience and creative impulses, he delighted in the congenial poetry of Scotland. Wordsworth's profound obligations to Burns were gratefully acknowledged, but his debts to Scottish poetry were also deepened—and enhanced by his friendship with Walter Scott.

4

Scott's Border Vision

Wordsworth's awareness of local attachment and its importance for poetry owed much to James Currie's edition of Burns, but his understanding deepened as he visited the country where Burns had worked until his death and met the living poet who was to become 'the Border Minstrel'. The Scottish Borders were the culmination of the six-week tour taken by William and Dorothy Wordsworth between July and September 1803. A trip that began with elegiac reflections by the grave of Burns ended with the convivial company of Walter Scott, whom they met in Lasswade at his summer home. From setting out as strangers in an unfamiliar country, the Wordsworths later enjoyed being honoured guests in an area soaked in traditional poems and stories. As Dorothy later recalled, Scott's name served as a kind of 'passport' wherever they went: 'Mr Scott is respected everywhere: I believe that by favour of his name one might be hospitably entertained throughout all the borders of Scotland.'[1] From a tiny, remote house in Clovenford to Dr Somerville's Manse at Jedburgh, Scott's friendship meant that doors opened readily to welcome the Englishman and his sister in their clapped-out Irish cart. Scott's work as the Sheriff of Selkirk took him on regular journeys through the Border towns, and, in between his professional duties, he was delighted to introduce the Wordsworths to the special character of the land he loved. Dorothy saw at once that Scott was 'passionately attached to the district of the Borders' and later reflected that his 'local attachments' were stronger 'than those of any person I ever saw'.[2]

Dorothy Wordsworth's praise of Scott was not just an expression of gratitude for his generous hospitality during their trip to Scotland, however, for their way had been prepared by the remarkable book he had compiled the year before. *Minstrelsy of the Scottish Border*, published in the Border town of Kelso in 1802, was an emphatic public statement of Scott's local attachments, which he was already extending to a third volume. Scott's astonishing knowledge of the Borders was evident in every line of the detailed editorial annotations to his collection of popular verses, ballads, and imitations. Though dedicated to the Duke of Buccleugh, the substantial work was clearly a declaration of deep personal attachment to the Scottish Borders. For Wordsworth, returning to the landscape of his childhood and realizing increasingly the value of the human experience intertwined within its familiar contours, Scott's pride in his own local culture was very inspiring. Scott was a direct contemporary and an aspiring poet, but he too chose to centre his world view many miles north of the Houses of Parliament. Like Wordsworth, too, Scott had come to understand fully the importance of his favourite region in adulthood, when his appreciation of the old ballads of the Scottish people was awakened by influences from beyond the Borders.

As a highly educated Edinburgh lawyer, Scott was not a Scottish poet of the kind portrayed by Currie, whose talents were nurtured in the parochial schools and sustained by local songs. He may have learned the popular Scottish ballads in his youth, when staying with his grandparents at their farm in Smailholm, but his own determination to collect and publish the Border ballads was just as much a result of the literary fashions of the 1790s as was Wordsworth's decision to compose *Lyrical Ballads*. Just as Wordsworth's awareness of the imaginative potential cradled in Grasmere was subsequently heightened by his experience of other places and cultures, so Scott's enthusiasm for collecting the popular poetry of the Borders was stimulated by the discovery of foreign literature. For both poets, recognition of their own deep attachments to the places familiar since childhood resulted from the desire for reconnection that came with the expansions of adult experience. For both poets, too, the distance inseparable from the very realization of this need gave their own work qualities that distinguished it from the traditional culture to which it was so powerfully drawn. Scott's *Minstrelsy* demonstrated both inwardness with traditional poetry and an external perception of its importance, but the doubleness of his perspective offered a model that was troubling as well as reassuring. Though Scott's local attachments provided corroboration for Wordsworth's mature project, the ambivalence of his Border vision provoked further questions about the nature of poetry.

Scott, Bürger, and Burns

Scott, like Heaney, became a poet when his roots crossed with his reading, but it was foreign rather than native literature that helped him to understand the value of his early domestic experience. The excitement over German poetry that seized British readers in the 1790s failed to entice him across the North Sea like Coleridge and Wordsworth, but he was just as affected by the craze for Bürger and the German ballad. As for Wordsworth, it was Scott's immersion in German culture that renewed both his interest in his homeland and his admiration for Burns. These dual influences affected him rather differently from Wordsworth, but both contributed just as much to his growth as a poet and to his first significant work, *Minstrelsy of the Scottish Border*.

Scott's first published poem was a ballad, but, far from being a recollection from his childhood experience in the Borders, it was inspired by hearing rave reports of Anna Letitia Barbauld's spirited performance of Bürger's *Lenore*, during her visit to Edinburgh in the autumn of 1795. When Scott obtained a copy of the German ballad that had been causing such a stir in British audiences since its appearance in English, he was prompted to compose his own version. His effort to render the ballad into English was so well received by friends that he decided to publish 'The Chase' and 'William and Helen', as well as contributing imitations of Bürger's poems to Matthew Lewis's *Tales of Wonder*. Although Scott's own translations were rapidly lost in the flood of new Germanic ballads, he was excited by the venture and determined to make his mark in the world of letters: 'I was more bent to show the world that it had neglected something worth notice, than to be affronted by its indifference.'[3] Scott's debut as a poet resulted from a desire to follow the latest literary fashion and to excel others in the field. It was hardly an expression of local attachment or a serious attempt to uphold the traditions of his nation. And yet, as is often the case, personal ambition rapidly led to the discovery of things of wider significance and to the recognition of local work as a legitimate basis for serious art.

Scott's approach to self-improvement was to engage in intensive study of existing ballads and, as his writing skills developed, so did his knowledge of the poetic traditions of Germany, Scotland, and England. He had already begun learning German a decade before Wordsworth, after hearing Henry Mackenzie address the Royal Society of Edinburgh on the extraordinary energy of modern German literature. Scott and his friends were gripped with excitement over a 'race of poets' apparently ambitious 'to spurn the flaming boundaries of the universe' and abandon 'the pedantry of the unities'.[4] Contemporary Germany seemed to offer a thrilling alternative to the classical, religious, and philosophical emphasis of modern Scottish universities. Particularly attractive to the Edinburgh students was the discovery of 'the remarkable coincidence between the German language and that of Lowland Scotland', which meant that learning to read the poetry of Goethe, Schiller, and Bürger was both new and, at the same time, oddly familiar. Where Wordsworth found the differences between German and Scottish poetry becoming more apparent as his understanding deepened, Scott was increasingly struck by the resemblances.

Once Scott had embarked on his translations and imitations of Bürger, he was reminded more and more of the native poetry of Scotland, while the widespread admiration for the German ballads made him see old, accustomed things in a new light. German poetry was a means to bring material long neglected as commonplace and unsophisticated back into the centre of Scottish consciousness. Work on Bürger's ballads allowed Scott to awaken figures buried deep within his memory and to deepen the shades of familiar, but half-forgotten, scenes. The terrifying ballads, with their recurrent motifs of wild rides and demon lovers, gripped German and British audiences in the 1790s and helped Scott recognize the rich imaginative potential of the traditional legends of the Scottish Borders. Why be content with *Lenore* when you could be transported by *Tam Linn*? In the 'Eve of St John', which Scott wrote for Matthew Lewis's *Tales of Wonder*, he set his Gothic ballad of a tryst, a murder, and a spectral lover in Smailholm Tower, the Border fortress that loomed over the imaginative landscape of his childhood.[5] For Scott, creative activity always involved acts of memory as well as imagination, and so his early poems fused materials familiar since childhood with modern influences.

As a boy, he had been entranced by Percy's *Reliques of Ancient English Poetry*, which he later remembered reading for the first time in the garden of his aunt's home by the Tweed. Even at the age of 13, Scott had the quasi-uncanny experience of finding that, as he opened the book, he was confronted with things he had always known: 'to read and to remember was in this instance the same thing.'[6] The thrill of discovering the kinds of poem he had loved since childhood, which lived in his mind as secret 'Dalilahs' of the imagination, stayed with him, but the faint guilt associated with his private enthusiasm was later countered by the intellectual demands of his scholarly research and language studies. Scott's admiration for the *Reliques* was divided between his love of the wild tales and his respect for the 'sober research, grave commentary and apt illustration' provided by the editor, whose academic approach seemed to bestow legitimacy on his materials.[7] At the same time, Percy also possessed a 'poetical genius capable of emulating the best qualities of what his pious labour preserved' and thus provided a model for the ballad collector that combined creativity with analysis, imaginative sympathy with historical knowledge. Percy had revealed to the young Scott that his childhood enthusiasms could become serious adult pursuits and that the composition of poetry could be encouraged by study. When Scott began work on the German ballads in the 1790s, he was reviving memories, not just of the old tales he heard as a small boy, but also of those he had read a few years later in Percy's *Reliques*: ballads were both thrilling Dalilahs and sterner schoolmistresses, from whom an inspiring young poet could learn much.

Translation of the ballad meant attending carefully to vocabulary and structure—Scott could now recall the poems he had known in his youth and see them as the work of skilful craftsmen, schooled in inherited techniques and fully conscious of their different effects on an audience. The repetitions characteristic of oral forms might be contributing more than a mere *aide memoire*, in poems that depicted the beating hooves of a galloping horse, the tramp of an army, or the curse of a betrayed lover. Simple vocabulary could, in the context of a chilling tale, prove far more powerful than elaborate Latinate diction. In the 1790s, when the craze for Gothic stories was at its height, readers were eager for poems that could make their spines tingle in the early hours, and so the pared-down language of a fast-paced ballad, with its narrative gaps and startling transitions, was just what was wanted.

The taste for ballads, established by Percy's *Reliques of Ancient English Poetry* in 1765 and renewed by the spectacular appearance of *Lenore*, had also helped modern urban readers to relish the idea of traditional culture and to recognize its place in the texture of a nation.[8] In Scotland, the willingness to revive older traditions and present them to an international audience was abundantly obvious in the enthusiasm for *The Poems of Ossian*, though Macpherson's endeavour had been bound up with his pride in the Highlands and his notions of poetry formed by a classical education. For Macpherson, ballads had represented the broken remains of a once-great culture, and his own work involved piecing together the fragments to restore the lost epics of Caledonia.[9] Scott, who studied modern German literature and caught the Gothic enthusiasms of the 1790s, was able to recognize the worth of Scottish ballads and to see that his own Lowland region held cultural treasures every bit as valuable as those of the bleak Highlands.

Though Scott's attachment to the Border ballads was rooted in childhood, then, its flowering in 1802 was actually brought about by the intellectual climate of Edinburgh. There contemporary literary trends were debated, developed, and modified and Scottish talent was especially welcome. Even more important to Scott's success than the vogue for ballads, perhaps, was the contemporary admiration for Burns. The students who heard Henry Mackenzie enthusing over contemporary German literature had already been directed to admire 'the heaven-taught ploughman', whose *Poems, Chiefly in the Scottish Dialect* commanded a laudatory essay from Mackenzie in *The Lounger* in 1786. The following year, Scott was introduced personally to Burns, who swept into the capital and was hailed as a natural genius by the Edinburgh literati. The impact of their meeting is apparent in Scott's cherished recollections of Burns's quick sympathy for the dead soldier depicted on the wall of an Edinburgh drawing room, his 'perfect self-confidence' in every company, and, above all, his expression: 'I never saw such an eye in a human head, though I have seen the most distinguished men in my time.'[10] For a young man with literary ambitions, Burns's arrival on the Edinburgh scene was at once startling and inspiring, since he demonstrated the possibility of impressing the most illustrious company simply through his skills with a pen.

The admiration that seized Scott in his late teens continued undiminished, despite the well-publicized difficulties that attended Burns's domestic life. As he reflected on his own career in the autobiography he began in 1808, Scott admitted that he had 'not been blessed with the talents of Burns or Chatterton'.[11] Since, by this stage, Scott was the best-selling poet of his era, the remark gives a measure of his high opinion of Burns. When he launched the *Quarterly Review* a year later, his first contribution was, accordingly, a generous tribute to the 'extravagance of genius' of 'this wonderful man'.[12] For Scott to have heard, in 1796, that his very first attempt at a German ballad was being compared with the work of Burns had, therefore, been encouraging, to say the least. His translation of *Lenore* was written for his friend, Miss Cranstoun, who had greeted his work as 'something of a cross between Burns and Gray'.[13] This was the highest praise she could have offered, since Gray was one of the most admired of modern British poets and Burns, widely recognized as an astounding natural genius.

If many readers of the 1790s saw Burns as a remarkable natural phenomenon, however, Scott's admiration was magnified by his awareness of Burns's accomplishment in imitating traditional poetry. In both the *Quarterly* and in a later 'Essay on Imitations of the Ancient Ballad', he praised Burns for the ability to infuse traditional poetry with an intensity that completely eclipsed the scattered sources he had collected.[14] This unusual skill was especially prized by Scott, for whom Burns was at once a great original and a brilliant restorer. Though he never translated German ballads, Burns's capacity to create remarkable poetry that blended the new and the traditional triggered in his younger contemporary a sense of the creative possibility hidden within the ordinary culture of Scotland. Scott saw that Burns had gathered material from agricultural labourers and alehouses and then turned it into songs that delighted people at every level of society. It was a remarkable achievement in an age when class divisions were as clearly marked by the way people spoke as by their homes, occupations, and incomes.

Burns provided more than an inspiring example, however. Scott's own talent had been evident to others from an early age, but his appeal to the literary circles in late-eighteenth-century Edinburgh was greatly enhanced by their complicated response to Burns. When John Lockhart was tracing the immediate enthusiasm for Scott's first publications, he saw at once that it coincided with the shock of Burns's early death: 'Scotland had lost that very year the great poet

Burns, her glory and her shame.'[15] Scott's kind reception was due at least in part to the 'general sentiment of self-reproach, as well as of sorrow...excited by the premature extinction of such a light'.[16] Scottish readers, suddenly bereft of their most brilliant contemporary, looked especially kindly on the young Walter Scott, while the poet himself began to aspire to the place that had suddenly been left empty. His consciousness of Burns's sudden celebrity is abundantly evident in the account of their only meeting, which also reveals the desire prevalent in late-eighteenth-century Edinburgh for a great Scottish poet. Despite the astonishing contemporary advances in science, medicine, philosophy, economics, and history, Edinburgh was not especially well blessed with creative writers. Burns had appeared, as if from nowhere, to provide modern Scotland with a national poet, but he had then declined and disappeared before having a chance to enjoy full recognition throughout the United Kingdom. As Scotland's 'glory and her shame', Burns paved the way for Scott, whose literary career was in many ways dependent on Burns's extraordinary example and untimely demise. By 1802, Scotland seemed to need a national bard as never before, and, in the essay that prefaced the *Minstrelsy*, Scott referred to Burns explicitly as 'the Poet of Scotland'.

For a writer as attracted to Scottish history as Walter Scott, Burns's ability to use traditional Scottish language, songs, and stories with such skill and feeling made him seem 'wonderful'. The songs of Burns had been published throughout the 1790s by James Johnson in the *Scots Musical Museum* and George Thomson in *Select Scottish Airs*.[17] Scott's own familiarity with the songs is obvious from the *Quarterly Review* essay of 1809, where he singled out for special notice songs from 'The Jolly Beggars' and praised Burns's general accomplishment as a lyricist: 'no poet of our tongue has ever displayed higher skill in marrying melody to immortal verse.'[18] His comments were prompted by Robert Cromek's new *Reliques of Robert Burns*, which included some hitherto unpublished songs as well as Burns's own notes and extracts from his Commonplace book. As Scott discovered Burns's private opinions on such matters as Scottish metres and the 'noble sublimity, and heart-making tenderness' of ancient ballads, he was able to see the full importance of traditional Scottish song culture to Burns's poetic growth as well as his skills as an adapter and restorer.[19] Though generally critical of Cromek's editing and Burns's excessive concentration on songs, the review nevertheless reveals Scott's admiration for the self-taught genius of Scotland. He responded warmly to the strong national feeling evident in Burns's comments and marvelled at his power to transform traditional materials with 'those magic touches, which, without greatly altering the song, restored its original spirit, or gave it more than it had ever possessed'.[20] Even in the late 1790s, when Scott was still labouring to establish himself as an original poet and preserver of ancestral culture, Burns had provided strong corroboration for both purposes. Cromek's detailed evidence of Burns's song-writing practices had not yet become available when Scott was working on the *Minstrelsy*, but it was abundantly evident from the songs themselves that Burns was at once a great poet, a great collector, and a patriot.

Burns's practice offered powerful justification for Scott's decision to publish poems that deviated so strikingly from Standard English. At a time when most Scottish writers laboured carefully over their work to weed out any trace of Scottish idiom or vocabulary, Burns had published a volume entitled *Poems, Chiefly in the Scottish Dialect* and proved that poetry of the highest quality could be composed in language that did not conform to the rules laid down by contemporary grammarians and dictionary-makers. In the *Quarterly Review*, Scott set the richness of Burns's Scots poetry against the impoverished nature of his English with its 'comparative penury of rhymes and the want of a thousand emphatic words which his habitual acquaintance with Scots supplied'.[21] It was the tribute of a practising poet, who knew only too well the advantages of possessing the most extensive vocabulary when attempting to compose rhyming stanzas. Scott was among the first to recognize that Burns's familiarity with Scots as well as English, far from being a limitation, actually furnished him with a special range of poetic possibility.

Burns's poems, though more complicated than those published in the *Minstrelsy*, offered a crucial precedent for allowing the old ballads into print in their unpolished but emphatically native language. Although Scott appeared to demonstrate his own distance from the unimproved language of his countrymen by writing his introduction in English and referring to Scots words as 'barbarisms', the evocation of Burns as a justification for retaining the traditional language of the ballads greatly enhanced their value for readers: 'Such barbarisms, which stamp upon their tales their age and nation, should be respected by an editor, as the hardy emblem of his country was venerated by the Poet of Scotland.'[22] In case anyone was unfamiliar with his reference, he included a version of the lines in which Burns had equated the Scots tongue with the national thistle:

The rough bur-thistle spreading wide
Among the bearded bear,
I turned the weeder-clips aside,
And spared the symbol dear.

The verse was from 'To the Guidwife of Wauchope House', which Burns had sent to Mrs Elizabeth Scott of Jedburgh, in response to her praise of the Kilmarnock edition. Burns replied to her verse epistle with a 'thank-you' poem, explaining his long-standing wish to make poems 'for poor auld Scotland's sake'—and hence his choice of diction.[23] Scots, like the thistle, might be deemed an intrusive weed in some places, but it was the natural growth of the tough northern landscape and remarkably hardy and tenacious. For Scott to translate traditional ballads into any language other than that of their original performers would be to make them unrecognizably weak and moribund.

The verse epistle to Mrs Scott was published for the first time in Currie's *Burns*, which suggests that Scott read the new edition with interest just as he was assembling the *Minstrelsy* (though he may also have seen a copy of the poem in Jedburgh). Indeed, Currie prepared the way for Scott's collection practically as well as culturally, for in his preface Scott referred any English readers of the *Minstrelsy* who might be baffled by 'the more common peculiarities of the Scottish dialect' to consult 'the excellent glossary' provided by Currie. Burns not only gave Scott the courage to publish the local poetry of the Borders, but also alerted him to the potential obstacles that his ballads might pose to English readers. By the time Scott published the *Minstrelsy* in 1802, Burns's poems were receiving renewed critical attention and so he was acutely aware of the difficulties attending the publication of materials in non-Standard English. The *Minstrelsy*'s elaborate essay and notes on the history and manners of Border society were designed to please an audience already conditioned, not only by contradictory admiration to Burns's life and works, but also by the widespread reservations about his language.[24]

At a time when so many contemporary writers were turning to German poetry or imitating English magazine verse, Currie's edition of Burns helped Scott as well as Wordsworth and Coleridge to recognize the value of native traditions. The emphatically Scottish character of Burns's work, which was brought to the fore by Currie's historical and social approach to the life and work, was nevertheless especially inspirational to Scott. The debates surrounding the new Union between Britain and Ireland, which came into effect in January 1801, had heightened consciousness of the distinct national traditions within the United Kingdom, but it was clear from every page of Burns's work that he had long been aware of the special strengths of Scottish poetry. Scott's desire to present the *Minstrelsy* as an offering to his native country echoes Burns's own expressions of patriotic feeling in the verse epistle to Mrs Scott, as well as many of the poems in the Kilmarnock edition. In the 'Epistle to John Lapraik', for example, Burns had paid tribute to Allan Ramsay and Robert Fergusson, the 'two justly admired Scotch Poets' mentioned in the preface to *Poems, Chiefly in the Scottish Dialect*, whose stirring examples had helped to kindle his own literary ambitions.[25] In 'The Vision', he had invoked the memory of William Wallace, while dedicating his own work as a poet to the Scottish Muse, Coila.

Scott had been familiar with Burns's expressions of allegiance to Scottish tradition since the first publication of his *Poems*, in 1786, but Currie's edition explicitly directed readers towards the social context, seeing in Burns's achievement, not just the signs of individual genius, but also broader national characteristics. Scott must have been as strongly affected as Wordsworth by Currie's analysis of the powerful local attachments that characterized the common people of Scotland, but his own interest in the native ballad took on a new dimension when seen in the light of Currie's views on the importance of traditional songs for nurturing Scottish patriotism. Since Scott had already begun collecting traditional Scottish ballads and composed several of his own by the time Currie's essay appeared, he would undoubtedly have been pleased by its evident admiration for popular culture. One of the footnotes even included an analysis of the old ballad of 'Edom o'Gordon', which praised its dramatic dialogue and compared it to the scriptures and Homer.[26] The arresting technique gave the old ballad an immediacy that guaranteed its emotive power—an insight that supported Currie's aesthetic preference for poets who belonged to 'a ruder condition of society' and painted 'individual objects' rather than making learned generalizations. Currie's approach, which would have seemed natural enough to Scott, recalled numerous Scottish Enlightenment essays on the progress of society, which routinely associated the most imaginative work with the 'ruder' stages. He was more or less quoting Hugh Blair's lecture on the Rise of Poetry, when he observed that 'Abstraction, so useful in morals, and so essential in science, must be abandoned when the heart is to be subdued by the powers of poetry or of eloquence'.[27] The French antiquarian Paul Mallet, whose *Northern Antiquities* had been translated into English by Thomas Percy, had attacked the use of 'abstract terms and reflex ideas' that turned modern poetry into 'nothing more than reasoning in rhyme, addressed to the understanding, very little to the heart', celebrating instead the imaginative freedom of the earliest poets of Northern Europe.[28] Where philosophers such as Adam Smith had tended to see an inevitable displacement of poetry by more rational discourses as society advanced, Currie, like Blair, Mallet, and other primitivist critics, was prepared to suggest that the power of poetry over the heart might actually be desirable. If the corollary of Enlightenment theories of social progress was the loss of truly imaginative, passionate poetry, then Burns's project of restoring old songs was a major contribution to national culture—a revival of the passionate character of the ancient literature of the North.

As already discussed in Chapter 3, Currie saw Burns's songs as his greatest contribution to the nation: 'there is no species of poetry... so much calculated to influence the morals, as well as the happiness of a people, as those popular verses which are associated with national airs, and which being learnt in the years of infancy, make a deep impression on the heart, before the evolution of the powers of understanding.'[29] Currie's emphasis on the effect of national songs on children would probably have struck Scott rather differently from Wordsworth, however, being a fellow-Scot and less given to exalting the child as father of the man. The observation that Burns's songs were capable of binding 'generous hearts to their native soil, and to the domestic circle of their infancy' was somewhat double-edged when read through an Enlightenment perspective on the progress of society, since it could imply a kind of arrested development among the 'Scottish peasantry' not entirely dispelled by their

unique education in the parochial schools.³⁰ Currie's critical
account of the formative years, nevertheless, made remarkable
claims for the larger importance of poetry in Scottish society and
may well have reinforced Scott's interest in the ways in which
poetry was integral to the lives and history of those in the
Borders.

Currie's emphasis on the location of Burns's songs could hardly
have escaped Scott when he read the essay during his own period of
intensive work on the *Minstrelsy*, since the place names in Scottish
lyrics were crucial to his argument about the long-term psycholo-
gical effects of song culture: 'the sentiments are given to particular
characters, and very generally, the incidents are referred to particular
scenery.'³¹ Tender situations took place not in any grove or purling
brook, but rather on the banks of the Nith or by the bush of Traquair.
These were popular songs, set in places well known to Scott. If
Burns's skills as a lyricist were so indebted to anonymous masters of
the past, then there must be some value in studying the popular oral
traditions of Scotland as well as the society that had given rise to
the poetry.

For Scott, Burns's later activities as a collector would have been
just as interesting as Currie's speculations on the effects of his child-
hood exposure to traditional songs. The extracts from Burns's journal
of his Border tour in 1787 would have been especially intriguing,
partly because it revealed a carefully planned expedition to discover
new areas of Scotland and collect the local songs, but mostly because
it contained the first impressions of an area Scott knew so well:
'Breakfast at Kelso—charming situation of the town—fine bridge
over the Tweed. Enchanting views and prospects on both sides of the
river, especially on the Scotch side.' ³² The journal recorded that,
only months after Scott's own, memorable meeting with Burns in
Edinburgh, Burns had travelled from Kelso to Jedburgh, from
Melrose to Selkirk, being entertained by many of Scott's own friends
and acquaintances. Currie might have been disappointed by the
dearth of fashionable picturesque description in the Border tour, but
Scott would have understood that Burns had responded primarily to
the people he met and to the human dimensions of the places he
visited. Occasionally, he pronounced the Tweed 'clear and majestic',
or Jedburgh 'charming and romantic', but he was generally much
more inclined to make observations on the residents, the agriculture,

and the local history ('a Holly-bush where James the second was accidentally killed by the bursting of a cannon'; 'Mr Sommerville, the clergyman of the parish, a man, and a gentleman, but sadly addicted to punning'[33]). For Burns, like Scott, the places he visited were inseparable from the people who lived there.

Currie's method of approaching Burns's songs through their Scottish settings, which worked rather better in relation to the Highland tour, nevertheless provided an instructive model for Scott, as he compiled materials for the *Minstrelsy*. That the simple poetry of ordinary Scottish people should merit extensive notes and a scholarly essay seemed reasonable enough after Currie's emphasis on the importance of particular environments to the overall moral health of the nation. Suddenly, it seemed to matter very much where poetry came from—and how it signalled its origins to readers. By attempting to provide an intellectual framework for understanding Burns, Currie had, inadvertently, helped lay the groundwork for a new readiness to welcome poetry that could prompt an immediate recognition of local truth. For Scott, however, local attachments were every bit as important as local truths.

Scott's Border Vision

When Scott prepared his own collection of ballads for the press in 1802, less than two years after the appearance of Currie's edition, he had an important precedent for emphasizing the connections between the poems in his anthology and the places where they originated. Like *Poems, Chiefly in the Scottish Dialect*, Scott's *Minstrelsy* was published in a small Scottish town, whose very name, Kelso, seemed to contribute to the volume's credibility. The specific regional associations of the publication were already obvious in its lengthy title: *Minstrelsy of the Scottish Border, Consisting of Historical and Romantic Ballads Collected in the Southern Counties of Scotland; with a few of Modern Date, Founded upon Local Tradition*. There seemed little doubt about where these poems originated, even though the question of who had written them remained invisible.[34] In the *Minstrelsy*, the place and the poems seemed far more important than the individual poet, for, instead of the conventional author's portrait, the frontispiece depicted the magnificent ruins of the Hermitage, a Border stronghold encircled by a river and the surrounding ridge of mountains. The old ballads were just as much a part of the rugged terrain of southern Scotland as its fractured castles and similarly marked by centuries of bloody feuds and power struggles. To present such rough material to readers whose taste had been polished by aestheticians and accustomed to the standardized language and sentimentality of magazine verse was a bold assertion of local loyalty.

Scott was a shrewd judge of his audience and so, while the *Minstrelsy* was very evidently local work, it was also carefully packaged to widen its appeal to those further afield. The frontispiece conforms to contemporary tastes for picturesque scenery, with a tree and solitary figure in the foreground, a ruin ringed by a river in the middle distance, and, in the background, the faint outlines of distant mountains. The silhouetted figure seems at once a participant in the landscape—a shepherd or a fisherman, perhaps—while also being a spectator, a reader within, gazing on the ruined castle. Like the ballad-collector, he is part of the local area and yet capable of looking on from a distance, of understanding what he sees and feeling the residue of the conflicts registered in the castle walls. A Borderer in the regional sense, he also suggests a kind of 'border-vision' later identified by Raymond Williams as the special quality of writers who retain old ties while still achieving a more detached view of their homes.[35] He is, in other words, the perfect mediator between the community and the wider world, because he is able to share both perspectives and thus alleviate potential misunderstandings.

When he defined 'border vision', Williams had in mind the barriers of class and education, but his own work also demonstrated that the conflicting compulsions to depart and return are often especially strong in those from Border regions. His own background in the Black Mountains imbued him with a distinct sense of local difference, which made 'both English and Welsh...foreigners'.[36] At the same time, he knew that the country to which he looked back fondly in adulthood was itself riven, 'a frontier zone which had been the location of fighting for centuries'.[37] His Border childhood had set him apart from the surrounding areas, but the development of his mature border vision placed his own remembered neighbourhood at a distance. The ability to combine inside and outside perspectives is characteristic of the poets who made local work the basis of their wider reputations. Williams's special insight into the additional complexity of Border vision for writers whose homes are in themselves Border areas is nevertheless of considerable importance for this book. For, in such regions, a stable viewpoint is neither easy to achieve, nor necessarily appropriate. In the frontispiece to Scott's *Minstrelsy*, the dark figure in the foreground is paralleled by the shadow in the shattered wall of the fortress. Though the engraving was depicting a view familiar to local residents and appealing to Romantic tourists, it was also introducing the collection of poems with an image of destruction. The Hermitage is a symbol of ancient power, but its history of shifting ownership, allegiances, and fortune is written into its very fabric. While easy to enjoy as a nostalgic image of a lost, chivalric past, the engraving depicts a region torn by warfare and political uncertainty.[38] Local attachments in such a region were passionately held but by no means conducive to peace and stability.

The castle provided a visual counterpart of the ballads in the collection—old, rooted, and recalcitrant. Shaped by centuries of communal action and reaction, Border poetry remained oddly elusive and, despite the contemporary taste for ballads, resistant to any easy absorption into the modern world. In his introductory 'Essay on the Borders', Scott acted as a kind of guide into dangerous terrain, offering the ballads as a way into unfamiliar parts and pasts. He described the Border region between Scotland and England as a 'stage, upon which were presented the most memorable conflicts of two gallant nations', and, although he was referring to the era preceding the successive Unions of the Crowns in 1603 and the Parliaments in 1707, his account had strong contemporary resonance for readers of 1802, in the wake of the United Irishmen's Rising and the Act of Union with Ireland. His theatrical metaphor may have softened the reality of Border warfare, but it could not conceal the fact that the ballads were the cultural legacy of a blood-soaked region.

Scott's own sense of local obligation is evident in his formal dedication to the Duke of Buccleugh, in whose family halls the ballads had been sung for centuries, but he also presented his work as a personal tribute to his 'native country':

By such efforts, feeble as they are, I may contribute somewhat to the history of my native country; the peculiar features of whose manners and character are daily melting and dissolving into those of her sister and ally. And, trivial as may appear such an offering, to the manes of a kingdom, once proud and independent, I hang it upon her altar with a mixture of feelings, which I shall not attempt to describe.[39]

Here was a volume that demonstrated not only love for the local area, but also a powerful sense of duty. It was a 'votive offering' just as much as the Greek image of Orpheus and the bird or St Kevin's vigil. Scott's allegiance to his native country is nevertheless couched in terms that emphasize his classical education and knowledge of other cultures, as he makes his offering to the 'manes'. Though a Borderer by descent and romantic inclination, he had been raised and educated largely in Edinburgh, the centre of Scottish Enlightenment progress and self-styled 'Athens of the North'.[40] Not only was his volume aimed at those whose cultural standards were similarly formed, but his own awareness of the benefits of modernity made him chary of the very culture that exercised such a powerful enchantment over him. Ballads were the traditional media for local expression, but, as Scott unleashed the old, unruly voices into the polite world of print, he was also making way for a complicated, personal response to his ancestral region. His collection was an act of homage, but it came with its own health warning, and the very emphasis on the steady dissolution of peculiar Border features was as much an act of containment as an attempted revival.

In the *Minstrelsy*, Scott demonstrated that the true character of a region could be found in its popular literature and local stories. Just as Currie presented native songs as part of the very fabric of Scottish life—the creation of a particular people, language, and landscape—so Scott saw the ballads he had collected as inseparable from the communities in which they had been recited for so many years. The difference was that, where Currie had painted a portrait of a peaceful, religious, hard-working rural community, Scott knew that the Borderers had been tough, warlike people, frequently engaged in feuds with local families or cattle raids on nearby farms. The *Minstrelsy* included extensive notes on the historical events, people, and places named in the verse, so 'The Battle of Otterbourne', for example, was framed with facts about the Gordons and the Graemes, their exploits in the East March, their tower in Annandale or Walls in Tweeddale. The result was that the battle commemorated in the ballad acquired the authenticity of historical and geographical fact, rather than seeming like something from legend or romance. Though he had loved the Borders since his childhood, his understanding of the region's peculiar qualities was influenced by the philosophical ideas prevalent in eighteenth-century Edinburgh, just as Currie's approach to Burns had been. His essay displays detailed knowledge of the historical figures and local features that had left their traces in the Border ballads, but the local details are combined with more detached analysis of the kinds of cultural forms produced by societies at different stages of civilization. The narrative of battles, raids, and sieges carried out by the Douglases, Percys, Armstrongs, and Murrays are set side by side with more general statements about the 'more rude and wild...state of society'.[41]

Scott was clearly conscious of the potential difficulty of presenting local culture to a wider audience and so he adopted the tone of the antiquarian or philosopher of history, who perceives the relics of older culture as evidence for an earlier stage of human society. The antiquarian tone helped to place at a distance the lawlessness of those featuring in the ballads, whose approach to life was so alien to Scott's own role in the modern society of the Borders. His dedication to the Duke of Buccleugh would also divert any dangerous suspicion about his political sympathies, for, though ballads might be admired by contemporary radicals as the popular entertainment of ordinary people, Scott was keen to show that they had once delighted the Clan Chiefs and the nobility of Scotland just as much.[42]

At a time when fears of a revolution within were compounded by the external threat of a French invasion, any reminder of the long period in which the United Kingdom had been convulsed by Border warfare might be generally unwelcome. To celebrate an era of native courage and local attachment was suitably patriotic, but to recall a culture distinguished by its disregard for state authority and operating according to regional loyalties was potentially provocative. The year 1803 saw both the publication of the third volume of the *Minstrelsy* and Robert Emmet's attempt to overturn the new Union between Britain and Ireland. Emmet failed, but his uprising, together with the outbreak of renewed war with France, demonstrated that the newly united kingdom was neither internally stable nor secure from foreign threats. Whether Scott's portrait of old Border society offered a chilling reminder of how recently Britain had been a wild, ungovernable land of feuding warlords, or whether it provided a model of the kind of spirit that Wordsworth found so lacking in modern England, was open to question. The editor's own political agenda was carefully concealed beneath the voice of the historian. Scott's objective tone lent authority to his prefatory essay and pre-empted charges of uncritical partiality to his homeland or dangerous sympathy for subversive groups. Inevitably, it also had the effect of emphasizing his own detachment from the society he described. If the volume was, as he claimed, a tribute to his native country, then Scott was also presenting himself as an external observer—a modern outsider rather than a genuine participant in the land of his fathers. Wordsworth often achieved a powerful doubleness of insider/outsider perspectives in his Lakeland poems by creating encounters between one who belonged to the place and a visiting stranger, but the dialogue between the speakers in poems such as 'Hart-Leap Well' suggests an attempt to find common ground. Scott's Border vision is obvious throughout the *Minstrelsy*, as the ballads, with their distinctive Scottish language and place names, are surrounded by learned expositions in elegant English prose. The controlled tone of the notes often seems at odds with the freedom of the ballad, however, while the sentiments in the poems resist conciliation. Both the prose and the poetry give hints of a writer grappling with contradictory impulses or, as Scott himself admitted, with 'a mixture of feelings' that he 'would not attempt to describe'.[43]

For, despite his careful mediations between the material in the collection and the wider audience, Scott's essay has moments when the polished surface suddenly opens to reveal attitudes a little less smoothly accommodated by the modern civilized state. His appar-ently offhand remark about poetry constituting 'the amusement of a very small part of a polished nation' is, after all, a succinct statement of the very problem Wordsworth had decried so vigorously in the preface to *Lyrical Ballads*, while his obvious admiration for the Border ballads and their vital role in traditional communities suggests criti-cism of any society in which poetry has ceased to be central.[44] Both Scott's essay and his collection of poems reveal a deep nostalgia for the more vigorous society that had spawned such stirring ballads and a strong sense of regret over the 'mediocrity' and 'slow, steady, progressive, unvaried occupation' that seemed to be the norm in a well-regulated modern life.[45] Despite the lawlessness of the Border raiders, Scott admired the simple diet, plain clothing, and lack of materialism among the Borderers, whose 'only treasures' were 'a fleet and active horse' and ornaments won for the 'females of their family'. Though his notion of traditional rural society was very much more chivalric and violent than Wordsworth's and his reference to the Borderers' 'paltry huts' lacked the reverence afforded to Michael's simple cottage, Scott's admiration for a people whose values provided such a contrast to the ostentatious consumerism of the modern British nation had much in common with Wordsworth's advocacy of 'plain living'.[46] Like Wordsworth, too, Scott was proud of his personal connection with a society that still seemed oddly distinct from the rest of Britain. His account of Border history conjures up a mini-state at odds with both the neighbouring kingdoms, and not unlike Wordsworth's later depiction of Cumbria as a 'Republic of Shepherds'. Though Scott made his allegiance to the established hierarchies of the United Kingdom clear in his dedication and in the urbane tone of his English prose, his imaginative attraction to a society where very different rules and values prevailed was only too apparent.

In the traditional communities of Scotland, the importance of the past, place, and poetry seemed beyond question. Those areas least affected by modern development still seemed to offer a living link to a very different existence, in which feelings had been 'frequently stirred to the highest pitch, by the vicissitudes of a life of danger and military adventure'.[47] The stories and songs commemorating local heroes had been passed down orally through generations, proving that poetry had an essential part to play in the continuation of a healthy community. In the southern Highlands, where 'the same families have occupied the same possessions for centuries', the warlike ballads about people who had lived there centuries ago still survived, furnishing Scott with the resources for his collection.[48] Despite its showy dedication, Scott acknowledged his real debts in the intro-ductory essay, to the shepherds and old people 'in the recesses of the Border mountains' who could still remember and recite the old songs and narrative poems.[49] It was as if the land not only shaped the char-acter of the Border songs in the first place, but then kept them alive in the hidden recesses of the hills. Generations of shepherds and drovers had spent dark evenings in Liddesdale, listening to 'Dick o' the Cow' or 'Kinmont Willie' and imagining the exploits of their predecessors through the familiar routes and refrains.

Scott was fascinated by the workings of the oral tradition and the way in which the identity of the original author became lost in the progress of the song: 'Whether they were originally the composition of minstrels, professing the joint arts of poetry and music; or whether they were the occasional effusions of some self-taught bard, is a question into which I do not here mean to inquire.'[50] What mattered more than authorship in the Scottish Borders was the means through which the songs survived. Just as important to society as the warrior chiefs who led their people were the poets who perpetuated their deeds in verse and ensured that they would never be forgotten. According to Scott's essay, each Border town had, until very recently, maintained its own piper, who was responsible for maintaining the local oral and poetic tradition and for taking songs to people in outlying areas. Like Wordsworth's 'Old Cumberland Beggar', they travelled from place to place, linking isolated communities and reminding them of their common connections. Like the ideal poet in the preface to *Lyrical Ballads*, the Scottish pipers helped to bind together 'by passion and knowledge' the scattered outposts of human society, 'in spite of things gone silently out of mind and things violently destroyed'.[51] They were an essential part of the community, maintaining its life through reaffirming its traditions, but their attachment was not that of the smallholder, tied by generations to his patrimonial acres.

Scott never described the local Border musicians in the elevated way that Wordsworth adopted for his argument, but his more down-to-earth, apparently factual account of poetry's role in an area he knew so well carried its own conviction. In his emphasis on the song rather than the singer, Scott was also inadvertently offering corroboration for the admonishments of 'Resolution and Independence' and reinforcing a different approach to the question of poetry's true purpose. That the kind of memories preserved in the Scottish ballads might prompt less conciliatory feelings than Wordsworth's warm faith in the universal 'human heart' was, however, beyond question. Rather than representing a conscious act of selfless generosity by the poets who composed them in the first place, the anonymity of the old poems might have something to do with the dangerous society in which they survived, where any expression of local affiliation might provoke hostility if overheard by someone from the other side. The poet, in a divided society of this kind, might be a potentially treacherous figure—given to stealing from other families or betraying the secrets of his own.

At times, Scott presented himself humorously as a kind of Border raider, pillaging the secret stores of his neighbours and making them his own.[52] This, of course, made him a true son of his native country—following the activities of his warlike predecessors in his own way—but it was not without a troubling dimension. The problem of emulating the example of earlier residents often confronts those who turn their homes into poetry, but it seems especially fraught for those whose native country has experienced bloodshed and local division. When Heaney observed in 'Digging' that he had no spade to follow men like his father and grandfather, he was articulating a sense of physical inferiority to practical men similar to that experienced by the young Walter Scott; and his answer was the same—to dig with his pen. Just as Scott's pen was employed in the cause of Border raids, however, so Heaney's would sit, 'snug as a gun'. Poems such as 'Digging' raise the question that is implicit throughout Scott's *Minstrelsy*, as to whether the modern writer's activity represents a peaceful advance on the more difficult life of his ancestors, or whether the work of writing can be just as tough, dangerous, aggressive even? The possibility that has troubled twentieth-century Irish writers from Yeats onwards—that writing might provoke certain kinds of action and unforeseen consequences—is implicit in the old ballads of the *Minstrelsy*. It was perhaps Scott's deep and intuitive understanding of Border culture that made him emphasize so clearly his affiliation to modern society and impose such a strong framework of notes and classifications on his potentially unruly material.

Border Writing

Scott's image of himself as a raider was, of course, a light-hearted reflection on his collecting activities. His son-in-law John Lockhart recalled that Scott was the first to drive a wheeled carriage through Liddesdale in the summer of 1798, on his seventh trip into the inaccessible stretch of country between Jedburgh and Moffat, gathering 'songs and tunes, and occasionally more tangible relics of antiquity'.[53] The trip was adventurous by modern standards, because the district was still so wild and remote, but, in comparison with the kinds of activity captured in the songs he was collecting, Scott's claims as a pioneer were somewhat tame. He was well treated on his collecting trips by people who had few visitors and was guided by Robert Shortreed, who knew the area very well. As Border raids went, it was remarkably amicable. Scott's adventure nevertheless brought him into direct contact with remote sites such as the Hermitage and with direct descendants of the moss-troopers who had followed the Earls of Douglas into battle and still preserved the ancient riding ballads. In the hidden 'recesses' of his native country were powerful traditions that operated mysteriously, enabling poems to survive without the public endorsement of print.

When Scott published the ballads he had collected in the *Minstrelsy*, he presented his work as a tribute to his native country, emphasizing his role as a preserver and commemorator of a country whose distinctive features were every day dissolving into those of her neighbour. Scott saw himself as the rescuer of Border culture—but he was also its elegist. As is often true of elegies, his work involved impressing on survivors that the object of the lament was really gone and that the living generation must move on to fresh woods: the manner and character of the old country were disappearing, the last piper of Jedburgh had been dead several years. For readers of his collection, however, a rather different perspective emerged very rapidly, since the ballads themselves speak from the pages of the *Minstrelsy* with startling clarity and freshness. There is little sense of cultural dissolution in the poems, whose heroes approach death with remarkable equanimity. Johnny Armstrong's 'Farewell to Gilnock' has the air of a man who knows that his unjust death will guarantee his permanent place in the minds of his successors—there is no sense at all of slow absorption into a larger entity.

Often the ballads seemed to create their own longevity, as in the closing lines of 'The Battle of Bothwell Bridge':

> Alang the brae, beyond the brig,
> Mony brave man lies cauld and still;
> But lang we'll mind, and sair we'll rue,
> The bloody battle of Bothwell-hill.[54]

The survivors of the battle are left to 'mind'—in three senses of the word—to take heed, to object to, and to remember. In other words, the ballad ends, not with a wistful note of regret, but with the tougher tones of obligation and perpetuation. Its simple language and strong rhythms ensure that listeners will keep the poem in mind, that it will be repeated and repeated. Many of these poems were neither consoling nor conciliatory—they were pledges to remember the wrongs of the past. Unlike Macpherson's Ossian, who seemed to foretell the utter disappearance of Celtic culture in his melancholy laments for the race of heroes, the often nameless speakers in Scott's Border ballads have a powerful sense of their ability to withstand the ravages of time. The long history of oral transmission demonstrated the longevity of the ballads and their special capacity to lodge in the minds of new generations. Where Macpherson picked up traditional stories and snatches of Gaelic verse and translated them into a safe image of the ancient Highlands in English prose-poetry, Scott was giving the Border ballads a new existence on the printed page. Although he altered the materials he had collected from local people, he retained the spoken language of Lowland Scotland and the traditional form of the ballads. As he insisted that the poems were part of a culture that had now been superseded, Scott seemed to be consigning them to the past, while simultaneously opening their secret doors to unknown and distant readers. The *Minstrelsy* was fraught with internal tensions, as the editor emphasized the age and remoteness of his materials and yet admitted that he had acquired them from the ordinary people of southern Scotland. The poetry was being presented, on the one hand, as old and commonplace, on the other, as unfamiliar and remarkable. The puzzling contradictions were part of Scott's Border vision: the internal divisions of a modern, educated editor, who was also a poet, deeply attached to the culture under discussion.

Although Scott presented himself in the *Minstrelsy* as a collector, it has long been known that his understanding of the editorial role was rather more creative than was generally apparent at the time. Some of the ballads were assembled by Scott, some emended, some expanded, some adapted, and some effectively his own creations. As an accurate transcription of local culture, the *Minstrelsy*, therefore, left something to be desired. As an expression of the complexity of local attachment, however, it was a very revealing collection. When Wordsworth had returned to the Lakes in 1800, the poems he wrote celebrated the strong domestic attachments of men such as 'Michael', who provided an inspiring example to the poet and, potentially, the nation. Currie, too, admired the local attachments of the common people of Scotland to the valleys and hillsides where they lived, following the ways of their families and strengthened by the traditional songs. Scott was just as passionately attached to the area where he had lived as a child and where his family had its roots, but the expression of his powerful local feeling was more contradictory or 'mixed'.

Since there were elements of traditional Border culture that had no place in the law-abiding world that he worked hard each day to maintain, Scott could not adopt the whole-hearted approval of the earlier generations of local inhabitants that Wordsworth advocated. The very aspects of Border history that seemed to fire his imagination most readily were those that, as a man of the law, he could least condone. The uneasiness of Scott's insider/outsider perspective resulted, perhaps, from his deep knowledge of the physical conflict that had always scarred his home country. Raymond Williams's identification of 'Border vision' was, after all, intensified by his own sense of coming from a Border region or 'frontier zone'.[55] The peculiar attachment to a Border region seems to involve inherent fissures and an instinctive sense of internal detachment.

Seamus Heaney has admitted to feeling similarly 'displaced' by his family circumstances, as part of a Catholic community in Ulster, for whom 'being in-between was a kind of condition from the start'.[56] Despite Heaney's warm memories of Mossbawn, he has always recognized that 'the country of community' was also 'the realm of division'.[57] Disputed areas, or 'frontier zones', like Derry were marked by centuries of antagonism and affiliation as much as by the natural contours or vegetation. Heaney knew from an early age that every field was a record of passionate local attachment— 'Broagh, The Long Rigs, Bell's Hill; Brian's Field, the Round Meadow, the Demesne; each name was a kind of love made to each acre'.[58] He was equally well aware that such strong bonds could give rise to violent dispute and intimidation. Heaney's background has made him acutely conscious that local attachment, however stirring or sustaining, can prove deeply problematic to the creative writer. His faith in the power of local work has never been an unthinking preference for the familiar and has been tested over many years by a clear-sighted recognition of the more disturbing aspects of attachments to home and family. Though so differently placed from Scott's situation in the late-eighteenth-century Scottish Borders, Heaney shows an acute understanding of the way in which old disputes can continue to determine modern action. His complicated explorations of local attachment, therefore, help to illuminate certain aspects of the *Minstrelsy*, which are rather different from Wordsworth's much less equivocal celebrations of Home.

Scott's fascination with local history made him especially alert to the way in which the Borderers had always formed such deep attachments to their native land, but it also revealed the destructive potential of such fierce loyalties. For a writer passionately attached to the 'Debateable Lands', the lines of connection were inevitably enmeshed with confrontation, while the situation of the poet was stained with blood. The traditional responsibilities of Border poets included memorializing the heroic deeds of the people, who in turn preserved the poetry through repeated recitals. Old stories and wounds remained fresh in the ballads, long after the poet who sang about them was forgotten, so the poems seemed to belong, not to any individual, but to those who still lived where extraordinary things had happened. The anonymity of the ballads made their places of origin all the more important to Scott, as he tried to impose a kind of order acceptable to the reading public of his day, annotating his material with facts and locations.

At the same time, the lack of attribution and the variations in the oral versions gave him the freedom to blend his own imagination with that of the older poets. A ballad such as 'Thomas the Rhymer' was a traditional tale, firmly associated with Ercildoune in Roxburghshire, but its uncertain authorship and incompletion meant that Scott could assume the mantle of the old Border minstrel and let his own words fuse with ancient tradition. Thomas's sojourn in Faery land provided a framework for Scott's own creative flight, and the old ballad can be read as a metaphor for the poet's thrilling transportation into a parallel world in which different laws operated. At the same time, the traditional depiction of Thomas being carried away by forces stronger than himself, through the blood that 'Rins through the springs o' that countrie', reflects that darker side of the Border poet's experience.[59] As Scott merged his creative identity with that of his local predecessors, he found that the ballads expressed both the perennial attraction and repulsion of the Border poet towards his native culture.

SCOTT'S BORDER VISION

Scott's recourse to the legends of his native land has parallels with Heaney's attraction to Irish myth. When Heaney translated *Buile Suibhne*, the medieval tale of Sweeney who took flight from the Battle of Moira in the form of a bird, he drew attention to his personal connection to the tale. Sweeney's kingdom was in County Antrim and County Down, neighbouring on Heaney's original 'nesting ground', and so, in responding to the legend, he was performing a role similar to that of the traditional Border poet, and retelling the local narrative for a new generation. Heaney also presented Sweeney as a Borderer, a figure of the 'in-between', caught between traditional pagan society, on one side, and the new Christian Ireland, on the other. It is Heaney's view of Sweeney as an image of the poet, however, that is most telling, and his interpretation of Sweeney's flight from the battle as the struggle of the 'free creative imagination' to escape 'religious, political and domestic obligation'.[60] Even as Heaney was attracted by the local myth and eager to reshape the old tale for a new audience, he recognized the impulse to escape the obligations of home. Sweeney is just as much a figure for the Border writer as Thomas the Rhymer, and like Scott's legendary predecessor, he embodies the conflict inherent in certain kinds of local work.

Sweeney is a memorable image of the Border poet, caught between cultures, ages, and responsibilities and firmly located in a place that is a home and a battlefield. His flight from the fray is exhilarating and terrifying—in the painful moment of transformation he is at once free and doomed to a guilty existence. As Sweeney broods over his experience, the dilemma of the Border poet is played out—is it better to stay with your people and fight, or to take flight and view things from a distance? Sweeney is compelled to fly, but then moves, maddened, from place to place, isolated from and pursued by those closest to him. He escapes physical combat, but is never really free, as he obsessively revisits the places and people of the past. Heaney's identification with Sweeney is more obvious in his own poetry—for example, at the end of *North*, where he portrays himself:

> I am neither internee nor informer;
> An inner émigré, grown long-haired
> And thoughtful; a wood kerne

> Escaped from the massacre,
> Taking protective colouring
> From bole and bark.[61]

The wild man, forced into taking refuge from the massacre, is an image of the poet caught in the Troubles and torn by conflicting loyalties to his art and his community:

> How did I end up like this?
> I often think of my friends'
> Beautiful prismatic counselling
> And the anvil brains of some who hate me
>
> As I sit weighing and weighing
> My responsible *tristia*
> For what? For the ear? For the people?[62]

The urge to escape from a massacre may be an experience more common among medieval warriors, but it provides a powerful metaphor for the modern writer whose work is confined by the hostile conditions of his home. In *North*, with its disturbing depictions of ancient sacrificial victims, the guilt of the modern poet is palpable. For Heaney, writing about the Troubles risked turning the poet into an 'artful voyeur', but choosing not to address the current turmoil risked seeming evasive or even treacherous.[63] By the time he composed *Station Island*, however, Heaney's guilty confusion had given way to greater clarity and confidence. When he revived Sweeney for 'The First Flight', the issue of local obligation was presented very differently:

> I was mired in attachment
> until they began to pronounce me
> a feeder off battlefields
>
> so I mastered new rungs of air
> to survey out of reach
> their bonfires on hills.[64]

Attachment to home, so sustaining to the Heaney of 'Mossbawn', was presented in *Station Island* as a mire. Rather than centring and staking the potentially wayward imagination, the local background in this poem seems to be boggy and restrictive. As Heaney meditated on poetic responsibility in 'The First Flight', the poet whose work is too closely connected to his local community is figured as a macabre bird of prey, feeding off the blood of his kin. Escape from the massacre is not necessarily a form of desertion, if staying at home makes the poet a kind of vulture.

Heaney's wrestle with the task of the poet during the Troubles may seem far removed from Scott's peaceful antiquarian enthusiasms, but his practice of reading contemporary concerns in local legends offers helpful insight. Although Scott's official role in the *Minstrelsy* was that of editor rather than poet, he used the collection of traditional materials to allow his own Border preoccupations a secret voice. In his haunting re-creation of the traditional ballad of the three ravens, 'The Twa Corbies', Scott's ambivalence about the role of the Border poet is apparent, especially when the poem is placed beside Heaney's versions of the Sweeney legend. Scott's poem is a dialogue between two crows, who have alighted by the body of a fallen knight:

> 'Ye'll sit on his white hause bane,
> And I'll pike out his bonny blue een.
> Wi' ae lock o' his gowden hair,
> We'll theek our nest when it grows bare.

> 'Mony a one for him makes mane,
> But nane sall ken whare he is gane:
> O'er his white banes, when they are bare,
> The wind sall blaw for evermair.'[65]

Unlike most Romantic images of the poet as a songbird—a nightingale, a skylark, a cuckoo—the corbies are anonymous and predatory, picking over the carcase, building their own nests from others' suffering. Like Heaney's guilty self-image, they are 'feeders off battlefields', dependent for survival on conflict and violent death. Scott's ballad suggests that the poet's desire to 'master new rungs of air', as Heaney put it, is not a straightforward issue of artistic freedom, or aversion to bloodshed, or even cowardice. It suggests instead a deep unease about the nature of Border culture and the poet's role in relation to society. For, if the poet is neither benefactor, leader, hero, nor historian, but rather a deceitful scavenger, feeding on the aftermath of other's actions, the moral value of his art must be open to question. Despite its beauty and dark humour, 'The Twa Corbies' presents an uncomfortable metaphor for a certain kind of local poetry.

The self-punishing view of the poet evident in 'The Twa Corbies' is indicative of a modern creative artist at work on old materials. The traditional dilemmas of the Border poet, which relate to local obligation and the duty to perpetuate the memory of old wrongs, are further complicated in the work of both Heaney and Scott, by notions of originality and belatedness. Weighing against the uncomfortable sense of the local poet as a scavenger, fattening on the troubles of his community, is a completely contrary anxiety relating to the difficulties of the modern, desk-bound writer whose life seems so inactive and feeble in comparison to that of his warlike predecessors— or contemporaries. The doubleness of 'The Twa Corbies' is entirely apt for the doubly conflicted experience of the modern poet whose local attachments are to a fighting zone, and whose creative sensibilities are both compelled and repelled by his immediate culture. Scott had to grapple, not just with the conflict between imaginative attraction to a wilder, freer, more physical society and a contrary awareness of the benefits of modernity, but also with the realization that, in the region to which he was most attached, the very wildness and freedom of the people meant that the subjects of the poetry were oddly prescribed and often far from admirable.

Although the blood in Scott's Border country was shed much longer ago than the events that surrounded *North, Sweeney Astray,* and *Station Island,* a region that had been the site of so many battles and skirmishes posed some of the same problems for the poet, albeit less urgently. Central to the local poet's dilemma was the question of where art belonged in a violent world. By the time he composed the Nobel Lecture, Heaney had arrived at a clear understanding of poetry's redemptive capacity and potential defiance of even the most brutal conditions. His earlier work, however, reveals with equal clarity the problems surrounding local poetry in troubled places.

In a sense, Scott could safely indulge his imagination in the history of bloody Border feuds, without fearing to reignite the old hatreds. Whether this was a proper part of the poet's duty was, however, another matter. For Wordsworth, grappling with ideas about the modern poet's responsibility to make a vital contribution to a society in sore need of help, the issues of local division and poetry's traditional function as a call to arms were troubling ones. In 1802, when Scott published the first two volumes of the *Minstrelsy,* Wordsworth was calling on the memory of Milton and lamenting the disappearance of 'great men' from his nation. Was it possible to look back to the seventeenth century, when Milton had composed his great epic, without seeing also the massive upheaval and bloodshed of the Civil War? Poetry of any value had to be true, but what if the truths it expressed concerning human nature were not of a peaceful Republic, but rather of a state of war? According to many influential eighteenth-century thinkers, the composition of great poetry actually required periods of turbulence, and the epics of Ancient Greece owed much to the first-hand experience of Homer: 'He saw Towns taken and plundered, the Men put to the Sword, and the Women made Slaves: He beheld their despairing Faces, and suppliant Postures; heard their Moanings o'er their murdered Husbands, and Prayers for their Infants to the Victor.'[66] Such approaches to the classics inevitably raised questions over whether a poet could equal the genius of Homer if he lived in less turbulent times.

At the end of 'Home at Grasmere', Wordsworth had rejected the idea of writing about battles, but the impulse to do so was real enough:

> Yea, to this day, I swell with like desire;
> I cannot at this moment read a tale
> Of two brave Vessels matched in deadly fight
> And fighting to the death, but I am pleased,
> More than a wise Man ought to be; I wish,
> I burn, I struggle, and in soul am there.   (ll. 928–33)

Though Wordsworth bade 'farewell to the Warrior's deeds', in a determined effort to dwell on loving, peaceful thoughts, his imaginative excitement over violent conflict is only too clear. For Wordsworth, the 'peaceful vale', where Nature's calming ministry was most in evidence, was a counter to tales of war and daring deeds. Not all traditional rural areas were so conducive to the composition of poems embodying the kind of hope, fortitude, and love that Wordsworth admired in Grasemere, however.

Scott's *Minstrelsy* was one of the most important collections to appear at the beginning of the new century, but, if it abundantly answered Wordsworth's demand for local truth, it also showed that local attachments did not necessarily ensure the peace and moral health of the community. Wordsworth's hopeful visions of a paradise recoverable in the ordinary world were challenged by Scott's revelations about the culture of the Borders, but the related questions about poetry's connection with violence were all part of a profound and cumulative exploration of the place of poetry in the modern world.

Wordsworth's Friendship with Scott

For Wordsworth, Scott's work not only provided corroboration for ideas he was developing in Grasmere, but also provoked further investigation into the nature of poetry, its relationship to place, and its role in modern society. When he made his extensive trip to Scotland in the year that the third volume of *Minstrelsy of the Scottish Border* appeared, Wordsworth was delighted to meet the man who seemed to combine the kind of local attachment he most admired with the self-consciousness of a highly educated and skilled modern interpreter of society. Scott, dividing his time between the literary and legal circles of Edinburgh and the more scattered communities of the Borders, was ideally placed to understand the value of traditional poetry and to present it in ways that might affect sophisticated contemporary readers. But, above all, Wordsworth was excited by being able to witness for himself the direct connection between poems that could be read from the printed page and the places where they had originated.

Wordsworth had long been interested in the Border region, which stretched away to the north-east of Cumbria and yet still seemed strange, unfamiliar country. When he tackled hard questions about the nature of human behaviour in the years following his return from revolutionary France, he had set his experimental drama, *The Borderers*, in the unsettled period long before the national boundary between England and Scotland had been agreed. Wordsworth's play had failed to find favour with London theatre-owners, but now Scott had succeeded in bringing the region into the public eye, complete with extensive history and transcriptions of medieval documents. For the Wordsworths, however, Scott's local knowledge was most engaging when delivered in person and prompted by places that were still very much part of contemporary experience. By September 1803, they had travelled extensively through Scotland, discovering the beautiful coastline of Argyll, visiting Rob Roy's domain and Ossian's Grave in Glen Almond, but what they had gathered so far was as nothing to the depth of Scott's understanding of his favourite region. As Dorothy recalled in her journal entry on their visit to Melrose Abbey with Scott: 'He was here on his own ground, for he is familiar with all that is known of the authentic history of Melrose and the popular tales connected with it. He pointed out many pieces of beautiful sculpture in obscure corners which would have escaped our notice.'[67] Just as her brother had explained to readers of 'Michael' that in the valley above Greenhead Gill was a heap of stones that they 'might see and notice not', so Dorothy was aware of the way in which a well-informed insider could reveal secrets that would otherwise remain invisible to the visitor.

It was not just Scott's knowledge of ecclesiastical architecture and carving that proved enlightening, however, but also his love of 'authentic history' and 'popular tales'. Some of Scotland's most cherished memories seemed to cluster around the High Altar in the ruined abbey, where not only Earl Douglas, hero of 'Chevy Chase', but also the wizard Michael Scott, and even the heart of Robert the Bruce himself were buried. A proper introduction to Melrose Abbey was a trip back to the fierce world of medieval Scotland and a startling reminder that, beneath the peaceful, atmospheric ruins lay memories waiting to spring into life, if released by the right man. Scott knew how to read a landscape, and this was what made him such an invaluable guide and exemplar. The Wordsworths might well have travelled down the Teviot without pausing at Carlanrig, if Scott had not advised them to 'look about for some old stumps of trees, said to be the place where Johnny Armstrong was hanged'.[68] Whether or not Scott had recited his favourite Border ballad too, the remote spot immediately gained significance because of its legendary associations. Johnny Armstrong still possessed heroic stature in the land he had dominated for years, living on in the ballads that bore his name, his fate retold to readers of the *Minstrelsy*. His lasting fame had been secured, not so much by his reckless deeds, as by his death, which occurred as a result of a courteous, but misleading, invitation from the King:

> The King he wrytes a luving letter,
>   With his ain hand sae tenderly,
> And he hath sent it to Johnie Armstrong,
>   To cum and speik with him speedily.[69]

When Armstrong arrived, he was summarily hanged with thirty-six of his men, an event that made a permanent record on local memory:

> John murdered was at Carlinrigg,
> And all his gallant cumpanie;
> But Scotland's heart was ne'er sae wae,
> To see sae mony brave men die—

The trees at Carlanrig, which were used as a makeshift gallows, were said to have withered away at the injustice of the execution, leaving gaunt skeletons to mark the local landscape.

The weather-torn trunks might hardly have arrested the attention of travellers on such a beautiful route, but Scott's local insight transformed the deserted slope into a site of human tragedy and royal treachery, its contours deepened by centuries of outrage. Dead stumps could be revived by poetry, which helped to impress their stark silhouettes on successive generations as the shape of a painful past. Unfortunately, the Wordsworths, unaccompanied by Scott at this stage of their journey, failed to find the withered trees, but they still felt an obligation to search the landscape for hidden meaning, because of his special understanding. Scott's passionate attachment demonstrated again and again the powerful conjunction of memorable poetry and a real sense of place. As Dorothy Wordsworth had found so often during her trip to Scotland, what appeared to be empty expanses or unnamed valleys were really 'inhabited solitudes'.[70] One of the aspects of Scotland most striking to the Wordsworths was the way in which memories of earlier individuals lived on in the minds of later generations, giving figures such as Wallace or Rob Roy the quality of living presences. Like Michael or the village priest described in 'The Brothers', the people of rural Scotland seemed able to read the country like a book, seeing, in what might appear to be a vacant stretch of moorland, local heroes and stories of unfailing interest.

Unlike the hidden stories of Grasmere, however, Scott's wealth of tales opened the eyes of his guests to the lasting effects of violent action on communal memories. Not only had the events recalled in the local ballads scarred the landscape permanently, but it seemed that violence provoked a particular kind of poetry. The terse narratives, with their uncompromising dialogue, sudden shifts, irregular rhythms, and familiar formulae were the literary counterpart of the bloody events from which they sprang. Was Scott's philosophical explanation, which saw the ballads as relics of a society in which the poet performed the task of local reporter and historian to his clan, sufficient to account for their character? Could it be rather that the poetic imagination was especially aroused by blood, conflict, and fear? Or that the poems responding to battlefields and executions had been most popular with their audiences? Or was it that poets had always responded to unsettled or oppressive circumstances by creating poems adequate to the conditions? What constituted an adequate poem at moments of upheaval, and what were the responsibilities of the poet to his people? These were troubling questions that arose insistently in a country where poems seemed to grow naturally from violent acts and, though Wordworth's own home country had a more peaceful history, he had experienced the shock of internal conflict in the aftermath of his return from Revolutionary France. In 1802, he had grappled with questions about the adequacy of poetry to the realities of a suffering world, but his attempts at resolution had sent him on further exploration. The Scottish tour of 1803 was a journey that was as much internal as external.

Since Scott's collection of Border ballads had only recently been published when the Wordsworths visited him, it is not surprising that he directed his guests to locations described in the *Minstrelsy*.[71] His enthusiasm for the area was not, however, confined to places marked by painful stories transmuted into song. He was a welcome guest in homes throughout the region and absorbed more private tales as well as the well-known legends. On the journey along the Teviot towards Hawick, Scott took his friends off the road to see a beautiful, secluded spot where a 'stone bridge crossed the water at a deep and still place, called Horne's pool, from a contemplative schoolmaster, who had lived not far from it, and was accustomed to walk hither, and spend much of his leisure near the river'.[72] The tranquil pool could hardly be more different from the withered stumps at Carlanrig and their secret history of violence, but it was still charged with human value rather like the spots immortalized in Wordsworth's 'Poems on the Naming of Places'.

Within a few miles, the Border landscape offered dramatic contrasts, not just in the physical variations between bare hillsides and tree-lined river valleys, but also between the different sites that brimmed with human meaning. Peaceful or violent, public or private, active or contemplative, religious or secular, recent or remote: the Borders offered an extraordinarily rich variety of places imbued with human feelings. If the poet needed the 'interchange of peace and excitation', as Wordsworth was coming to recognize, then this was a place in which the creative genius should thrive.[73] The dawning realization that violence was not after all incompatible with poetry may also have helped him to come to terms with his own traumatic experiences in revolutionary France, however reluctantly. Perhaps, after all, the peaceful life of Michael was not in itself sufficient to inspire great art? Perhaps it was the startling contrast between the traditional manners of rural Grasmere and the more brutal behaviour evident elsewhere that imbued the story of Michael's quiet endurance with such power? As Paul Fussell realized when trying to make sense of the poetry of the First World War, the pastoral seemed to spring from the knowledge of man's brutality. When Wordsworth returned to serious work on *The Prelude* a couple of years after his trip to Scotland, the early recollections of his Lake District childhood were skilfully woven around the much more turbulent episodes in France. By then, the boy's destructive tendencies and the extreme violence of which societies were capable all seemed to be contributing something essential to the growth of the poet's mind—and certainly to the creation of adequate poetry. As Heaney emphasized in his Nobel Lecture, 'necessary poetry' is able to 'touch the base of our sympathetic nature while taking in at the same time the unsympathetic reality of the world to which that nature is constantly exposed'.[74] To do so requires taking a good look at the unsympathetic reality.

For the visitor privileged enough to be introduced by Scott, the Border country possessed both surface beauty and unexpected depths. Like the Heaneys' backyard at Mossbawn, the ground was rich in hidden colour for anyone who delved below, but what might be revealed there prompted a 'mixture of feelings' every bit as unmanageable as those written into the field names of rural Derry. Though the Border feuds recorded in the Scottish ballads were less immediate than those surrounding Heaney's youth, Scott's vivid imagination meant that his own encounters with the local landscape were fraught with remembered fears. Recollected violence was nevertheless a strange source of personal power. Scott's local attachments had grown over years of familiarity with the windings of the rivers, with the crevices in the rocks, and, most importantly, with the stories that clung to each. It is evident from Dorothy Wordsworth's personal admiration, and her accounts of the way in which 'the Sheriff' was regarded by people throughout the Borders, that his local knowledge was a major source of his extraordinary reputation. Scott's enthusiastic desire to share the secrets of his land turned him into a kind of wizard, like his namesake, Michael Scott, who makes such a memorable appearance in *The Lay of the Last Minstrel*. Broken branches seemed to become whole as he spoke, while empty stretches of grey scenery filled with raiders or supernatural processions. Scott's initial standing in the local community depended on his modern legal training and professional experience, but his growing fame depended on his imaginative connection to the Borders. Though born in Edinburgh, he seemed almost more able to participate in the land than those who had lived and worked there throughout their lives, because local knowledge gave him links to the past as well as to the immediate fields. His experience of the capital city also made Scott more conscious of his attachment to the Borders, which could never be taken for granted and seemed to demand perpetual renewal.

As a child, he had spent time with his grandparents at their farm in Roxburghshire, an experience that proved crucial to his later success as an editor, poet, and novelist. Looking back in later life, he realized that the stories he heard from his grandmother and her servant had nurtured his fascination with local history and helped him discover that the landscape could yield unexpected rewards. In *Marmion*, Scott admitted that his 'poetic impulse' had been 'given, | By the green hill and clear blue heaven', a personal insight that also suggests that the corroboration Wordsworth found in Scott's work was entirely mutual. Both poets gained enormously from their friendship, and, although *The Prelude* had not been published by 1808 when *Marmion* appeared, the self-reflective passages interspersing the 'Tale of Flodden' suggest that Wordsworth's explorations into his growth as a poet and with the relationships between the present and past were of great interest to Scott.

Marmion opens with reflections on the 'wintry' state of contemporary Britain, following the deaths of Pitt, Fox, and Nelson, that recall the anxieties raised in the sonnets Wordsworth had just published in

1807. Scott included a clear echo of 'The Immortality Ode' as he contrasted his faith in the vernal sun bestowing new life 'Even on the meanest flower that blows' with doubts about whether modern Britain will be revived by another spring.[75] It was in the third book, however, that Scott developed his most Wordsworthian introduction, when he presented his own creative inspiration as having its roots in the physical experiences of childhood:

> It was a barren scene, and wild,
> Where naked cliffs were rudely pil'd;
> But ever and anon between
> Lay velvet tufts of loveliest green;
> And well the lonely infant knew
> Recesses where the wall-flower grew,
> And honeysuckle lov'd to crawl
> Up the low crag and ruin'd wall.[76]

Within the 'barren scene' were hidden secrets, and, as the apparently unyielding cliffs opened to reveal life and growth, the 'lonely infant' was translated from a vulnerable figure to one of vital strength.

Local knowledge had been a source of power from his earliest days. Scott's exploration of his growing local attachments involved greater emphasis on human presences of a rather different kind, however, from those Wordsworth celebrated in Grasmere. In the autobiographical fragment written in the same year that *Marmion* was published, Scott described how his 'love of natural beauty', awakened by the Borders, was intensified when the grand features of the landscape were 'combined with ancient ruins, or the remains of our father's piety or splendour'.[77] The verse epistle in *Marmion* makes the same point, as it moves from the generally 'barren scene' to focus on the special imaginative nourishment provided by the peel tower at Smailholm:

> And still I thought that shatter'd tower
> The mightiest work of human power;
> And marvell'd as the aged hind
> With some strange tale bewitch'd my mind,
> Of forayers, who with headlong force,
> Down from that strength had spurr'd their horse,
> Their southern rapine to renew,
> Far in the distant Cheviots blue,
> And home returning, fill'd the hall
> With revel, wassel-rout, and brawl.   (*Marmion*, iii. 179–88)

The barren hills might offer the unexpected pleasure of a wallflower or honeysuckle, but it was the shattered towers and Border peels that really fired Scott's imagination.

In his sonnet 'Written in London, September 1802', Wordsworth had used Milton's powerful word 'Rapine' to express his abhorrence of modern metropolitan society, where 'Rapine, avarice, expense' were idolized. For Scott, on the other hand, far from being a pejorative term, 'rapine' conjured up the thrilling raids of his Scottish forebears as they harried the enemy south of the Border. The dramatic tales he heard from the older people in Roxburghshire fused with his own ideas about the ruined strongholds to create a mental landscape crowded with terrifying figures and violent action:

> Methought that still with trump and clang
> The gateway's broken arches rang;
> Methought grim features, seam'd with scars,
> Glar'd through the window's rusty bars,
> And ever by the winter hearth,
> Old tales I heard of woe or mirth
> Of lovers' slights, of ladies' charms,
> Of witches spells, of warriors' arms;
> Of patriot battles, won of old
> By Wallace wight and Bruce the bold;
> Of later fields of feud and fight,
> When pouring from their Highland height,
> The Scottish clans, in headlong sway,
> Had swept the scarlet ranks away.   (*Marmion*, iii. 189–201)

For a boy whose reason for staying with his grandparents in the countryside was his own physical disability, the idea of heroic men of action was especially gripping. As the adults worried about his lameness, little Walter imagined himself on a Border raid or following the Bruce into battle. His recollections of a rural childhood were, therefore, rather different from those re-created by Wordsworth in *The Prelude*. Instead of casting himself as a kind of savage, delighting to plunge into streams or hang from cliffsides, plundering birds' nests, Scott knew that his imaginative resources had been fostered by the old stories and historical remains that studded the Border landscape. Always at one remove from what he described with such passion, Scott's Border vision allowed him to participate imaginatively in the lawless society of old, while maintaining a detachment that brought a different kind of freedom.

The image of the young boy finding wallflowers in the 'recesses' of 'low crags and ruined walls' was at once a literal recollection and a metaphor for the collector, editor, and adapter of Border ballads. Scott learned early in life how to uncover remarkable stories from the natural and man-made features of his favourite region and never lost the childlike excitement they provoked. His self-consciously educated tone may have suggested a modern perspective on a less sophisticated stage of human society, but much of Scott's work betrayed a sense of loss rather than gain. His awareness of the centuries of action that had gone before meant that he was always a newcomer to the great collective Border story, filled with imaginative energy but labouring under an inevitable sense of physical inadequacy and general belatedness. The image of the little boy playing out the great battles of Scottish history with his pebbles and shells is both an affectionate recollection and an ironic comment on the modern descendant of the Border chiefs.

Despite the sense of physical inferiority, Scott's inner strength nevertheless developed with his intimate knowledge of familiar territory. The 'shattered tower' of Smailholm, which figured as largely in Scott's mind as any of the natural features, was there for anyone to see, but its real meaning could be discovered only from someone on the inside. In an area like that of the Borders, there was hardly a cave or a broken tower that had not been magnified by human associations, but these 'recesses' were known only to those who had attended carefully to the land for many years. True understanding of the place gave tremendous power to the writer, whose decision to publish Border material was at once an act of homage to the area, an act of generosity to those outside, and an assertion of special wisdom. Scott's reputation in the Borders was obvious to the Wordsworths as soon as they met him and showed that a modern poet could still be regarded as a figure of immense importance to those outside the fashionable literary circles. Scott went on to demonstrate, too, that poems grounded in regions unknown to those elsewhere could still attract enormous numbers of readers. After the second edition of the *Minstrelsy*, Scott turned his hand to more open composition, publishing *The Lay of the Last Minstrel* in 1805, with its unapologetic references to 'Minto Crags',

'Eskdale-moor', 'Warkworth, or Naworth, or merry Carlisle'. From this point onwards, he became the most popular poet of the period, attracting huge sales, creating a market for historical poems, and, inadvertently, transforming the Scottish tourist industry.[78] Although Wordsworth attracted contemptuous criticism for his decision to draw inspiration from the Lake District, Scott's popularity in the early nineteenth century demonstrated beyond any reasonable doubt that poems set firmly in a recognizable region had the power to speak to readers from far and wide. The poetry of local attachment was not restricted to those familiar with its place of origin, but could capture the imagination of any sympathetic reader. And, if Scott became more conscious of the workings of the imagination through his friendship with Wordsworth, Wordsworth's awareness of the complexity of local attachment was deepened through his encounters with Scott and the Scottish Borders.

5

Robert Burns's Addresses

The Wordsworths' trip to Scotland in 1803 ended well, with the sun smiling on their last week's travel westwards through the Borders back to the Lakes. As they finally rejoined their outward path at Longtown, however, Dorothy noted that, although 'the fair prospect of the Cumberland mountains' was now in view, they could not 'look along the white line of the road to Solway Moss without some melancholy emotion'.[1] She was, of course, recalling their very first destination, six weeks before, when they had visited Burns's home in Dumfries and the graveyard where he was buried. The Wordsworths were deeply affected by their experience, which seemed to drive all other thoughts from their minds as they travelled slowly through the places he had lived and worked for, as Dorothy recalled, there was nothing connected 'with Burns's daily life that is not heart-depressing'.[2] When her brother responded to his experience in 'At the Grave of Burns, 1803', the poem, written in Standard Habbie, almost overflowed with echoes of Burns's poems and the deep melancholy of the situation. Wordsworth had been horrified enough by reading Currie's account of Burns's brief life, but now, confronted with the two unmarked graves of the young poet and his little boy in the corner of the churchyard, thoughts that had darkened 'Resolution and Independence' acquired the full force of first-hand experience. Wordsworth knew Burns's 'A Bard's Epitaph' by heart, and, as he repeated it by the grave, he was painfully struck by the prescience of the poet who had chosen to close his first published volume with a poem on his own death.

'At the Grave of Burns' includes perhaps the most succinct statement of Wordsworth's personal sense of indebtedness to Burns:

> I mourned with thousands, but as one
> More deeply grieved, for He was gone
> Whose light I hailed when first it shone,
>   And showed my youth
> How Verse may build a princely throne
>   On humble truth.[3]

Burns's importance as a poet of truths, acquired not by an extensive academic education, but through deep understanding of those immediately around him, had been brought home to Wordsworth again and again since his trip to Germany. Now, standing on Burns's own 'unpoetic ground', it was abundantly reaffirmed.[4]

For Wordsworth, Burns was a kindred spirit, joined 'heart with heart and mind with mind', whose work had given him hope for the future of contemporary British poetry. As the poem emphasizes, his affinity with Burns was further strengthened by their close proximity on either side of the Solway Firth,

> Alas! where'er the current tends,
> Regret pursues and with it blends,—
> Huge Criffel's hoary top ascends
>   By Skiddaw seen,—
> Neighbours we were, and loving friends
>   We might have been.   (ll. 37–42)[5]

As Wordsworth meditated on Burns's untimely death, afflicted by thoughts of what might have been, he was also articulating his gratitude to Burns as an inspiration and guiding light. Burns was the poet who had shown Wordsworth the way to write poetry that mattered, who had risen 'like a star' but whose real strength had been in 'touching earth'.

When he returned to his poem many years later, to compose 'Thoughts suggested the Day Following, on the Banks of Nith, near the Poet's Residence', Wordsworth had the added authority of hindsight in his assessment of Burns's greatness:

> Through busiest street and loneliest glen
> Are felt the flashes of his pen;
> He rules mid winter snows, and when
>   Bees fill their hives;
> Deep in the general heart of men
>   His power survives.   (ll. 43–8)

The sequel poem was published almost forty years after Wordsworth had first stood at the grave of Burns in 1803, and by then Burns's lasting contribution to the world was assured.[6] The poetry of humble truth had reached far beyond its origins in south-west Scotland to delight men and women across the world. It was quintessentially 'local work' in Heaney's terms and as travelworthy as it was trustworthy. Burns's universal popularity was, as Wordsworth's later poem suggests in its self-allusive metaphor, proof of the faith expressed in *Lyrical Ballads* that 'we have all of us one human heart'.

Wordsworth's desire to visit the places associated with Burns and to compose poems in the very locations where he felt the great 'Spirit, fierce and bold' is a testimony to the powerful local dimensions of Burns's work. To pay proper tribute to Burns, it seems, Wordsworth had to feel the very places in which Burns had been moved to compose his immortal poems. Burns was a key figure in the aesthetic shift from seeking truth in wide, general observation to particular experience—and to the creation of a local poetry whose appeal depended on feeling not description. The powerful attraction James Currie had attempted to analyse in relation to Burns's work was very similar to what readers were experiencing in 'Tintern Abbey' and what Coleridge longed for in 'Dejection'—an environment that is not just *seen*, but *felt* along the blood. Though Burns was not given to thanking 'Nature' for her ministering care in quite the same terms as Wordsworth and Coleridge, his creation of a completely convincing world meant that any sympathetic reader could share the emotions embodied in his poems. Despite its unassuming appearance and prefatory claim that the poems had been composed purely to amuse the poet and his immediate circle, *Poems, Chiefly in the Scottish Dialect* reached both a local audience and the most influential literary circles of the day. As a result, many readers became fascinated by the world in which their idol had lived and eager to see for themselves the little cottage at Alloway where he was born or the graveyard where he was buried. Burns may initially have attracted literary visitors from neighbouring areas—Samuel Thomson, the Ulster poet, William Wordsworth and Robert Anderson, from Cumbria—but in the centuries that followed, numerous tourists made pilgrimages to the area that rapidly became known as the Burns Country.[7] Interest in the special character of Scottish rural life had been stimulated by Currie's edition, but for many early nineteenth-century travellers, and especially the Wordsworths, the impetus to explore south-west Scotland came from Burns himself.

A Lad Born in Kyle

Burns's own attachment to the area around Alloway was evident throughout the Kilmarnock edition, and, when he came to reflect on his life a few months after the publication of his first collection, a strong sense of place seems to have been fundamental to his mature sense of self. As he explained in a letter to the Revd Greenfield in December 1786: 'I have long studied myself, and I think I know pretty exactly what ground I occupy, both as a Man, & a Poet.'[8]. Burns was defining himself in terms of his confident knowledge of his place in the world and used the same expression in a long, auto-biographical letter sent to Dr John Moore the following August: 'To know myself had been all along my constant study.—I weighed myself alone; I balanced myself with others; I watched every means of information how much ground I occupied both as a Man and as a Poet.'[9] Burns's sense of his own 'ground' was essential to his psyche and his songs—and hence his importance to any study of local attachments. His relationship with his local community was not without complications, however, nor was the scope of his work circumscribed by its strong attachments to particular places, despite the different ways in which Burns's identification with Ayrshire has influenced readers.

Successive collections of poetry are normally designated first, second, or enlarged editions, but Burns's early volumes are generally distinguished from each other through the circumstances of their original publication—the Kilmarnock edition, the Edinburgh edition. Such identification inevitably locates them in particular places—these are volumes of poetry that seem to come with their address labels firmly attached. Though partly an accident of critical history, the widely accepted terms reflect something intrinsic to the volumes in question as well as emphasizing the personal history of Burns himself. The two names of Kilmarnock and Edinburgh have always influenced the reception of Burns's poetry, by emphasizing both his regional origins and his larger importance as the poet of

Scotland. Burns is seen both as a local lad and as 'Caledonia's bard'—doubly situated in rural Ayrshire and the capital city.[10] For many poets, a move from provincial obscurity to national fame is a mark of literary success: praise from established experts and sales to anonymous readers afford a different kind of esteem from the enthusiasm of affectionate friends and family. And who prefers to remain known only to a local audience when national celebrity is within grasp? Burns's astonishing appearance on the Scottish literary scene was a triumph of natural ability over privilege and convention, as his talent was recognized immediately by readers far from Kilmarnock. The publication of his second volume of *Poems, Chiefly in the Scottish Dialect* in the capital city less than a year after the original modest production in Ayrshire symbolized Burns's new status as national bard and, as David Daiches observed many years ago: 'The Edinburgh edition, with its imposing list of subscribers...and its equally imposing "Dedication to the Noblemen and Gentlemen of the Caledonian Hunt", established his fame as a poet throughout Britain and beyond.'[11] And yet, from the time of the first biographies by Robert Heron and James Currie, Burns's career was rarely seen as a straightforward success story, with readers perennially registering unease about his later development and declaring a preference for the early work. Even in the twentieth century, when the worldwide popularity of Burns's songs was so well established, Catherine Carswell still asserted in her biography, 'what may be called the body and soul of his work falls well within the first two years he lived at Mossgiel'.[12] Seventy years later, Don Paterson introduced his personal selection of Burns's work with a similar observation: 'after the age of twenty-seven, he wrote very little poetry of any merit.'[13] Far from tracing a triumphant progress from obscure beginnings to national fame, biographers and editors, early and late, have presented Burns's career as something of a tragedy, characterized by the onset of unhappy intellectual influences, emotional chaos, financial difficulty, and, whether as the result or the companion of these misfortunes, the 'dereliction of his muse'.[14] Continuing admiration for the poems written before Burns's departure from his childhood home shows that his early reliance on local knowledge was very well judged. However, close consideration of Burns's later career also reveals that the ability to embody local truths in poetry was not restricted to the area where Burns grew up and that the works that travelled furthest were often those composed after his departure from Ayrshire.

The Kilmarnock Edition

Poems, Chiefly in the Scottish Dialect opened with 'The Twa Dogs', which effectively located the entire volume: "Twas in that place o' *Scotland's* isle |That bears the name o' auld king COIL."[15] Burns's collection came from Scotland, as the title made plain, but readers were made aware of the specific connection with Kyle as soon as they got inside the boards. Persistent references to his native region made plain Burns's sense of the ground that he occupied 'as a man and a poet'; but what was less obvious to his first readers was that these local attachments formed the foundation of his personal literary agenda. The Kilmarnock edition was introduced by a modest address that masked Burns's real ambitions. His preface assumed the voice of the unknown country poet, whose 'little creations' were a respite from hard agricultural labour and who begged that his humble 'Education and Circumstances of Life' might be taken into account by the public.[16] It was only when readers got as far as 'The Vision' or the verse epistles that they began to discover serious literary aims being articulated in highly sophisticated ways. By then, however, many had taken the pose of the simple bard at face value, enjoying his poems about dogs, sheep, whisky, and country life and not anticipating anything more profound. In *Tristram Shandy*, one of Burns's 'bosom favorites', Sterne had delayed the 'Author's Preface' until he was halfway through the third book, but he did at least signal clearly to his readers that it was there.[17] Burns, on the other hand, hid his manifesto within his apparently unassuming collection, conveying his aspirations in a series of poems.

Often, when he wanted to approach the most serious topics, Burns projected a comic image of the poet. In 'The Vision', for example, the opening images of the speaker's self-rebuke, 'stringing blethers up in rhyme | For fools to sing', is the prelude to an astonishing revelation of Burns's literary aims, his creative inspiration and growth.[18] In this key poem, the crucial contribution of the local area for Burns's creative development is conveyed through the Scottish Muse, 'Coila', who is effectively dressed in a map of Ayrshire.

The startled poet describes her wonderful mantle, recognizing a landscape 'well-known' to him from his earliest days:

> Here, DOON pour'd down his far-fetch'd floods;
> There, well-fed IRWINE stately thuds:
> Auld, hermit AIRE staw thro' his woods,
>   On to the shore.[19]   (ll. 79–82)

Coila, the symbol of Kyle, saves Burns from abandoning poetry by explaining that she has nurtured him from the cradle to be her bard, watching his early enthusiasm for rhymes, his adolescent delight in the local shoreline and familiar fields, and guiding his burgeoning love of his fellow men—and women. Rather than address the natural world or the local community directly, in 'The Vision' Burns adopted an allegorical structure, acknowledging his sources of inspiration through the imaginative encounter with a visitor at once heavenly and earthly. In the process, Kyle is elevated to quasi-divine status, even as the poet himself is being instructed to strive in his own '*humble sphere*' (l. 260). In urging humility, 'The Vision' actually makes huge claims for the apparently limited sphere that is to be Burns's source and subject—and hence Wordsworth's gratitude to the poet who had shown him how 'Verse may build a princely throne | On humble truth'.

In 'The Vision', Burns was developing ideas that he was also sketching out in his Commonplace Book. In August 1785 he recorded his admiration for Allan Ramsay and Robert Fergusson, but knew that it was alloyed by his strong sense of local pride. 'I am hurt to see other places in Scotland, their towns, rivers, woods, haughs, etc., immortalized in such celebrated performances,' he wrote, while lamenting that his own 'dear native country' remained unknown.[20]. Even though Ayrshire could boast famous men, historic events, and beautiful scenery, it had yet to acquire an imaginative life beyond its borders, as he went on to complain: 'we have never had one Scotch Poet of any eminence, to make the fertile banks of Irvine, the romantic woodlands and sequestered scenes on Aire, and the heathy, mountainous source, and winding sweep of Doon emulate Tay, Forth, Ettrick, Tweed, etc.' Such a clear articulation of the perceived rivalry between different Scottish regions shows that, for Burns, local poetry was far more than a fashionable subgenre of the eighteenth century—it was an expression of loyalty as well as literary skill. Although he was eager to remedy the general neglect of his home, Burns was also aware of both the scale of his ambition and the disadvantage of his situation: 'Alas! I am far unequal to the task, both in native genius and education.'[21] Despite these misgivings, the task of immortalizing his own 'dear native country' was one that Burns undertook with considerable determination, as evident in the strong sense of local consciousness that characterizes many of his early poems.

Rather than content himself with loco-descriptive couplets reminiscent of Denham and Pope, however, Burns approached the challenge of immortalizing Ayrshire in a variety of ways. 'The Vision' is a dramatized version of the internal dialogue Burns jotted down in his notebook in August, complete with an allegorical figure for local inspiration. The depiction of Ayrshire on Coila's mantle was a way of conveying poetry's capacity to reveal extraordinary wonders in the most familiar things, though the comic irony of describing as 'well-known' a land unfamiliar to the majority of British readers helped pre-empt any unhelpful mockery of the supernatural device or inappropriate use of epic convention. Burns's comic use of classical devices avoided not only the derisive tendencies of mock-heroic verse (since his intention was to elevate rather than to undermine the little world of Mauchline), but also the ridicule that might attend a serious poem about the epic potential of Ayrshire. The dazzling and disconcertingly serious Muse nevertheless presented many readers with a challenge, since those who could not recognize the geographical features on her robe were being asked to imagine stunning scenery they had never seen, in order to understand its importance to the poet. Through the voice of Coila, Burns was explaining his own development and literary purpose, while posing as the humble bard who had more or less abandoned his time-wasting rhymes. It was an experiment in self-division that suggests a poet torn between his desire to write about what mattered to him and his awareness of an audience that might not be like-minded.

Later in the volume, Burns chose the verse epistle, with its implicitly dialogic character, as another form for addressing the widespread neglect of Ayrshire. Points made in the Commonplace Book were now emphasized through the heavily rhymed stanzas of Standard Habbie, as Burns lamented 'Auld Coila's' absence from the world stage, his comic exasperation rising with each new line:

> Nae *Poet* thought her worth his while
> To set her name in measur'd style
> She lay like some unkend-of isle
>   Beside *New Holland.*[22]

Since 'New Holland', now better known as Australia, had been discovered by Europeans only fifteen years before, Kyle's remoteness was hardly being understated by her literary champion. The epistle accordingly invites Willie Simson of Ochiltree to join Burns in answering the poets of other regions:

> *Ramsay* an famous *Fergusson*
> Gied *Forth* and *Tay* a lift aboon;
> *Yarrow* and *Tweed*, to monie a tune,
>   Owre Scotland rings,
> While *Irwin, Lugar, Aire* an' *Doon,*
>   Naebody sings.   (ll. 43–8)

The comic colloquialism of the verse letter helped mask Burns's seriousness and thus deflect any scorn that might be heaped on an obscure dialect poet who dared to aspire above his station. To argue too earnestly for the cultural importance of Kyle would be to invite the contempt of city-centred critics, and so Burns wisely adopted a more playful, self-knowing tone. In what seemed an unobjectionable appeal to a fellow Ayrshire resident, Burns laid out a remarkable poetic programme in fulfilment of the promise made to Coila a few pages before.

Not content with setting the rivers of Ayrshire on a par with the Tweed and Yarrow, Burns's aims were international and eternal:

> Th' *Illissus, Tiber, Thames* an' *Seine,*
> Glide sweet in monie a tunefu' line;
> But *Willie* set your fit to mine,
>   An' cock your crest,
> We'll gar our streams an' burnies shine
>   Up wi' the best.

> We'll sing auld COILA's plains an' fells,
> Her moors red-brown wi' heather bells
> Her banks an' braes, her dens an' dells,
>   Where glorious WALLACE
> Aft bure the gree, as story tells,
>   Frae Suthron billies.   (ll. 49–60)

Burns was nothing if not ambitious. 'To W. S*****n' proposed that the rivers of Ayr should become as famous as those of classical Greece and Rome or modern London and Paris. By invoking Ayrshire's most famous son, William Wallace, Burns was also making a stand for liberty and casting himself and fellow poets as local heroes. He was, in effect, anticipating Byron's only half-humorous observation that the lasting memory of great men, great deeds, and great places depended on the skills of a great poet ('they shone not on the poet's page, | And so have been forgotten'[23]). Where Byron chose an Italian stanza for his exploration of the poet's place in the world, however, Burns employed the distinctively Scottish form of the verse epistle in Standard Habbie, as both a tribute and a challenge to Ramsay and Fergusson.

'To W. S*****n' suggested that a region achieved full existence only once it had been recorded, mythologized, and given imaginative life. Burns was casting himself, not merely as the recorder of Kyle, but also, in part, as its creator. Despite his intermittent self-doubt and public insistence on being the bard of a humble sphere, he was seized with a desire to equal or to excel the great poets who inspired his creations, so his elevation of the local had a personal as well as a communal dimension. The epistle to Simson was composed in 1785, when Burns was still sometimes using his father's north-eastern version of the family surname 'Burness', so the wordplay on making 'our streames and burnies shine, up wi' the best' was especially pronounced.[24] *Poems, Chiefly in the Scottish Dialect* includes an array of different poetic kinds, which enabled Burns to demonstrate his mastery of complicated Scottish metres and rhyme-schemes and his understanding of the adequacy of certain distinctive stanzas. In 'The Holy Fair', for example, he chose the traditional verse form of 'Christis Kirk on the Green' for a poem celebrating Scottish folk festivities, with its lively, alternately rhyming lines of eight and seven syllables, and short refrain.[25] Like Standard Habbie, it was an old form, already revived by Ramsay and Fergusson and perfectly suited to the high-spirited scenes of 'The Holy Fair'. Scottish metres were the most appropriate choice for poems designed to glorify Kyle, not least because the most distinctive examples had their origins in south-western Scotland. As Douglas Dunn pointed out in his brilliant essay on 'Burns's Native Metric', Alexander Montgomerie, whose elaborate stanza was adapted by Burns for the 'Epistle to

Davie', 'To Ruin', and 'Despondency', came from an Ayrshire family, while Robert Sempill of Beltrees, whose elegy gave 'Standard Habbie' its familiar name, was from just across the Ayrshire border in neighbouring Renfrew.[26] Through the celebration of Ayrshire's life and culture, Burns himself hoped to shine, 'up wi' the best'— though, once he had actually experienced fame, his desire to be as 'well-known' as Ayrshire was to those who lived there waned considerably.

While Kyle remained the centre of his world, Burns's poems seemed propelled by centripetal as well as centrifugal forces, because of their strong sense of an audience. Many of the poems in his first collection were addressed to very specific objects. In addition to 'To W. S****n', there were verse epistles to other poets and friends—to John Lapraik, David Sillar, John Rankine, James Smith—as well as numerous poems of address: 'A Dedication to Gavin Hamilton', a mock birthday ode to George III in 'The Dream', 'The Author's Earnest Cry and Prayer to the Right Honourable and Honourable Scotch Representatives of the House of Commons', 'The Cotter's Saturday Night, inscribed to Robert Aikin', 'The Farmer's New Year Salutation to his Auld Mare, Maggie'; and the Farewells—to the Brethren of St James's Lodge, Tarbolton, to Eliza, to 'Poor Mailie'. Even poems that seem to be directed towards more generic objects, such as a mouse, a louse, a mountain daisy, turned out to have been prompted by an individual example of the kind—it was the mouse whose nest was destroyed by the poet's plough, the particular louse whom the speaker spotted in church. Though their larger meaning is not restricted to the audience designated by the title, many of the poems take their cue from a specific moment of encounter or imagined dialogue. It was as if the poet found himself through his perception of others, while his sense of the ground he occupied was almost always of shared ground. As the volume unfolds, the distinctive voice of a man moved by powerful feelings emerges at the centre of a completely convincing, communal world. The verse epistles, in particular, cumulatively create an image of a lively, self-sustaining community of brother-bards, living and working quite independently of Edinburgh and London. The idea of poems being exchanged in an atmosphere of 'muckle fun and jokin' makes a convincing enough case for poetry's vital social role without any need for abstract argument. Liam McIlvanney has also pointed out that the assertion of the 'non-material values—good-fellowship, fraternity, sympathy—against the corrupt self-seeking of the governing class' had a strong political cast in the years between the American and French revolutions.[27] The radical potential of such conversation between friends and related insistence that hearts mattered more than titles, rank, or wealth was certainly not lost on readers such as Wordsworth and Coleridge.

Readers of the late 1780s, who had only Burns's own glossary to help them, might not have been able to identify all the recipients of his poems, but the specificity and the tone of the poems seemed to confirm that these were real, living people and not fantasy figures. In fact, some of the first readers did know the identity of 'J. L', 'W. S', 'G. H.' or 'R. A', and for them the initials served as a kind of short-hand. The substitution of initials for proper names, though some-times seen as an attempt to make the poems 'less local', actually intensified the sense that the poems were addressed to real people, whose privacy should be respected even as the personal tribute becomes public.[28] The sense of things so familiar that no further explanation is necessary pervades Burns's first volume, deftly conveyed by his skilful use of the definite article—'the ingle-cheek', 'the auld clay biggin'—or his evocation of the habitual 'When winds frae aff Ben Lomond blaw', 'That merry night we get the corn in'. Just as Burns's friends are mentioned in a way that seems to assume their familiarity to readers, so too are the local place names. Gener-ally, the surrounding area is treated, not as the subject for poetry, but as a given, and it emerges all the more convincingly as a result. In 'Epistle to J. L*****k', for example, the poet has been told that the song he is enjoying was composed by someone from Muirkirk, and he responds by issuing an invitation to Mauchline. No concessions are made to a readership unfamiliar with rural Ayrshire. Burns's confident voice refers so clearly to things he knows well that any reader will trust his words and enter imaginatively into the world he has created through these minimal, but unmissable, references. Burns was a true parishioner, which is why he was also universal, as Heaney recognized when he described 'the liberation and amplifi-cation of parish truth in Burns's poetry', at the Burns Bicentenary celebrations in 1996—a year after the Nobel Lecture.[29]

The objects of Burns's poems are so well defined that the speaker's situation seems just as secure: the poet's home address is effectively created through a series of poetic addresses. The primary meaning of 'address' is of a communication directed at a particular audience, and so the clearly signalled objects of Burns's directions contribute much to the reader's larger sense of the poetry's origins. In a volume filled with verse epistles, salutations, laments, farewells, prayers, and dedications, it is possible to read most of the poems as a kind of address, since each seems to be directed both to a specifically identified object, as well as to the wider readership of the printed page. 'Epistle to a young friend', for example, is clearly meant for Andrew (Hunter Aikin), whose name appears in the second stanza, but the observations on 'mankind' are relevant to any reader. The poem has multiple addressees, including the poet himself, as the final, ironic self-rebuke makes plain:

> In *ploughman phrase*, GOD send you speed
> Still daily to grow wiser;
> And may ye better reck the *rede*
> Than ever did th'Adviser!   (ll. 85–8)

As in many of the poems, direct engagement with another leads to deepening self-knowledge—a pattern that helped Wordsworth to develop his own poems of encounter and to recognize the importance of Burns's 'humble truth'.

Burns's frequent self-admonishments provided a judicious balance for the unmistakable confidence of his poetic voice and soaring literary ambition. For, despite the pose of the 'simple bard' and professions of contempt for critical opinion, the desire for an extensive audience is clear enough in 'The Vision', the epistles, or the Commonplace Book. To establish Ayrshire on the world's cultural map, Burns needed to attract rather than alienate distant readers, so his local material had to be mediated by the inclusion of elements common to those beyond Kyle. His work was not merely a patriotic project, however, and his own love of English literature meant that the language of Shakespeare and Milton came just as readily to mind as Scottish poems. Though he used Scottish verse-forms with self-conscious skill, his poetry also drew on non-native literary traditions, as his roots crossed with his reading. This is one of the reasons that his poetry has remained so congenial to Heaney, who has expressed gratitude for Burns's willingness to open 'his doors to a great variety of linguistic comers', welcoming Beattie, Thomson,

Pope, and Milton as well as Ramsay, Fergusson, Montgomerie, or his neighbours.[30] Wordsworth, too, though also sufficiently familiar with the speech of Lowland Scotland to have no difficulty with Burns's local vocabulary, was just as impressed by poems that were composed predominantly in English, such as 'Despondency' or 'A Bard's Epitaph'. Burns's ability to reach a wider audience depended, not on the embodiment of local truths alone, but also on the rich inheritance of earlier poetry, Scottish and English, which strengthened his immediate knowledge of the world. Just as the full power of 'Resolution and Independence' depended on a fusion of literary recollections and first-hand experience, so Burns's poetry drew on the written and remembered as well as on his sympathetic, personal observations.

Roots and Reading

In the Kilmarnock edition, sudden shifts between familiar Scots and literary English are perhaps most obvious in 'Address to the Deil', where Milton's presence is signalled plainly in the epigraph ('*O Prince, O chief of many throned pow'rs,* | *That led th'embattl'd Seraphim to war*'). Though concerned with local beliefs, the poem approaches the 'Deil' through a complicated web of references to contrasting traditions and linguistic registers, making its point of origin seem less clearly defined than many in the volume. The only poem in the volume to be called an 'Address', it immediately emphasizes the difficulties of choosing an appropriate title and identifying its real object:

> O thou, whatever title suit thee!
> Auld Hornie, Satan, Nick, or Clootie'—

Though the tone is as familiar as that of the verse epistles, the recipient is much less clearly defined. On the one hand, the lines are dismissive and humorous, on the other, fearful of a subject able to adopt different identities and pervade every culture. Auld Hornie, Nick, or Clootie make him seem part of Scottish cultural tradition, but 'Satan' has also slipped in, a Miltonic intruder into the more familiar company.[31] Though apparently synonymous, the linguistic disjunction of 'Satan' hints of mock-heroic incongruity and inverted hierarchies, especially as the lines evoke Pope's address to Swift in *The Dunciad*.[32] As Burns reels off the possible titles, his comedy boosted by recollections of Swift and Pope, he seems to be adapting Augustan satire for traditional Scottish material. Since 'Halloween' is introduced by a prose note offering the poem's 'Charms', 'Spells', and 'Prophecy' as 'entertainment to a philosophic mind', the use of the mock-heroic may be similarly designed to emphasize a distance between the educated speaker and the traditional beliefs that form much of the poem.[33]

The 'Address' has often been read, accordingly, as the work of an enlightened author, sympathetic to progressive, Moderate Presbyterianism. Mockery of 'the Deil' was a way of satirizing the Hellfire sermonizing of hardline Kirk ministers bent on terrorizing their congregations into compliant virtue.[34] In 'The Holy Fair', the poem immediately preceding, Burns conjured up just such a figure, only to deflate him when his flock, half asleep, start up at what sounds like the roar of Hell, but turns out to be nothing more than 'some neighbour snoran' (l. 197). Burns commented that 'The fear o Hell's a hangman's whip, | To haud the wretch in order' in his 'Epistle to a Young Friend', which explicitly rejected the practice of enforcing morality through fear in its celebration of personal integrity and independent thought. The Devil, who so often seemed the most powerful ally of certain local ministers and their 'preaching cant', was an attractive candidate for mock-heroic treatment.[35] If the 'Address' is adapting Milton and Pope to satirize small-mindedness, however, its real power derives from a deep uneasiness about the subject and its implications, artistic and moral. The energy of Burns's poem is dynamic, generated by the struggle to bring opposing, potentially incompatible forces into line, which makes it more like a dramatic monologue than a verse epistle. The speaker's initial inability to name his object—so different from most of the poems—emphasizes his uncertainty over the location of power. Burns's Deil goes by many familiar names, but remains ultimately unknowable. As Murray Pittock has suggested, though 'ostensibly a figure from oral culture...this rusticity is everywhere problematized and undercut'.[36]

Burns makes comic capital from the elusiveness of his quarry, but his apparently light-hearted evocation of Milton also recalls one of the serious preoccupations of *Paradise Lost*—the mystery surrounding the principal Fallen Angel. He is described as 'The arch enemy, And hence in Heaven called Satan', when he makes his first speech in Hell, but this is not his original name, as Raphael later makes clear: 'Satan, so call him now, his former name is heard no more in heaven.'[37] When Burns included Satan in his list of possible titles, he was both evoking Milton but also recalling the way the great opponent had evaded the grasp of a poet who belonged, inevitably, to a fallen world. What was Satan's real name? In *Paradise Lost*, Milton had been faced with the dilemma of what to call the fallen angels, who were caught in a kind of nominal limbo since their true names had been 'blotted out and razed | By their rebellion, from the book of life'.[38] Though they came to be 'known to men by various names, and various idols through the heathen world', their true, original names remained hidden beneath ostentatious, but false titles—'O Prince, O Chief of many throned powers!'[39] For anyone as conscious of his own name as Burns, Milton's obsession must have been intriguing. Naming, as made clear by Adam's prelapsarian duties, is a way of asserting power, which means that failure to give a proper name may suggest diminished authority.[40] The more names Burns fires at the Deil, then, the less certain does his command of the situation appear.

With no name to fix his address, it is likely to miscarry—a problem compounded by the absence of any fixed abode. For the Deil appears in as many different places as he has titles. The poem rises brilliantly to the challenge of making the unknown knowable by its insistent use of Scots to depict a faintly ludicrous figure with 'smoutie phiz' and 'reeket duds', scalding poor wretches in a 'brunstane cootie', but at every turn it seems to be wrong-footed by the Deil's refusal to stay put: 'An tho' yon *lowan heugh*'s thy hame, | Thou travels far' (ll. 15–16). Where is the Deil to be found? The poem offers a surprising range of possibilities, rising to quasi-epic, cross-cultural heights as it recalls him, 'ranging like a roaran lion, | For prey, a holes an' corners tryin',' or 'on the strong-wing'd Tempest flyin', and is only just reined back by the short, familiar, vernacular, 'Tirlan the kirks' (ll. 19–21). The confident voice and regular stanzas seem to resemble Burns's other poems, but they are repeatedly challenged by the not quite known. 'Address to the Deil' is much less securely anchored by particular times and places, pushing on from verse to verse in an attempt to close in on its subject, which seems, at every turn, to be elsewhere. The fear that the Deil might actually be closer to home than he seems is, however, even more unsettling. The specificity of the speaker's 'douse, honest' Graunie,

> Aft 'yont the dyke she's heard you bumman,
> Wi' eerie drone;
> Or, rustling, thro' the boor tries coman,
> Wi' heavy groan,   (ll. 33–6)

seems much more menacing than the remote devil in 'yon cavern grim an' sooty' (l. 3). Burns's skill in embodying local material works against the voice of the enlightened, highly literate speaker, because it lends authenticity to Grannie's account, rather than dismissing it as an old wives' tale.

If the epigraph from *Paradise Lost* initially seemed to suggest light-hearted mockery of superstitions, as the poem gathers momentum it begins to reveal that Burns's Deil is just as unsettling as Milton's Satan. The account of the speaker being startled out of his wits on a dreary winter night in stanzas 7 and 8 is obviously a comic, Gothic parody, especially as the 'Deil' does nothing more than squatter away like a duck. Even as the stanza mocks misplaced fears, however, it acknowledges the imaginative grip exerted by the Deil. The choice of language, though seemingly designed to minimize the threat, actually magnifies the sense of a largely unknown but powerful opponent, for behind the Scottish loch with the duck is another dim recollection of *Paradise Lost*. When Satan appears in the opening Book he is 'stretched out huge in length … | Chained on the burning lake', a monstrous sea beast surrounded by darkness. He is neverthe-less able to 'put on swift wings' (II. 630), when necessary, and is later found 'Squat like a toad' at the ear of Eve, before his transformation into a serpent. With Milton in mind, Burns's recollection of seeing something that subsequently 'squattered like a drake | On whistling wings' seems a little more sinister than at first. If the Deil is not, after all, Auld Hornie, Nick, or Clootie, making mischief among the local community, but a being of the stature evoked by Milton, then the poet has just cause to be alarmed by this close encounter. Both the Scots idiom and epic epigraph, introduced to mock Burns's object, now seemed to have joined forces with the enemy in subduing the speaker. For the comic deflation of the Deil—whether he is bumman in a ditch, standing up like a bull rush, or coming to Paradise incog—repeatedly recoils on the speaker to reveal his own confusion. Local

ROBERT BURNS'S ADDRESSES 193

and literary tradition fuses brilliantly to create a poem that brings
large philosophical questions down to earth and, in doing so, renders
them terrifyingly personal. Does the Prince of Darkness really walk
the earth, or is he a projection of the human mind, fed by fears, folk-
lore, and theology? Or worse still—is the reason why he cannot be
fixed in any particular place that he has been hiding within all the
time?

The real horror of an inner demon emerges in the fourth stanza,
which drops abruptly from its global survey to find the Deil lurking
invisibly 'in the human bosom' (l. 23). While this may be another
satirical jibe at the unco guid—the Holy Willies who are so concerned
with others' wickedness that they fail to see their own—it may also
reflect the poet's anxieties about his personal failings and propensity
to err and stray. Burns mocked the Kirk Elders who rebuked him so
severely for his sexual conduct, but he was immune neither to their
condemnation nor to prevailing fears about the Last Judgement and
final division of mankind into sheep and goats. As Walter McGinty
has argued, Burns was brought up to feel responsible for his actions
and believed in 'a retributive scene of existence beyond the grave'.[41]
Although Burns's remark was prompted by his sense of the 'positive
injustice' apparent in the world, the less comforting corollary of
divine judgement would also have been obvious to him, especially
after experiencing public censure for actions deemed sinful by the
Kirk.

For all the exuberance of *Poems, Chiefly in the Scottish Dialect*, there
are numerous moments when the future seems a terrifying prospect,
from 'To a Mouse', to 'The Epistle to Davie', to 'Despondency', to
the final 'Bard's Epitaph', even though the 'Prayer on the Prospect of
Death' finds hope in a forgiving God. 'Address to the Deil' may
seem altogether lighter and more ebullient, but it still concludes with
the possibility of a final descent into Hell. Although the speaker
seems to be extending his enlightened sympathy towards even the
irredeemable figure he has been addressing, there is a strong vein of
self-interest and self-mockery in the hope that Auld Nickie-ben will
mend *before* he sends the poet to his black pit. Fear of Hell was real
enough in rural Scotland and provides an equivalent shadow behind
Burns's poetry. Indeed, his work gained conviction from its refusal
to gloss over the less congenial aspects of his community, which
were just as much part of Ayrshire as the beautiful rivers, traditional

poetry, and lively companions. Local attachment, as Scott recognized when he began to collect his Border ballads, often involved wrestling with the darker dimensions of the immediate world, whether internal or external.

Though Wordsworth and Coleridge were both delighted to find in Burns's work evidence of the great poet's ability to find paradise in the light of common day, it also showed that the same imaginative power could just as easily discover Hell. As Milton had suggested in his own portrait of Satan, the mind was capable of creating its own infernal pit, so there was no need to be looking out for the Deil in particular glens or kirkyards. It is not surprising that Burns made so much effort to realize the Deil as a visible, recognizable figure, because the horror of him lurking within was far greater than any external encounter. And hence, perhaps, his choice of title, since 'Address to the Deil' suggests something more public and oratorical than a verse letter, prayer, or salutation. It is also more purposeful, with its additional meaning of getting to grips with a problem and of setting things to right. Any private form of communication with the Deil would be far too dangerous, but an 'address' is a defence against intimacy. At the same time, however, Burns's Deil, magnified by recollections of Milton's Satan, is an object of intense fascination, not least because of his imaginative potential. The poem's relentless pursuit conjures up a most energetic figure, with mysterious forces at his command, a body of female followers, and a capacity for shape-shifting. His appeal to the poet is abundantly obvious, and, even though his power is terrifying, there is something marvellous in the way the idea of the Deil transforms ordinary places into sites of thrilling drama. The 'Address' is as much a celebration of the human imagination as an exposure of its irrational tendencies and hence its real affinity with Romanticism rather than the Augustan satire it playfully invokes.

Burns, like other Romantic poets, was enraptured by Milton, but his Satan was only partially indebted to *Paradise Lost*. It was the diffusion of his reading into other, much earlier influences that gave Burns's work such a distinctive character, as he himself realized when he attempted to explain his growth as a poet in the long, autobiographical letter to Moore. Crucial to his development, he reflected, was his education in modern literary classics and his 'vicinity to Ayr', which further enlarged his social and intellectual horizons.[42] Despite the emphasis on his reading, Burns also knew that his imagination was fundamentally indebted to traditions that flourished outside the local schools and libraries. Among these formative influences was an 'old Maid' of his Mother's, 'remarkable for her ignorance, credulity and superstition', but nevertheless in possession of 'the largest collection in the county of tales and songs concerning devils, ghosts, fairies, brownies, witches, warlocks, spunkies, kelpies, elf-candles, dead-lights, wraiths, apparitions, cantraips, giants, inchanted towers, dragons and other trumpery'.[43] She was the source, in other words, of many details that eventually found their way into the 'Address to the Deil'.

Though Burns dismissed Betty Davidson's old beliefs as 'trumpery', he still acknowledged their long-term effects: 'to this hour, in my nocturnal rambles, I sometimes keep a sharp look out in suspicious places; and though nobody can be more sceptical in these matters than I, yet it often takes an effort of Philosophy to shake off these idle terrors.' If the old maid left him mentally scarred, she had also 'cultivated the latent seeds of Poesy' and had a powerful effect on the young boy's imagination. The same ambivalence that emerges in the 'Address to the Deil' is evident in Burns's reflections on his creative development, which suggest a mind conditioned by sceptical resistance to delusion but deeply stirred by imaginative intensity and the unexplained. The philosophy that rescued modern man from the idle terrors of the past came at a heavy price. For Burns, the imagination might be potentially diabolical, but it was essential to sowing the latent seeds of poetry—and their proper cultivation. His metaphor, at once agricultural and biblical, could not be more telling. Burns's poetic growth was enriched by his reading and watered by the invigorating intellectual climate of his day, but it sprang from the local culture of Ayrshire.

Although Burns's local loyalty was proclaimed in 'The Vision' and the epistle to Simson, it was only after he had travelled more widely that he really understood the nature of his early influences. When he moved beyond his native county for the first time in the winter of 1786, he found himself in a very different environment where everything that seemed normal to him struck those he met as strange. The letter to Moore reflects both an interest in the philosophical probing into human nature that engaged intellectual circles in Edinburgh and a heightened consciousness of his own distinctive background.

Women like Betty Davidson might seem ludicrously out of place in the elegant salons of the modern capital, but by August, when he wrote to Moore, Burns had realized that she possessed something of inestimable value to him as a poet. Though much indebted to his reading for his technical and philosophical development, without a creative impulse that seemed to go back to his earliest years, his work would never have acquired its special character and might, indeed, never have been written.

Burns and Edinburgh

In the cold winter following the publication of *Poems, Chiefly in the Scottish Dialect*, Burns found himself in Enlightenment Edinburgh, fêted as a poetic genius while being patronized as a heaven-taught ploughman, out of place in the capital city but no longer the farmer he had grown up to be, saved by his sudden literary success from emigrating to Jamaica and yet still faced with grave difficulties concerning his future. Not only was he the father of three children by two different mothers, Elizabeth Paton and Jean Armour; he was also becoming entangled with Meg Cameron, pursuing Christina Lawrie and Margaret Chalmers, while still recovering from the untimely loss of Margaret Campbell, 'Highland Mary', who had died suddenly in October.[44] The man who had projected an image of himself as 'the simple bard' on the reading public was finding life anything but. As he admitted to Dr Moore, his future was far from secure because his 'keen Sensibility and riotous Passions' were so likely to 'make him zig-zag'.[45] Writing was a way out of financial and personal embarrassments, but even composing poetry, which had once come so easily, was now fraught with the difficulties of eager public expectation and a barrage of contradictory critical opinion. At the very moment when young Walter Scott was marvelling at the arrival of the wonderful genius with his unforgettable countenance, the poet himself was racked with inner confusion. In December 1787 he confessed to Robert Aiken: 'Various concurring circumstances have raised my fame as a Poet to a height which I am absolutely certain I have not merits to support; and I look down on the future as I would into the bottomless pit.'[46] The very blackness of Burns's future made him reflect on his life so far and to realize that the question 'Who am I?' was closely related to another: 'Where do I come from?'

Burns's sense of himself as a native of Ayr became more pronounced once he had left home, as is only too obvious in the few poems he wrote during his visit to Edinburgh.[47] The song he composed for his twenty-eighth birthday in January, for example, begins unequivocally: 'There was a lad was born in Kyle.'[48] For the first time in his life, Burns was resident in a big city, and the mixed feelings it inspired colour his 'Address to Edinburgh', whose very title suggests a public pose to cover private anxieties. Burns generally used the form when confronting something unknown or unmanageable—the 'Deil', the 'Unco Guid', or 'the Toothache'—not for expressing intimate feelings. Although apparently a tribute to the Capital, the 'Address to Edinburgh' is really an attempt to engage with something resistant to his familiar style. The voice that hails 'Edina' is very much less assured than that of the earlier *Poems*, and, as the poem circles back on itself, repeating the first stanza as its conclusion, the self-image presented could hardly be less like that of the vigorous bardie surrounded by friends and brothers:

> From marking wildly-scatt'red flow'rs,
>   As on the banks of *Ayr* I stray'd,
> And singing, lone, the ling'ring hours,
>   I shelter in thy honor'd shade.   (ll. 5–8, 61–4)

Burns's recollection of Ayr in the first stanza seems to conjure up an obscurity and lack of purpose, which has now been put behind him in favour of Edinburgh's exciting opportunities. By the end of the poem, however, it returns as a kind of wistful refrain, its stilted echo of 'To W. S****n' only emphasizing the gulf between Burns's Ayrshire self and his new situation. The repetition of the stanza seems to invite reconsideration of what has gone before, while the strange syntax allows for an alternative reading. If a longer pause is taken after the word 'singing', the lines now suggest a different contrast, between the bard who had strayed about freely, singing in response to the natural delights of his rural home, and the figure who now finds himself alone, enduring 'lingering hours' and forced to shelter in the shade. The studied language only widens the gulf between the past and present, its second-hand quality and contrived repetition too feeble to enable a proper return.

Although the poem begins and ends with reference to Edinburgh's 'honor'd shade', in the letters Burns wrote at this time 'shade' is a recurrent and far from positive word. There, he often expressed anxiety about being confined to the shades—usually associating the image with his early obscurity, as when he observed to Greenfield: 'I am willing to believe that my abilities deserved a better fate than the veriest shades of life.'[49] A few months later, he was anticipating a return to his 'shades', telling friends and acquaintances what he would take back with him.[50] To the Earl of Buchan, he imagined himself, somewhat disingenuously, 'stealing through my humble Shades', but warmed by the memory of the Patronage he had enjoyed.[51] The metaphor of rural shades, however, often reflected a deep disquiet over the celebrity status he experienced in Edinburgh, and his letter to Greenfield continued with a major qualification: 'But to be dragged forth, with all my imperfections on my head, to the full glare of learned and polite observation, is what, I am afraid, I shall have bitter reason to repent.' A similar sentiment was expressed to Hugh Blair, on the eve of Burns's departure in May: 'I often felt the embarrassment of my very singular situation; drawn forth from the veriest shades of life to the glare of remark.'[52] From the letters it appears that, though the shades of obscurity might be undesirable, the 'glare of remark' held terrors of its own.

The poet's portrayal of himself sheltering in Edina's 'honor'd shade' may, therefore, be a polite irony, expressing discomfort with the 'glare' of attention, but it also suggests more complicated feelings. Burns was adopting a pose of humility in the poem to flatter his eminent subscribers, but his words indicated a sense of displacement and uncertainty. Being in the shade depends on the direction of the light, so perhaps, in Edinburgh, Burns felt overshadowed by the great men who dominated the city, or by language of the polite society he was being encouraged to adopt and which seemed instead to shut him out from the sun? For a poet who was coming to realize that the seeds of poetry had been planted and nurtured in rural Ayrshire, the 'shade' of the city, however 'honor'd', was probably not the most fertile environment. Burns's recognition that the sources of his inspiration had sprung up naturally in Kyle may have been brought into sharp relief by the thought that life in Mossgiel was now only a memory.

If the 'Address to Edinburgh' was a rejection of Ayrshire, then it seems as forced as the language in which it was expressed. In a letter to John Ballantine, written a few weeks later, Burns admitted to 'Some life-rented, embittering Recollections' that 'whisper me that I will be happier anywhere than in my old neighbourhood', while he confessed to Muir, 'I have now neither house nor home that I can call my own, and live on in the world at large. I am just a poor wayfaring Pilgrim on the road to Parnassus.'[53] Arrival in Edinburgh was attended by a sense of self-induced exile from Ayrshire, and so the image of the poet sheltering in the shade may suggest, above all, a need for refuge. It was not that Edina lacked inspiring opportunities—the poem is a virtual catalogue of possibility and makes clear that the poet is being welcomed with opened arms. Throughout, however, the excitement is balanced by thoughts of loss, as contemporary wealth is set against memories of Scotia's kings, now laid low. The abstract 'Architecture' of modern Edinburgh fails to ignite the poet's imagination as readily as the 'rough, rude Fortress' of the Old Town, and everywhere the poet is a spectator, who 'sees', 'watches', 'views' but feels no personal connection with the sights. The only individual to be named in this poem is 'Fair B——', who seems decidedly distant, as she strikes his adoring eye like Heaven's beauties. Burns explained in a letter that 'Fair B——' was 'the heavenly Miss Burnet, daughter to Lord Monboddo', adding: 'There has not been any thing nearly like her, in all the combinations of beauty, Grace and Goodness the Creator has formed, since Milton's Eve on the first day of her existence.'[54] But the image of the speaker in the poem, who 'shelters in the shade', is more reminiscent of Milton's Satan than of Adam, for he seems to have alighted in a world of other people's wonders. In *Paradise Lost*, too, 'shades' are associated with Satan, who moves into Eden, like a black mist, and waits in the shade for Eve.

Once Burns had arrived in Edinburgh, his interest in Satan, so apparent in 'Address to the Deil', took on a new dimension. When he wrote to Mrs Dunlop in April, he announced his intention to 'study the sentiments of a very respectable personage, Milton's Satan—Hail horrors! Hail infernal world!'[55] In this letter, Burns was adopting a very different attitude to patronage from that of the flattering letters to Buchan or Greenfield, exclaiming proudly 'I set as little by kings, lords, clergy, critics &c as all these respectable Gentry

do my Bardship—I know what I may expect from the world, by and
by; illiberal abuse and perhaps contemptuous neglect.' By now, Satan
was emerging in Burns's imagination as a model of 'dauntless magna-
nimity, intrepid, unyielding independence, desperate daring and
noble defiance of hardship'—a Romantic rebel against an unjust
society and an inspiring master of rhetoric.[56] Equally attractive to
Burns was the thought of 'that great Personage, Satan' being a fear-
less exile who faced expulsion from heaven without admitting
defeat.

As Burns agonized over his own uncertain future, he turned to
Paradise Lost, saying: 'Give me a spirit like my favourite hero, Milton's
Satan,

'Hail horrors! hail,
Infernal world! and thou, profoundest Hell,
Receive thy new possessor! one who brings
A mind not to be chang'd by *place* or *time*!'[57]

The emphasis on place or time reveals Burns's own sense of depend-
ence on both, for, after quoting Satan's speech with admiration, he
berated himself in miserable contrast: 'I cannot settle to my mind…If
I do not fix, I will go to Jamaica. Should I stay, in an unsettled state at
home, I would only dissipate my little fortune, and ruin what
I intend shall compensate my little ones, for the stigma I have brought
on their names.' The letter was written in Mauchline, almost a year
after the publication of his poems, but shows that Burns's national
triumph had failed to secure his future or the well-being of his
children. The sense of displacement first registered so strongly in
Edinburgh persisted after his return to Ayrshire and, with it, self-
punishing reflections on his own destructive character. His favourite
hero, by now, was Satan, because Milton had shown how a strong
character could still rise above a self-induced Hell to display admirable
qualities. Satan was permanently exiled from his original home in
heaven and could not 'find place or refuge' on earth—but he did not
give up.[58] Not only did Satan represent unyielding independence—
something Burns valued very highly—but also a consistency irre-
spective of location. Resemblance to Satan, which had once seemed
horrifying, now afforded a kind of cold comfort.

Beneath Burns's irreverent bravado was an even more complicated
identification with Milton's character and his self-created misery.

During the summer of 1787, Burns, gripped with anxiety over his inability to settle 'to the serious business of life', tried to analyse his restlessness: 'I have almost ruined one source, the principal one indeed, of my former happiness; that eternal propensity I always had to fall in love. My heart no more glows with feverish rapture. I have no paradisical evening interviews stolen from the restless cares and prying inhabitants of this weary world. I have only *****'.[59] The letter goes on to describe a recent conquest, but Burns's self-presentation as 'an old hawk' bringing down a 'mounting lark' suggests that his victory had brought little satisfaction. This moment of self-disgust and rueful reflection suggests a different kind of identification with Milton's Satan from those of his more bullish statements. It also sheds further light on the shades of his 'Address to Edinburgh', whose circularity and lack of direction may reflect that of a poet who feared the fate of Satan, even as he resigned himself to it:

> Me miserable, which way shall I fly,
> Infinite wrath and infinite despair?
> Which way I fly is Hell, myself am Hell.[60]

'Address to Edinburgh' is a farewell to Mossgiel on landing in a new world, but its lack of progress and lame conclusion point to the same kind of uncertainty that Burns was experiencing: 'I am still "dark as was Chaos" in respect to Futurity.'[61] There is very little sense that the road ahead was clear or that Burns was poised for greatness—in his letters the future is painted as, at best, a zig-zag, at worst, a black pit. Despite Burns's personal uncertainty and the critical tradition of seeing a post-Kilmarnock downward slide, however, it is also possible to see his experimentation with entirely new voices as a crucial part of his growth as a poet. Burns, having made such an accomplished poetic debut, was faced with an especially difficult version of the 'second book syndrome'—but out of his struggle came works of art that may have been different in kind but were great nonetheless.

Edinburgh was a difficult environment, but it was there that Burns began to understand the real value of his background and, especially, of Scottish song culture. As his appreciation of Scottish song deepened, he did not abandon his earlier techniques, but developed them in new directions for his creative energies. Unlike the uneasy voice that addressed Edinburgh, the song lyrics allowed the colloquial immediacy reminiscent of the Kilmarnock poems in forms accessible to everyone. To become Caledonia's Bard was initially rather daunting, but the songs that flowed in the wake of the Edinburgh edition had a new inclusiveness that seemed to embrace the whole of the Scottish people. Some of his songs would be tributes to his new home in Dumfriesshire, some to places he visited only briefly, and some would transport singers and audiences back to the time of the Bruce, Mary Queen of Scots or the Jacobite Risings. As a song-writer, Burns began to discover what he admired so much in Milton's Satan—something that remained the same, unchanged by place or time.

Burns's song-writing has sometimes been understood largely as a response to commissions from Edinburgh publishers—a matter of business rather than of personal artistic expression. The question of authorship adds a further complication, since many of the songs attributed to Burns are either adaptations of earlier pieces or written entirely by someone else. Such a problematic body poses difficulties to those whose judgements of great poetry assume that originality and single authorship are fundamental. Song collecting, adapting, and writing nevertheless formed a crucial part of Burns's development as a poet—and as a man. As he explained to Mrs Dunlop in a letter written on his thirty-first birthday, 'Old Scots Songs are, you know, a favourite study & pursuit of mine', and it was because he took the pursuit so seriously that his work has been so successful and long-lasting.[62]

Scottish Songs

Burns's desire to write about his local area and please his old companions did not diminish, but he could not remain unaffected by the wider audience for his work after his visit to Edinburgh. Though deeply unsettled by his sudden fame and associated expectations, he was being lauded as a genius and knew that he had things to teach those who considered themselves his social superiors. The difficulty lay in persuading them that his ideas and sentiments were worth taking seriously, rather than merely courting attention as a natural prodigy or curious phenomenon. One way to achieve a more serious response to his work was to present rural, Scottish material in conjunction with elements drawn from other cultures, while still

maintaining the inherent value of the homegrown. This was one of
the strategies used in 'To W. S.', with its reference to the Illissus and
preference for the Doon. When he came to write 'The Banks of the
Nith' for the *Scots Musical Museum* in 1790, Burns once again elevated
a Scottish river through comparison with a more famous southern
counterpart, asserting that, though 'The Thames flows proudly to
the sea, | Where royal cities stand…sweeter flows the Nith, to
me, | Where Cummins ance had high command'. Even as Burns
attempted to make his local stream shine more brightly, however, his
language was recalling Dryden's celebration of the Thames in 'Annus
Mirabilis' and thus reminding his audience of the much-admired
glories of the famous English river. The task of elevating his own
country was fraught with complications, for, if the rhetorical strategy
of drawing comparisons with well-established coordinates actually
turned the mind of his audience to thoughts of earlier poems and
other places, it was decidedly counter-productive. On the other
hand, it was crucial to Burns's enterprise that he should include signs
of his broader knowledge, for fear of being regarded as, at best,
narrow and provincial, and, at worst, downright ignorant. To insist
that your own river is the best in the world seems unpersuasive to
those who suspect you have never heard of any others.

Burns could reveal his knowledge only with great care and
subtlety, however, since his self-presentation as the 'simple bard' was
crucial to his popularity, as well as to the persuasive power of his
writing. So, he was faced with something of a dilemma. How could
a poet elevate his local area, without reference to places better known
and more richly drenched in cultural associations? In the verse epistle
'To W. S****n', he had dealt with the problem by projecting his trans-
formation of Ayrshire into the future and couching his ambitions in
a light-hearted, colloquial exchange with another local poet. When
it came to writing poems in direct celebration of neglected spots,
however, it was more difficult to open the gates to other literary
rivers without the risk of inundation. He might assert that the Nith
flowed more sweetly than the Thames as far as he was concerned,
but whether this would be persuasive to those more familiar with the
Thames was another matter. Burns was the first major poet to grapple
with the perennial difficulty facing writers whose work is essentially
local—its capacity to interest those who are not already familiar with
the location. This was one of his major attractions for Scott, who was

to become the Border Minstrel, and for Wordsworth, the Lake Poet.

The need to reveal wider knowledge in order to give weight to his admiration for local culture was a key element in the development of Burns's mature work. In the Kilmarnock edition, he had tried to indicate that his language and subjects resulted from choice rather than necessity by including several poems in Standard English on topics fashionable in contemporary literary circles. The volume's reception showed that not everyone had noticed this, however, and so Burns needed other ways of asserting his authority. He needed patrons, but hated being patronized, as his outbursts about 'kings, lords, clergy, critics, &c.' make clear, but it was a difficult situation for a poet of his ambition, ability, and background to negotiate.

Burns's desire to tour Scotland and collect songs from different parts of the country was part of his response to the difficult situation that developed after the publication of the *Poems, Chiefly in the Scottish Dialect*. Having decided to launch himself on the public as a rustic bard, Burns felt the need to disguise many of his literary borrowings, but he could be quite open about a wide knowledge of Scotland's landscape and history. These were things that would give him authority, without smelling too much of the lamp. Touring would provide materials for the kinds of comparison needed to make his local celebrations more persuasive, and so, in 1787, after the publication of the Edinburgh edition, he embarked on tours of the Borders and the Highlands. Before he left, he wrote to Mrs Dunlop with a patriotic flourish:

The appellation of, a Scotch Bard, is by far my highest pride; to continue to deserve it is my most exalted ambition.—Scottish scenes, and Scottish story are the themes I could wish to sing.—I have no greater, no dearer aim than to have it in my power, unplagu'd with the routine of business, for which Heavens knows I am unfit enough, to make leisurely pilgrimages through Caledonia; to sit on the fields of her battles; to wonder on the romantic banks of her rivers; and to muse by the stately tower or venerable ruins, once the honored abodes of her heroes.[63]

Burns's aims were still consistent with those expressed in 'The Vision', but now, crucially, he was extending his sphere beyond Kyle to the whole of Scotland.

As he travelled through the different parts of the country, he collected experiences, images, songs, and measures, which prompted some spontaneous composition and provided materials and models for the rest of his creative career. Sometimes, he composed on the spot, inspired by his encounter with a lovely sight or beautiful melody; at other times different elements took longer to fuse. When he reached Aberfeldy in Perthshire, the composition prompted by the beautiful Falls was conditioned by an older song, 'The Birks of Abergeldie'. Abergeldie was much further north, near Balmoral, but, for Burns, the sound of a place, its literary qualities, and its associations were just as important as its physical beauty. Despite the contemporary assumption that Burns was an untutored genius, whose poems burst out like a force of nature, he was a highly skilled and discriminating reader and listener, with an extraordinarily retentive memory. He possessed not only a wonderful eye for the world around him, but also a sharp ear for airs and snatches and, crucially, an inner ear that turned what he absorbed into a rich internal landscape of rhythmic lines and rhymes. Burns had been experiencing traditional songs since his childhood and now he was actively replenishing this vital resource and, in the process, his own creative talent. He had embarked on an expedition of discovery—and recovery.

Burns's skills in fusing first-hand experience with acquired material were honed through touring. 'The Banks of the Devon' was a compliment to Charlotte Hamilton, sister of Gavin, Burns's friend, patron, and recipient of the 'Dedication to G***H****', who now lived in Clackmannanshire, but it was set to a Gaelic air that he heard being played in Inverness. The song was a rapid response to a number of different influences—human, musical, and geographical—but Burns was also storing impressions away, waiting for just the right combination of influences and circumstances. He visited the site of Bannockburn, for example, in September 1787, but several years passed before he composed 'Scots wha hae'. By that time, Burns had heard the air that was believed to be Bruce's battle march all over Scotland and, prompted by the outbreak of war with Revolutionary France in 1793, he composed words to fit the tune. The famous song was partly a personal response to a place, but the meaning of the place itself had been created over centuries and took on an urgent contemporary dimension during the moment of international crisis.

Burns's songs blended old and new, private and public, which is why they instantly appealed to his contemporaries and have continued to draw in audiences ever since. Burns's treatment of

public and historic themes almost always emphasized a personal
dimension, whether derived from his own experience or from his
imaginative sympathy with those involved. Seeing a place properly
involved the imagination just as much as the eye and, as Words-
worth noticed, 'natural appearances rarely take a lead' in Burns's
poetry, because his prime interest was always in human feelings and
stories.[64] When Wordsworth followed Burns in touring Scotland in
1803, his own views were constantly coloured by Burns's work, and
later he reflected that, when Burns spoke of 'rivers, hills, and woods,
it is not so much on account of the properties with which they are
absolutely endowed, as... to local patriotic remembrances and
associations, or as they are ministerial to personal feelings, espe-
cially those of love'.[65] No wonder Dorothy Wordsworth found the
apparently empty stretches of Scottish countryside to be 'inhabited
solitudes'.

As Burns travelled across Scotland, he was collecting more than
songs, sights, and stories—he was deepening his understanding of
human nature and discovering just what man had made of man. His
heart may have stirred at the memory of Wallace or the Bruce, but it
was just as affected by thoughts of the unsung heroes and the feelings
of those whose names had not been recorded in public history. By
recovering and rewriting popular songs, Burns was giving a new life
to something that belonged to the Scottish people. While he politely
paid lyrical compliments to those who graciously invited him into
their castles, he was just as inclined to pick up a piece of a drinking
song and make it whole. During his tour of the Borders, Burns jotted
down the first lines of a traditional song, 'There was a lass they called
her Meg', and developed it into a much more down-to-earth love
song than some of the 'compliments' he offered to wealthy ladies.
'All the Lads o' Thornie Bank' celebrated the ale-house at Buckie, a
fishing village on the east coast, which Burns visited in September
1787 on his way to meet relatives at Stonehaven. In widening his
horizons and discovering other areas of Scotland, he was also recov-
ering parts of himself—and recognizing that personal identity, like
local and national identity, was as much a confluence as a single pure
source. Song was, therefore, the perfect medium for Burns, allowing
him kinds of freedom that seemed unattainable to a poet so much in
the public eye. The cherished ideal of Liberty might, after all, be
realized through anonymity.

His songs drew on traditional materials that belonged to everyone and no one, but they were blended with personal references—to people Burns met, to places he visited, to things he had done, and to opinions he held. The formulaic nature of Scottish song meant that the personal could be disguised within the traditional and, conversely, the private could be immortalized within the universal. In 'Yon Wild Mossy Mountains', for example, Burns created a timeless folk song about a 'sweet Lassie' who lived by the Clyde, but he admitted in a note that 'the song alludes to a part of my private history, which it is of no consequence to the world to know'.[66] Whether he was referring to a secret love affair remains unclear, but the reference to 'private history' might also be a way of signalling to the political sympathies of a poem celebrating a lassie 'humble as humble can be' (l. 15), which were becoming dangerous to express by 1792 when the song was published. Whatever the private history might have been, through song, Burns both kept it hidden and gave it permanent existence. Often Burns seemed to be striving for the impersonality of timeless lyric, while leaving his distinctive traces everywhere. 'The White Cockade', for example, evokes the campaign of Charles Edward Stuart, but, even as Burns turns the traditional ballad into a Jacobite song, he still put part of himself into it, because the chorus, 'O he's a ranting roving lad', is so like that of his autobiographical song, 'There was a Lad'. The use of formulaic phrases and refrains allowed for additional dimensions to the simplest lyrics. Once a connection has been made between 'There was a Lad' and 'The White Cockade', Burns's own sentimental Jacobitism, stirred during the Highland tours, becomes evident, as well as his awareness of the human costs associated with those rare, charismatic, rantin, rovin lads, who inspire such a devoted following. Burns's travels were imaginative and internal as well as physical, so his songs are a testament, not only to his skill as an adapter, but to his progress as 'a man and a poet'.

Burns's poems were never a straightforward record of the world immediately around him. Though first-hand observations and habitual experience of his home ensured a documentary truthfulness, he was never first and foremost a local reporter. Ayrshire was vital to his sense of self, but it was not the sole source of his writing, which always tempered its parish detail with the formal adequacy of well-made verse. Thomas Carlyle described Burns's talent as a

fountain, bursting from 'the depths of the earth, with a full gushing
current, into the light of day', but his talent was more like a more
mature river, into which numerous tributaries flowed.[67] Currie had
seen the importance of traditional songs for the growth of Burns's
poetic talent and local attachments, but his mind was also well
stocked with the lyrics he had read. His poems frequently drew on
inner wells of oral and literary memory to meet the needs of the
moment, but his resources were not exclusively Scottish. Burns's
skill in fusing different cultural streams meant that he could adapt
very varied sources and still produce a song that seemed entirely
natural and native. If the different influences had seemed to collide
almost unmanageably in 'Address to the Deil', the lyrical beauty of
Burns's songs made any incongruities evaporate. Even where some
elements had most obviously been drawn from remote places,
Burns's mastery of Scottish metres and accents meant they could
still be blended into a harmonious whole. It is obvious from the first
line of 'O were I on Parnassus Hill' that the songwriter is keen to
emphasize his knowledge of classical literature, but, as the idiom
shifts to Scots, the opening line gives way to a celebration of local
inspiration:

> O were I on Parnassus Hill;
>   Or had o' Helicon my fill;
> That I might catch poetic skill,
>   To sing how dear I love thee.
> But Nith maun be my Muses well,
> My Muse maun be thy bonie sell;
> On Corsincon I'll glowr and spell,
>   And write how dear I love thee.[68]

Burns has invoked classical tradition humorously in order to acknowl-
edge, in Scots, the more immediate inspiration of the Nith and his
beloved. If in one sense, Burns mocks himself for being restricted to
his Scottish surroundings, his allusion to the classical 'Muses well'
demands a plural and thus opens the verse to another meaning—that
the Nith will offer inspiration just 'as well'. In other words, it can be
a personal Helicon not unlike Heaney's.
    Although the song can therefore be read as a rejection of book-
learning in favour of first-hand experience, which gives it affinities
with some of the verse epistles, the speaker's attitude is complicated
by the deeply allusive character of the song. As Kinsley noted in his

commentary, the idea of not being at Parnassus was itself borrowed
directly from Dryden's translation of the Persius—

> I never did on cleft *Parnassus* dream,
> Nor taste the sacred *Heliconian* Stream.[69]

The very words chosen to celebrate his local sources were weighted
with the sediment of earlier writings—for beneath Burns's verse was
Dryden and beneath Dryden, Persius, himself a Roman poet
lamenting his distance from classical Greece. What appeared to be a
simple, comic rejection of literary tradition was actually an echo of
a complaint stretching back through centuries, which linked Burns
to a distinguished band of self-effacing poets. Dryden's introduction
to his translation explained that Persius's design was to 'conceal his
name and quality' by presenting himself as nothing but a 'beggarly
poet', when in fact his aims were serious and political. It is easy to see
the attraction of such a figure for Burns, who was paying a subtle,
and entirely appropriate, tribute to this secretive poet, even as he
appeared to uphold the satisfactions of the simple life. Although
Burns had not concealed his social background, his own presenta-
tion as a ploughman had provided a cover for expressing serious
literary and political opinions, which he continued to articulate in
his songs.

   Though songs such as 'O were I on Parnassus' were not overtly
political, the desire to celebrate the value of his homely muse was
fundamental to Burns's sense of himself as a spokesman for the
common man. The political charge of his love songs derived not so
much from their patriotic dimension, but from the social outlook
and insistence that fundamental aspects of the human condition are
shared by rich and poor alike. In his letter to Moore, Burns had tried
to explain the importance of love to those not blessed with material
fortune: 'To the sons and daughters of labor and poverty', he wrote,
these 'are matters of the most serious nature: to them the ardent
hope, the stolen interview, the tender farewell, are the greatest and
most delicious part of their enjoyments'.[70] Unlike the love lyrics of
court poets, the songs sung by those employed in hard agricultural
labour reflected the most important thing in their lives—as Burns
observed succinctly in one of his bawdier numbers, 'Poor bodies hae
nothing but mowe'.[71] In 'O were I on Parnassus', Burns was keen to
show that a humble sphere was no bar to classical and literary

knowledge, but he also emphasized that his 'muse' was a full-bodied lass, with 'tempting lips' and 'roguish een', offering, in other words, a kind of inspiration that could move men at every social level. The song was at once a display and a rebuttal of his education, reflecting the complicated conflicts confronting Burns after the publication of his *Poems*.

The complicated strategies Burns developed for blending allusions into his songs were also helpful for adapting the different literary traditions of Scotland. 'Song.—Composed at Oughtertyre on Miss Euphemia Murray of Lentrose', for example, used Burns's newly acquired knowledge of different areas of Scotland to pay tribute to 'a bonier lass | Than braes o'Yarrow ever saw' (l. 4). The singer appears to uphold the authority of empirical truth by showing that his assessment is based on extensive observation:

> The Highland Hills I've wander'd wide,
>   And o'er the lawlands I hae been;
> But Phemie was the blythest lass
>   That ever trode the dewy green.   (ll. 17–20)

Beneath the gently self-mocking voice of one whose eye for a pretty woman has been carefully trained in his travels, however, lay the same awareness of literary geography that Burns had addressed so forthrightly in the epistle to Simpson. Thoughts of competing places were now more carefully submerged, however, in lines that seemed to flow from the central emotion of the lyric. When Phemie is described as 'bonnier than braes of Yarrow ever saw', Burns was recalling William Hamilton's well-known ballad, 'The Braes of Yarrow', and thus making a further retort to the more famous rivers of Scotland. As literary rivalry was absorbed into a love song, however, its undercurrent merely added quiet depths rather than diverting listeners into other channels of thought.

The shift of focus from the rivers of south-west Scotland to other regions, such as Strathearn in the Highlands, demonstrates that, though Burns had challenged himself to sing about his own surroundings, he was no longer motivated by a desire to prove that Kyle was the best place in the world. It might be dear to him and therefore the setting of some of his poetry, but there was no reason to persuade readers that his home was better than their own. In fact, when Burns urged Willie Simson to sing about Kyle, just as Ramsay and

Fergusson had sung about the Tay and the Forth, he may not after all have been suggesting that Ayrshire was more beautiful or more important historically, but rather that it was *equally* fertile ground for poetry. When he moved to Dumfriesshire in 1787, he commented that 'The Banks of the Nith are as sweet, poetic ground as any I saw', and, if it flowed more sweetly than the Thames, it was because of his personal attachment to the place.[72] Even when Burns composed songs that indulged in local boasting, such as 'Braw, braw Lads on Yarrow braes', it is obvious that the singer's admiration for the lads of Galla rather than Yarrow is based on her very personal attachment to one of them. Burns was again playing down the braes of Yarrow as inferior, but the song makes clear that the assessment is not being made on literary grounds.

This helps to explain why Burns could write such moving lyrics about places that he visited for the first time only in 1787. By then, his purpose was not so much the elevation of Ayrshire at the expense of the rest of the country, but rather the revelation of the special character of numerous places and, especially, their human dimensions. If he had initially felt that his purpose was to elevate auld Kyle above the rest of Scotland, his travels helped him to understand that almost everywhere had imaginative value, because everywhere was steeped in hidden stories and human experience. In song after song, Burns captured particular feelings, thus colouring the names of the places in the songs with human emotions and hidden narratives. In 'The Vision' he had expressed his local attachments through the figure of a strikingly physical young woman, but in many of his later compositions the Scottish landscape simply becomes part of a love song. The rivers flowing through the songs often reflect the speaker's feelings and acquire a particular personality in the process, which imbues them with a mythic power that yet seems entirely natural.

'Afton Water' demonstrates Burns's power to mythologize a landscape, as he urges 'Sweet Afton' not to disturb the dreams of his slumbering Mary. The tender song is typical of Burns's capacity to link love, poetry, and natural surroundings with a melody that blends them perfectly. If it suggests a quiet idyll quite remote from the tough life and rural poverty experienced by Burns himself, the feelings expressed still carry conviction because of the real setting. Just as Currie noted in relation to traditional Scottish song, the particular place and authentic details gave the human emotion credibility. If the dove at Afton Water seems to have flown in from conventional pastoral poetry of the period, it is given substance by becoming a stock-dove, surrounded by whistling blackbirds and screaming lapwings. The sounds of the scene evoke real birds, while at the same time imbuing them with human characteristics, so they provide a natural chorus for the murmuring stream at the centre of the song. The lapwing is also 'green-crested', a detail that suggests first-hand observation of the bird in bright sunlight, as well as carrying romantic suggestions of a knight protecting Mary as she sleeps. The existence of Afton Water as a real not imaginary place enabled Burns to create the idealized image of 'Mary' and her cot, in a song that could convey delicate feelings and still ring true. As Burns explained to Mrs Dunlop:

There is a small river, Afton, that falls into Nith near New Cumnock, which has some charming, wild romantic scenery on its banks.—I have a particular pleasure in those little pieces of poetry such as our Scots songs, &c, where the names and landskip-features of rivers, lakes, or woodlands, that one knows, are introduced—I attempted a compliment of that kind, to Afton.[73]

The song is 'a compliment' to the place—'Flow gently, I'll sing thee a song in thy praise'—but, as with so many of Burns's best songs, it seems to be about something other than the place itself. Human feelings imbued places with meaning, just as the detail of the real place made the emotion credible—their wholeness embodied local attachment.

Though Burns was evidently engaging in the same sort of project that he had outlined in 'The Vision', the letter about 'Afton Water' reflects his widening range in the years following the publication of the *Poems*. The choice of the Afton, a tributary of the Nith in Dumfriesshire, shows a willingness to extend his scope beyond Coila's domain and to enter the feelings of those less familiar to him personally. As Wordsworth realized, Burns avoided writing directly about places, but nevertheless developed ways of giving their names an unforgettable resonance. The situations of his speakers are rarely spelled out, but their moods are conveyed with great clarity— whether blithe, melancholy, tender, or indignant. Scottish place names accordingly become fixed in the minds of listeners with an accompanying emotional charge, which enables a powerful imaginative response to places encountered only through song. Burns had discovered that places acquired their value through the special feelings invested there and by the skills of those whose metres matched the states of mind. His songs were a celebration of human passion and a means of making permanent something that was inevitably mortal.

As Burns attempted to capture moments that were at once profound and fleeting, he often turned to the kind of natural images that could convey such elusive feelings. Again and again, his songs featured rivers, streams, and flowing water. This was partly a natural response to his upbringing in a country with fine, varied streams—so much a part of Ayrshire and yet the means of connection to the wider world. The image of a local river offered the security of the familiar, while resisting any sense of stagnation, its endless movement a perpetual source of life and energy. Burns was also inspired by the impressive sights he encountered on his travels—the Falls of Aberfeldy, the pass at Killiecrankie, the River Devon, the Earn, the Clyde. Some of his subjects were recognized beauty spots, some deserved to be much better known. Burns paid compliments to the renowned and neglected alike. His choices were influenced, too, by venerable traditions of river writing, Scottish, English, classical, which Burns admired and wished to emulate in his highly individual manner. In 'The Vision', he had followed literary example by referring to the rivers in human terms—'Well-fed Irwine' and 'Auld hermit Aire' recalled the parade of rivers in 'Lycidas', which in turn alluded to Virgil's addresses to the Mincius. In his songs, Burns continued to bring the landscape to life, but in a less studied way, so that the words, perfectly blended with the music, seemed as natural as the rivers themselves.

But, beneath it all, ran a deeper sense of affinity with the eternal movement and variety of Scottish rivers. Burns's identity with the local streams—the burns that he wanted to make shine—ran deep. He described his own life in terms of a 'flow', and, in 'To W. S****n', he painted the young poet discovering his Muse and himself on the banks of a stream:

> The *Muse*, nae *Poet* ever fand her,
> Till by himsel he learn'd to wander,

> Adown some trotting burn's meander,
>   An' no think lang;
> O sweet, to stray an' pensive ponder
>   A heart-felt sang!   (ll. 85–90)

This is an image not just of a young poet, drinking his inspiration
from his natural surroundings, but of one who is searching for self-
knowledge, since wandering down 'some trotting burn's meander' is
a metaphor for Burns's constant study of the zig-zags in his life.
When Wordsworth concluded his own sonnet sequence on 'one of
the most beautiful streams of his native country', he quoted this verse
to illustrate 'the power of waters over the minds of poets' in all
times.[74] For both Wordsworth and Burns, however, the wild, flowing
waters of their mountain homes had special meaning.

   Rivers offered Burns a way of representing his own internal jour-
neys, as well as providing images of human life in general. Though
many of his poems celebrated the creative energy of the youthful
bardie, there were also numerous reflections on the passage of time
and the fear of dim-declining age. In the songs, the human situation
being evoked often suggests a deep awareness of transience, the very
power of the lyric depending on the underlying current of wistful-
ness. Feelings are intensified by the acute sense of actual or immi-
nent change, while the flow of the river mirrors both the movement
of the music and the endless passage of time. The lyric, so beautifully
constructed, so firmly in place, both arrests the flow momentarily
and emphasizes its unstoppable power. The rhythmic lines are easily
memorized and so rapidly acquire a permanent place in the mental
landscape, even as the words themselves are reminders of the brevity
of an intense moment. Rivers have a similar permanence in the land-
scape that is rarely achieved by towns and cities, even though the
water that rushes along is different from one hour to the next. Free
and uncontainable, like Burns's songs, rivers could be enjoyed by
everyone, high and low, young and old, male and female.[75] Songs
offered Burns a new kind of freedom, because they seemed to acquire
a life of their own as they passed from person to person, and from
place to place. In song-writing, the name of the lyricist is often much
less familiar than the lyrics and so, if Burns could write songs that
would immortalize the rivers of his own land, his own identity
would be permanently assured, though oddly invisible. The indi-
vidual might dissolve in song, but, through this very immersion, he

would live for ever: his words shining through the burns that were being sung by distant audiences and generations.

Burns had announced his intention to 'sing' auld Coila's 'banks and braes' in 1786, and, within five years, he had composed the song that would make the 'Banks and Braes of Bonny Doon' familiar to people all over the world. It was a very beautiful song, destined to be enjoyed by generations of people, many of whom would know nothing of the River Doon or its poet. The verse nevertheless carries the sense of real human feeling in a real place, thus enabling audiences to participate in its emotion. The broken-hearted speaker sees the eternal beauty of the Doon as a sign of the river's indifference to her plight, but then comes to understand its perpetual movement as an image of passing time. Initially at odds with the scene, she is rapidly absorbed into it—her happiness as irretrievable as the waters that flow away into the sea:

> Ye banks and braes o' bonie Doon,
>   How can ye bloom sae fresh and fair;
> How can ye chant, ye little birds,
>   And I sae weary, fu' o'care!
> Thou'll break my heart, thou warbling bird,
>   That wantons thro' the flowering thorn:
> Thou minds me o' departed joys,
>   Departed, never to return.   (ll. 1–8)

The language is carefully chosen to convey the powerful yearning for departed joys, for nothing rhymes exactly with Doon, though many of the words seem to be reaching towards it—'bloom', 'thorn', 'return'—and, in the second stanza, 'twine', 'mine', and 'thorn' again. The Doon is emphatically there, yet for ever slipping away like the false lover and the delights of youth. It is both a distillation of broken love in all time and places and a love poem to Burns's dear, but now distant, native country, uttered in the distinct language of his home.

Burns was still aiming to create places that would attain a permanent place in the minds of people near and far, but 'The Banks of Doon' was neither an argument nor a manifesto. The form of such a poem seems perfectly suited to the situation, the feeling, and the setting, creating a wholeness or 'in-placeness', which is self-sufficient as well as inviting. Instead of expressing rivalry with other places, many of Burns's songs had an inherent beauty that transcended the

need for comparison. And, once Burns's expressions of local attach-
ment are seen not in competition with other traditions, communi-
ties, and places, but rather as part of his own personal quest for poetic
truth, then their astonishingly widespread and long-lasting appeal is
easier to understand. Burns hailed his editor, James Johnson, as a
great Scottish patriot and benefactor, because he had come to believe
in the power of song to outlive 'the neglects of idle fashion, & defy
the Teeth of time'.[76] In 'The Banks o'Doon' or 'A red red rose', Burns
acknowledged that water was a moment bright, then gone for ever,
while rose petals, however lovely, cannot last long. Though the songs
often insisted on the eternal nature of feeling, they also reminded
audiences of the inevitable course of life and the impossibility of
resisting change and decay. Their beauty was nevertheless intensified
by what it resisted, whether the dryness of life's moving sands or the
bare thorns of the plucked rose. Even the apocalyptic horror of rocks
melting into the sun were quietly answered by the harmonious flow
of the lyric, which seems momentarily more powerful. Through
singing auld Coila, Burns had learned to create the most mobile kind
of poetry.

Remember Tam o'Shanter's Mare

The new confidence that came from Burns's work as a songwriter
also infused some of the poetry he composed after the move to
Dumfriesshire. Now that he had realized the creative potential of
resuscitating traditional materials, new possibilities began to open
up. His sense of himself as a national figure with a responsibility
to include rather than exclude fellow countrymen is evident in the
'Address to the People of Scotland', which he published in the
Edinburgh Evening Courant:

> Hear, Land o' Cakes, and brither Scots
> Frae Maidenkirk to Johny Groats!—[77]

Burns was once again adopting the 'Address' for a public poem,
whose audience is less easily defined than an individual object, but
this poem had neither the satirical assertiveness of the addresses 'to
the Deil' or 'the Unco Guid', nor the uncertainty of the 'Address to
Edinburgh'. Instead, his tone was generally fraternal, as he directed

brither Scots to welcome an unlikely English visitor—the 'fine, fat, fodgel wight | O' stature short, but genius bright'—Captain Francis Grose, the antiquarian. When the poem finally turned to address Grose himself, its affectionate camaraderie was entirely consistent with the preceding description. Burns was ready enough to point out the comic aspects of Grose's antiquarian pursuits, but the joke was being shared with Grose and the entire Scottish nation. It could hardly differ more from Burns's satires, with their specific targets and delight in mockery. Burns had not abandoned his more hard-hitting style, but he was also turning his hand to a new kind of art, reminiscent of earlier poems, but less assertive about its specific regional origins.

By 1793, when the poem was included in the enlarged edition of Burns's *Poems*, Francis Grose was dead and the 'Address' became 'On the Late Captain Grose's Peregrinations through Scotland'. As he renamed the poem, Burns was paying a debt of gratitude to the man who had prompted the composition of 'Tam o' Shanter', which he recognized as his most accomplished work, displaying 'a force of genius and a finishing polish' that he despaired of ever excelling.[78] It was also the poem that allowed Burns to return imaginatively to Kyle, reconsidering his earlier aims and influences, reviewing his life and achievements, and reaffirming his skill in creating truly adequate poetry. Burns's Muse had not abandoned him when he left Mossgiel for Edinburgh in 1786, but she had led him to new regions that required different kinds of poetry.

'Tam o'Shanter' made its first public appearance in Francis Grose's handsome two-volume quarto, *The Antiquities of Scotland*, in April 1791. Burns and Grose met at the home of mutual friends and quickly discovered common interests in local history, non-standard speech, and convivial company.[79] Burns was happy to help Grose identify the Ayrshire sites worthy of inclusion in his magisterial antiquarian survey of Scotland, but made a special request that Kirk Alloway be included. Grose agreed, on the condition that Burns composed an accompanying poem based on local legend, partly perhaps because he could not find a great deal to say about the little ruined Kirk. When the volume appeared, each of the Alloway pages had only three lines of Grose's prose, but underneath ran more than 200 lines of Burns's poetry: 'Tam o'Shanter' is probably the most important footnote in literary history. The engraving of the modest church stands out among the castles, abbeys, and archaeological sites even before the reader encounters the startling voice below the lines of the official text. This is Burns's real 'Address to the People of Scotland', because it gives the people who had neither estates nor power a vital place in Scotland's history. When restored to its original context in the antiquarian guidebook, its intimate connection with Alloway— Burns's birthplace and the site of his father's grave—is abundantly clear. Through his friendly deal with Grose, Burns secured a place for his father among the antiquities of Scotland, in a magnificent volume, leather-bound for posterity.

'Tam o'Shanter' reveals Burns as both Caledonia's bard and the lad born in Kyle, as a poet true to his roots and his reading. Its imaginative force gains conviction from the details of local places and the human associations that make them so memorable:

> By this time he was cross the ford,
> Whare, in the snaw, the chapman smoor'd;
> And past the birks and meikle stane,
> Whare drunken Charlie brak's neck-bane;
> And thro' the whins, and by the cairn,
> Whare hunters found the murder'd bairn;
> And near the thorn, aboon the well,
> Whare Mungo's mither hang'd herself.—   (ll. 89–96)

The catalogue of local horrors is delivered as if by someone speaking to an audience who will know the full stories behind drunken Charlie's accident and Mungo's mother's suicide. It was a technique developed in the Kilmarnock edition, which Burns was now revisiting as he returned, imaginatively, to Alloway. The witches tale gains credibility from the preparatory local detail, but the terrifying stories that mark Tam's nocturnal progress suggest a certain ambivalence about his intimate knowledge of the route. Burns's tale exploits the power of local truth, but in doing so reveals his resistance as well as attraction to the area that had been home for most of his life. As Scott found when he began working on the Border ballads and as Burns himself had explained to Dr Moore, local attachments were not without their darker sides.

Burns was now drawing imaginatively on Betty Davidson's legacy, by reviving the kind of tale that had made such an indelible impression on his young mind. 'Tam o'Shanter', as he explained to Grose, derived from the 'many Witch Stories...relating to Aloway Kirk',

absorbed in youth and restored in adulthood, like snatches of song.[80]
The self-conscious return to early memories seemed to demand
distancing strategies, but now, instead of the antiquarian headnote
he had written for 'Halloween', Burns indicated his perspective
through his choice of form and narration. The tetrameter couplets,
so well suited to Tam's ride, were unlike any of the forms in the
Kilmarnock edition and suggested the combined influences of
Ramsay and Fergusson, Swift and Butler. Burns's new poem, like his
songs, blended memories of local experience with brilliant invention
in a well-tried literary form that was fully adequate to the purpose.

Though insistently grounded in Alloway, the skilful use of the
third person imposes a distance between the narrator and his story,
insisting on its wider interest:

> While we sit bousing at the nappy,
> And getting fou an unco happy,
> We think na on the lang Scots miles,
> The mosses, waters, slaps, and styles.   (ll. 5–8)

Though different in kind from Burns's song lyrics, the narrative
poem still shares their inclusiveness and ability to crystallize general
truths in simple language, while retaining the earlier poems' capacity
to mock their own speaker. 'Tam o'Shanter' is similarly addressed to
both the wider audience of traditional song and the more immediate
objects of the poems, its listeners undefined by name but understood
by nature. Burns adopts the voice of an experienced storyteller, who
might be entertaining people in an Ayrshire pub, but it also invites
attention from anyone who might be reading the poem:

> Now, wha this tale o'truth shall read,
> Ilk man and mother's son, take heed.   (ll. 219–20)

'Tam o'Shanter' begins and ends by emphasizing its own truths,
which are both local and universal, while the body of the poem
explores the nature of belief. Its status as fiction is persistently empha-
sized, but so are its non-literal truths.

The poem's self-reflexive character is most apparent when the narra-
tive flow is broken by direct addresses to 'Tam!', the 'gentle dames'
who might be reading the tale, or 'Inspiring bold John Barleycorn!',
who gives Dutch courage to all comers. Burns was incorporating
the poetic address into the longer poem in order to add suspense

and mock morality with well-timed interruptions—'O *Tam*! Hadst thou but been sae wise, | As ta'en thy ain wife *Kate's* advice!' (ll. 17–18), 'Now, *Tam*, O *Tam*, had they been queans, | A' plump and strapping in their teens...But withered beldams, auld and droll, | Rigwoodie hags wad spean a foal' (ll. 151–60). By including addresses within the fast-paced and mounting excitement of the main narrative, Burns was able to draw attention to the shared nature of the narrative—'But to our tale' (l. 37). For all its local truth and the documentary accuracy of its detail, 'Tam o'Shanter' persistently emphasized its formal truth as a good story well told in the rhymes, rhythms, metaphors, and allusions that helped to create its final power. If Burns drew on the traditional stories of his child-hood, he was also recalling the self-consciousness of the modern novels he was reading in 1790 when he wrote the poem.[81] *Tristram Shandy* frequently masqueraded as a conversation with different readers and devoted as much attention to its own status as a creation as to any narrative action.

Burns's literariness is nowhere more evident than in 'Tam o'Shanter', for all its pretence to being a simple local tale retold for the entertainment of readers of antiquities. For in 'Tam O'Shanter', as Burns meditated on Alloway, his birthplace and perhaps his own final destination, he was also revisiting his own imaginative life. While the comic-Gothic reflected contemporary literary tastes and the oral tales he had known since his youth, it was also revisiting his own exploration of mental belief in 'Address to the Deil'. Numerous poems are present in 'Tam o'Shanter', from the obvious recollections of 'John Barleycorn', 'Scotch Drink', 'Halloween', 'The Auld Mare, Maggie', and 'The Brigs of Ayr' in the detail of the main story, to the allusive rhymes, such as 'bonnet/sonnet' and 'skellum/bellum', which Burns had used in his verse epistle 'To the Rev. John Macmath'.[82] The meditation on pleasure being 'like poppies spread; | You seize the flower, its bloom is shed' is a reminiscence, not just of past pleasures, but of Burns's recurrent literary treatments of transience and his recourse to the natural world for images of human experience. The blend of nature, sexuality, and melancholy, which characterized 'The Mountain Daisy' and so many of the songs, finds an echo in 'Tam o'Shanter' and thus contributes to the dim feeling of familiarity that the poem exudes even when being read for the first time. As Tam sees Doon pouring 'all his floods', Burns recalls

'The Vision', 'To W. S****n', and his own project of making Ayrshire famous, now being both reaffirmed and questioned in a highly innovative, oddly traditional, poem.

The self-referencing was a literary device, which worked to create the crucial sense of the communal and the already known, as well as providing a means for Burns to address himself, surreptitiously. In 'Tam o Shanter' he was revisiting his earlier self, from a position distant in time and place, and reflecting on his poetic achievement. 'John Barleycorn' was one of Burns's pseudonyms, so the address to 'Inspiring bold *John Barleycorn*!' (l. 105) was not merely an apostrophe to whisky or to his early allegorical ballad. The figure of Tam, reluctantly returning home late and drunk, is, as Robert Crawford has emphasized, a mocking self-portrait of the wayward Dumfriesshire Exciseman, while his fondness for 'some auld Scots sonnet' underlines his resemblance to Robert Burns, the song collector.[83] As Tam approaches Alloway, however, he is moving into an earlier phase of his creator's existence, revisiting the mother-country of his imagination and demonstrating, beneath the mockery, his success in fulfilling Coila's decree. When Tam reaches the Kirk, Burns shows that he now has no difficulty in representing the Deil, who appears very clearly as 'auld Nick, in shape o' beast' | A towzie tyke, black, grim and large' (ll. 120–1). The Deil's connection with the poet is now similarly transparent, since Auld Nick's function is well defined—'To gie them music was his charge' (l. 122). Indeed, the horror of Tam o' Shanter—and hence its comic power—lies in the clarity of the detail and lack of equivocation.

Despite his self-acknowledged mastery of the new form, however, the sudden ending—where poor Maggie is simply left with 'scarce a stump'—disappointed readers such as Alexander Tytler, who felt that, though 'the preparation was fine, the result was not adequate'.[84] The abrupt shift from Tam's ride to the final moral reflection seemed startling because it tore apart the carefully created illusion of narratorial intimacy. To see this as inadequate, however, is to miss its rich implications. The final line is an explicit address to the reader— 'Remember Tam o Shanter's mare'—but one that pushes Tam into the past and underlines his condition as a figure in a story. Burns's composition was partially an act of memory, and perhaps, as it came to a close, he felt that some part of his imaginative life was behind him. Echoes of his earlier poems run throughout 'Tam o Shanter', and so the final glimpse of Tam fleeing from the witches is, among other possibilities, an image of a poet pursued by the admirers of his work, or even by thoughts of the poems themselves. Tam's frantic retreat was from something he had created himself. The old question, raised in 'Address to the Deil', of whether even the most vivid supernatural experience was really a projection of the human mind was being posed again in a most elaborate manner.[85] But, as in so many of Burns's poems, a more personal question lurked beneath the philosophic, for 'Tam o'Shanter' can be read as an exploration of the private fears of the creative artist whose very success is ultimately self-destructive. Behind the injunction to 'Remember Tam o Shanter's mare' may be an echo of old Hamlet's 'Remember me', appropriate enough in a poem about the site of his father's grave, which dwelled on whether he had fulfilled his original intentions. The final injunction to 'remember' was also a closing allusion to the poem that took the last place in his own collections of poetry—'A Bard's Epitaph', with its reflection on the author's 'thoughtless follies' and advice to readers to 'attend'.

If 'Tam o Shanter' was a kind of valedictory poem on his earlier work, the sophistication of Burns's handling of the poet's growth meant that it was also breaking new artistic ground and preparing the way for future experiments. The poem was both a return and a new departure, for it revealed a talent for sustained narrative that was not evident in the earlier work. Had Burns lived longer and in less taxing circumstances, he might have developed his narrative capacities or embarked on another kind of poetry still. After 1791, however, Burns, with a large and growing family to support, accepted a full-time post with the Excise and further commissions from Thomson and Johnson. As contemporary politics took on a new urgency, with the Revolution in France and the outbreak of war, Burns was less able to express his democratic sympathies directly, but he continued to find a way of giving voice to the people of Scotland by writing song lyrics. Many of his best-known and most enduring works stem from the 1790s—'Ae Fond Kiss', 'John Anderson, my Jo', 'The White Cockade', 'The Campbells are Comin', 'A Man's a Man for a That', 'My Love is like a Red, red, rose', 'Robert Bruce's March to Bannockburn'—the list goes on. His songs are often seen as Scotland's greatest contribution to international culture in the nineteenth century, even though they were so firmly attached to real locations that remained unfamiliar to many of their audiences. Currie recognized in 1800 that the intrinsic power of Burns's songs meant that they would be sung 'with equal or superior interest, on the banks of the Ganges or the Mississippi, as on those of the Tay or the Tweed' and by 1811, Josiah Walker had extended this sweep to the Ohio.[86] By the time of the celebrations for Burns's 250th birthday in 2009, he was being celebrated not just as Caledonia's Bard, but as part of a global network.

When Wordsworth heard about plans to build a national monument to Burns in 1819, he observed that Burns had already 'taken permanent root in the affections of his Countrymen' and had therefore 'raised for himself a Monument so conspicuous, and of such imperishable materials, as to render a local fabric of Stone superfluous'.[87] In other words, Burns had accomplished exactly the task Wordsworth had set for himself, of creating poetry that would live on, proving more durable even than stone. Heaney's ideal of local work was also embodied in Burns's songs, whose parish truths and lyric adequacy gave them the power to travel across the world and the centuries. With such a remarkable example of the travelworthiness of local work, it is therefore surprising that neoclassical notions about particularity and detail continued to survive into the nineteenth century and that Arnold should still have been dismissing regional literature as narrowly provincial in the 1870s. Burns proved an inspiration to Wordsworth and Scott, who kindled at his flame and made their own enormous contributions to international culture, but, while both followed him in celebrating their own favourite regions, his ability to create lyrics whose buoyancy was as remarkable as their anchor was perhaps even more important for those who did not enjoy such a secure sense of local attachment. His distinctive stanzas and use of Scots were followed by a host of poets who suddenly felt emboldened to regard their local speech as a poetic language, but he also offered a vital, if less immediately visible, model for those with the highest literary ambitions, including the young aspiring English poet, John Keats.[88]

6

Keats's In-Placeness

In his *Life of Robert Burns*, Lockhart praised his subject for remaining true to his background—'he ever announced himself as a peasant, the representative of his class, the painter of their manners, inspired by the same influences which ruled their bosoms.'[1] Despite Lockhart's obvious sense of his own distance from the 'peasants', he still admired Burns's power to break down social barriers by revealing the common humanity of wealthy and humble alike: to read Burns meant embracing 'the whole family of man'. Such egalitarian sentiments are entirely consistent with the claims Wordsworth had made for poetry and closely resemble the views on Burns expressed by John Wilson, fellow contributor to *Blackwood's*. They come as something of a surprise, however, when read in conjunction with an essay Lockhart had written ten years earlier. In 1818 he had adopted a very different attitude to Burns's influence, presenting it not as a force for social redemption but as a kind of infectious delirium:

> Of all the manias of this mad age, the most incurable, as well as the most common, seems to be no other than the *Metromanie*. The just celebrity of Robert Burns and Miss Baillie has had the melancholy effect of turning the heads of we know not how many farm-servants and unmarried ladies; our very footmen compose tragedies, and there is scarcely a superannuated governess in the island that does not leave a roll of lyrics behind her in her band-box.[2]

Lockhart was dismayed not by Burns, whose fame was fully justified, but by the effect of his success on the lower orders—the numerous working men and women whose lives had been transformed by the discovery that a ploughman could also be a poet. The sudden proliferation of poets in every walk of life seems to have horrified Lockhart, and, far from applauding Burns's influence, his essay reveals his anxiety over the threatening flood of lower-class publications and the swell of misguided ambition. For modern readers, Lockhart's essay is most remarkable, however, not for its general condescension to the poets inspired by Burns, but for its identification of the young man most afflicted by the epidemic— John Keats.

The elaborate image of a virulent disease sweeping the nation was preparing the way for a devastating critique of Keats, who had been 'bound apprentice some years ago to a worthy apothecary in town', but was now laid low: 'Whether Mr John had been sent home with a diuretic or composing draught to some patient far gone in the poetic mania, we have not heard. This much is certain, that he has caught the infection and caught it thoroughly.'[3] The heavy humour runs throughout Lockhart's hostile review, which concludes by ordering the hapless victim 'back to the shop Mr John, back to "plasters, pills and ointment boxes" etc.' Although Burns had inspired working poets and proved to publishers the existence of a market for lower-class and dialect poetry, the legacy of his success had not been wholly positive. John Clare's perceived similarity to Burns, for example, not only helped the 'Northamptonshire peasant' into print, but also led some of his admirers to fear for his character, drinking habits, and morals. Keats, though an apothecary rather than a farmhand, was still lowly enough to alarm the Tory reviewers and supply an arsenal of jokes and critical objections to fill their magazine.

As recent scholarship has shown, the *Blackwood's* assault was largely political, being prompted by Keats's association with the radical poet and publisher Leigh Hunt.[4] Lockhart's essay nevertheless has significance beyond the question of Keats's reception. It reveals, very concisely, the contemporary hostility to certain kinds of poetry and the continuing difficulties for poets associated too firmly with particular places. When Shaw made Henry Higgins boast that he could 'place any man within six miles', he was pointing out to the audiences of *Pygmalion* that language was a means to power.[5] To 'place any man', in this context, meant to identify his local dialect, but it also conveyed the sense of assigning him to his proper station. Putting someone in his place means reminding him that he is in the company of someone better—whether the superiority lies in knowledge, social standing, or even natural justice. Lockhart's review was an attempt to put Keats in his place—to reveal to the young upstart, very publicly, that others were in a better position to compose poetry than he could ever be. To make Keats a member of a 'Cockney School' was a way of emphasizing his lower social origins and consequent ignorance of correct language. As a 'cockney', Keats was being presented to the reading public, not only as a native of the great metropolis, but also as a Londoner whose speech was far from perfect.

Unlike Burns, who had 'ever announced himself as a peasant' and confessed from the start to writing 'chiefly in the Scottish Dialect', Keats had the audacity to publish first a collection simply entitled *Poems* and then the long poem *Endymion*. For a man whose education had not stretched to Greek, such unfounded ambition was asking for a severe rebuke: modern poets, in Lockhart's view, should know their place. The review of Keats was the fourth in a series of essays on the Cockney School, which had begun in October 1817 with the very first issue of *Blackwood's*. Running throughout were reminders that Hunt, Keats, and their circle had not enjoyed the benefits of a classical education, nor even proper instruction in the use of English. This was what lay behind Byron's double-edged compliment to Keats as a poet who 'without Greek | Contrived to talk about the Gods of late, | Much as they might have been supposed to speak' (*Don Juan*, xi. 60). Contemporary admiration for Keats's poetry was perpetually impeded by knowledge of his educational and social limitations and related prejudices about his vulgar, fanciful, second-hand classicism.

'Cockney' had a number of connotations, but what it chiefly conjured up was an image of lower-class Londoners with unattractive accents. For the well-educated reviewers of Edinburgh, who had grown up in a culture where the mastery of correct English was every bit as important as classical attainment, the publications of the 'Cockney School' were an irresistible target. Jeffrey's decision to launch their successful Whig rival, the *Edinburgh Review*, with his assault on the 'Lake School' was a further prompt. If the *Edinburgh* had achieved fame and sales by putting Wordsworth, Coleridge, and Southey in their place, *Blackwood's* would match their success through similar strategies. The Romantic period may have embraced the wide movement towards the local in literature, but the consciousness of writing being attached to particular regions was raised as much by those hostile to the trend as by those who contributed.

Unlike Wordsworth, Scott, or Burns, Keats had no sense of attachment to the region of his childhood and, if anything, became anxious to separate himself from the local associations emphasized by hostile Scottish critics. His life was a succession of temporary lodgings, and his poetry seemed to inhabit a world largely free of specific place names, regional manners, or historical records. This does not mean, however, that Keats was cut off from the literary and social concerns of his day, nor beyond the reach of the great modern poetry of local attachment. He was profoundly influenced by Wordsworth and Burns, but his response was not that of a country poet learning to value his native community in the light of their work. Keats found corroboration for his own endeavour in Wordsworth, just as Wordsworth had in Scott and Burns, but it was different in kind and never took the form of uncritical gratitude. For Keats, issues of local origin and the proper environment for poetry had to be explored in conjunction with related questions about the moral, political, philosophical, and aesthetic purposes of art. His fascination with Wordsworth and Burns nevertheless demonstrates that the poetry of local attachment spoke as strongly to the rootless as to those parishioners who understood that the world must come to them. His poetry can be read as a retort to contemporary critics who equated regional writings with narrowness, because it shows how truths that might have emerged in Grasmere or Alloway still had meaning for those in very different places. Keats's careful engagement with the competing claims of the local and universal also demonstrates brilliantly the way in which true lyric verse is ultimately able to carry its anchor within.

Keats's poems were singled out by Heaney as representative of the richest 'note of truth' achievable in the lyric, and their contribution to the Romantic affirmation of the place of poetry in the modern world cannot be overstated. But Keats's achievement did not come easily. It was only through the painful oscillations of aspiration and despair, through his obstinate questioning of everything understood intuitively, through finding both crucial corroboration and inevitable limitation in the work of other writers that Keats found his own distinctive place in English poetry. Hostile reviewers set him firmly in Leigh Hunt's circle, but Keats's interactions were far more varied and complex than the caricature in the periodicals suggested. From the beginning, he was open to numerous influences—personal and intellectual, oral and printed.

He was always engaged, simultaneously, in intense internal dialogues with himself. As his letters demonstrate, correspondence for Keats was multi-layered, involving not only himself and the friend he was addressing, but also the numerous writers who dominated his imagination and the different moods, tones, and tendencies that seemed to stalk his mind so unmanageably. The pursuit of poetry's place in the world was inseparable from inner exploration, even though Keats's full realization of his art involved both literary and physical discovery as well.

Keats's Place

Even before the *Blackwood's* wits had turned their unwelcome attention towards the 'Cockneys', Keats had begun to ponder the question of where he lived and its possible effects on his poetry. His consciousness of living in the city is evident in his earliest published poem, 'To Solitude', which begins:

> O Solitude! if I must with thee dwell,
>   Let it not be among the jumbled heap
>   Of murky buildings; climb with me the steep,—
> Nature's observatory—whence the dell,
> Its flowery slopes, its river's crystal swell,
>   May seem a span; let me thy vigils keep
>   'Mongst boughs pavillioned, where the deer's swift leap
> Startles the wild bee from the fox-glove bell.[6]

Keats had moved into London in October 1815 to complete his medical training at Guy's Hospital, in Southwark. The striking contrast between his new surroundings and those of Edmonton, where he had spent much of his childhood and early teens, is obvious in the desire to escape the 'jumbled heap of murky buildings' for 'flowery slopes'. The crystal rivers and wild bees probably owed as much to Renaissance pastoral as to the familiar countryside on the northern edge of London, but Keats's sonnet reveals both his awareness of contemporary ideas about the kind of environment most suited to healthy growth and a desire to find a language suitable to his sentiments.

In 'Frost at Midnight', Coleridge had explicitly contrasted his own stunted psychological development, 'reared in the great city, pent mid cloisters dim', with what he hoped his son would experience in the freedom of the rural world. His poem was a beautiful expression of views he had discussed with Wordsworth and conveyed in a letter to George Dyer, who had been a frequent visitor at the Dissenting school in Enfield that Keats attended: 'the best of us are liable to be shaped and coloured by surrounding Objects—and a demonstrative proof, that Man was not made to live in Great Cities!'[7] When Coleridge thought of the moral benefits of life in the countryside, where 'all around us smile Good and Beauty', he lamented the misfortune of those forced to 'wish and wish away the bitter Little of Life in the felon-crowded Dungeon of a great City!'[8] Like those of other radical thinkers of the 1790s, Coleridge's attitudes reflected the associationist thinking of David Hartley, whose elaborate physiologically based theory of the mind emphasized the benefits of positive early influences, including a rural childhood. At school, Keats, too, was encouraged to see God's work in the natural world and to study both the distant constellations and the nearby plants in the headmaster's garden.[9] If first-hand experience of the natural world was so important to the proper mental and moral growth, however, being lost among murky buildings could hardly be the ideal environment for a budding poet. It was difficult to make intellectual and spiritual progress through observing God's visible creation, when even the stars were blacked out by tall houses, smoke, and lamplight.

For a young man hungry for things of beauty, Guy's Hospital was not a very attractive prospect. Keats was deep in the city, surrounded by towering buildings, grimy brickwork, and streets crowded with boys in rags and disabled war veterans. Were these the sights to strengthen a sensitive mind? Keats's new life in a modern hospital seemed quite alien to the delicate beauty of poetry. His poems so far, even when dealing with politics, had been filled with rich, exotic imagery of hummingbirds, amber rays, silver doves, and laughing cerulean skies. It was not just a question of whether central London could offer inspiration, but whether the various pressures of city life rendered poetry entirely irrelevant. As Keats listened to the cartwheels striking the cobblestones, or smelled raw sewage pouring into the river, or gazed at the exhausted surgeons in the operating theatre, he must have sometimes wondered what kind of art could survive there.

In the sonnets Keats wrote some months after his move to Guy's, he gave vent to the feelings of relief afforded by a brief escape into the countryside:

> To one who has been long in city pent,
> 'Tis very sweet to look into the fair
> And open face of heaven.   (ll. 1–3)

Behind his sonnet lay 'Frost at Midnight', with its 'city pent' consciousness of the blessings of natural surroundings, but behind Coleridge's lines stood Milton's Satan, bursting from Hell:

> As one who long in populous City pent,
> Where Houses thick and Sewers annoy the Aire,
> Forth issuing on a Summer's Morn to breathe
> Among the pleasant villages.   (*Paradise Lost*, ix. 445–8)

The populous City often seemed to have struck poets as a hostile environment, destructive to its residents and the innocent countryside beyond. Wordsworth's recent sequence of sonnets 'Written in London' had dismissed the capital as 'a fen | Of stagnant waters', filled with 'selfish men' wearing 'their fetters in their souls', so it is not surprising to find his younger contemporaries turning to the countryside for inspiration.[10]

Even as Keats's sonnets acknowledged the attractions of 'Nature's beauty', however, they also emphasized that this 'sweet reprieve' was an opportunity to think hard about 'Milton's fate' and 'Sidney's bier'[11]—in other words about the Republican heroes whose absence from contemporary London had been lamented by Wordsworth. However enticing the Edenic sensations of the countryside after weeks in a suffocating hospital ward, they were not enough for Keats. The sub-Miltonic language of the 'balmy zephyrs' ushered in, not just a summer eve, but the 'stern form' of Milton himself, who rose to admonish the escapist and recall the moralist. As Wordsworth had reminded contemporary readers, Milton's example showed that a poet could create things of consummate beauty and still maintain a commitment to society. Art did not have to be kept away from human suffering, even though the poet's task of remaining true to both was a hard one.

Keats knew that through medicine he might do mankind some good, but he also came to realize that art had its own, vital contribution to make. The tension between his responsibilities as a doctor and his compulsion to write were never resolved absolutely, but his short career demonstrates a conscious decision to opt for a life of creative rather than medical practice. While natural aptitude obviously played a part in his choice, Keats's long-standing commitment to improving the world, or, at least, to easing some of its pains, continued to inform his creative endeavour. In his more optimistic moments Keats understood fully the place of poetry in human society, even though in darker periods he questioned both its chances of survival and its therapeutic power. Many of his best poems are poised between hope and doubt, braced by internal tensions and astonishingly resistant as a result.

Throughout his writing life, Keats was engaged in questions and among them was the cause of creativity. While he was pursuing his training at Guy's, he was also enjoying literary evenings with friends, including another young poet, George Felton Mathew. In October 1815, Mathew published a verse epistle to an unnamed 'Poetical Friend' in the European Magazine, which addressed the possible sources of creative talent. Mathew approached his friend's apparently inexplicable talent, with questions characteristic of their age: 'O where did thine infancy open its eyes? | And who was the nurse that attended thy spring?'[12] In Mathew's eyes, Keats's poems posed a challenge to fashionable opinions about environmental influences, because they had greater affinity with the warm climate of the 'glorious East' than with the 'frigid skies' of Britain. In a direct rejection of Wordsworthian principles, Mathew declared somewhat clumsily to his friend:

> It is not the climate, or scenery round,
>   It was not the nurse that attended thy youth
> That gave thee those blisses which richly abound
> In magical numbers to charm and to soothe.   (ll. 25–8)

Instead of his surroundings, Keats had been nurtured by the Queen of 'the gay fields of Fancy', by which Mathew presumably meant his innate imaginative power and his reading. He was nevertheless concerned that Keats's medical studies might now be forcing 'the spirit of Poesy' to sleep.

For all its awkward phrasing, Mathew's poem was raising crucial questions for Keats or any poet living in the city at a time when leading writers were advocating the superiority of a rural existence. Was a poet's creativity determined by the beauty of his surroundings or by his own natural ability? Must he have had the kind of experience recalled by Wordsworth, of bounding like a roe wherever nature led?

Whatever Mathew might say about the irrelevance of early environments, Coleridge's fears of the long-term consequences of his London schooling seemed to have been realized, judging by the vivid account of creative paralysis described in 'Dejection'. Mathew was offering a consolatory response to Keats's sonnet 'To Solitude', which he echoed in his closing lines, but his denial of formative external influence was not wholly convincing. Within a month of reading Mathew's epistle, Keats had composed a reply, expressing gratitude for their friendship, but still setting out his own, independent view of poetry and its relationship to the world at large. The fanciful notion that he should be waking the spirit of poetry irrespective of circumstances was quickly dismissed:

> But might I now each passing moment give
> To the coy muse, with me she would not live
> In this dark city.   ('To George Felton Mathew', ll. 31–4)

The proper setting for Mathew's idea of poetry would be 'Some flowery spot, sequester'd, wild, romantic', complete with Druid oaks, dark-leaved laburnum, nightingales, bees, cowslips and preferably 'a ruin dark, and gloomy'. In other words, Mathew was urging retreat into the fields of Fancy—fit for escapists but not for someone concerned with the troubles of the real world. Instead of a delicious fantasy, Keats needed somewhere for contemplating 'humanity', inspired by writers who had used their art to combat the pains of 'the pitiless world' and by heroes who had fallen 'in the cause of freedom'—Chatterton, Shakespeare, Milton, Alfred, William Tell, Wallace, and Burns. The epistle was an early expression of a resolution Keats would often reiterate, as he put aside the enchanting world of the senses in pursuit of intellectual or moral self-discipline. As he put it in the later sonnet 'On Sitting down to read *King Lear* again', the golden tongue of romance must be silenced if the aspiring poet were to tackle the fiercer, bitter-sweetness of the human condition. At the same time, his earliest poems also reveal a strong awareness that only certain physical conditions could furnish the mental concentration necessary for meditation and composition. Whether these were essentially rural was as yet unclear, but, from the beginning of his career, Keats was testing the conventions of pastoral and examining his own attraction to natural beauty as part of his commitment to becoming a serious poet.

The Sense of Real Things

In the programme of personal literary development Keats devised a year later, the instinctive appeal of the pastoral is only too clear. 'Sleep and Poetry' presents the young poet sleeping on grass, feeding on apples and strawberries, and biting the shoulders of 'white-handed nymphs in shady places', before turning resolutely away from such pleasures to embrace the demands of tragedy and epic:

> And can I ever bid these joys farewell?
> Yes, I must pass them for a nobler life,
> Where I may find the agonies, the strife
> Of human hearts...   (ll. 122–6)

As in 'To George Felton Mathew', Keats saw that the true poet was tasked with exploring the deepest passions of humanity, however compelling the delights of pastoral.

Just as Keats's conception of pastoral owed more to Renaissance conventions than to Wordsworth's stripped-down revival of the mode, however, his idea of epic was similarly inspired by rich, mythological painting:

> for lo! I see afar,
> O'er sailing the blue cragginess, a car
> And steeds with streamy manes—the charioteer
> Looks out upon the winds with glorious fear:
> And the numerous tramplings quiver lightly
> Along a huge cloud's ridge.   (ll. 126–30)

According to Richard Woodhouse, this was Keats's 'Personification of the Epic Poet, when the enthusiasm of inspiration is upon him'— hence the speaker's wish that he too 'might know | All that he writes with such a hurrying glow'.[13] Even as Keats imagined himself turning resolutely from romance to epic, he was expressing his ideas through the enticing figure of the Greek god Apollo, flying through clouds, talking to trees, gazing on 'shapes of delight, of mystery and fear', and glimpsing 'a lovely wreath of girls' (ll. 137–50). The self-disciplined movement from the unreal world of pastoral produced a new train of images, equally vivid but equally remote from the sights and sounds of Keats's London. The mythological figure of Apollo, inspired by Poussin's painting of *The Realm of Flora* hardly seemed closer to the 'noble strife of human hearts' than the white-handed nymphs left behind by the ambitious poet. It is as if the poem registers its own self-doubt—about the very language chosen to embody the poet's conceptions. For, just as the wish for Apollo's godlike power is uttered, the tone changes and the imaginary flight falters:

> The visions all are fled—the car is fled
> Into the light of heaven, and in their stead
> A sense of real things comes doubly strong,
> And, like a muddy stream, would bear along
> My soul to nothingness...   (ll. 155–9)

Keats's poetic vision, unable to withstand the pressure of 'real things', rapidly becomes a memory whose survival depends on the poet's determination to 'strive | Against all doubtings' and keep alive 'The thought of that same chariot, and the strange | Journey it went' (ll. 159–62). The epic vision suddenly seems to have faded far away, as if it never really existed.

Once the sustained flight of Apollo has been broken, the poet's struggle against doubt provokes a sequence of standard questions about the progress of English poetry, triumphant in the age of Shakespeare, languishing during the age of satire. Beneath it lay a deeper anxiety about the ultimate survival of poetry in modern society. As Keats pondered questions that had troubled Gray over whether the imagination could fly as freely 'As she was wont of old' (l. 165), he was confronting more than the Enlightenment commonplace that the creative arts flourished most vigorously in the earliest stages of society. When the speaker confesses to the great English poets that he could not 'trace | Your hallowed names, in this unholy place, | So near those common folk' (ll. 209–11), he was referring explicitly to the polluting effects of Restoration literature. The lines also suggest, however, Keats's frustration with his personal circumstances and uncongenial cultural milieu. For Keats, 'place' was as much temporal as geographical or social, for the temples, rooms, gardens, and landscapes that filled his writings were often spatial metaphors for moments in time. Despite the doubts that make 'Sleep and Poetry' twist and turn from its initially clear course, Keats had not given up hope for his own age, for his poem announces a new, 'fairer season', witnessed by music 'upstirred | From out its crystal dwelling in a lake' (in other words, by Wordsworth) and pays tribute to the 'fine sounds' of Leigh Hunt (ll. 221–9). Conditioned by the very neoclassical standards he despised, Keats inevitably regarded epic and tragedy as the highest kinds of literature, but his instincts urged him to admire Wordsworth and Hunt, whose work seemed predominantly pastoral. What 'Sleep and Poetry' revealed was not, after all, a straightforward plan for the young poet's development, but rather a series of complications and reversions, of opposing ideas that seemed hard to resolve. Keats was driven by the desire to move forward, enriching the world in new ways while honouring what had gone before, even though his progressive impulses were hemmed in by personal doubts and by uncertainties over the capacity of poems to survive in the inhospitable climate of today or the unknown hazards of tomorrow. At the same time, the poem drew hope from the example of modern poets whose work was part of the very mode dismissed in favour of higher things. 'Sleep and Poetry' was a manifesto for a poet who felt part of an exciting new movement and hopeful of surpassing even those he most admired, but it also reflected the erratic experience of a dreamer, drifting into excitable consciousness during a sleepless night.

Mathew's suggestion that Keats was the poet of enticing escapism had not been at all welcome, but in the years that followed Keats struggled hard with the tendency to perceive high art as being fundamentally opposed to 'real things'. In 'Sleep and Poetry' he introduced epic as the 'noble strife of human hearts', but this grand idea did not seem able to survive when confronted by reality. Poetry might, in theory, be dealing with the profoundest aspects of human society; all too often it seemed to be carrying its enthusiasts away into a world remote from human concerns. Conversely, the concentration required to create fine art was prone to interruption from the pressing business of daily life in a London hospital, by public events, or by distressing news of private misfortune. If at times Keats regarded the escape into art as a denial of social responsibility, at others he was more troubled by the way in which his quick sympathies seemed to prevent him from achieving the single-mindedness of the true artist. Keats's determination to succeed was twinned with doubt about the best way to proceed. As he plunged into *Endymion*, an astonishing feat of over 4,000 lines ('Did our great Poets ever write short pieces?'[14]), the equivocations of 'Sleep and Poetry' took on an ambitious allegorical form. Keats's hero is a young man whose troubling vision of ideal beauty leads him to abandon his family and social responsibilities in pursuit of his dream. Although Keats seems to be following Wordsworth's lead at the outset, announcing his intention to begin while he could not 'hear the city's din' (l. 40) and proclaiming the saving power of things of beauty, in spite of 'despondence, of the inhuman dearth | Of noble natures, of the gloomy days', thoughts of 'Tintern Abbey' and *The Excursion* soon become submerged in a dazzling world inspired by Renaissance painting and poetry. The initial emphasis on wreathing a 'band to bind us to the earth' recedes almost as soon as the scene shifts to an imaginary Latmos, where fleecy lambs remain 'unworried | By angry wolf, or pard with prying head' (ll. 74–6). Eventually, Wordsworth's insistence on finding paradise in the common day helps to recall Endymion from his visionary pursuit to more familiar ties and responsibilities, but the very recollection of Wordsworth is complicated by being pressed into an epic simile:

> Those two on winged steeds, with all the stress
> Of vision search'd for him, as one would look
> Athwart the sallows of a river nook
> To catch a glance at silver throated eels—
> Or from old Skiddaw's top, when fog conceals
> His rugged forehead in a mantle pale,
> With an eye-guess towards some pleasant vale
> Descry a favourite hamlet faint and far.   (iv. 390–8)

The personification of Skiddaw in his mantle seems more attuned to those on the winged steeds than to the unseen residents of the favourite hamlet, which can hardly hope to engage Endymion as passionately as his goddess has been doing. Though *Endymion* appeared to follow Wordsworth and Scott by introducing the final book with an apostrophe to the 'Muse of my native land' (iv. 1), the same line reappeared a little later, this time with a question mark— 'Muse of my native land, am I inspired?' (iv. 354). Endymion's return from his spiritual journey is far from easy: 'His first touch of earth went nigh to kill' (iv. 614). Recovery of solid ground brings about a new clarity of purpose, as Endymion recognizes his own error:

> Presumptuous against love, against the sky,
> Against all elements, against the tie
> Of mortals each to each, against the blooms
> Of flowers, rush of rivers, and the tombs
> Of heroes gone! Against his proper glory
> Has my own soul conspired.   (iv. 639–44)

Since so much of the poem prior to this moment has been a vivid, sensuous re-creation of Endymion's exotic pilgrimage, however, his dismissal of the dream as 'nothing' (iv. 637) is hardly convincing, and he admits that 'the past doth prison' him (iv. 691). The competing attractions of the ideal visionary pursuit and the responsibilities of human society were not easily separated, especially in a poem where the mythic figures seemed altogether more physically appealing than the images of the real world. *Endymion* concludes with a reconciliation between the ideal and the earthly, but its somewhat baffling process tends to thwart the overall allegory and leaves the reader, like Peona, to return home in wonderment.[15] What was clear from Keats's experiment, nevertheless, was the seriousness with which he undertook his task and the way in which his exploration of the nature of art prompted intense creative expression. The struggle to resolve artistic and moral questions was embodied in the very form of the poem, with its rapid shifts of scene and style, its creation and deflation of dreams, and frequent internal dialogues. As Keats finished his remarkable exploration, he realized that 'the simple imaginative Mind may have its rewards in the repetition of its own silent Working', in other words, the journey was more important to a good poem than the destination.[16] He had come to feel certain about some things, at least—'the holiness of the Heart's affections and the truth of Imagination'—but how to develop a kind of poetry adequate to his deepening understanding of art's relationship with life was far from obvious.[17]

Keats's reply to Mathew had eschewed the 'sequestered, wild, romantic' retreat and advocated the pursuit of more serious moral and political topics, but, in the verse letter he sent to John Hamilton Reynolds in March 1818, Keats lamented his inability to sustain the

ideal realm of art. As in 'Sleep and Poetry', Keats called on Apollo
for god-given words to recreate the Enchanted Castle, which he
remembered from one of Claude Lorrain's paintings, but the illusion
is broken by thoughts of the poor herdsman, failing in his attempt to
tell friends of the sweet music emanating from the castle—'they
believe him not'.[18] The vision, once again, falters—this time in the
face of disbelief. Keats, aware of the vulnerability of certain kinds of
art to a sceptical audience, again chose the essentially dialogic form
of a verse epistle to debate aesthetics, interspersing vivid imaginative
flights with hard questions. As he probed the desirability of imagi-
native freedom, Keats exposed, in startling clarity, the difficulty of
realizing a fully adequate kind of art. It was not just that the ideal
represented by Claude's painting might be rejected by those obliv-
ious to its enchantment, but rather that the very people most suscep-
tible to its appeal had their own inherent powers of destruction. The
dilemmas of *Endymion*, which had also been explored by Shelley in
Alastor, were now revisited in a verse letter written to a sick friend,
but the answers still remained elusive.

The poem is framed by recollections that reveal the alarming
waywardness of Keats's mind, from the 'disjointed' images that had
visited him in bed the night before to the 'mysterious tale' of a quiet
moment that turns into a waking nightmare:

> I was at home
> And should have been most happy—but I saw
> Too far into the sea, where every maw
> The greater on the less feeds evermore—
> But I saw too distinct into the core
> Of an eternal fierce destruction,
> And so from happiness I far was gone.   (ll. 92–8)

The recognition that there are few 'who escape these visitings'
recalls the young poet of 'Resolution and Independence', afflicted
suddenly and inexplicably by gloom. Where Wordsworth had left
his speaker dwelling on the bracing truths embodied in the leech-
gatherer, however, Keats's poem ends with a determined retreat into
the very world of romance that he had rejected elsewhere—'I'll
dance, | And from detested moods in new romance | Take refuge'
(ll. 110–13). Keats had written eloquently on his resolution to turn
from romance to seriousness, but his poetry now acknowledged

the difficulty of attaining the ideal world once fully conscious of the suffering inherent in the mortal one. It now seemed that even a lovely, picturesque setting could not guarantee peace for someone sensitive to the struggles of the natural world and conscious of man's destructive instincts. Beauty might, after all, be as hard to achieve as the sublime.

In 'Sleep and Poetry' the vision of Apollo was overwhelmed by a 'sense of real things', but, by the time Keats composed his verse epistle to Reynolds, the question of what actually constituted reality had complicated matters even further. Was Keats's perception of the 'eternal fierce destruction' beneath the beautiful surface of the natural world 'real'—a truth denied by certain kinds of dazzling art? Or was it a projection of a tainted, individual imagination, unable to find peace and happiness even at home? Was it, in other words, merely an alternative vision, whose reality depended on the artist who gave it a recognizable form? When Reynolds reviewed Keats's *Poems* in 1817, he praised him for seeing natural objects with his mind rather than the eye, but in the verse epistle Keats seemed to be questioning which was the more reliable means to truth.[19] The contrast between the artist's idealized representation of the sea and the poet's recollection raised hard questions about the nature of art and the kind of environment most conducive to its creation. Keats wrote to Reynolds from the Devon coast at Teignmouth, but the experience presented in his verse letter was rather different from that suggested by Claude Lorrain's calm, shimmering expanses. Which was more real—a powerful image controlled by a great artist and enjoyed by generations, or a former medical student's perception of the perpetual flux and destruction that constituted the material universe? In order to resolve the creative crises that gripped his early verse epistles, Keats turned increasingly to contemplate the work of other writers, searching for guidance on his own strange journey.

Keats's Poets

A few weeks after composing the verse epistle to Reynolds, Keats wrote several letters to friends, reflecting on his life since he had taken the momentous decision to give up medicine in favour of poetry. By now, some of the tensions explored in the early poems had apparently been resolved: 'I have been hovering for some time between an exquisite sense of the luxurious and a love for Philosophy—were I calculated for the former I should be glad—but as I am not I shall turn all my soul to the latter.'[20] Keats was once again attempting a self-disciplined move away from the 'luxurious' towards the acquisition of knowledge and wisdom, which, as he explained to John Taylor, would involve him in years of 'study and thought'.[21] Keats had realized that there were different ways of 'doing some good for the world', but having chosen the literary road he now needed to strengthen its foundations and widen his mental horizons. Some days later, he told Reynolds that he was planning to learn Greek and Italian, in order to master the wisdom of the Ancients: abandoning medicine did not mean abandoning his studies. Ever since he had encountered the stunning artistry of the Elgin marbles, which had been bought for the British nation in 1816, Keats had been fascinated by Ancient Greece.[22] He felt increasingly frustrated, therefore, by his inability to enter Homer's famous demesne except through translations and reports from other, more educated authors. *Endymion*, which had occupied so much of his time and energy the year before, had had to rely on classical handbooks, Renaissance poetry, and mythological paintings, but it was impossible not to feel a great distance from the fountain, to experience a longing that could not be fully understood. As Keats was giving *Endymion* the finishing touches, the first scathing attack on the Cockney School appeared in *Blackwood's*, so he was acutely conscious of the critical contempt that might be heaped on poets who inadvertently revealed their ignorance.[23] Keats was only too aware of the cultural deficiency of being, as Byron would put it, 'without Greek', but, as he acknowledged to Haydon in a sonnet on the Elgin Marbles, 'what I want I know not where to seek'.[24]

Although he had now taken a clear decision to devote himself to writing, Keats was still afflicted by anxiety, as evident in a revealing comment to Reynolds: 'For although I take poetry Chief, there is still something else wanting to one who passes his life among Books and thoughts on Books.'[25] Keats may have recognized that his true talents lay in the field of literature, but he was still tormented by the sense of 'something else wanting'. A week later he wrote again, admitting that he was 'glad at not having given away his medical Books' and resolving to keep alive what he had learned at Guy's.

Keats's literary road had taken him into a labyrinth, but even in his confusion he was sustained by the very thing that had led him there—poetry. Wordsworth, in particular, was the greatest 'help'.[26]

As Keats explored the different kinds of genius embodied respectively by Milton and Wordsworth, he addressed the questions that aggravated Jeffrey, Byron, Peacock, and Hazlitt, as to whether Wordsworth had 'an extended vision or a circumscribed grandeur', but his own answer took the form of an extended simile, comparing human life to a 'mansion of many apartments'.[27] The movement from the Chamber of Maiden thought ('where we see nothing but pleasant wonders, and think of delaying there for ever in delight') was very similar to the pattern envisaged in 'Sleep and Poetry', in which the speaker passed from the pleasures of pastoral to the noble duty of epic. This time the shift was perceived, not as a conscious choice, however, but as the corollary of the awakening intellect—of understanding that the world was full of 'Misery and Heartbreak, Pain, Sickness and oppression'.[28] The bright Chamber of the dawning imagination led only to a choice of doors into the dark—the very situation now facing Keats. And it was here that Wordsworth seemed strong enough to help—for in 'Tintern Abbey', gazing into 'the burthen of the mystery', he had articulated exactly what Keats was trying to say. Since Wordsworth's subsequent work could be seen as a courageous exploration of the 'dark passages' that led in all directions from the light, intoxicating Chamber of Maiden-Thought, Keats should follow his example, venturing into the darkness and 'thinking into the human heart'.

Far from being wilfully self-limiting, as many of his contemporaries had insisted, Wordsworth's poetry struck Keats as being more profound even than Milton's—an achievement he attributed not so much to individual superiority as to the collective advances that had taken place since the late seventeenth century. For Keats, who had trained to be a doctor, the notion that poetry drew positively from the progress of other intellectual disciplines was important personally, as well as being a counter to the depressing views of men such as Peacock. Though *The Four Ages of Poetry* was published a year after Keats's letter, both were influenced by widespread assumptions that modern science had made steady progress since the Renaissance, while literature had not. Keats had imbibed a literary-historical narrative of sorry descent from the Golden Age of Elizabeth into

satire and rocking-horse rhythms, but his own reading of Words-
worth helped to convince him that the decline had been temporary
rather than absolute. There were still lingering doubts, nevertheless,
even in relation to Wordsworth. For the very strength that Keats
identified—his power to understand human misery—might also be
preventing Wordsworth from fulfilling his destiny as an epic poet.
Keats regarded *The Excursion* as 'one of the three things to rejoice at
in this age' and knew from the preface that Wordsworth found in the
human heart the 'main region' of his song.[29] Still haunted by thoughts
of epic as the artist's ultimate achievement, Keats puzzled over
whether this was a kind of poetic martyrdom, and wondered if
Wordsworth lacked Milton's intense concentration on his artistic
vocation—his 'epic passion'. Perhaps even for a modern genius like
Wordsworth, there was still something else wanting.

Although Keats was reading Wordsworth's new publications with
such care and intelligence, his programme of study was constantly
arrested by thoughts of his own inadequacies. Despite his deep admi-
ration, Keats acknowledged that he was not really in a position to
judge the whole truth of Wordsworth's poetry—'we find what he
says true as far as we have experienced and can judge no further but
by larger experience.'[30] At once, the flaw in his plan to devote himself
to reading was apparent—for 'axioms in philosophy are not axioms
until they are proved upon our pulses: We read fine—things but
never feel them to the full until we have gone the same steps as the
Author.'[31] Only a week before, Keats had announced his intention to
devote several years to study and thought; already it seemed that this
was inadequate preparation for the creation of poetry that mattered.
Passing one's life among books was all very well, but it could not
provide the fullness of meaning that came only from personal expe-
rience. Or that, at least, was what Keats thought on 3 May.

Various things emerge from the seeming randomness of the
letters Keats wrote in spring 1818—one is his growing belief that
there was, after all, 'something real in the world' and that the 'some-
thing' mattered to poetry. Rather than fear 'real things' as destruc-
tive to art, Keats now saw that great art absolutely required a sense
of the real. What also emerges from his tentative correspondence
over the questions raised in poems such as 'Sleep and Poetry' was
the need for help from other writers. Keats's personal aesthetic
enquiries had been pursued through the various letters to brother

poets, but at every turn Keats sought guidance from the examples of the established greats—Shakespeare, Milton, and, increasingly, Wordsworth. Keats's conviction that there was something real in the world was part of his profound engagement with Wordsworth, whose work revealed that there was no necessary opposition between the pastoral and the real world of misery, pain, and heartbreak. As he dwelled on Wordsworth's deepening achievement, however, he became aware that his own feelings of incompleteness might have something to do with inexperience. Unless he could share the thoughts of a great writer through having participated in similar actions or life events, it was impossible to 'feel them to the full'. Mere intellectual understanding was inadequate—Keats desired a more complete connection, involving ideas, feelings, observations, and memory. Reading had always been a passionate pursuit for Keats, but he now feared that even burning through the finest English poetry might not furnish him with the kind of knowledge needed to develop his own art.

The limitations of poets who relied too much on books for inspiration had been underscored in the first, devastating *Blackwood's* essay on Leigh Hunt and the Cockney School, which had appeared in October 1817:

Mr Hunt is altogether unacquainted with the face of nature in her magnificent scenes; he has never seen any mountain higher than Highgate-hill, nor reclined by any stream more pastoral than the Serpentine River. But he is determined to be a poet pre-eminently rural, and he rings the changes— till one is sick of him, on the beauties of the different 'high views' which he has taken of God and nature, in the course of some Sunday dinner parties, at which he has assisted in the neighbourhood of London.[32]

If Hunt's poetry was being lambasted for revealing its ignorance of nature's magnificence so plainly to those of wider experience, there seemed little hope for Keats without some drastic remedy. As he grew to admire Wordsworth more and Hunt less, however, Keats began to wonder whether the elusive 'something' might be an acquaintance with nature at her most magnificent. If the *Blackwood's* essay shocked Keats into reconsidering his admiration for Hunt's version of pastoral, its emphasis on first-hand experience of the natural world was reiterated by the lectures he began attending in January 1818. Here he listened to Hazlitt's passionate admiration for the naturalness and force of the greatest poetry. Shakespeare, especially, was 'the poet of nature', and, unlike so many modern writers, he had the deepest sense of 'what was grand in the objects of nature, or affecting in the events of human life'.[33] Instead of examining Shakespeare's literary and historical sources, Hazlitt represented the familiar characters as 'real beings of flesh and blood', who spoke 'like men, not like authors'. Shakespeare possessed 'the genius of humanity', capable of creating every kind of person and becoming anything he wanted. It was a kind of complete knowledge that did not seem, at least in Hazlitt's account, to have depended very much on books. The difference between these ideas and the programme of poetic growth set out in 'Sleep and Poetry' must have given Keats pause for thought. Nor could he be confident any longer that classical study would necessarily equip him for achieving the kind of Shakespearian wholeness that was embodied in fully adequate poetry. According to Hazlitt, Homer himself was a poet of the real world, not a literary scholar.

Shakespeare towered above almost every other poet in the lecture series, but Hazlitt was prepared to concede that at least one modern writer had demonstrated some of the same qualities—Robert Burns. 'The pulse of his poetry', Hazlitt had remarked, 'flows as healthily and vigorously as Shakespeare's', and Burns apparently possessed the 'same magnanimity, directness, and unaffected character'.[34] For Keats, desperate to strive towards Shakespeare's astonishing heights, the discovery that among the moderns only Burns seemed to be measuring up to Hazlitt's ideal must have been quite startling. It was Burns alone who seemed capable of recovering the kind of physical, manly energy that distinguished Shakespeare: 'He had a strong mind, and a strong body, the fellow to it. He had a real heart of flesh and blood, beating in his bosom—you can almost hear it throb...he held the pen and the plough with the same firm, manly grasp.'[35] There was nothing about Burns having excellent classical attainments— his physical strength and close connection to the earth seemed far more important. Unlike Leigh Hunt, Burns had found his material not in books but in the living world around him—'for the artificial flowers of poetry, he plucked the mountain-daisy under his feet; and a field-mouse, hurrying from its ruined dwelling, could inspire him with the sentiments of terror and pity'. In Hazlitt's vivid account, Burns was as much the poet of nature as Shakespeare.

His imagination and sympathy flowed so quick and deep that the great tragic emotions could be prompted by nothing more elevated than a mouse.

Keats had included Burns in the roll-call of heroes he sent to Mathew, but the verse epistle gave no hint that Burns possessed the Shakespearian magnitude discerned by Hazlitt. That he figured at all indicates nevertheless that Keats was aware of Burns from the start of his writing career—which is not surprising, given the controversy prompted by Peterkin's new edition of Burns and the campaign to erect a memorial in Dumfries.[36] Burns's life was the talking point of London when Keats arrived in 1815. The journal that published Mathew's 'To a Poetical Friend' had carried a lengthy tribute to Burns in its July issue, together with a frontispiece depicting the new monument. The *European Magazine* had referred to Burns's 'wildly original, though uncultivated genius, arising superior to all the restraints of adversity, and the shackles of situation', in a way that could hardly fail to ignite Keats's interest.[37] The description of how Burns 'blazed like a meteor on the poetic world, and was hailed with the same enthusiasm which greets a newly discovered planet of the astronomer' may well have lodged in Keats's retentive mind, re-emerging a year later when he expressed his own amazement on discovering Chapman's Homer. Burns, after all, offered a similar kind of hope to poets anxious about their linguistic limitations as Chapman provided for those unable to read Greek. He was a liberator and a patriot, unashamed of his native language and thus a source of inspiration to his fellow countrymen.

The essay offered stirring claims for the vital role of poetry in society, arguing that it was not an 'idle art', but one that led to 'the noblest efforts of which the human mind is capable'[38]—ideas that would have been very congenial to Keats, as he tried to reconcile his impulse to write poetry with his strong sense of duty to society. Equally striking was the essayist's confidence that Burns's poetry had made a major contribution to his own land and even its history. Since Burns had given 'a new and superior interest to every spot which his muse had to celebrate', it was now impossible to visit Scotland's historic fields 'without feeling the power of him, who, in appropriate strains, has sung the glory of her chieftains, and, as it were, revived WALLACE, BRUCE, and all those who so long slumbered with them in their *gory bed*'. Poetry was not a merely reflective art, capable of transcribing observation or imitating earlier writings—it also had the power to transform the world for future generations and to recast the past in ways that made sense to the living. When Keats listened to Hazlitt extolling Burns's powers in 1818, the lecture would thus have rekindled thoughts sparked some years before. Hazlitt's emphasis on Burns's quick responses to his immediate surroundings were in keeping with the *European Magazine* writer's obvious enthusiasm for 'the rivers, the valleys, the mountains' of Burns's native country and both were indebted to prevailing assumptions about the crucial relationship between the poet and his environment. Though Keats had been troubled by the equation of rural poetry and *retreat*, both Burns and Wordsworth showed that living in the country meant neither evading responsibilities to their fellow men nor producing inadequate poetry, but rather the opposite. Their versions of pastoral included close observation of the rural world and a deep sympathy with the truths embodied in communities so often ignored by the ruling classes.

Keats had allowed himself to write in direct response to his immediate experience of the physical world in poems such as his early verse letter 'To my Brother George', but, in the months before he attended Hazlitt's lectures, he had been working to complete *Endymion*, with its fantastic settings and mythological figures. Though not without vivid seasonal descriptions of 'daffodils', 'juicy stalks', and bees humming about 'globes of clover', the poem owed more to Keats's reading than to his first-hand experience of the natural world. Its dazzling texture seemed woven from scattered strands of classical myths and ultimately as vulnerable to the pressure of 'real things' as the visions of 'Sleep and Poetry'. Rather than remedying his approach to classical subjects through further study of ancient Greek, Keats began to wonder whether a very different kind of knowledge would be more beneficial. Homer's own genius had, after all, been nourished by his wide experience of different kinds of human society, according to influential classicists such as Blackwell. The great Greek bard had received only fairly brief discussion in Hazlitt's lecture series, because his place in world literature was unassailable, but what had been stressed was Homer's wide knowledge of the world: 'he grapples with all the objects of nature, and enters into all the relations of social life. He saw many countries and the manners of many men; and he has brought them all together in his poem.'[39] He was, in other words, another poet of nature.

If Keats hoped to understand Homer's power, knowledge of many countries and many men might be what was needed—and certainly some experience of the countries that had produced the most original poets of recent times. In *Endymion*, he had attempted to pay tribute to the Muse of his native land, but the language of his poem refused to match its subject: 'O first-born on the mountains! by the hues | Of heaven on the spiritual air begot! | Long didst thou sit alone in northern grot' (iv. 2–4). Keats's poem did not much resemble those of the northern Muse's modern heirs, who all seemed variously committed to the language really spoken by men. In *Endymion*, he had acknowledged the saving power of the 'touch of earth' to recover the visionary from his pursuit of empty dreams, but the ground he conjured up was not quite as solid as the argument demanded. Within months of hearing Hazlitt's lecture on Burns, Keats was heading north to see for himself the land of his native Muse.

The Same Steps

The desire to go 'the same steps' as Wordsworth in order to understand his poetry fully took a surprisingly literal course, as Keats walked from Liverpool to Rydal Mount, before continuing his journey to Scotland. The ambitious tour shows Keats's determination to enlarge his experience and to encounter unfamiliar landscapes at first hand. Although he had already visited numerous places in the south of England—from Margate to Teignmouth, from the Isle of Wight to Oxford—none of these had offered the magnificent mountain scenery that Wordsworth had celebrated in *The Excursion*. As he explained to Benjamin Bailey, when he reached Inveraray:

I should not have consented to myself these four Months tramping in the highlands but that I thought it would give me more experience, rub off more Prejudice, use [me] to more hardship, identify finer scenes load me with grander Mountains, and strengthen more my reach in Poetry, than would stopping at home among Books, even though I should reach Homer.[40]

Learning Greek was all very well, but Keats was trying a new path to knowledge. By the time he wrote this letter, he had been travelling for a month, but the life-changing effects of his adventure had been obvious from the start.

Once he arrived in the Lake District, Keats began recording his impressions in a journal letter to his brother, Tom. His excitement shines through the detail:

> First we stood a little below the head about half way down the first fall, buried deep in trees, and saw it streaming down two more descents to the depth of near fifty feet—then we went on a jut of rock nearly level with the second fall-head, where the first fall was above us, and the third below our feet still—at the same time we saw that the water was divided by a sort of cataract island on whose other side burst out a glorious stream—then the thunder and the freshness. At the same time the different falls have as different characters; the first darting down the slate-rock like an arrow; the second spreading out like a fan—the third dashed into a mist—and one on the other side of the rock a sort of mixture of all of these. We afterwards moved away a space, and saw nearly the whole more mild, streaming silverly through the trees.

As he attempted to re-create his experience of the waterfall at Ambleside, Keats adopted simple vocabulary, which nevertheless assumes great force through the accumulation of rhythmic phrases, almost orchestral in their varied and simultaneous movement. There is none of the self-consciousness of so many of his letters, nor the classical embellishment of his early poetry, nor the vacillation between opposing ideas that characterized almost everything he wrote. The prose concentrates on the representation of a particular moment. As he commented a few lines further on, Keats was living 'in the eye', while his 'imagination, surpassed, is at rest'.

Again and again, on his northern tour, Keats found that the ideas formed from his reading were inadequate to the reality of the scene before his eyes. Just before his account of the waterfall, he evoked the passage from *Paradise Lost*, which celebrates natural profusion in contrast to artificial knot gardens, but then insisted that the Lake District was even wilder: 'Milton meant a smooth river—this is buffeting all the way on a rocky bed ever various.' The 'thunder and freshness' of the waterfall were blasting away old assumptions from Keats's interior landscape. His travelling companion, Charles Armitage Brown, later recalled Keats's amazement at seeing the Cumbrian mountains for the first time: 'even he, with all his imagination, could not, until he beheld them, suggest to himself a true idea of their effect on the mind.'[41] Keats had heard about mountains, read about mountains, seen paintings of mountains, but, as Brown observed, 'language and art are equally inefficient. The reality must be witnessed before it can be understood.' The very questions that Keats had broached to Reynolds were now being resolved practically—proved on the pulses. As he tried to explain to Tom, it was 'the tone, the coloring, the slate, the stone, the moss, the rock-weed; or if I may so say, the intellect, the countenance of such places' that were so astonishing.[42] The distinctive physical attributes all combined to create a specific, regional quality unlike anything Keats had ever encountered. It was not so much the scale of the landscape, for 'the space, the magnitude of mountains' had been 'well imagined' in advance, but nothing had prepared him for the peculiar character of the Lakes: 'this countenance or intellectual tone must surpass every imagination and defy any remembrance.'

In 'Sleep and Poetry', Keats had represented Apollo 'o'er-sailing the blue cragginess', but such generalized, painterly images would no longer suffice. The encounter with the Cumbrian mountains was decisive: 'I shall learn poetry here', he wrote, 'and shall henceforth write more than ever, for the abstract endeavor of being able to add a mite to the mass of beauty which is harvested from these grand materials, by the finest spirits, and put into ethereal existence for the relish of one's fellows.'[43] It was not that all art was useless, for, in celebrating his own epiphany, Keats acknowledged Wordsworth, who had harvested beauty from this very landscape. His phrasing alluded to the preface to *The Excursion*, where Wordsworth had given thanks for

> Beauty—a living Presence of the earth,
> Surpassing the most fair ideal Forms
> Which craft of delicate Spirits hath composed
> From earth's materials.   (ll. 42–5)[44]

Keats's visit to the Lakes had confirmed that books could not be a substitute for physical experience and helped him understand the inspiration Wordsworth drew from earth's materials.

Keats's correspondents might reasonably have expected from his letters that he would return with a bag full of poems composed on his tour. In fact, he wrote very little between June 1818 and his return in late August. What does survive, apart from the vivid letters, is either light verse written to entertain family and friends or short poems registering some kind of inadequacy. For his excitement in the Lakes rapidly gave way to a less confident sense of his creative future, and, by the time he reached Ben Nevis, nothing seemed clear:

> Here are the craggy stones beneath my feet;
> Thus much I know, that, a poor witless elf,
> I tread on them, that all my eye doth meet
> Is mist and crag, not only on this height,
> But in the world of thought and mental might.
>
> ('Read me a Lesson, Muse',ll. 10–14)

If Keats had hoped that his trip would bring a better understanding of the world, it seemed only to have plunged him into deeper confusion—the clarity achieved in Ambleside had turned to mist. Weeks of living in the eye might have laid his imagination to rest, but it hardly seemed to be making the dark passages of human experience any easier to penetrate.

Although visiting Scotland had been a corrective to his book-learned notions, the reality of first-hand experience was not always refreshing to the creative spirit. Burns country had been a strange mixture of surprises and fulfilled expectations. Ayrshire was much more beautiful than Keats had imagined ('O prejudice! It was rich as Devon'), but in the midst of the startling scenery were the most familiar landmarks—'the "bonny Doon", with the Brig that Tam O'Shanter cross'ed—Kirk Alloway, Burns's Cottage and then the Brigs of Ayr.'⁴⁵ More disconcerting to Keats than the fertile hills, however, was what he found inside Burns's Cottage—'a mahogany faced old Jackass who knew Burns—He ought to be kicked for having spoken to him'.⁴⁶ Keats's tirade against the 'flummery of the birthplace' reveals the profound discomposure he experienced in Alloway, when he discovered that the cradle-place he had journeyed so far to reach was dominated by a coarse drunkard who cashed in on having known Burns. At once, Keats's belief in the need to experience reality collapsed and the desire to have his imagination surpassed seemed ludicrously misplaced:

> Fancy is dead and drunken at its goal:
> Yet can I stamp my foot upon thy floor,
> Yet can I ope the window-sash to find
> The meadow thou hast tramped o'er and o'er.
>
> ('This Mortal Body', ll. 8–11)

Keats had come to Alloway determined to write a sonnet, but the encounter with the real rather than the imagined place produced only a poem that Keats refused to show his friends. The shocking revelation forced him to reconsider his entire programme, as he confessed to Reynolds

I cannot write about scenery and visitings—Fancy indeed is less than a present palpable reality, but it is greater than remembrance—you would lift your eyes from Homer only to see close before you the real Isle of Tenedos—you would rather read Homer afterwards than remember yourself—One song of Burns's is of more worth to you than all you could think for a whole year in his native country.[47]

Perhaps he would, after all, have gained more from stopping at home and studying ancient Greek.

What Keats was learning in Scotland was nevertheless of the utmost importance to his own development. Having been troubled by the shortcomings of his own experience and exhilarated by the discovery that Wordsworth was creating art from his personal interactions with the external world, he now realized that true poetry was not, after all, dependent on certain kinds of landscape alone. Visiting the Lakes and Ayrshire might offer insights into the poetry of Wordsworth and Burns, but it would not enable Keats to write in their style. As he confessed in the sonnet 'On Visiting the Tomb of Burns':

> Burns! with honour due
> I have oft honoured thee. Great shadow, hide
> Thy face! I sin against thy native skies.   (ll. 12–14)

Both Burns and Wordsworth composed local work—true to their own felt experience. To achieve similar strength in his own poetry, Keats needed to be true to his own responses and not attempt to imitate others.

Alloway was, in a sense, the end of his pilgrimage, because it showed that he had once again been on the wrong track and that Burns could be found more reliably in his songs than in his cottage. Seeing Scotland revealed to Keats not a landscape with special qualities to nurture the budding genius, but an environment full of surprises and contradictions. If anything, Burns's poetry had suffered from certain aspects of his homeland—his disposition was 'southern', his sensitive and sensual nature crushed by the oppressive 'kirkmen', who 'banished puns and laughter and kissing'.[48] For a poet who had once assumed that poetic growth depended on subduing the senses in the pursuit of deeper knowledge, the possibility that Burns's naturally 'luxurious imagination' had been obliged 'in self defence to deaden its delicacy in vulgarity' was a sobering thought. Far from following Currie's presentation of the peasant poet nurtured by his special Scottish upbringing, Keats recoiled from the austerity of the Kirk and the mediocrity of the cottage. If Wordsworth and Scott understood the enabling influence of Burns's local attachments, Keats found it hard to reconcile his reading of the poetry with his experience of the circumstances.

The disorientation resulting from Keats's visit to Burns's birthplace is evident in the poem he wrote afterwards, 'There is a Joy in Footing Slow', which admits that 'a longer stay | Would bar return, and make a man forget his mortal way' (ll. 31–2). In this strange reflection on his trip, it is memory that saves the literary pilgrim from losing his mind 'on mountains bleak and bare'. Ironically, pursuit of the 'real' Burns had turned out to be more like Endymion's search for vision than his recovery of solid ground. Keats's journey had still confirmed the ultimate importance of personal experience, however, because it was through separation from the familiar that Keats began to see what mattered most:

> O horrible! to lose the sight of well remember'd face,
> Of brother's eyes, of sister's brow, constant to every place;
> Filling the air, as on we move, with portraiture intense,
> More warm than those heroic tints that fill a painter's sense,
> When shapes of old come striding by and visages of old,
> Locks shining black, hair scanty grey, and passions manifold.
>
> (ll. 33–8)

Keats's 'inward sight' was not after all dependent on scenery, but sustained by mental images of deeply felt relationships far more powerful than immediate visual stimulation. He had made Endymion realize, with guilty horror, that visionary obsession had carried him away from the loving 'tie of mortals each to each' (iv. 641), but now that he had experienced for himself the acute alarm of disconnection, he clung to saving memories:

> No, no, that horror cannot be—for at the cable's length
> Man feels the gentle anchor pull and gladdens in its strength.
>
> ('There is a Joy', ll. 39–40)

Far from being a rejection of Wordsworthian ideas, however, Keats was discovering, with renewed gratitude, the truths of 'Tintern Abbey'. For, although Wordsworth represented rural memories as his imaginative stronghold against the din of towns and cities, Keats recognized that his own mind was just as much the dwelling place of lovely forms. Nature was Wordsworth's anchor and guide in 'Tintern Abbey', but it had taken Keats some time to realize the nature of his own 'gentle anchor'. The individual journey of exploration was made possible by the sense of internal stability residing in memories of loved ones, 'constant to every place'. A few months before, Keats had announced that 'Fancy is the Sails, and Imagination the Rudder' of Poetry, but now he realized that an anchor was just as necessary if the ship were ever to be properly launched.[49] With his elder brother making the long sea voyage to America, Keats's awareness of emotional ties and the mind's crucial contribution to their maintenance was acute.

Keats's anchor was a metaphor not only for personal relationships, but also for the strong ties of poetry. Just as Wordsworth had drawn on earlier poets to articulate his sense of natural connection with the life of things, so Keats affirmed his own network of personal bonds through memories of the poets whose homes he had now visited. 'Tintern Abbey' was clearly helping him across the silent plain, but Burns, too, had written about the need for an unfailing lifeline 'when on Life we're tempest-driven', before concluding that 'A correspondence fix'd wi' Heav'n, | Is sure a noble *anchor*!'[50] The complicated emotions stirred up in Burns's Country demanded a language steeped in literary associations and ideas that Keats was both echoing and challenging. As John Middleton Murry noticed many years ago, 'There is a Joy' is indebted in thought and cadence to Wordsworth's 'Star Gazers', which had been published in *Poems, in Two Volumes* with the political sonnets, the Scottish poems, 'Resolution and Independence', and 'The Immortality Ode'.[51] Keats's opening line was drawn from Wordsworth's speculation on the 'grave and steady joy' that might possess 'him who gazes, or has gazed', but his entire Scottish experience was raising the question posed by Wordsworth, of whether 'Hills of mightiest fame . . . betray us when they're seen?' The star that had led Keats to seek the low-cradle-place had not, after all, given rise to the kind of revelation he craved.

Wordsworth's unresolved exploration of the baffling experience of returning to the self after gazing on something long imagined provided a resonant model for Keats, who echoed 'Star Gazers' in word, phrase, and idea. His most obvious debt, however, was to the long rhyming couplets, which were adapted to create a sense of 'footing slow across the silent plain'. The verse was also reminiscent of Burns's 'Man was Made to Mourn', with its alternating four-beat and three-beat lines, which, if read aloud, sound very similar to the rhyming fourteeners used by Wordsworth. Since Keats's poem referred explicitly to Burns, he was using an appropriate form for the purpose, while also revealing the submerged presence of Burns in 'Star Gazers'. Both Burns and Wordsworth had offered hope of 'recompense' for the disappointed and dejected figures in their poems, but it was the form, metre, and language as much as their wisdom that provided a lifeline to Keats. The formal adequacy of poetry could not be achieved by responding only to personal experience: Keats's anchor was strengthened by earlier poems whose tried and tested lines offered him the stability to move onwards.

Wordsworth had himself paid tribute to the power of art to capture the intense but fleeting nature of experience in his sonnet on Sir George Beaumont's painting of a 'Bark upon the glassy flood | For ever anchored in her sheltering bay'.[52] The true artist could embody a moment of physical experience in forms that continued to give delight, long after the initial impulse was heard or seen no more. His own poems sought to rescue essential truths from the messy confusion of experience and make them permanent. As he explained in *Lyrical Ballads*, the poet was 'the rock and defence of human nature; an upholder and preserver, carrying everywhere with him relationship and love'.[53] Despite Wordsworth's emphasis on the poet's relationship with the real world, Keats now understood that the challenge was to find an adequate language, and, to embody his own experiences fully, he needed to incorporate the poems that conditioned his perceptions. Reynolds had been right when he praised Keats for looking at natural objects 'with his mind...and not merely with his eye', but it took time for Keats to develop a kind of poetry strong enough to stand up to the force of his imaginative energy.[54] The letters written in Scotland are a remarkable record of his mature poetry in the making.

As he moved north, away from Ayrshire, Keats continued to reflect on the places he encountered, but became increasingly frustrated by the inadequacy of mere description. Fingal's Cave, especially, brought home the limitations of straightforward representation in the face of such a staggering natural wonder. 'I am puzzled how to give you an Idea of Staffa', he wrote to Tom, and, even after a valiant attempt to conjure up the vast cave and its basalt pillars, concluded flatly, 'it is impossible to describe it'.[55] The poem that follows conveys the inexpressibility of his experience through a series of negatives:

> Not Aladdin magian
> Ever such a work began.
> Not the Wizard of the Dee
> Ever such a dream could see;
> Not St John in Patmos' isle
> In the passion of his toil,
> When he saw the churches seven,
> Golden aisled, built up in heaven,
> Gazed at such a rugged wonder.   (ll. 1–9)

The place that Keats had visited was not like anything else created, dreamt, or seen in a vision; but, as the baffled speaker searches for words, the sleeping figure of Lycidas comes to the rescue, awakened by a gesture at once tenderly human and yet charged with traditional meaning. The memory of Milton frees Keats from the difficulties of descriptive language and restores him to imaginative expression. Although both setting and sentiment are drawn from Keats's new experience, the figure of the young poet resuscitated by a kiss comes from his earlier, passionate pursuit of poetry. The poem reveals a strengthening synthesis between reading and personal experience, and, with it, a renewed sense of kinship with congenial literary predecessors.

Keats had not abandoned his ambitions to compose an epic in the Grecian manner, but his recent struggle with the nature of poetry meant that he would embark on his new task with rather more care than in his earlier plunge. During the Scottish tour, he had grappled with competing sources of truth, the limitations of language, and recalcitrant materials for future creation. Ideas for a mythological poem suddenly acquired a new kind of reality in Staffa, when Keats realized that the only way to conjure up its awe-inspiring magnitude was through an elaborate simile:

The finest thing is Fingal's Cave—it is entirely a hollowing out of Basalt Pillars. Suppose now the giants who rebelled against Jove had taken a whole Mass of black Columns and bound them together like bunches of matches—and then with immense Axes had made a cavern in the body of these columns...such is fingal's Cave.[56]

He had attempted to explain his own mental development to Reynolds through an extended image of the 'mansion of many apartments', but now Keats evoked human action to express the stunning natural architecture of Staffa. There was no clear division between the external world of nature and the internal workings of Keats's mind, and, at last, he was beginning to realize that he needed to re-create this dynamic interchange if his art were to achieve proper strength and buoyancy.

Wordsworth had led him to understand that nature should be his teacher, but it was the difficulty—and futility—of writing about scenery and 'visitings' of various kinds that helped him grasp the whole truth. Although 'Tintern Abbey' had pointed towards the dark passages of the human mind, Keats wanted to see the landscape that influenced Wordsworth's growth before submitting to such uncharted exploration. On his travels, he had learned to test ideas assumed from his reading against the facts as he perceived them, but direct observation of a greater variety of people and places did not prompt much spontaneous composition. The northern tour had initially heightened Keats's awareness of the misleading potential of poetry, when he recognized that his own notions were built on the sandiest ground. As he progressed, however, he saw that the best poetry had a way of distilling experience and rendering it into beautiful, lasting forms that could be shared by numerous readers, whose own memories were all too often fragmentary, arbitrary, or merely ordinary. By the time he travelled across Mull to the tiny island of Staffa, Keats was more concerned with finding ways to express his feelings than with worrying about whether what he saw was more real than what he had anticipated. His task was to create beauty for the relish of his fellow men.

New Direction

When he returned home to nurse his younger brother, Tom, Keats was helped through the distressing months by a new sense of personal direction. A letter to George and Georgiana, written in October, displayed a quiet confidence: 'I think I shall be among the English

Poets after my death.'[57] Despite Lockhart's blistering essay, Keats insisted that the only thing that could affect him was personal doubt over his ability, from which he seldom suffered ('and I look with hope to the nighing time when I shall have none').[58] He had come home with a much clearer sense of where he stood and now knew that he was not confined to any contemporary regional 'school': 'I feel more and more every day, as my imagination strengthens, that I do not live in this world alone but in a thousand worlds—No sooner am I alone than shapes of epic greatness are stationed around me.'[59] Keats might be caricatured as an ill-educated London apothecary, but he had been on a journey as profound as it was arduous. Nothing that the reviewers could throw at him would deflect him from his course, even though his brother's agonizing decline meant that he was unable to write very much during the last, painful months of 1818.

The poems Keats wrote in the year following his return from Scotland constitute his highest achievement and demonstrate a new intensity of focus. It was not that the questions had been solved, but they now seemed less of an impediment—'I have made up my Mind never to take any thing for granted', he wrote to George and Georgiana in December, without any suggestion that his creative progress would cease because of this insistent, restless probing.[60] A few lines later, he described his dawning sense of being able to apprehend truths at last: 'I never can feel any truth but from a clear perception of its Beauty—and I find myself very young minded even in that perceptive power.' Eight months earlier, Keats had doubted his ability to 'feel' the fine things that he read without having shared some of the author's experience, but now he recognized that developing the capacity to perceive and create beauty was as important as other kinds of experience. He was not rejecting the everyday, quotidian world for a separate aesthetic realm, for he had come to understand Wordsworth's insistence that beauty waited upon his steps and could be perceived in all kinds of surprising places. For a poet whose 'discerning intellect' was properly wedded to the universe 'in love and holy passion', beauty was 'a simple produce of the common day'.[61] Keats was affirming his faith in the capacity of art to embody the truths that could be discovered anywhere and thereby become a long-standing friend to man. However fragile it might seem, a thing of beauty had a kind of power that defied the tyrannies of fashion, physical decay, oppressive government, and even time itself. To confront adversity by composing poetry to the best of his ability was a gesture of defiance and hope.

Since his return from Scotland, Keats had concluded that the 'bodily eyes' could see only 'the fashion and Manners of one country for one age'.[62] Although he had set off eager to expand his knowledge, he soon realized that first-hand observation would always have limitations. However many people and places he might encounter, he would still be restricted by having only his own perspective at a particular moment of human history—'No man can live but in one society at a time'. Keats now thought that 'manners and customs long since passed whether among the Babylonians or the Bactrians are as real, or even more real than those among which I now live', and recognized that personal experience was not after all the only thing that mattered: 'The more we know the more inadequacy we discover in the world to satisfy us.' As the inadequacy of knowing the world became apparent, so did the realization that the power of art was not to be explained by straightforward mimetic—or documentary—qualities. *Caleb Williams*, for example, had been admired by Hazlitt, not for its accurate transcription of the world, but for its 'intense and patient study of the human heart, and by an imagination projecting itself into certain situations, and capable of working up its imaginary feelings to the height of reality'.[63] The beauty Keats wished to achieve in his own work was not a cold, detached quality to be assessed by the eye or ear alone, but a complete, overwhelming force, felt in the heart and mind as well as all the senses.

Keats's renewed preoccupation with art and literature might suggest that his own attempt to 'learn poetry' in the Lakes and Scotland had been misguided. Certainly, the toll taken on his body must, in one sense at least, have outweighed any benefits of the tour. If he had concluded that art should not be a transcription of the external world, the point of loading himself with finer scenes and grander mountains was perhaps annulled. The experience of hard travel in unfamiliar places had nevertheless enriched his imagination and, crucially, demonstrated to him the way in which poetry could act as both ship and anchor to those responsive to its special strengths. It was no good trying to re-create the places that lived in others' writing unless he could feel their beauty personally, but he could learn much from the modern poets whose work had the strengths of Shakespeare or Milton. Keats had been disappointed by Wordsworth's absence from Rydal Mount, especially since it was due to Lord Lowther's Tory campaign, and plunged into deeper dismay by the reality of Burns's cottage. In neither case were the facts, as perceived by a young visitor on a particular day, able to come close to the deeper truths and long-lasting beauties of the poetry written in these very locations. This did not, however, diminish the poetry in any way, or its astonishing power to convince readers of its trustworthiness.

Keats's northern tour was vital to his developing understanding of art and to allaying the anxieties that had so often made him doubt his own direction. The local landscape and people were essential to both Burns's and Wordsworth's work, but it was their emotional relationship with the world around them and with existing poetry that helped them to create things of beauty. Though Keats had been excited to see the landmarks featured in Tam's drunken ride, Burns's real importance for him lay in the poems he knew by heart.[64] In 1816 he had written sonnets about escaping into the countryside to compose poetry; by April 1819 he had decided that it was better to live in town, 'for the sake of Books, which cannot be had with any comfort in the country'.[65] His Scottish journey had apparently given him a big enough 'doze of the Picturesque' for the time being.[66] Keats still found the social constraints of the city wearing, but he needed books in order to write. It was from reading Wordsworth and Burns rather than from visiting the Lakes and Ayrshire that he learned about both the human heart and the mind's ability to project imaginary feelings into poetic reality.

'Hyperion'

As he returned to work during the winter of 1818–19, Keats drew on the experiences of his tour, but not with an eye to the picturesque traveller. He was reviving his ambition to attempt an epic poem and casting his Titans in a cold, northern environment, inspired by his experiences:

> It was a den where no insulting light
> Could glimmer on their tears; where their own groans
> They felt, but heard not, for the solid roar

> Of thunderous waterfalls and torrents hoarse,
> Pouring a constant bulk, uncertain where.
> Crag jutting forth to crag, and rocks that seem'd
> Ever as if rising from a sleep,
> Forehead to forehead held their monstrous horns;
> And thus in thousand hugest phantasies
> Made a fit roofing to this nest of woe.
> Instead of thrones, hard flint they sat upon,
> Couches of rugged stone, and slaty ridge
> Stubborn'd with iron.   ('Hyperion', ii. 5–17)

The realm of Flora was left far behind, as Keats's new conception of
the 'naked Grecian manner' fused memories of Staffa with the Elgin
marbles, to envisage Thea and Saturn 'postured motionless | Like
natural sculpture in cathedral cavern' (i. 85–86).

Rather than probe the differences between art and reality, imag-
ined and observed, human and natural, internal and external, Keats
was developing a kind of poetry that obliterated such distinctions
and thus overwhelmed critical objection with the sheer force of the
passage as a whole. It was a very different kind of beauty from that
of *Endymion*, but one that demanded a response from the ear, eye,
body, and mind. The reader almost hears the force of the waters
repeated in the 'roar...hoarse...pouring', while the hugest fantasies
seem to seethe from half-animated, monstrous rocks. Unlike the
clear analogies Keats had used to depict the Ambleside waterfall, he
was now dissolving conventional distinctions between the workings
of his imagination, the physical setting, and the ideas of his new
narrative in order to demolish false oppositions between the external
universe and the astonishing world within. The mythical figures are
inseparable from their surroundings, for their groans are part of the
waterfalls' roar and they themselves, 'scarce images of life', lying
'like a dismal cirque of Druid stones, upon a forlorn moor' (ii. 33–5).[67]
When their individual voices are heard, they assume the sound of
water through simile and onomatopoeia: Clymene, 'like timorous
brook...lingering along a pebbled coast', Enceladus, with 'ponderous
syllables, like sullen waves | In the half-glutted hollows of reef-rocks'
(ii. 300–6). Keats was drawing creatively on the images that had
haunted his mind since his tour—the stone circle at Keswick, Fingal's
Cave, the shores of Mull, the numerous streams running down to
the sea—but each was flowing along with other ideas and sympathies.

Rather than attempt a traditional narrative poem, Keats was creating something new in which thoughts could not be separated from the texture of the verse, but burst upon the reader, embodied in imaginary beings and their surroundings.

Burns had conveyed his own gratitude for the inspiration of his region by creating a full-bodied muse, knocking on his cottage door, wrapped in a mantle of rivers, mountains, and local heroes. Keats's Titans were less domesticated, but nevertheless shared some of the concrete qualities of Burns's allegorical imagination. In neither poem was there any sense of intellectual concerns being detached from the facts of the body or the feelings of the heart. Keats recognized in Burns a kindred spirit, whose poetry celebrated the body, even as it underlined its mortal nature. He had not been able to write an adequate sonnet in Alloway, but Burns had nevertheless guided him towards paths that were now leading into his own, as yet, undiscovered territory.

Keats learned from both Burns and Wordsworth in order to make his own contribution to the collective advance of modern culture. Both had written poetry that brought their observations, feelings, and moral vision together in language fully adequate to the world in all its beauty and ugliness. The trip to their homelands made him realize, however, that his own imagination demanded a kind of poetry less obviously tied to the manners of one country in one age. When he turned to his new epic poem, he was revisiting the Wordsworthian insights mooted to Reynolds in May, but his own understanding of how to explore the dark passages leading from the Chamber of Maiden Thought had been enlightened by his trip. When Hyperion's feet touch upon a granite peak to dazzle the fallen Titans with light, he is re-enacting the illumination of a poet who suddenly sees more clearly into the darkness.

Although 'Hyperion' was based on Greek legend, it marked the beginning of Keats's serious exploration of the crucial topic for modern poetry: the mind of man. The narrator's descent into the den with no insulting light represented his own journey into the unknown depths unplumbed by Wordsworth. It was the entrance to the 'untrodden region' that Keats ventured into for his 'Ode to Psyche', with its grateful echoes of Wordsworth and yet evident desire to move beyond his achievement. In 'Hyperion', Keats discovered ways of conveying mental action more vividly than through literal description, and so his poem presented an ideal of cultural progress directly through speech and indirectly through its own peculiar form and language. The grand march of the intellect, which Keats had outlined to Reynolds, was clearly articulated by Oceanus, when he reminds his fallen companions of the inevitability of their defeat by successors 'more strong in beauty' (ii. 213). Unlike his namesake in *Endymion*, the Oceanus of 'Hyperion' recalls the fatalistic attitude of the ancient Celtic bard, Ossian, whose name he adapts and to whom Burns, Wordsworth, and Hazlitt had each paid tribute. Keats was blending the classical Oceanus with native poetic traditions and his own experience of the Atlantic as it roared through Fingal's Cave. The result was a modern version of an ancient world, proud of its own power and yet prepared to concede to an even greater beauty:

> We are such forest-trees, and our fair boughs
> Have bred forth, not pale solitary doves,
> But eagles golden-feather'd, who do tower
> Above us in their beauty, and must reign
> In right thereof; for 'tis the eternal law
> That first in beauty should be first in might.   (ii. 224–9)

Hazlitt had seen Ossian as the 'decay and old age of poetry' and thus inadvertently provided Keats with a way of countering the Enlightenment equation between the earliest stages of society and the most energetic, vigorous poetry.[68] In 'Hyperion', which heralds the arrival of Apollo's warmth and beauty in the desolate, northern den of the Titans, Oceanus emphasizes the antiquity of ancient poetry and the desirability of new life. His image of the forest tree, reminiscent of Macpherson's renderings of the old Gaelic poetry, effectively reverses the anxiety felt by Keats in relation to the Elgin marbles. There, the impotent modern was a sick eagle gazing at the perfection of the ancient world; here, the ancients looked up to the moderns, whose beauty and knowledge had been nurtured in their boughs. The wasting of time, as visible in Greek marbles as in British stone circles, registered in Keats's portrayal of 'grey-haired Saturn, quiet as a stone', whose 'old right hand lay nerveless, listless, dead | Unsceptred' (i. 4, 18–19). The vivid physical imagery embodies the abstract idea of passing centuries and the associated feelings. Instead of the great mansion with its apartments, Keats was adapting imagery from nature, the visual arts, and earlier poetry to create a medium capable of conveying his idea of beauty overwhelming all other considerations. The stunning power of his own figures was in itself an answer to the troubling oppositions that he had been so keen to resolve, for his language blended the disparate and resistant elements into a new form.

'Hyperion' seemed to absorb Greek sculptures and Scottish seashores, ancient epic and modern philosophy, as the natural prelude to a new divinity, whose godliness depends on the acquisition of 'Knowledge enormous'(iii. 113). The modern poet derived strength from the accumulated wisdom and suffering of the world, which was so much older now than when Homer composed his great epics— 'Names, deeds, grey legends, dire events, rebellions, | Majesties, Sovran voices, agonies, | Creations and destroyings' all contribute to the painful power of Apollo (iii. 113–15). Keats had discovered that human history was as important to the poet as his immediate experience of the world, but, in order to make something meaningful from this collective deluge, he also needed to be able to distil its essential beauty. This was where Burns's powers of personification, Wordsworth's mastery of blank verse, and both poets' astonishing lyric abilities helped Keats to fulfil his ambition.

'Hyperion' remained incomplete, however, and the climactic moment of Apollo's deification is followed by empty space. Whether this should be read as the 'nothingness' that followed the epic vision of 'Sleep and Poetry', or as an invitation to modern readers to take up Apollo's challenge is open to question. Biographical evidence suggests, on the one hand, that Keats abandoned 'Hyperion' because of its excessive debts to Milton, and, on the other, that its composition was interrupted by that of the great poems of 1819.[69] Subsequent composition suggests that 'Hyperion' was abandoned only temporarily, even though it was published in his *Poems* of 1820. The 'Fragment' was, after all, a fitting form for a poem that attempted to convey the antiquity of Greek and Celtic epic within itself. Though the form might seem to undermine the poem's progressive philosophy by questioning the capacity of a modern poet to sustain the epic, as a 'Fragment' it could also stand, not as a relic of ancient perfection, but as a thing unfinished, poised in anticipation of fresh composition. Like a beautifully finished detail surrounded by blank canvas, the 'Fragment' was endlessly intriguing to any imaginative reader. In 'Hyperion', Keats had created a sequence of intensely realized images that suggested things much larger than any straightforward paraphrase could convey. By remaining independent of any particular historical moment, his poem could have many different kinds of meaning, personal, literary, political. At the same time, 'Hyperion' demonstrated that it was only through intense focus on the fully realized moment that any imaginative power could be achieved.

Keats and In-Placeness

'Hyperion' remained a tantalizing fragment, but its intensity heralded the vast idea of beauty Keats now hoped to realize fully in his poetry. Work on the epic had helped him develop methods of fusing together the different elements of his own experience—his reading, his ideas, his sensory perceptions—into poems that betrayed no awkward faltering or shifts of topic. Though incomplete, 'Hyperion' had a fullness and sense of inevitable movement, of words that earned their place by being self-evidently right. As Keats turned to different forms and subjects in 1819, many of his new poems achieved the same imaginative fusion and intensity discovered in 'Hyperion' and thus the self-sufficient 'in-placeness' so admired by Heaney. For his epic, Keats adopted the challenging form of blank verse, in the great tradition of Shakespeare, Milton, and Wordsworth, but his new sure-footedness made him eager to experiment with different metres, adapting various forms and making them his own. When he wrote 'The Eve of St Mark' in January, he borrowed his title from Scott, his heroine from Chatterton, his tetrameter from Burns and Coleridge, and his local detail from Chichester. The result was not quite like any of his sources, however, and shows a distinctive voice emerging, strengthened by the new clarity of purpose.

If *Endymion* had paid lip-service to the native muse, Keats was now devoting his full attention to medieval architecture, ballads, tales, and folklore, infusing traditional British material with new, exotic elements. 'The Eve of St Agnes' seizes the traditional northern ballad, charging it with warmth and colour to create a richly realized world that touched the senses, emotions, and intellect. Just as Apollo's triumphant appearance in 'Hyperion' reddened everything with warm air, so the bitter chill of St Agnes Eve is dispelled by the sight of Madeline with 'warm gules' on her breast, and 'rose-bloom' on her hands. It was as if Keats was redeeming British poetry through an infusion of Mediterranean blood. The sensual 'southern disposition', suppressed in Burns by the prevailing religious climate, was being freed to run riot in Keats's poems—and seemed all the more vital because of the cold surroundings. When Porphyro, flushed with passion, finally melts into Madeline's dream, 'as the rose | Blendeth its odour with the violet', the warm imagery is thrown into powerful relief by the surroundings—'Meantime the frost-wind blows | Like Love's alarum pattering the sharp sleet | Against the window-panes' (ll. 320–4). The kirkmen may have banished puns and kissing from Burns's world, but Keats had restored them to his own native poetry. Bards, in Keats's new collection of *Poems*, were not old, cold, melancholic Ossians, but figures of 'passion' and 'mirth', whose souls were found on earth as well as in heaven.

'The Eve of St Agnes' demonstrates a new boldness in its choice and vivid treatment of a subject that could be enjoyed on the level of straightforward narrative or through a variety of possible interpretations. As in 'Hyperion', Keats was binding together aesthetic and political ideas with emotional and physical impulses to create a poem resistant to unweaving, even as it offered the most tempting threads. His use of the Spenserian stanza and references to faeryland seemed an invitation to allegorical reading, but, at the same time, the elaborate rhyme-scheme offers its own satisfaction, irrespective of additional interpretative meaning. Stanzas such as this carry their own conviction, because of the beautiful vowel sounds, alliteration, and aural patterning:

> And still she slept an azure-lidded sleep,
> In blanched linen, smooth, and lavender'd,
> While he from forth the closet brought a heap
> Of candied apple, quince, and plum, and gourd,
> With jellies soother than the creamy curd,
> And lucent syrops, tinct with cinnamon;
> Manna and dates, in argosy transferr'd
> From Fez; and spiced dainties, every one,
> From silken Samarkand to cedared Lebanon.   (ll. 262–70)

The flatness of the word 'heap' helps to sustain the astonishing illusion that is being created in the reader's mind, while emphasizing the difference between Madeline's blissful oblivion ('sleep') and Porphyro's quietly urgent activity. The final 'p' in heap anticipates those of the 'apple' and 'plum', which in turn prepare the way for the more unexpected jellies, lucent syrups, and exotic fruits that follow. The sheer pleasure of the language makes the reader complicit with Porphyro's preparations, since each line whets the appetite aurally and imaginatively for the next.

Keats's growing awareness of sound effects made him revisit forms that he had already mastered, with renewed excitement. Although he still experimented with the Shakespearean sonnet, he was also bent on devising an entirely new rhyme-scheme, in which every stress was weighed, every rhyme counted. Even technical discussions demanded a wholeness of form, image, and meaning, so the constricting rhyme-scheme of a traditional English sonnet was figured as Andromeda, beautiful, naked, but chained to a rock. Keats was still paying tribute to Apollo, the God of poetry, medicine, and sandal-makers, but his mythological reference fused with an elaborate conceit involving the metric feet of poetry being fitted with 'Sandals more interwoven and complete'.[70] Keats had been criticized very publicly for the more unfortunate rhymes in *Endymion*, but he knew that rhymes, far from being fetters, could provide the anchor chains that gave poems their paradoxical stability and movement.[71] Although many sonnets were marred by their 'pouncing rhymes' and concluding couplets, their limited focus and tightly regulated shapes offered a possible prototype for the intense beauty Keats hoped to achieve.[72] Having already filled the Spenserian stanza with an unparalleled richness of language and imagery, Keats was moving on to create a kind of poetry equal to his high aspirations, weaving words together into intricately textured stanzas, resistant to all odds. As he wrote to George and Georgiana in America, mingling his literary thoughts with the English spring, the travelworthiness of poetry seemed ever more important: her sandals must be winged as well as interwoven.

In 'If by Dull Rhymes' Keats challenged himself to see what could be achieved 'by ear industrious, and attention meet'. Within weeks, he had written a series of poems that he called Odes even though their rich, regular, heavily rhymed stanzas differed considerably from those of Wordsworth's and Coleridge's great Odes. Both 'Ode to a Nightingale' and 'Ode on a Grecian Urn' dwell on the 'ear', whether in response to the song of a bird in a darkened garden or to the 'unheard' melodies that play from the images on the urn. Both have an almost Burnsian sense of direction, because of their focus on a single object, and yet each possesses multiple meanings, held in play by a structure that brings a meaning of its own. The Odes are intensified by contrasts between art and life, happiness and despair, youth and age, colour and darkness, stasis and flight, oblivion and immortality, but each seems to belong naturally to the other. The hollow urn is both empty and overflowing, silent and yet full of songs, pipes and 'that heifer lowing at the skies' (l. 33). Keats was still exploring the relationship between different kinds of reality and finding words whose literal meaning often criss-crossed with their physical, acoustic power. The semi-personified 'quietness' of 'The Grecian Urn', for example, ushers in both an idea that recurs throughout and a sound-set that binds different words together almost imperceptibly:

> Thou still unravish'd bride of quietness,
>   Thou foster-child of silence and slow time,
> Sylvan historian, who canst thus express
>   A flowery tale more sweetly than our rhyme!   (ll. 1–4)

The 'i' of 'quietness' looks back to 'bride' before leading on to 'child', 'silence', and 'time', while the final consonant recalls 'still' and anticipates 'foster', 'silence', 'slow', 'Sylvan', 'express', and 'sweetly'; 'foster', in turn, introduces 'historian' and 'canst', which glance backwards and forwards to 'Sylvan' and 'than'. The dense pattern of internal assonance and alliteration counters any 'pouncing' end-rhyme, even though Keats's new verse owed much to traditional Shakespearian and Petrarchan sonnets. The carefully interwoven, ten-line stanzas, rhyming ababcdedce or ababcdecde condensed both sonnet traditions and abandoned the elegiac couplet, so that each verse seems complete in itself, while open to its companions within the greater whole. The Odes are almost like miniature sonnet sequences, though their radical adaptation of earlier form allowed a freedom for each poem to possess its own peculiar music, rhythm, and atmosphere. The short lines in 'Ode to a Nightingale', for example, gesture to the nightingale's beautifully unpredictable song and offer opportunities for startling shifts of tone ('But here there is no light'), or affirmation ('And purple-stained mouth'), or flight ('In the next valley glades').

The Odes meditated on questions that had preoccupied Keats for some years, but, unlike the somewhat untethered movements of the earlier epistles and dream visions, his ideas were being tightly reined into beautiful shapes that allowed them to remain unresolved without seeming out of control. Thoughts that had previously taken up entire poems and long letters were distilled into single lines, in words chosen so carefully that a train of other poems could be found within. 'Ode on Melancholy' fused recollections of Milton, Shakespeare, Thomson, Wordsworth, Coleridge, and Burns into lines whose central image commanded full attention, while radiating a dim awareness of earlier rainbows, morning roses, or sipping bees. Keats was still expressing his personal experience as truthfully as he could, but, since his mind was peopled by poems, exploration of its dark passages meant discovering literary shades. In the 'Ode to Psyche', Keats drew on both the classical myth of Cupid and Psyche, as conveyed through Adlington's translation of Apuleius, as well as his medical lectures and textbooks, in order to create an extended image of his own mind, more beautiful than the 'Mansion of many apartments' or the 'Vale of soul-making'. As he dressed 'the wreathed trellis of a working brain', Keats was creating a kind of poetry that embodied rather than merely described his thoughts and feelings.

As memories of sights, sounds, and feelings blended with poetic allusions, philosophical concerns, and factual knowledge, Keats achieved a literary beauty possessed of its own self-evident truth. 'Ode to a Nightingale', for example, re-created Keats's distinctive experience through sensual detail, brilliant acoustics, and recollection of nightingales in the poems of Wordsworth, Coleridge, Milton, Shakespeare, Ovid. His ode was, among other things, an answer to Coleridge's 'The Nightingale', because, through enriching its own sinuous lines with traces of earlier poems, it showed that, far from 'filling all things with himself', the poet could lose himself in the abundance of echoes. To suggest that earlier poets had somehow prevented their successors from seeing the 'real' world truthfully was to deny the truth of their poems and their vital place within the mind. There was no clear distinction between external and internal realities: the 'shadows numberless' were in fact full of poetic 'numbers' and similar understated puns. The obliteration of any opposition between reading and reality is especially obvious in the evocative image of Ruth, in tears amid the alien corn. For the song she heard 'when, sick for home' was the same that Keats caught far away in the Hebrides, though his ears were tuned by Wordsworth's Solitary Reaper. It was the song of all poets whose lyrics spoke to those who listened and that continued to provide a sense of connection, despite the alienating forces of time, scepticism, thoughtlessness, ill health, poverty, and even death. When a poet attained the true, 'unappeasable note', which Heaney has recognized in Keats, then his song was part of the nightingale's eternal life.

Once the immortality of art could be seen as the true friend of man, rather than as a kind of cold pastoral, mocking the transience of its audiences, the creation of poetry became the truly generous act that Keats had always hoped to accomplish. The strongly braced form of the Odes nevertheless enabled him to continue to question his tentative beliefs, avoiding complacency and creative paralysis. Their very wholeness meant that a sense of irresolution—and therefore, possibility—could be maintained, capturing the excitement of the fragment within the completeness of a fully realized poem. The Ode allowed for multiple meanings without any loss of overall clarity. The complexity of 'Ode on a Grecian Urn' is apparent by its second word—since 'still' could be an adjective, meaning tranquil or motionless, or a qualifier for 'unravished', which suggests a movement towards violence. Keats had long admired Shakespeare's capacity to be in 'uncertainties, Mysteries, doubts, without any irritable reaching after fact & reason' and now he had developed his own way of presenting the multi-layered nature of human existence.[73] Keats was attempting a kind of poetry equal to the achievement of the unknown creator of the ancient Greek urn, whose work had a beauty powerful enough to 'obliterate all consideration' or, as he put it in the poem, to 'tease us out of thought'.[74]

In 'Ode to a Nightingale' the poet is in the dark, and so, being forced to 'guess' rather than accurately identify what is at his feet, he creates a work that is at once true to his immediate experience and able to embody his rich memories, hopes, and fears. As he echoed 'Tintern Abbey' in the 'weariness, the fever and the fret', Keats was taking up the challenge that Wordsworth had held out and was exploring the darkness within the mind as well as the shadows cast by circumstance. His response was to create a poem so rich in reference to strong, corroborative poetry, so braced by internal rhymes, wordplay, assonance, and alliteration, that, although the world where youth grows pale and spectre-thin and dies is acknowledged unflinchingly, it is made to seem an integral part of the overall beauty. Keats responded to the pessimism of Burns's 'Despondency' or Coleridge's 'Dejection' and the bracing admonishment of 'Resolution and Independence' by creating an Ode that demonstrated the creative rewards of melancholy. Keats's resolution was to accept the human condition, with all its pain and sorrow, overcoming either despair or consolation with an intense concentration on the inherent beauty of the living moment. The melancholy fit did not lead inevitably to creative paralysis, nor to despondency and madness, but descended from 'heaven like a weeping cloud'. Keats knew as well as Burns and Wordsworth that melancholy was the inseparable companion of delight, but his image of the poet as one who could 'burst Joy's grape against his palate fine' meant that the recompense was abundant enough.

'To Autumn' offered no escape into the lost songs of spring, embracing instead the different, full-throated chorus of maturity. With such an overwhelming present, neither lament for lost joys nor hope in those to come seemed necessary. The full-grown lambs bleated as loudly as the Urn's lowing heifer, but the gathering silence is held triumphantly at bay in the intensely realized moment. In fact, hints of the swallows' imminent departure only heighten the significance of their present twitterings. Keats knew the proximity of born and 'bourn', and his poetry celebrated the power of language to transform the awful ironies of existence into eternal puns and kisses.

In 1819, following the death of his younger brother, his engagement to Fanny Brawne, and the realization of his own fatal illness, Keats meditated on the capacity of the most fragile forms to survive. Though his poems acknowledged the destructive nature of human society, the beauty of his language remained quietly defiant. The Odes Keats composed during his last intensely creative year were more than equal to his own harsh, personal circumstances and historical moment and to those of readers in very different times and places. As the American poet Philip Levine found when growing up in the unpromising industrial landscape of modern Detroit, Keats showed that he did not need 'to live apart from the daily difficulties of the world' in order to create things of beauty.[75] Keats had learned by 1819 that lyric poetry carried its own anchor and was, therefore, free to travel across the oceans of space and time. If he had once cast himself as an early voyager gazing out on the Pacific, he had come to realize that aspiration and frustration, desire and despair, could all be eternally present as long as the poem was properly buoyant, braced, and ballasted.

7

In the City

For Keats, there was no psychological pump in the backyard from which to draw imaginative draughts, but his intense responses to the immediate world fused with a rich, inner life of memories, books, and personal relationships. His attraction to Wordsworth and Burns nevertheless demonstrates the power of local attachment irrespective of shared regional origins: someone with little experience of low and rustic life could still hope to aspire to the high ideals set out by Wordsworth or respond with deep feeling to the songs of Burns. Keats showed that the hopes of the previous generation had not been misplaced by finding corroboration for his own creative journey in their poetry. For later readers, who felt far more distant from the earth than either Burns or Wordsworth, Keats held out the possibility of achieving the same kind of fully embodied art, persuasive enough to carry its own in-placeness. His significance for all those to whom cities and suburbs are more familiar than lakes or mountains is immense, since his poetry has the trustworthiness of local work while remaining much less obviously tied to an unchanging landscape. Numerous nineteenth-century poets followed Burns and Wordsworth in celebrating their attachments to rural regions, from Clare in Helpstone to Housman in Shropshire, while many followed Scott's example in re-creating their favourite countryside in both poems and novels, from Hogg in Ettrick or the Brontës in Yorkshire to Hardy in Dorset. As George Eliot reflected in *The Mill on the Floss*: 'These familiar flowers, these well-remembered bird-notes, this sky with its fitful brightness, these furrowed and grassy fields, each with a sort of personality given to it by the capricious hedgerows—such things as these are the mother tongue of our imagination, the language that is laden with all the subtle inextricable associations the fleeting hours of our childhood left behind them.'¹ Local attachments and local truths contributed as much to the great nineteenth-century novel as to the poetry of the Romantic period. What is perhaps less immediately obvious, however, is that local truth was just as important for those living in cities.

For Keats, local truth meant the creation of a kind of poetry capable of overwhelming readers everywhere with its beauty. Many other urban writers responded to the great Romantic poetry of local attachment by finding expression for their own familiar worlds, irrespective of whether these conformed to conventional aesthetic notions of fine architecture, or whether poetry was their form of choice. Burns and Wordsworth found second selves not just among the poets most able to admire their lyric beauty, but in a host of prose writers and novelists, for whom local attachment was the mother tongue of the imagination, even though their homes were not among hedgerows and grassy fields. To attempt an account of the massive legacy left by Burns and Wordsworth over the past two centuries would be foolhardy at this late stage, but a brief exploration of local attachment in urban writing will help to show that this crucial aspect of the Romantic revolution was not confined to lyric poems any more than to particular landscapes.

Attachment and Alienation in London

As soon as Charles Lamb received the newly enlarged edition of *Lyrical Ballads* in 1800, he wrote to Wordsworth excitedly: 'Separate from your company, I don't much care if I never see a mountain in my life—I have passed all my days in London, until I have formed as many and intense local attachments, as any of you *Mountaineers* can have done with dead nature.'² Wordsworth's celebration of the Lake District in 'Michael', 'The Brothers', and the 'Poems on the Naming of Places' prompted Lamb to recognize the psychological importance of home: 'My attachments are all local, purely local.' Where Wordsworth drew creative energy from the fells and lakes, Lamb's inspiration sprang from 'the Lighted shops of the Strand and Fleet Street, the innumerable trades, tradesmen and customers, coaches, wagons, playhouses, the bustle and wickedness about Covent Garden, the very women of the Town, the Watchmen, drunken scenes, rattles'.

The pulsating life of London, its sounds, smells, and endlessly shifting sights, fed his heart and stimulated his writing just as surely as Wordsworth drew sustenance from the swarm of sensations in Grasmere vale.

Lamb's outburst of metropolitan loyalty was not so much a counter to the rural bias of *Lyrical Ballads* as a sympathetic endorsement of Wordsworth's faith in the universal meaning inherent in local attachments. He was among the first to respond with real understanding to Wordsworth's bold affirmation of the profound importance of local work and to see at once how it related to his own, innermost feelings. *Lyrical Ballads* helped Lamb to recognize what he already felt—that local attachment depended, not on conventional ideas of picturesque beauty, but on the psychological bonds fostered there. A place could fall far short of Gilpin's guidelines on a beautiful landscape but still provoke the most passionate feelings in its residents and therefore the most powerful literature. Whatever Coleridge might say about the disastrous consequences of an urban education, Lamb knew that his own impulse to write was fostered by the city. Born 'under the nose of St Dunstan's steeple' at Temple Bar, Lamb formed deep attachments to the City of London, just as Wordsworth's heart was anchored in the Lakes.[3] In each case it was the familiarity of the environment and the distinct human dimensions that proved so sustaining. For Lamb, the encounter with someone else's celebration of local attachment startled his own grateful sense of being a Londoner into prose.

Although Lamb's statement of his own local attachments was one of the most perceptive responses ever made to *Lyrical Ballads*, it was not very well received by Wordsworth. His reply has not survived, but Lamb's summary suggests that his friend had taken offence: 'he was sorry his 2d vol. had not given me more pleasure (Devil a hint did I give that it had *not pleased me*).'[4] Wordsworth may have been hurt by a specific criticism or by the general tone, but it is most probable that he was discomforted by his friend's witty dismissal of 'dead nature' and unaccountable preference for the city. For, although Wordsworth's collection revealed that paradise could be recovered from within the world of all of us, it also betrayed lingering concerns about the tendency of certain environments to stifle better impulses. When he outlined the forces threatening contemporary society in the preface, Wordsworth singled out 'the accumulation of men in cities' as something destructive to the human spirit, while, in 'Tintern Abbey', it was the condition of being 'in lonely rooms, and mid the din | Of towns and cities' that demanded the redemption offered by rural memories. In *The Prelude*, the profound anxieties associated with the city would demand an entire book.

The city, in Wordsworth's poetry, was often a source of restless, negative energy and not conducive to the recovery of hidden stories, personal spots of time, or the essential passions of man. The images of London and Paris in *The Prelude* were rather the means by which Wordsworth emphasized the depth of his gratitude for the permanent gift bestowed by the very different landscape and people of his home country. Wordsworth's claims to universality and longevity were nevertheless substantiated by sympathetic readers such as Lamb, who showed that his poetry could awaken a creative response in those living in a wholly different physical environment. Beneath their local distinctions lay fundamental similarities in the relationship between the individual and his familiar world, for Wordsworth's difficulty with London was not so much that it was a *city* as that it was unfamiliar. London appears in *The Prelude* like a grotesquely distorted mirror image of the Lake District scenes, reminiscent of the challenge posed by Pandemonium to the divine creation in *Paradise Lost*. For a young man brought up in the Lakes, London had once seemed as enticing as the fabulous cities of legend, so *The Prelude* is recording a moment in which imaginative expectation collapses in the face of first-hand experience. The degree of turmoil that London stirred up in Wordsworth was even greater than that of Burns's encounter with Edinburgh or Keats's visit to Alloway and is registered in the brilliantly re-created struggle to find a language adequate to the overwhelming circumstances. Book VII portrays the terrifying prospect of old familiar things being submerged by an unmanageable present, as the 'reality' of the new world displaces local trust with falseness and superficiality.

Wordsworth's horror at the perceived threat posed by the city to man's natural attachments helps to shed light on Lamb's very different response. Unlike Lamb, Wordsworth was profoundly troubled by the perpetual movement of the crowds and Hackney coaches, the Comers and Goers in the overflowing streets, conveying his sense of bombarded bewilderment in the unspecific 'Face after face . . . Shop after shop' (vii. 173–4). It was a world that offered no secure foothold to the traveller, no welcoming hand to guide him to safety. In the village communities of the North, people knew each other so well that they had no need of epitaphs or public records, but here Wordsworth found that 'the face of every one | That passes by' was a mystery (vii. 597–8). His imagery often emphasized the disorientation that came from feeling so cut off from his familiar terrain, as memories of the Derwent, of Greenhead Gill, or the Cocker were utterly submerged beneath the 'endless stream of men, and moving things' (vii. 158). What had always been real turned into a terrifying metaphor. Even when he took refuge from the thronging streets, Wordsworth found in the popular panoramas and spectacles only 'mimic sights that ape | The absolute presence of reality' (vii. 248–9). In London, everything was present, but always oddly unreal, while the roar of the external world seemed to blast any budding poetic impulse.

Especially disconcerting were the strangers from abroad. The ironic account of heading 'homeward through the thickening hubbub', like Satan flying through Chaos, includes 'among less distinguishable shapes, | The Italian, with his Frame of Images | Upon his Head', the Jew with his basket and the 'slow-moving Turk' with a 'freight of slippers piled beneath his arm' (vii. 228–31). As the description continues, specific types become little more than a haphazard catalogue of nationalities:

> The Swede, the Russian; from the genial South,
> The Frenchman and the Spaniard; from remote
> America the Hunter-Indian; Moors,
> Malays, Lascars, the Tartar and Chinese,
> And Negro Ladies in white muslin Gowns.   (vii. 239–43)

The uneasy rhythms in the list of dislocated nouns register Wordsworth's anxiety over what seemed an unnatural display of universal displacement. It was a nightmare of uncreation, of order overturned by uncontrollable forces, where the great races of the Enlightenment world view—The European, Negro, Chinese, Tartar, and American— had all been jumbled together as if in mockery of God's divine plan.[5] Instead of remaining distinct individuals with their own homes, connections, personal histories, and inner lives, everyone who arrived in London seemed to turn into the same kind of indistinct 'shape'. Wordsworth's London was an 'undistinguishable world', where all those living 'amid the same perpetual flow | Of trivial objects' were steadily 'melted and reduced | To one identity' (vii. 696–704). The thronging streets, filled with a bewildering mass of merchants, immigrants, and foreign visitors, were completely antithetical to his ideal of hardy individuals rooted in their native soil.[6] The sameness and narrowness of experience that he considered necessary for the essential passions to take root were parodied by contemporary London, where, instead of feeling that 'we have all of us one human heart', people were unconsciously melted into one characterless mass. The stagnant 'fen' was as stifling to the individual as it was destructive of local and national attachments. Above all, it cut him off from the world he knew, rendering him a stranger in his own country just as surely as did the war with Revolutionary France. Wordsworth was dismayed by the sight of 'Swedes', 'Lascars', and 'Negro Ladies', not because they were foreign, but because they were images of his own sense of homelessness.

Though the somewhat exaggerated account was partly a rhetorical strategy to emphasize the underlying stability of Wordsworth's earlier attachments and to offer a dramatic backdrop for the striking individuals who stood out from the crowd, the confusing lists of disconnected sights and sounds convey a genuine difficulty. Wordsworth's fears were far more personal than the traditional concerns about metropolitan corruption that had been gathering force as 'luxury' became a fiercely political issue.[7] For the poet who believed that his imagination had been nurtured by a countryside steeped in childhood memories and local stories, the physical facts of London were deeply problematic. The sheer volume and variety of sensory experience overpowered his internal equilibrium, laying 'The whole creative powers of man asleep' (vii. 655), while many of the truths revealed in London pointed to the defeat rather than triumph of the human spirit. London had overwhelmed the young northerner on his first visit and continued to threaten his faith in poetry's capacity to embody essential truths or to withstand competing distractions.

Although Wordsworth's supposed imaginative failure was being countered by the quality of his account, the horror of Book VII is powerful enough. The difficulty of creating beauty from the chaos of London is underlined when the poem turns, in seeming desperation, to the archaic trope of invoking a muse:

> For once the Muse's help will we implore,
> And she shall lodge us, wafted on her wings,
> Above the press and danger of the Crowd.   (vii. 656–8)

The urge to look down on the crowded streets was an expression of a deep need for order and meaning amid the fragmentation of city experience. Surrounded by endlessly moving, disconnected sights and sounds, Wordsworth could not experience the reassuring continuity of the deeply felt and meaningful landscape, and so, like Sweeney flying from the battlefield, he imagined an ascent into clearer vision. The motif of the muse provided a saving memory from an era when the city could be seen as part of a larger whole, as imaged in medieval and Renaissance paintings, walled and surrounded by green hills.[8] As Wordsworth projected himself above London, he adopted Miltonic language to contain the 'anarchy and din, | Barbarian and infernal!' within the ancient hills of his mental landscape. Like Keats in the Highlands, the very articulation of his fears revealed the power of poetry to combat otherwise overwhelming experience. Memories of *Paradise Lost* were strong enough to help Wordsworth express his response to London and to provide a sense of attachment when confronted by a nightmare of disconnection.

The very tone of his ascent above the 'danger of the Crowd' nevertheless reveals a sense that some literary conventions were not as travelworthy as others and that his own response to London was relying on the language of a vanished era. The half-humorous evocation of a muse was an acknowledgement that the modern city could not be contained by any comforting vision of 'order in variety' and burst out with a miscellaneousness defiant of transcendent meaning.[9]

As he re-created his impressions of London in 1805, Wordsworth could look back on a time when cities had their proper place in a divinely ordered world, but he was standing at the beginning of a century in which cities changed for ever and, with them, art and literature. As Wordsworth turned momentarily to the muse, he was both demonstrating a desire for transcendent order and conceding that traditional ways of understanding the world might not survive in the modern city. He rounded up his own disturbing memories with a reaffirmation of the spiritual resources of his mountain childhood, but the images of the city remain troubling to the grand scheme of *The Prelude* and have contributed to the long-standing charge that Wordsworthian Romanticism, taking refuge in a rural idyll that had ceased to exist for most British people, was fundamentally a poetry of retreat. When regarded in this way, his Victorian popularity seems as much an 'elegiac record of humanity's sense of alienation from its original habitat in an irrecoverable, pre-capitalist world' as nineteenth-century British landscape painting.[10] The increasing attraction of particular rural scenes in the Romantic period can, of course, be understood as a symptom of rapid urban expansion and the erosion of personal connection to the land. Lamb's response to *Lyrical Ballads*, however, provides a bracing counterblast to any accusations of nostalgia by showing explicitly that Wordsworth's appeal was not that of the countryside *per se*, but of real human beings in a convincing world. Lamb was as strongly influenced by his intelligent engagement with Wordsworth as Keats, but his choice of literary form and direction were very different.

For all Wordsworth's misgivings, Lamb's London was a personal place, pulsating with intimate feeling, bound with emotional ties and associations, and overflowing with imagined life. Unlike Wordsworth's idealized family farms, where domestic affections were inseparable from a sense of inherited responsibilities, the modern city streets belonged to no one and everyone. Their freedom was in this sense closer to Burns's rivers than to Michael's patrimonial fields. London was open to all and yet oddly exclusive, its residents bound by the familiarity of their environment and yet aware of their inevitable insignificance in the midst of so many people. Wordsworth's astonishment that in London 'men lived | Even next-door neighbours... yet still | Strangers, and knowing not each other's names' was simply the norm for those born and brought up in the metropolis.[11] For Lamb, the 'passion for crowds' that came so naturally to a Londoner made rural situations seem intolerably quiet and empty: 'a mob of happy faces crowding up at the pit door of Drury-lane Theatre, just at the hour of six, gives me ten thousand sincerer pleasures, than I could ever receive from all the flocks of silly sheep that ever whitened the plains of Arcadia or Epsom Downs.'[12]

Lamb's response to *Lyrical Ballads* led him to develop his thoughts into an essay, which appeared in the *Morning Post* under the title 'The Londoner'. Here he declared his loyalty to the city and affection for its citizens by answering contemporary assumptions about the health-giving effects of the countryside with a humorous defence of London's therapeutic atmosphere: 'The man must have a rare *recipe* for melancholy, who can be dull in Fleet-street. I am naturally inclined to hypochondria, but in London it vanishes, like all other ills.'[13] In an echo of the city-induced 'weariness', 'fever', and 'fret' of 'Tintern Abbey', Lamb suggested that his own recovery from such moods depended on London:

> Often, when I have felt a weariness or distaste at home, have I rushed out into her crowded Strand, and fed my humour, till tears have whetted my cheek for unutterable sympathies with the multitudinous moving picture, which she never fails to present at all hours, like the scenes of a shifting pantomime.[14]

Rather than turning inwards to memories of natural beauty and former happiness, Lamb combated his darker moments by plunging into the very streets that Wordsworth had found so oppressive.

Far from rejecting Wordsworth's work in his celebration of the city, however, Lamb was drawing personally from its revelations. The Lake District was almost as remote as Scotland, but Lamb passionately admired both Wordsworth and Burns, because he responded so powerfully to the feelings embodied in their work.[15] He could understand 'The Vision' or 'Michael', for his own local attachment was just as deep: 'I love the very smoke of London because it has been the medium most familiar to my vision.'[16] Affection grew from habit, so 'the very deformities of London, which give distaste to others' delighted Lamb.[17] If Wordsworth had paid tribute to Nature as his nurse, guardian, and guide, Lamb would give thanks for his upbringing in London, 'Nursed amid her noise, her crowds, her beloved smoke'.[18] Like Wordsworth, Lamb also experienced the creative benefits of encountering other places—his own preference for noise and crowded streets had been confirmed when Coleridge invited him to Somerset and then published a poem portraying him, in city pent, pining and hungering after the Nature.[19] Just as Keats realized in Alloway that he would never write an adequate Scottish song simply by visiting Ayrshire, Lamb discovered through his friendship with Wordsworth and Coleridge that his own work flourished best in his own world.

Adequate Forms

Lamb rose enthusiastically to the Romantic challenge of writing local work, but, where Keats would respond to the jumble of murky buildings by delving into the dark passages of his own mind and developing poetry strong enough to withstand external pressures, Lamb's London-based writings were largely prose. This was a consequence partly of contemporary magazine culture, partly of personal inclination, and partly for financial reasons. Besides the various practical considerations, however, was an artistic impulse to find the medium best suited to the experience of the modern city writer—a form adequate to the world he knew. Pope, Swift, and Johnson had all responded to London in rhyming couplets, but there was something about the random variety of the city streets—the endlessly shifting pantomime—that seemed especially suited to representation in prose. Wordsworth's uneasy revival of the muse in London and his heavy Miltonic allusions suggest a sense of disjunction between the high blank verse of *The Prelude* and the fleeting, distinctly unheroic series of images that stream through Book VII. When Lamb chose to express his own Wordsworthian practice of extracting meaning 'from the commonest incidents of a town life' in 'The Londoner', he used the form of the familiar essay as the best medium for what he had to say.[20] His writing was as true to his personally felt experience as Wordsworth's, but better suited to prose than to the magisterial movement of blank verse or the charged intensity of the lyric poem. Like other local work, Lamb's drew strength, not just from his immediate environment, but also from the earlier writers— and those who had drawn most from their daily experience of living in the metropolis had generally produced essays or novels.[21]

Prose was the natural choice for 'The Londoner'. Lamb's *Essays* were heir to a tradition that had been flourishing in London for a century, even though his own contribution was defined as much by difference as by similarity. Early eighteenth-century London had spawned a mass of new journals, pamphlets, and chapbooks, which offered financial rewards to a growing network of writers and publishers and helped create a sense of common ground for people entirely unknown to each other.[22] For the first time, publications were being written, not for a patron or coterie, but for an anonymous readership. Often, they reflected a metropolitan awareness of survival among strangers: Ned Ward's caustic observations on the contemporary city, for example, were published under the title *The London Spy*.[23] Almost as soon as publishing became economically viable for a mass audience, the people of London were buying local work whose continuing existence depended on entertaining those it portrayed. Ned Ward's hugely popular *Spy* presented the bewildering variety of city life in long, winding sentences full of physical details, down-to-earth similes, and colloquial expressions. The new journals appealed to people's fascination with themselves and with aspects of everyday human life neglected by more well-established media. This was not local work of the kind admired by Wordsworth or Heaney, since the essays were generally neither sympathetic to those depicted, nor ambitious to please posterity, but they were nevertheless subject to empirical tests of truth, because they aimed at readers who would recognize the real world in their words.

Addison and Steele borrowed from such works to create the more detached and less voyeuristic persona of the *Spectator*, whose short, beautifully finished, essays seemed designed to impress readers with their elegance and charm them into polite discussion. Although many of their remarkable essays were concerned with political, philosophical, and aesthetic questions, they also celebrated the multiplicity of ordinary life in the city, turning the attention of an avid readership towards London cries and coffee houses, playhouses and face patches, booksellers and banks, Smithfield and St Paul's, street signs, fashions, parks, and jokes and anything else that caught the eye of Mr Spectator. Often an essay would begin with a casual reference to everyday, personal experience of London—'Passing under *Ludgate* the other Day . . .', 'I was yesterday in a Coffee-House not far from the *Royal Exchange* . . .'—so that the issues under discussion were grounded in a recognizable world already familiar to readers.[24]

Addison's approach to the cosmopolitan character of contemporary London could hardly have been more different from Wordsworth's dismay, for, instead of emphasizing the isolation of displaced strangers, he perceived distinct groups and bodies among the larger crowd. The newly built Royal Exchange seemed a 'kind of Emporium for the whole Earth', where every fashionable visitor symbolized the power of the British nation to share its energy and prosperity with the most distant nations. All the world seemed to meet there, but, far from finding the spectacle distasteful, Mr Spectator revelled in being 'lost in a Crowd of Jews', or 'a Body of Americans' or 'a Group of Dutchmen'.[25] Rather than suggesting loss and displacement, the long list of different nationalities struck Addison as evidence of London's power to 'knit Mankind together', an ideal to which he also aspired in his writing.[26] In the metropolitan environment where, as Wordsworth saw with horror, people often did not know their nearest neighbours, the new print culture offered a vital means of shared experience. Addison, anticipating Benedict Anderson by three centuries, actively promoted among strangers the idea of a 'Fraternity of Spectators' and encouraged discussion of his ideas in homes and coffee houses.[27]

The *Spectator*'s popular success and critical acclaim meant that it continued to offer connections to isolated individuals years after its original publication. When Boswell moved to London from Edinburgh in 1762, for example, his journal recorded that he 'was full of rich imagination of London, ideas suggested by the Spectator'.[28] Like many other visitors, Boswell learned to read the city by reading the *Spectator* while his own prose gained confidence from knowing that others had walked down the very same streets. His journal was written in direct response to first-hand experiences, but it was also prompted by the essays that helped him see what was there. Addison's and Steele's essays provided a model for expressing the potentially bewildering experience of the thronging metropolis and, though impelled neither by Wordsworth's aspiration to permanence, nor by Burns's or Scott's regional loyalties, nor by Keats's pursuit of beauty, demonstrated a flexibility of style and plurality of voices that seemed quite equal to an environment where anonymity and mobility were the norm.

Like Addison and Steele, Lamb wrote with easy grace of things familiar to himself and readers, but his reflections on everyday life were much more personal and less detached than those of the *Spectator*. Despite the obvious debts of any London essayist to Addison, Lamb was eager to distinguish himself from his eighteenth-century forerunners and, in doing so, revealed the special character of local attachment in Romantic literature. When he reviewed Hazlitt's *Table Talk* in 1821, Lamb took the opportunity to emphasize the difference between modern essayists and those of the previous century, singling out the *Spectator* for particular criticism. Addison's chief limitation, in Lamb's eyes, was the creation of a persona who never came to life: 'He writes finely upon all subjects—but himself. He sets everything in a proper light—but we do not see through his spectacles. He colours nothing with his own hues.'[29] Detached spectatorship was not enough to create writing of a kind to move mankind, for Lamb, like Wordsworth and Burns, regarded feeling as fundamental to literary power.

Addison might have been familiar with the London streets, but his observations lacked the warm sense of a sympathetic relationship with his world and his fellow men. There was no sense of attachment to his community, nor any recognizable personality behind the prose. It was not that the observations were lazy or inaccurate, but they were lacking in emotion and therefore any real sense of belonging: 'They describe indeed with the utmost felicity all ages and conditions of men, but they themselves smack of no peculiar age or condition.'[30] Rather than writing from the heart, Addison excelled in 'wit', 'criticism', and 'morality', but his work failed to inspire readers of Lamb's generation because of the 'cold generalities' that militated against true attachment to the world. Lamb, who had been brought up on Burns and Cowper and fostered by Coleridge and Wordsworth, shared the Romantic admiration for writing that celebrated the particular, the personal, and the local. Without these vital human relationships, literature was in danger of seeming sterile, abstract, and irrelevant. The attachment of a writer to a real place meant that his work had an underlying fullness and unity—something absent from the *Spectator*, which, in Lamb's view, was 'little more than bundles of Essays... hanging together with very slender principles of bond or union.'[31]

The objections to the *Spectator* are most illuminating for Lamb's own practice and help to delineate the differences between London writing in the early eighteenth century and the Romantic period. In his *Elia* essays, Lamb was determined to maintain a consistent voice and to colour everything with the hues of his own mind and heart, even though his emphatically personal response to familiar places was prompted as much by reading as by residence. Elia's approach to 'The South Sea House', for example, was as much a reply to Addison's 'Royal Exchange' as 'The Londoner' had been inspired by Wordsworth's expressions of attachment to the Lakes. Lamb's opening address to his audience, 'Reader, in thy passage from the Bank—where thou hast been receiving thy half-yearly dividends', borrowed the *Spectator*'s formula, but imbued it with a more personal tone, emphasizing individual relationships.[32] As the essay unfolds, the personality of the writer is everywhere apparent, from the opening elegiac description of fading grandeur to the sympathetic accounts of the different cashiers and accountants, each named and fondly remembered. Lamb was composing a memorial to the once great house of trade and answering Wordsworth's anxieties about the anonymity and perpetual variations of city life. As he described the South Sea House, he evoked both Wordsworth and Addison in his prose:

Situated as thou art, in the very heart of stirring and living commerce,— amid the fret and fever of speculation—with the Bank, and the 'Change, and the India-House about thee, in the hey-day of present prosperity, with their important faces, as it were, insulting thee, their *poor neighbour out of business*—to the idle and merely contemplative,—to such as me, old house! There is a charm in thy quiet:—a cessation—a coolness from business—an indolence almost cloistral—which is delightful![33]

The passage that follows so naturally from Lamb's opening description of the South Sea House countered Wordsworth's famous equation of the city with 'fever' and 'fret' and ironized Addison's celebration of the energy of the Royal Exchange. Since 'the city' was filled with different feelings and fortunes, neither generalized dismissal nor exaltation of London was adequate to its complicated life and hidden stories. Lamb could write about favourite buildings with the same sense of their special character as Wordsworth conveyed in his Grasmere poems; in the process, he revealed the limitations of Addison's observations. Lamb's reminder of the South Sea Bubble and focus on the moths and dust now encrusting the one-time 'centre of busy interests' revealed that Mr Spectator's short-sightedness extended to economics as well as human beings. Though ultimately indebted to Addison, Lamb's thoughtful reflections on the ways in which a onetime hub could become a Herculaneum helped him stake his claim for a new kind of prose and a modern urban readership.

'The Great Cockney'

Lamb's adaptation of Wordsworthian ideals shows that the desire to convey the personal and particular was not exclusively the province of poetry. In the nineteenth century, numerous writers followed Lamb's example, creating prose works that demonstrated strong local attachments in the midst of what Wordsworth regarded as the least congenial environment for any such feelings. The city that Wordsworth thought likely to lay 'the whole creative powers of mind to sleep' actually worked like an awakening breeze on one of the nineteenth century's greatest exponents of local attachment— Charles Dickens. Dickens's London is already the subject of numerous studies, but some consideration of his early career offers insight into the way in which the Romantic literature of local attachment contributed to the Victorian novel.

Dickens launched his writing career in the newspapers, with the descriptions of everyday life in contemporary London that became *Sketches by Boz*. The essays were presented as the work of 'a regular Londoner', whose authority came from his intimacy with the places described and affection for the residents.[34] 'Boz' was evidently writing as an insider, entirely at ease in the maze of streets. Like Scott and Wordsworth in their native territories, Dickens was both satisfied with the world immediately around him and eager to share its secrets, but he followed Lamb in his choice of prose as the medium adequate to his experience.

Dickens was fascinated by the 'gin shops' and 'dirty, straggling houses' in the parts of London less frequently visited by writers, but, far from presenting them as objects of disgust or shame, his overriding tone was of affectionate excitement.[35] Instead of apologizing to a middle-class audience, Dickens preferred to whisk them along the busy streets, pausing to consider the door knockers, cabs, and shop windows, while eavesdropping on conversations to catch Kensington accents or cockney slang. The illusion created in his early prose was of immediate proximity to the scene and spontaneous re-creation of real life—as expected from a 'sketch'. At the same time, his essays revealed an awareness of contemporary prejudices about 'low life' and the literary conventions relating to the city. When Wordsworth had struggled to re-create his experience of London in 1805, the image of Milton's Hell, with shades of Dante and Hades, had risen irrepressibly.[36] Dickens, equally aware of such associations, employed them playfully, to very different effect. When he evoked the Underworld, it was for a sketch of Monmouth Street, the 'burial place of the fashions', where the 'extensive groves of the illustrious dead' stood open for readers to enter.[37] Dickens acted as a guide, conducting his companions through a world thick with human history and emotion. Among the cast-offs of unknown

Londoners, Dickens could feel the strangers who had passed through the same streets over the years, leaving traces of their lives, even though their names had disappeared. London's rapidly changing history was hung on the old racks: 'Pilot greatcoats with wooden buttons have usurped the place of ponderous lace coats with full skirts; embroidered waistcoats with large flaps, have yielded to double-breasted checks with roll-collars'. The tailors and their original customers were now untraceable, but packed into the tight racks was a throng of almost-present strangers, their stories woven into tired fabrics. Second-hand clothes shops furnished Dickens with a rich metaphor for the city and the people who constituted its endlessly altered life.

Ringing the changes on Addison's Royal Exchange, Dickens's witty metaphor encompassed clothes, cities, and the human condition. Several of the old garments might have belonged to the same person at successive stages of life, from the blue suit of the small boy to the coarse frock of the prisoner: as he measured out a life in coat sizes, Dickens demonstrated the writer's ability to breathe life and meaning into the discarded and outgrown. Instead of recoiling in confusion from the shifting surfaces of London, Dickens gathered together pieces that particularly caught his eye and made them into something marvellous. Memories of the dead, the outmoded, and the outwitted crowded the second-hand shop, but a fresh eye and skilful craftsmanship turned them into serviceable goods, ready for recirculation. Dickens also delighted in cutting old, familiar materials into new patterns, for stitched into the background of 'Monmouth St' was Lamb's essay on 'Old China', where memories of different outfits had served as an index to fluctuating happiness and prosperity.[38]

Lamb was one of the unnamed but benevolent shades haunting Dickens's entire series of *Sketches*, along with Johnson and Addison, who had helped to create the literary form so well suited to capturing the variety of the capital. As with so many local writers, recollection of freshly imprinted observations acquired extra depth from Dickens's reading. In 'Monmouth Street', he was paying tribute to a living city, whose rich meaning depended on its numerous residents— including the writers. Though the title of his collection, *Sketches by Boz*, suggested rapid responses to immediate experience, Dickens's apparent spontaneity had been greatly helped by earlier masters of the form. 'Sketches', even more than Romantic fragments, also carried a promise of more substantial work to come.

When Dickens turned his hand to writing a novel set in London, it made sense to use materials and methods similar to those of his successful *Sketches*. In *Oliver Twist*, the melodramatic images of Fagin, 'skulking only through byways and alleys', work because the byways and alleys are evidently part of a world that is deeply familiar to the narrator: 'Near to the spot on which Snow Hill and Holborn Hill meet, there opens: upon the right hand as you come out of the city: a narrow and dismal alley leading to Saffron Hill.'[39] Although the scene is so different, the technique is reminiscent of the opening lines of 'Michael', where the narrator's local knowledge not only authenticates his tale, but also invites readers to listen to what he has to say. Dickens's careful use of detail suggests first-hand experience, but passages of apparently straightforward reportage are also rich in allusion, alliteration, internal rhyme, and symbolic significance:

In its filthy shops are exposed for sale, huge bunches of second-hand silk handkerchiefs, of all sizes and patterns; for here reside the traders who purchase from the pickpockets. Hundreds of these handkerchiefs hang dangling from pegs outside the windows, or flaunting from the door-posts; and the shelves within are piled with them. Confined as the limits of Field Lane are, it has its barber, its coffee-shop, its beer-shop, and its fried-fish warehouse. It is a commercial colony of itself: the emporium of petty larceny: visited at early morning, and setting-in of dusk, by silent merchants, who traffic in dark back-parlours; and who go as strangely as they come.[40]

The observation of the various shops offers an apparently objective guide to readers unfamiliar with the area, but the passage is also pulsing with an undercurrent of insider excitement over the thrilling sight of 'huge bunches of second-hand silk handkerchiefs' and their tempting, ominous situation, hanging and dangling outside. Dickens's portrayal of Field Lane harks back to Addison's Royal Exchange, his strange merchants and 'emporium of petty larceny' mimicking the *Spectator*'s proud 'emporium for the whole earth'. The thin lines between theft and trade, commerce and crime, are only too evident in Dickens's description, which self-consciously deals in its own second-hand materials, even as it asserts the authority of first-hand knowledge. When he wrote his novels, Dickens was trading different parts of himself—reshaping early essays and techniques, drawing on books and personal experience, remembering stories gathered in the London streets. David Copperfield would subsequently offer helpful insight into his creator's imaginative development by describing 'the manner in which I fitted my old books to my altered life, and made stories for myself, out of the streets, and out of men and women'.[41] By 1850, Dickens was sufficiently established to reflect publicly on the growth of a London writer, but his skills in making stories from the streets and fitting old books to a rapidly altering life were evident from his earliest work.

For a city novelist, whose work was to be published in monthly parts, careful strategies were needed to avoid the narrative collapsing into disconnected episodes. The huge cast of characters necessary for a convincing representation of London life demanded methods quite different from those appropriate to writers in rural areas. As Words-worth realized with a shock, rural communities were largely based on face-to-face relationships among people who knew each other by name and nature, whereas, in the city, the very idea of a community seemed somewhat misplaced.[42] The challenge for Dickens was to create a sense of personal connection within his London fiction, even as he conjured up jostling crowds of passing strangers. In *Oliver Twist*, the plot was constructed in such a way that characters initially introduced as strangers to each other would gradually discover connections, but the often-contrived plot mechanisms are tolerable largely because of the more subtle use of recurrent images and ideas, which form links between different chapters and quietly create the community of the novel.

Among the motifs developed by Dickens to construct a fictional community equal to the opacity of the modern city was that of the second-hand clothes, first explored in 'Monmouth Street'. Just as Wordsworth had urged a stripping-away of superficial differences in the quest for a common humanity, Dickens was only too conscious of 'the power of dress':

What an excellent example of the power of dress young Oliver was! Wrapped in the blanket which had formed his only covering, he might have been the child of a nobleman or beggar…But now that he was enveloped in the old calico robes which had grown yellow in the same service, he was badged and ticketed, and fell into his place at once—a parish child.[43]

Oliver was placed more definitively by the social than the geograph-ical coordinates of his birth. If Wordsworth looked for social recovery in rural areas, however, Dickens was alert to the potential problems of a small community in which the accidents of birth often determined lifelong prospects. London might be intimidating and even dangerous, but it nevertheless offered the possibility of shedding an existing identity and constructing a new one among strangers. The aspect of metropolitan life most troubling to earlier observers such as Mandeville or Smollett, who deplored the misleading appearances of well-dressed, upwardly mobile Londoners, was explored and re-explored by Dickens.[44] To those used to the transparency of an eighteenth-century rural community, the misleading surfaces of the city seemed fraught with danger, but, when Oliver Twist watches his old rags being carted off by the second-hand trader, he is freed from an unhappy childhood and ready for a new life. Dickens knew only too well that some familiar communities could be stifling rather than enabling and that the sheer size of London offered a prospect of recovery to those who could never create a new self at home. The rag stalls of Field Lane and the second-hand clothes shops of Monmouth Street were the burial place of identities as well as fashions, but not necessarily sites of lamentation.

Dickens was as alert as Wordsworth to the possibility of being engulfed by the uncaring crowd, as his later images of the Gordon Riots in *Barnaby Rudge* or of little Florence Dombey, robbed of dress, class, and identity, 'repulsed and pushed about, stunned by the noise and confusion', demonstrate, but the complexity of his novels allowed him to point to the positive dimensions of anonymity and changing identity as well.[45] His own career had, after all, benefited greatly from a press culture of anonymity, which gave new journalists a chance to present their work by the side of more established writers. Once given the opportunity, however, he was eager to create a distinctive literary identity for himself and dreaded being re-submerged. *Oliver Twist* was only the first of a series of remarkable novels that charted the interlocking and precarious identities of numerous characters in a city whose local truth was so persuasive that anything seemed possible.

For Dickens, clothing imagery was more than a tool for the social satirist. In *Oliver Twist*, for example, the movement of fabric was a key narrative principle, not only indicative of changing fortunes, but also forming crucial links between apparently unconnected people, ideas, and places. As John Jordan has pointed out, the 'patchwork coverlet' that wraps Oliver Twist's dead mother at the outset haunts the rest of the novel in the shape of surprisingly mobile pieces of cloth.[46] The 'huge bunches of second-hand silk handkerchiefs' in Field Lane may seem little more than a local detail, but in retrospect they connect the particular scene to the larger purposes of the whole. As the novel progresses, handkerchiefs become a crucial motif, used by Fagin to train his boys, by Noah Claypole for his belongings, by Sikes to encircle his neck like a noose, and by Nancy to plead for mercy. Handkerchiefs link Oliver to Fagin and his gang, to Mr Brownlow and Rose, to Noah, Sikes, and Nancy. They are a means of connection in an environment that might otherwise seem irredeemably various: a device whereby Dickens could create meaning without sacrificing the realistic sense of streets swarming with strangers. At the same time, the handkerchiefs worked allusively to link Dickens's London to earlier texts, hinting to Victorian readers that the new serialized novel might have secret aspirations to become 'a Newgate *Othello*'.[47] The stolen handkerchiefs lead just as readily to *Moll Flanders*, where Defoe's criminal heroine lifts clothes and accessories in the London crowd with a degree of self-possession more than equal to that of the Artful Dodger. They also flag up Dickens's twentieth-century heirs—in Eliot's 'silk handkerchiefs' floating down the Thames or Joyce's 'snot-green' image of Irish writing and, more recently, in Ali's *Brick Lane*, where the menacing Mrs Islam dictates to her husband through coded hankies.[48] Handkerchiefs are passports into the underworlds of the novel—to the hidden groves of writers dead or still to come.

The scraps of material circulating in *Oliver Twist* therefore provide links between the disparate characters, themes, social spheres, and successive instalments of a serialized novel and also between Dickens, his heirs, and predecessors. Dickens, like the Dodger, stole from Defoe and laid in stocks of material for future writers. The buildings he described and the people he sketched were inevitably transient, but his writing had the capacity to survive centuries of physical disruption and to provide connections and continuities with other texts. In a place where multiple occupancy was the norm and property for ever under new ownership, writers' materials changed hands easily, often reappearing in unexpected new forms. London had long been a great centre for trade, but within the capacious form of the Victorian novel were riches from the past and gifts for the future, as well as a perpetual interchange of contemporary materials and voices.

The very pleasure derived from rapidly changing scenes and characters, so abundantly obvious in Dickens's early work, also generated a need for connection and stability. The richness of the London experience meant that any true representation risked becoming fragmentary and ultimately rather meaningless. When he wrote *The Pickwick Papers*, in 1835–6, Dickens was fulfilling a commission from Chapman and Hall to create a comic gentleman's sporting club in a series of monthly parts, not unlike a series of sketches. As his characters developed, however, he became frustrated by the format, wishing 'that these chapters were strung together on a stronger thread of general interest'.[49] His new novel, accordingly, took the name of its central character, 'Twist', which meant, among other things, a thread for sewing different parts together.

The connections necessary to make artistic sense of a potentially unwieldy narrative were constantly being twisted through irony, contrasting scenes, opposing viewpoints, and recollections of earlier moments. Images were passed on from one novel to another, their meaning altering in the process. David Copperfield's recovery, material and emotional, for example, recalled Dickens's earlier insights into 'the power of dress' when Mr Dick advises that the ragged boy be 'measured for a suit of clothes directly'.[50] In *Great Expectations*, however, Pip's visit to Mr Trabb the tailor is the beginning of his slide away from the loving guardian of his youth. When Joe pays his visit to London, the difference between his solid virtue and Pip's misplaced obsession with status is symbolized through their contrasting appearances, as Joe holds tightly to his hat 'like a bird's nest with eggs in it', while his eyes roll 'round and round the flowered pattern' of Pip's new dressing-gown.[51] The excruciating comedy of the scene is a telling comment on the opportunities afforded by the city to those who wished to don a new identity and hide an unwanted background under a glossy new coat. Life in the city all too easily became a means to detachment—as Wordsworth emphasized and Dickens sometimes admitted. Though Pip's childhood had hardly been a happy one, the contrast between his ostentatious new dressing-gown and Joe's well-worn bird's nest hat is a powerful reminder of the value of old, familiar, far-off things, despite the excitement of the new. As Biddy and the reader recognize, Joe is a worthy man, whose goodness remains unchanged by circumstances and whose empty bird's nest defies the dazzling world of expectation. Dickens understood local attachments as well as anyone, but possessed the satirist's ability to present his own mental landscape as an alien environment for a character anchored elsewhere.

Scott had already seen that the novel offered a flexible form for presenting familiar communities from inside as well as out, and his border perspectives had proved to be perfectly trained for Scottish historical fiction. When he read *Castle Rackrent*, he had admired Edgeworth's ability to mediate between those within the novel and those turning the pages in astonishment, recognizing her quasi-diplomatic contribution to relations between Britain and Ireland. In *Waverley*, Scott had developed the device of the English visitor in Scotland, which enabled him to present parts of his own country from an unfamiliar angle and thus introduce familiar details to distant readers. 'Auto-exoticism' offered scope for sympathy and satire, participation and alienation, attachment and detachment.[52] The arrival of a newcomer in London had been a popular motif for comic satirists from Wycherley to Egan, but, because Dickens shared Scott's personal attachment to the settings of his fiction, his social observation was often rounded out with deeper emotion. Oliver Twist's vulnerability on arrival in London prompts alarm as much as amusement, his incomprehension underlined by the knowing insider who pops up to lead him through the darkness. Dickens could have followed Smollett in presenting the bewildering unfamiliarity of London as a terrifying mass of streets, houses, and passing strangers. Instead of leaving his tiny protagonist to wander and wonder, however, he immediately introduced a memorable voice: 'Hullo, my covey, what's the row?' The Artful Dodger's opening remark instantly distinguishes him from the crowd, from other characters, and from the narrator. Readers encounter his voice before any description of his appearance, and begin to learn about his world as he translates for Oliver. Like Scott, Dickens knew that the skilful use of local language was a way of helping readers participate in its imaginative life. For all those for whom 'cockney' meant foreign, the Artful Dodger was a mediator and guide. In a matter of sentences, Dickens juxtaposed the two worlds of the Dodger and Oliver, revealing through a contrasting comprehension of the simplest words how their understandings had been determined by their respective

local backgrounds: '"I suppose you don't know what a beak is, my
flash com-pan-i-on." Oliver mildly replied that he had always heard
a bird's mouth described by the term in question.'[53]

Dickens's attachment to London did not preclude sympathy with
those from elsewhere, and the representation of his home ground
was enhanced by an awareness of the city's capacity to baffle outsiders.
The London underworld into which the Artful Dodger leads readers
is just as threatening as the city represented in *The Prelude*, but there
is no sense in *Oliver Twist* of an indistinguishable stream of figures,
melted and reduced to one identity. Dickens's London, as both Henry
James and James Joyce subsequently recognized, was full of remark-
able, vital individuals, but it was also a place criss-crossed with
different kinds of connection.[54] The capacious chapters of the Dick-
ensian novel seemed to offer space to every kind of character and
every corner of London, while maintaining an overall sense of
internal connection. Dickens's novels were local work—trustworthy,
travelworthy, and overflowing with gratitude to the place from
which they drew life.

Dickens was just as attached as Lamb to the crowded streets of
London and often found other environments imaginatively sterile.
When he visited Italy, he wrote home wistfully about his failure to
make any headway with his new story 'Put me down on Water-loo
Bridge at eight o'clock in the evening, with leave to roam about as
long as I like, and I would come home, you know, panting to go
on.'[55] As Chesterton observed wryly: 'Amid the pictures of the Uffizi
he starved for something beautiful, and fed his imagination on
London fog.'[56] Dickens's imagination was nourished by memories of
his familiar landscape just as much as Wordsworth's, and so even the
breathtaking beauty of Botticelli and Michelangelo were less
inspiring than the London streets. When he travelled to Preston in
1854 to see the weavers' strike, he was similarly disappointed; 'I shall
not be able to get much here,' he confided in a letter to John Forster.[57]
When he was faced with an unfamiliar industrial landscape, Dick-
ens's imagination was as hard to ignite as the unmanned mill engines.
In Preston he remained a distant spectator, but in London he was
part of the place. As Joyce commented with admiration, London was
'the breath of his nostrils: he felt it as no writer since or before his
time felt it'.[58] Joyce understood from reading Dickens's work that his
local surroundings were essential to his emotional and imaginative

force: 'If Dickens is to move you, you must not allow him to stray out of the hearing of the chimes of Bow Bells. He is there on his native heath and there are his kingdom and his power.' No matter that Dickens was actually born in Portsmouth—Joyce was responding as one great parishioner to another, feeling the truth of Dickens's writing as local work. The *Blackwood's* reviewers had hurled the charge of being a cockney at Keats as a badge of shame, but in Joyce's eyes Dickens was a great writer because he was 'the great Cockney'.[59]

Post-Romantic Attachments

Heaney's affection for local work is rooted in his own childhood home in County Derry, but his understanding of its importance to the modern world has been opened and deepened over many years by his love of poetry. Wordsworth, especially, has proved a sustaining presence throughout his career and remains, for Heaney, a truly adequate poet. To assume that, since both Heaney and Wordsworth enjoyed a country childhood, their preoccupation with local attachment is primarily a rural concern would, however, be mistaken, as this study has attempted to demonstrate. The diversity of nineteenth-century literary responses to the Romantic discovery of local attachment suggests that local work thrives just as vigorously in cities as in the countryside—and may indeed occupy an even more important place in a predominantly urban society.

By the middle of the nineteenth century, the Romantic literature of local attachment had inspired varied and vigorous responses from poets, essayists, and novelists, whose work demonstrated that local truths could be discerned in the modern city just as readily as in the countryside. As urban life became the norm for the majority of the British population, its literature proved adaptable enough to survive in the most challenging conditions. When Victoria came to the throne in 1837, cities existed where before there had only been fields and villages.[60] As Birmingham, Manchester, Liverpool, Glasgow, Sheffield, Derby, Leeds, or Bradford became vast physical facts, millions of people found themselves living in places with no established literary traditions, no history of local attachment—so they had to create their own. The transformation of Victorian Britain and

Ireland brought into being unprecedented, self-authenticating local cultures that operated under different aesthetic laws and created their own traditions. Poets such as Edwin Waugh, 'The Lancashire Burns', for example, or Samuel Laycock, whose dialect poems sold in thousands, were part of a lively circle of brother bards, writing from and for the northern industrial cities of Victorian Britain.[61] Though not aiming necessarily to be among the English greats after their deaths, they were reaching out to vast contemporary readership, and their local attachments, not inappropriately, were tested by spatial rather than temporal boundaries.

During the eighteenth century, the new foundries and steam engines had attracted spectacular paintings and poems on the wonders of the modern world, but, as the great powerhouses of the Industrial Revolution became a permanent part of the landscape, they began to generate different challenges.[62] On the one hand, the increasing associations of the Victorian city with dirt, disease, and slum dwelling meant that Keats's questions about the kind of art fit for survival in the modern city took on a new urgency. On the other hand, now that the industrial cities had become home to so many, distant perspectives that looked on mills with either amazement or horror were no longer adequate to the situation. When Elizabeth Gaskell attempted to re-create Manchester in fiction, she was offering a challenge to metropolitan assumptions about art by attempting to give voice to people who had no place in the existing literary tradition, because their peculiar place in society was a by-product of the steam-powered loom.[63]

By the 1840s, the population of Manchester was six times greater than it had been when *Humphry Clinker* was published, and so Smollett's depictions of the elegant spa towns and university cities of northern Britain were no more helpful than distant vistas of dark factories silhouetted against a flaming sky.[64] Like Dickens introducing his *Sketches* as the work of a 'complete Londoner', Gaskell emphasized her inside knowledge of Manchester, translating the streets into words, transcribing local songs onto the printed page, and transporting readers into the homes of those who worked in the mills. Although the modern industrial city could hardly have been more different from rural Kyle or the Lakes, for *Mary Barton* the poems of Burns and Wordsworth offered models even more helpful than Dickens's metropolitan fiction. Their poems had shown the world that it was not necessary to inherit an estate, acquire a profession, or attend university in order to command respect or feel the most tender emotions. What really mattered was common to everyone, irrespective of class or country—but it was internal, rather than evident in the clothes they wore or the accents in which they spoke. The poetry of Burns and Wordsworth demonstrated in different ways that people who might be dismissed by some as an ignorant mass had not only equal rights, but often qualities far more admirable than those who failed even to see them as human beings. Their local attachments were, if anything, more powerful than those of their employers, because they were largely confined to a small area and did not enjoy the privileges of easy travel or country houses. Wordsworth's capacity to seek poetry in the most unassuming quarters was a constant inspiration to Gaskell, as she realized, with gratitude, 'the Poetry of Humble Life... even in a town, is met with on every hand'.[65] In *Mary Barton*, she included street songs and dialect poems such as 'The Oldham Weaver', but the poetry of her novel was also to be found in the Wordsworthian depths of emotion and the sympathetic creation of individual men and women whose hidden stories mattered so much.

Although some Victorian authors wrote largely for the expanding regional audiences outside the old cultural capitals of Britain and Ireland, others created local work that spoke powerfully to people with no first-hand knowledge of the great modern cities. In their very different ways, Keats, Lamb, Dickens, and Gaskell all rose to the challenge of composing work that was at once equal to their immediate circumstances and capable of reaching out to those elsewhere. The adequacy of local work, as Keats discovered when he made his pilgrimage to Alloway, was dependent not on realistic representation of the external world, but rather on truthful expression, which could take many forms. Browning's 'Fra Lippo Lippi', for example, though set in Renaissance Florence, advocates local truth just as passionately as Wordsworth or Heaney. Realistic description was crucial to the Victorian novel, but many writers also followed Keats's example, responding to the Romantic literature of local attachment with work truthful to their inner lives as well as to outward circumstances.

The well-known reactions of modernist writers against literary realism might suggest that local truth ceased to matter in the early twentieth century. Heaney's argument, however, points to the opposite conclusion—that it has never been more important. Whether we follow his examples and consider Yeats's 'Meditation in the Time of Civil War', or turn to the rather different case of Joyce in *Dubliners*, it is evident that twentieth-century writers have been just as indebted to ideas of local truth as their Romantic predecessors. The political situation in Ireland may have made the very notion of inherited traditions problematic, but it has also added impetus to the creation of local work that is both native and international.[66] In Scotland, too, Burns's desire to make his unkenn'd region known throughout the world has been matched in the years leading to devolution by poets and novelists determined to give modern Glasgow her cultural dues.[67] In the twentieth century, poets in England, Ireland, Scotland, and Wales drew on both the rich poetic traditions of the islands and the experimental form of the novel, which evolved side by side with the aesthetic ideal of local work. Though generally less inclined than their Romantic predecessors to adopt certain traditional metres and rhyme schemes, they have nevertheless adapted their reading to suit their roots and created work that measures up just as courageously. Their roots have often been in concrete parks and new estates rather than open fields, however, and even those born in the country have been shaped by life in the modern city.

Although Heaney has continued to draw deep draughts from the old pump at Mossbawn, his poetry has been deeply affected by the experience of Belfast, the city where he lived between 1961 and 1972. His profound sense of poetry's crucial place in the world and the value of local work developed through a period of extreme violence, which is one reason why Yeats's poems have such resonance for him. Heaney's faith in the staying power of poetry was severely tested throughout the Troubles, which means that his mature statements carry the conviction of well-tried truths. For his own belief in the deep human need for art in the direst circumstances has been corroborated by a host of poets who have demonstrated the same truth by creating adequate poetry during the Troubles. Even in a city subject to violent destruction, the desire to discern permanent truths remains: though the volatility of the immediate environment may make it seem unwritable, poets still find ways of sharing local experience and defying the destruction.

The mobility of the modern city, so disconcerting to Wordsworth and so thrilling for Dickens, had a particular edge in Belfast during the 1980s. 'Turn Again', the first poem in Carson's *Belfast Confetti*, refers to a map of the city that shows 'the bridge that was never built' and 'the bridge that collapsed'.[68] The poem brilliantly captures the sense of imminent disaster and uncertain survival through the extended metaphor of the map: 'The linen backing is falling apart—the Falls Road hangs by a thread.' Echoes of Yeats's grand apocalyptic utterances are both ominous and ironic, for Carson conveys the bewildering sense of being part of History, but without any clear direction, of being at home and yet permanently displaced. 'Turn Again' nevertheless carries the conviction of local work, its documentary accuracy evident in the details of the Belfast street names, its formal adequacy in the beautiful long lines running over their allotted space to leave odd words below, as if hanging by a thread.

Despite the extraordinary challenge to poetry, Belfast has inspired local work of the most powerful kind. At times, older motifs emerge from the experimental long lines, as in 'Patchwork', where both the Romantic preoccupation with childhood memory and the Renaissance trope of viewing the city as a map are evoked:

> Nearly at the summit, we could see the map of Belfast. My
>   Father stopped
> For a cigarette, and pointed out the landmarks: Gallaher's
>   Tobacco factory,
> Clonard Monastery, the invisible speck of our house, lost in
>   All the rows[69]

What Carson reveals are prospects of the mind every bit as powerful as those that inhabit the poems of Heaney and Wordsworth, and every bit as conscious of their own precarious existence. Unlike the local work of poets whose mental landscapes feature hills and fields, however, Carson's dwells amid the torn and fragmentary. 'Patchwork', for example, gradually stitches together the raw edges of a barbed wire tear, a ripped white shirt, an appendectomy, an unravelled jumper, a map of Belfast and the generations living there. The poem threads its way through the disparate and the broken, until it has created the dominant image of the patchwork quilt, which wraps the body of the speaker's grandmother. This is not a Dickensian social comment on the power of dress, but a meditation on the survival of memory through art, for the scraps of material are physical emblems of a past no longer visible—a square from a distinctive dress, a tangible remnant of a particular day. The patchwork demonstrates both a patient defiance of loss and a practical attitude that makes change serviceable rather than devastating. In its understated way, the quilt shows how new patterns and life can be created from the discarded remnants of a battered community, just as Carson's poem has been.

In his autobiographical prose work *The Star Factory*, the same image of quilting recurs when thoughts of the bombed-out Smithfield flea market trigger reflection on the vitality of personal memory and odd fragility of buildings. All that was left after the fire at the market were old books, 'their margins charred, but the dense compact volumes of their interiors intact'.[70] The mental thread leads from book-burning to images of early Christians, memorizing forbidden texts: 'where two or three of them were gathered... they would stitch their remembered episodes together, pretending to make a quilt for a wedding or a funeral; and the temporal authorities could not suppress the stories of this collective phoenix.' The communion of language, the collective creation of tales strong enough to confront the most oppressive circumstances, again finds a symbol in the unassuming patchwork quilt. From the common ragbag of broken memories and quotation comes something marvellously resistant to destruction, a quiet assertion of continuity from the heart of the wreckage.

Unlike those of Burns, Wordsworth, Scott, or even Heaney, Carson's recollections involve numerous, unreconciled images joined by a shared location—but his Belfast is very much a 'felt' landscape, where the sense of local attachment is just as strong. 'The Smithfield of my memory', he wrote in *The Star Factory*, 'is no more'.[71] Still the memory is re-created on the page, together with both the description of its destruction and earlier impressions of Smithfield, culled from Victorian guidebooks and histories of Belfast. Each moment is laid carefully beside the next and stitched into a chapter by an author whose 'patchwork' principles inform the entire book.[72] Writing about Belfast is not just a matter of first-hand experience, as emphasized when Carson finds an emblem of Smithfield in a photograph of men picking up books in the shell of a bombed library during the Blitz. His response to local catastrophe finds a parallel in the unknown wartime readers, for, within the charred but 'rock-solid' book covers, imprinted with their 'five thistle motifs', is a corresponding reaffirmation of human value and hope for a better society.[73]

Notes

INTRODUCTION

1. Seamus Heaney, 'Crediting Poetry', in *Opened Ground: Poems 1966–1996* (London, 1998), 462.
2. The family radio is described in more detail in Dennis O'Driscoll, *Stepping Stones: Interviews with Seamus Heaney* (London, 2008), 360.
3. 'Crediting Poetry', 464.
4. 'St Kevin and the Blackbirds', in *The Spirit Level* (London, 1996), 20.
5. 'Crediting Poetry', 460.
6. Ibid. 459.
7. Matthew Arnold, 'The Literary Influence of Academies', in *Lectures and Essays in Criticism*, ed. R. H. Super (Michigan, 1962), 249. For helpful discussion, see Robin Gilmour, 'Regional and Provincial in Victorian Literature', in R. P. Draper (ed.), *The Literature of Region and Nation* (Basingstoke, 1989), 51–60; Simon Trezise, *The West Country as Literary Invention* (Exeter, 2000), 10–13.
8. Seamus Heaney, 'The Placeless Heaven: Another Look at Kavanagh', in *The Government of the Tongue* (London, 1988), 3–14, at 9.
9. Patrick Kavanagh, 'Parochialism and Provincialism', in *A Poet's Country*, ed. Antoinette Quinn (Dublin, 2003), 237.
10. Arnold, 'Literary Influence of Academies', 249.
11. Patrick Kavanagh, *Collected Poems*, ed. Antoinette Quinn (London, 2005), 184.
12. 'The Placeless Heaven', 6.
13. Thomas Hardy, *The Life and Work of Thomas Hardy*, ed. Michael Millgate (London, 1984), 151.
14. Thomas Hardy, 'General Preface to the Novels and Poems', in *Tess of the D'Urbervilles*, vol. i of *The Wessex Edition of the Works of Thomas Hardy*, rev. edn., 24 vols. (London, 1912–31), p. viii.
15. Thomas Hardy, *The Woodlanders*, vol. vi of *The Wessex Edition*, 4–5.
16. 'General Preface', i, p. ix.
17. Ibid.
18. See Chapter 2 below.
19. Clarence Graff, Speech at Chawton, in *Jane Austen Centenary* (Steventon, 1917); cf. Reginald Farrer, 'Jane Austen. Ob. July 18, 1817', *Quarterly Review*, 452 (1917), 1–30.

20. Brian Southam, *Jane Austen and the Navy* (London, 2000), 51–2, 255.
21. Paul Fussell, *The Great War and Modern Memory* (Oxford, 1975), 231.
22. Paul Nash to Gordon Bottomley, *c.*23 Aug. 1917, in Paul Nash, *Poet and Painter: Letters between Gordon Bottomley and Paul Nash 1910–1946*, 2nd edn. (Bristol, 2000), 86.
23. Seamus Heaney, 'Place and Displacement: Recent Poetry from Northern Ireland', in *Finders Keepers: Selected Prose, 1971–2001* (London, 2002), 112–33, at 114.
24. Seamus Heaney, *The Redress of Poetry* (London, 1995), 191.
25. Ibid.
26. Simone Weil, *The Need for Roots* (1949), trans. Arthur Wills (London, 2002), 163.
27. Ibid. 170.
28. Ibid.
29. Ibid. 172.
30. Seamus Heaney, 'Orange Drums, Tyrone, 1966', in *North* (London, 1975), 68; *Station Island* (London, 1984), 65.
31. 'Crediting Poetry', 460.
32. Richard Kearney, 'Myths of the Motherland', in *Postnationalist Ireland: Politics, Culture, Philosophy* (London and New York, 1997), 121.
33. George Watson, 'From Hanover Street to the Garvaghey Road: Growing Up in Portadown', *Ideas*, 8/2 (2001), 24–35, at 32. See also Watson's earlier essay, 'England: A Country of the Mind', in Draper (ed.), *Literature of Region and Nation*, 147–59.
34. Joep Leerssen, *Remembrance and Imagination: Patterns in the Historical and Literary Representation of Ireland in the Nineteenth Century* (Cork, 1996), 27.
35. On the 'ancestral dreads' associated with nationalism, see, e.g., Tom Nairn, *After Britain* (London, 2000), 257–9; Steven C. Bourassa, *The Aesthetics of Landscape* (London and New York, 1991), 139–40, discusses objections to the architecture of 'critical regionalism' on the grounds of its possible links to Nazism. Anthony D. Smith, *Nationalism and Modernism* (London, 1998), provides an excellent overview of recent theories of nationalism.
36. 'Crediting Poetry', 460.
37. Ibid. 465.
38. William Wordsworth, *Lyrical Ballads, and Other Poems, 1797–1800*, ed. James Butler and Karen Green (Ithaca, NY, and London, 1992), 752–3.
39. 'Crediting Poetry', 464.
40. Ibid.
41. Arnold, 'On the Modern Element in Literature', and 'Heinrich Heine', in *Lectures and Essays on Criticism*, ed. Super, 132. Arnold's term may be indebted to Spinoza, for whom the concept of an 'adequate idea' is related to truth (Benedict de Spinoza, *On the Improvement of the Understanding,*

The Ethics, Correspondence, trans. R. H. M. Elwes (New York, 1955), 106–10, 395).

42. For careful discussion of Heaney's situation and the need for an 'adequate response', see Fran Brearton, *The Great War in Irish Poetry* (Oxford, 2000), 217–51.

43. 'Place and Displacement', 119.

44. Seamus Heaney, 'Osip and Nadezhda Mandelstam', in *Government of the Tongue*, 83; *Lyrical Ballads*, 752.

45. William Wordsworth, 'Resolution and Independence', ll. 118–19, in *Poems, in Two Volumes, and Other Poems, 1800–1807*, ed. Jared Curtis (Ithaca, NY, and London, 1983), 128. From 1827, 'strong admonishment' became 'apt admonishment'.

46. *The Fenwick Notes of William Wordsworth*, ed. Jared Curtis (London, 1993), 14. For discussion of the poem's growth, see Jared Curtis, *Wordsworth's Experiments with Tradition: The Lyric Poems of 1802* (Ithaca, NY, and London, 1971).

47. 'Crediting Poetry', 466.

48. Points reaffirmed in O'Driscoll, *Stepping Stones*, 448–9.

49. Seamus Heaney, 'Belfast', in *Preoccupations: Selected Prose 1968–1978* (London, 1980), 37. In addition to Heaney's extensive critical prose, details of his reading appear in O'Driscoll, *Stepping Stones, passim*.

50. David Jones, *Epoch and Artist* (London, 1959), 29.

51. Wordsworth, *The Prelude*, xiii. 311–12, in *The Thirteen-Book Prelude*, ed. Mark L. Reed (Ithaca, NY, and London, 1991).

52. Wordsworth included a note on l. 107, observing that it had 'a close resemblance to an admirable line of Young, the exact expression of which I cannot recollect' (*Lyrical Ballads*, 119).

53. 'Osip and Nadezhda Mandelstam', 84–5.

54. Seamus Heaney, 'Faith, Hope and Poetry', in *Preoccupations*, 218.

55. Wordsworth's note on 'Thoughts Suggested the Day Following on the Banks of the Nith', in William Wordsworth, *Last Poems, 1821–1850*, ed. Jared Curtis (Ithaca, NY, and London, 1999), 475. See Chapters 3 and 5 below.

56. 'Crediting Poetry', 466.

57. John Keats, 'Lines Written in the Highlands after a Visit to Burns's Country', ll. 39–40, in *The Poems of John Keats*, ed. Jack Stillinger (Cambridge, MA, 1978). See Chapter 6 below.

58. Seamus Heaney, 'viii', in *Seeing Things* (London, 1991), 62. For Heaney's comments on the poem, see O'Driscoll, *Stepping Stones*, 321–2.

59. 'The Placeless Heaven', 13; 'Place and Displacement', 118.

60. 'Crediting Poetry', 467.

61. Marilyn Butler, 'Introduction', in Maria Edgeworth, *Castle Rackrent and Ennui* (London, 1992), 2.

62. Ibid. 62; 'Michael', l. 19, in *Lyrical Ballads*, 253.

304 NOTES

63. James Boswell, *The Life of Samuel Johnson*, ed. George Birkbeck Hill, rev. L. F. Powell, 6 vols. (Oxford, 1934–50), ii. 433.

64. Leo Damrosch, 'Generality and Particularity', in *The Cambridge History of Literary Criticism*, iv, ed. H. Nisbet and Claude Rawson (Cambridge, 1997), 382.

65. Locke's influential *Two Treatises of Government* (1690) revealed the political and social implications of empiricism. See also M. H. Nicolson, *Mountain Gloom and Mountain Glory* (New York, 1959).

66. J. Fauvel, R. Flood, M. Shortland, and R. Wilson (eds.), *Let Newton Be!* (Oxford, 1988); R. Westfall, *Never at Rest: A Biography of Isaac Newton* (Cambridge, 1980); Edward Casey, *The Fate of Place* (Berkeley and Los Angeles, 1997), 133–79.

67. See, e.g., John Ray, *The Wisdom of God Manifest in the Works of Creation* (London, 1690).

68. John Toland, *The Life of Milton* (London, 1698), 84. Felicity Nussbaum, 'Biography and Autobiography', in *Cambridge History of Literary Criticism*, iv, ed. Nisbet and Rawson, 306.

69. Samuel Johnson, *The Lives of the English Poets*, ed. Roger Lonsdale, 4 vols. (Oxford, 2006).

70. For Joseph Spence's interests in the 'wonderful phaenomenon of Wiltshire', see William Christmas, *The Lab'ring Muses* (Newark and London, 2001), 75.

71. Bernard Smith, *The European Vision of the South Pacific*, 2nd edn. (New Haven and London, 1985); Anthony Pagden, *European Encounters with the New World* (New Haven and London, 1993); Neil Rennie, *Far-Fetched Facts* (Oxford, 1996).

72. James Beattie, *Essays on Poetry and Music* (London, 1776), 182; *The Minstrel, or the Progress of Genius* (1770), with Memoirs of the Life of the Author by Alexander Chalmers (London, 1811), 176–7.

73. Samuel Johnson, 'The Vanity of Human Wishes', l. 2, in *The Yale Edition of the Works of Samuel Johnson*, vi. *Poems*, ed. E. L. McAdam Jr. with George Milne (New Haven and London, 1964), 91.

74. Samuel Taylor Coleridge, *Biographia Literaria*, ed. J. Engell and W. J. Bate, 2 vols. (Princeton and London, 1983), ii. 7.

75. To Dr Trusler, 23 Aug. 1799, in *The Letters of William Blake*, ed. G. Keynes (London, 1968), 30.

76. See Hazlitt's admiration for Burns's 'manly grasp', in *Lectures on the English Poets* (1818), in *The Complete Works of William Hazlitt*, ed. P. P. Howe, 21 vols. (London, 1930–4), v. 128.

77. Robert Burns, 'The Vision', l. 23, 'Epistle to Davie', l. 142, in *The Poems and Songs of Robert Burns*, ed. James Kinsley, 3 vols. (Oxford, 1968), i. 103, 69.

78. William Wordsworth, 'Third Essay upon Epitaphs', in *The Prose Works of William Wordsworth*, ed. W. J. B. Owen and Jane Worthington Smyser, 3 vols. (Oxford, 1974), ii. 180.

79. *Lyrical Ballads*, appendix on poetical diction, 761.
80. 'Third Essay upon Epitaphs', ii. 85.
81. William Wordsworth, *The Excursion*, ed. James Butler and Sally Bushell (Ithaca, NY, and London, 2007), 38.
82. Ibid. 40.
83. M. H. Abrams takes the lines from 'Home at Grasmere', which became the 'Prospectus to The Recluse' in the preface to *The Excursion*, as the starting point for his influential account of Romanticism, *Natural Supernaturalism* (New York and London, 1971), 26.
84. William Wordsworth, 'Home at Grasmere', ll. 1031–4, in *Home at Grasmere. Part First, Book First, of the Recluse*, ed. Beth Darlington (Ithaca, NY, and London, 1977), 106.
85. *Biographia Literaria*, i. 304.

CHAPTER I

1. *Opened Ground: Poems 1966–1996* appeared in 1998; *Finders Keepers* in 2002. The most extensive interviews appeared in O'Driscoll, *Stepping Stones*, in 2008.
2. 'A Sense of Place', in *Preoccupations*, 145.
3. 'Mossbawn', in *Finder's Keepers*, 3.
4. Wordsworth, 'Ode: There was a Time', l. 82, in *Poems, in Two Volumes*.
5. On the nest as an image of 'the origin of confidence in the world', see Gaston Bachelard, *The Poetics of Space*, trans. Maria Jolas (1964; London, 1994), 103.
6. 'Digging', in *Opened Ground*, 4. 'Digging' was the first poem in Heaney's first collection, *Death of a Naturalist* (London, 1966), 1.
7. 'Personal Helicon', in *Death of a Naturalist* (London, 1969), 44.
8. *The Prelude*, iv. 247–59.
9. *The Two-Part Prelude*, ll. 289–90; when the passage was revised in 1805, 'fructifying' became 'renovating' (*Prelude*, xi. 259). *The Two-Part Prelude* was first published in 1974, and could not therefore have been a direct influence on 'Personal Helicon', despite the striking affinity. William Wordsworth, *The Prelude, 1798–9*, ed. Stephen Parrish (Ithaca, NY, and London, 1977).
10. *The Prelude*, xiii. 278.
11. 'xlviii', in 'Squarings', *Seeing Things*, 108.
12. On Heaney's 'archaeologies' see Helen Vendler, *Seamus Heaney* (London, 1998), 38–57.
13. The title of his *Poems, 1966–1996*, is a quotation from the last line of 'Act of Union', in *North*, 50, and from 'Glanmore Sonnets', I and II, in *Field Work* (London, 1979), 33, 34.
14. 'Mossbawn', 6.

15. 'xli', in 'Squarings', *Seeing Things*, 101.
16. 'Mossbawn', 6. On Heaney's articulation of the sense of division, internal and external, see Seamus Deane, ' "Unhappy and at Home": Interview with Seamus Heaney', *The Crane Bag*, 1/1 (Spring 1977), 61–7; Neil Corcoran, *The Poetry of Seamus Heaney* (London, 2002), 236; Eugene O'Brien, *Seamus Heaney and the Place of Writing* (Gainesville, 2002), esp. chapter two.
17. 'Mossbawn', 6.
18. Wordsworth's use carries eighteenth-century associations of landscape theory, as well as Latinate and Miltonic resonances (*Paradise Lost*, xi. 380); for more recent, evolutionary ideas on landscape, see Jay Appleton, *The Experience of Landscape* (London and New York, 1975).
19. *Station Island*, 82–3. See also Ciaran Carson, 'Escaped from the Massacre?', review of *North*, *The Honest Ulsterman*, 50 (Winter 1975), 183–6; Edna Longley, *Poetry in the Wars* (Newcastle, 1986), 140–69; David Lloyd, *Anomalous States: Irish Writing and the Post-Colonial State* (Dublin, 1993), 14; Brearton, *The Great War in Irish Poetry*.
20. Jerome McGann, *The Romantic Ideology* (Chicago, 1983); *The Beauty of Inflections* (Oxford, 1988); Marjorie Levinson, *Wordsworth's Great Period Poems* (Cambridge, 1986); Alan Liu, *Wordsworth: The Sense of History* (Stanford, 1989); Kenneth Johnston, *The Hidden Wordsworth* (New York, 1998).
21. 'Wordsworth's Skates', in *District and Circle* (London, 2006), 22.
22. *The Prelude*, x. 4; Yeats's 'Meditation in the Time of Civil War' is discussed in these terms by Heaney in 'Crediting Poetry', 464. For a perceptive discussion of 'Heaney and Violence', see Dillon Johnston's essay 'Violence in Seamus Heaney's Poetry', in *The Cambridge Companion to Contemporary Irish Poetry*, ed. Matthew Campbell (Cambridge, 2003), 113–32.
23. 'Home at Grasmere', ll. 949–51.
24. *The Prelude*, i. 640.
25. Ibid. 649–50.
26. 'ii', in 'Lightenings', *Seeing Things*, 56.
27. *The Two-Part Prelude*, the first version of *The Prelude*, as well as 'Nutting' and 'There was a Boy', were all written in Goslar in 1799. For composition, see *The Prelude*, *1798–9*, ed. Parrish, and Mark Reed, *Wordsworth: The Chronology of the Early Years*, *1787–1799* (Cambridge, MA, 1967), 331–2. For biographical detail, see Stephen Gill, *William Wordsworth: A Life* (Oxford, 1989), 156–75. Heaney's interest in Wordsworth as a displaced figure is evident in the lecture he delivered at Dove Cottage in 1984, 'Place and Displacement: Recent Poetry from Northern Ireland'.
28. To Coleridge, 14 or 21 Dec. 1798, in *The Letters of William and Dorothy Wordsworth*, i. *The Early Years*, *1797–1805*, ed. Ernest De Selincourt, rev. Chester L. Shaver (Oxford, 1967), 238.

29. *Early Years*, 238; *The Two-Part Prelude*, ll. 156–69; *The Prelude*, i. 460–73.
30. 'Home at Grasmere', ll. 156–60. Although the earliest surviving manu-script of the poem dates from 1806, there is compelling evidence to suggest that the poem was largely composed in 1800.
31. *The Prelude*, x. 249–74; see Chapter 3 below.
32. Wordsworth's headnote to 'Hart-Leap Well', in *Lyrical Ballads*, 133. The poem's initial inspiration—an encounter at Hart-Leap Well on the wild winter journey from Sockburn—and subsequent composition during a difficult patch on 'The Brothers' were later described by Wordsworth, *Fenwick Notes*, 15.
33. Geoffrey Hartman suggested that the hart's 'final, gigantic leaps' are emblematic of Wordsworth's homing instinct—'the vigor with which the separated imagination seeks its native country' (*Wordsworth's Poetry 1787–1814* (New Haven, 1964), 142). James Butler noted the personal significance for Wordsworth of this account of a 'tragic return to a birthplace' in 'Tourist or Native Son: Wordsworth's Homecomings of 1799–1800', *Nineteenth-Century Literature*, 51/1 (1996), 1–15.
34. 'Advertisement', published with the 'Poems on the Naming of Places', in *Lyrical Ballads*, 241. For details of the natural features recorded in Wordsworth's literary landscape, see David McCracken, *Wordsworth and the Lake District: A Guide to the Poems and their Places* (Oxford, 1985).
35. 'There is an Eminence', l. 17, in *Lyrical Ballads*, 247.
36. 'Joanna's Rock', ll. 82–3, 69–70.
37. 'Emma' refers to Dorothy Wordsworth; see Gill, *William Wordworth*, 179–214.
38. *Fenwick Notes*, 8, 98–9; *Lyrical Ballads*, 379–82.
39. Wordsworth's Note on 'The Brothers', in *Lyrical Ballads*, 381–2.
40. *Lyrical Ballads*, 382. See also the more extensive discussion in the *Essays upon Epitaphs*.
41. T. W. Thompson, *Wordsworth's Hawkshead*, ed. Robert Woof (London, 1970), p. xvi. Thompson includes a wealth of fascinating detail about Ann Tyson and other local residents. See also Gill, *William Wordsworth*, 21–6.
42. As I have argued at greater length in 'Plain Living and Ungarnish'd Stories: Wordsworth and the Survival of Pastoral', *RES* ns 59 (2008), 118–33.
43. *Lyrical Ballads*, 258, 403.
44. Ibid. 751.
45. Ibid. 753.
46. Some scholars have judged Michael more severely, including Annabel Patterson in *Pastoral and Ideology: Virgil to Valéry* (Oxford, 1988), 206–14.
47. Matt. 5: 16.
48. To Mathews, 8 June 1794, in *Early Years*, 125. Nicholas Roe sets the radical, Godwinian context for Wordsworth's image, and notes the reference to

Isa. 9: 2 ('The people that walked in darkness have seen a great light') in *Wordsworth and Coleridge: The Radical Years* (Oxford, 1988), 184–5.

49. Although Michael's lamp seems chiefly indebted to the Sermon on the Mount, both 'the Evening Star' and Wordsworth's image of his own lamp hung up in Heaven also suggest Dan. 12: 3 ('And they that be wise shall shine as the brightness of the firmament; and they that turn many to righteousness as the star for ever and ever').

50. To Fox, 14 Jan. 1801, in *Early Years*, 313.

51. Ibid.

52. Ibid. 315.

53. Wordsworth's dismay over the end of cottage industry in Westmoreland is visible in sonnets on the silence of the spinning wheel: William Wordsworth, *Shorter Poems*, ed. Carl H. Ketcham (Ithaca, NY, and London, 1989), 108–9, 124–5, 520.

54. *The Prelude*, x. 448.

55. Ibid. See also Roe, *Wordsworth and Coleridge*; and *The Politics of Nature: William Wordsworth and Some Contemporaries* (Basingstoke, 2002); Howard Erskine-Hill, *Poetry of Opposition and Revolution from Dryden to Wordsworth* (New York, 1996).

56. *Stepping Stones*, 119. Heaney worked at Queen's University, Belfast, between 1966 and 1972. Internment—or the suspension of habeas corpus—was introduced in Northern Ireland in 1971.

57. 'Field of Vision', in *Seeing Things*, 22.

58. *The Prelude*, x. 725–8.

59. *Lyrical Ballads*, 753.

60. *North*, 38; *Sweeney Astray* (London, 1983), preface; 'Fosterling', in *Seeing Things*, 50.

CHAPTER 2

1. Dedication to *Don Juan*, stanza 5, ll. 7–8, in *Lord Byron: The Complete Poetical Works*, ed. Jerome J. McGann, 7 vols. (Oxford, 1980–93), v. 4.

2. Sales of *Lyrical Ballads* rapidly warranted further editions, but the critical response to the volume was limited and largely hostile. For full details see Robert Woof (ed.), *William Wordsworth: The Critical Heritage*, i. *1793–1820* (London and New York, 2001).

3. Francis Jeffrey, review of Robert Southey's *Thalaba*, *Edinburgh Review*, 1 (Oct. 1802), 63–83.

4. John Clive, *Scotch Reviewers: The Edinburgh Review, 1802–1815* (London, 1957); Leslie Mitchell, '*The Edinburgh Review* and the Lake Poets 1802–1810', in *Essays Presented to C. M. Bowra* (Oxford, 1970), 24–38.

5. Jeffrey, review of Wordsworth's *Poems in Two Volumes*, *Edinburgh Review*, 11 (Oct 1807), 214–31; review of *The Excursion*, *Edinburgh Review*, 24 (Nov. 1814), 3.

6. Dedication to *Don Juan*, stanza 5, ll. 3–5.

7. Thomas Love Peacock, *The Four Ages of Poetry* (1820), in *The Halliford Edition of the Works of Thomas Love Peacock*, ed. H. F. Brett-Smith and C. E. Jones, 10 vols. (London and New York, 1924–34), viii. 17.

8. Preface to Cantos I and II (not published until 1901), in *The Complete Poetical Works*, ed. McGann, v. 683–4; *Four Ages*, viii. 19.

9. *Four Ages*, viii. 17.

10. Ibid. 21.

11. Ibid.

12. Ibid. 24–5.

13. To William Wordsworth, 30 May 1815, in *The Collected Letters of Samuel Taylor Coleridge*, ed. Earl Leslie Griggs, 6 vols. (Oxford, 1956–71), iv. 575.

14. *Biographia Literaria*, ii. 43.

15. Stephen Gill, 'Wordsworth and *The River Duddon*', *Essays in Criticism*, 57/1 (2007), 22–41.

16. Unsigned review, *Literary Gazette*, 4 (25 Mar. 1820), 200–3, in Woof (ed.), *William Wordsworth: The Critical Heritage*, i. 752.

17. Unsigned review, *Literary Chronicle and Weekly Review*, 2 (July 1820), 420–2, in Woof (ed.), *William Wordsworth: The Critical Heritage*, i. 767.

18. Unsigned review (Lockhart and Wilson), *Blackwood's Edinburgh Magazine*, 7 (May 1820), 206–13.

19. Unsigned review, *The British Review*, in Woof (ed.), *William Wordsworth: The Critical Heritage*, i. 777–8.

20. *Lyrical Ballads*, 744.

21. To John Wilson, 7 June 1802, in *Early Years*, 355.

22. Johnson, *Lives of the English Poets*, i. 238. This is the first recorded use of the term 'local poetry'.

23. Ibid.

24. *Windsor Forest*, ll. 1–2, in *The Poems of Alexander Pope*, ed. John Butt (London, 1963), 195. For discussion of the political dimension of these poems, see R. Aubin, *Topographical Poetry in XVIII-Century England* (New York, 1936); J. Turner, *The Politics of Landscape* (Oxford, 1979).

25. 'The Third Discourse' (1770), in Joshua Reynolds, *Discourses on Art*, ed. Robert R. Wark (New Haven and London, 1997), 49.

26. 'The Fourth Discourse' (1771), in ibid. 69.

27. *Rasselas* (1759), in *The Yale Edition of the Works of Samuel Johnson*, xvi, ed. Gwin J. Kolb (New Haven and London, 1990), 43–4. For discussion of the philosophical context, see Damrosch, 'Generality and Particularity'.

28. George Eliot, *Scenes of Clerical Life*, ed. Thomas A. Noble (Oxford, 1985), 42; 'The Natural History of German Life', in *Selected Critical Writings*, ed. Rosemary Ashton (Oxford, 1992), 261.

29. Arnold, *Lectures and Essays in Criticism*, 249, and Introduction, above.
30. See, e.g., Adam Smith, *Lectures on Jurisprudence*, ed. R. L. Meek, D. D. Raphael, and P. G. Stein (Oxford, 1967); Henry Home, Lord Kames, *Sketches of the History of Man*, 3 vols. (Edinburgh, 1774); Adam Ferguson, *An Essay on the History of Civil Society*, ed. D. Forbes (Edinburgh, 1966).
31. Hugh Blair, *Lectures on Rhetoric and Belles Lettres*, 2 vols. (London, 1783). See also Robert Crawford (ed.), *The Scottish Invention of English Literature* (Cambridge, 1998).
32. 'Spring', l. 819, 'Winter', l. 169, 'Spring', ll. 468–75, in James Thomson, *The Seasons*, ed. James Sambrook (Oxford, 1981).
33. 'The Third Discourse', 49. See also John Barrell, *The Political Theory of Painting* (New Haven and London, 1986).
34. See Andrew Wilton and Ilaria Bignamini (eds.), *Grand Tour: The Lure of Italy in the Eighteenth Century* (London, 1996). For the impact of continental travel on native artists, see, e.g., Andrew Wilton, *Turner Abroad* (London, 1982); Judy Egerton, *Wright of Derby* (London, 1997); Timothy Wilcox, *Francis Towne* (London, 1997); Ann Crookshank and the Knight of Glyn, *Ireland's Painters, 1600–1940* (New Haven and London, 2002).
35. Nicholas Penny (ed.), *Reynolds* (London, 1986).
36. Byron to Leigh Hunt, Sept.–30 Oct. 1815, in *Byron's Letter and Journals*, ed. Leslie A. Marchand, 13 vols. (London, 1973–94), iv. 318–19.
37. Michael Dobson, *The Making of the National Poet* (Oxford, 1992); Jonathan Bate, *Shakespeare and the English Romantic Imagination* (Oxford, 1986); Lucy Newlyn, *'Paradise Lost' and The Romantic Reader* (Oxford, 1993); Richard Terry, *Poetry and the Making of the English Literary Past* (Oxford, 2001); Nick Groom, *The Making of Percy's Reliques* (Oxford, 1999); Katie Trumpener, *Bardic Nationalism: The Romantic Novel and the British Empire* (Princeton, 1997).
38. Roy Porter, *London: A Social History* (London, 1994), 157.
39. John Sekora, *Luxury: The Concept in Western Thought from Eden to Smollett* (Baltimore, 1977); Maxine Berg and Elizabeth Eger (eds.), *Luxury in the Eighteenth Century* (Basingstoke, 2002); Maxine Berg, *Luxury and Pleasure in Eighteenth-Century Britain* (Oxford, 2007).
40. Tobias Smollett, *The Expedition of Humphry Clinker*, ed. Angus Ross (Harmondsworth, 1967), 119.
41. Vivien Jones, 'The Coquetry of Nature: Politics and the Picturesque in Women's Fiction', in Stephen Copley and Peter Garside (eds.) *The Politics of the Picturesque* (Cambridge, 1994), 120–44. See also Ina Ferris, *The Romantic National Tale and the Question of Ireland* (Cambridge, 2002); Trumpener, *Bardic Nationalism*.
42. Leerssen, *Remembrance and Imagination*, 35–8.
43. *Castle Rackrent*, 63.

44. Walter Scott, General Preface to *Waverley* (1814), which was added to the Edinburgh edition of his novels in 1829; *The Waverley Novels*, 24 vols. (London, 1924), i.
45. Christmas, *The Lab'ring Muses*, 98–100.
46. Mary Waldron, *Lactilla, Milkwoman of Clifton* (Athens, GA, and London, 1996); Christmas, *The Lab'ring Muses*, 235–66.
47. Jeffrey Cox, *Poetry and Politics in the Cockney School* (Cambridge, 1998).
48. See John Brewer, *The Pleasures of the Imagination: English Culture in the Eighteenth Century* (London, 1997); William St Clair, *The Reading Nation in the Romantic Period* (Cambridge, 2004); C. R. Johnson, *Provincial Poetry 1789–1839: British Verse Printed in the Provinces: The Romantic Background* (Otley, 1992) provides a useful bibliography.
49. Robert Burns, 'Epistle to J. L****k, An Old Scotch Bard', ll. 55–60, in *Poems and Songs*, i. 87.
50. Robert Crawford, *Devolving English Literature* (Oxford, 1992), 108.
51. Linda Colley, *Britons: Forging the Nation, 1707–1837* (New Haven and London, 1992).
52. *Watson's Choice Collection*, ed. Harriet Harvey Wood, 2 vols. (Edinburgh and Aberdeen, 1977, 1991); Allan Ramsay, *The Ever-Green* (Edinburgh, 1724). See also Crawford, *Devolving English Literature*.
53. Edmund Burke, *Reflections on the Revolution in France*, ed. Conor Cruise O'Brien (Harmondsworth, 1968), 135.
54. Ibid.
55. See Raphael Samuel, *Island Stories, Patriotism*, 2 vols. (London, 1996, 1998), ii. 60.
56. Michael Baron, *Language and Relationship in Wordsworth's Writing* (London and New York, 1995), 24.
57. William Cowper, 'Retirement', l. 62, in *The Poems of William Cowper*, i. *1748–1782*, ed. John D. Baird and Charles Ryskamp (Oxford, 1980), 379.
58. 'The Deserted Village', l. 52. All references to Goldsmith are to *The Poems of Gray, Collins and Goldsmith*, ed. Roger Lonsdale (London, 1969).
59. See Roger Lonsdale's annotations and, for a more recent approach, Michael Griffin, 'Delicate Allegories, Deceitful Mazes: Goldsmith's Landscapes', *Eighteenth-Century Ireland*, 16 (2001), 104–17.
60. See Appleton, *The Experience of Landscape*; Denis E. Cosgrove and Stephen Daniels (eds.), *The Iconography of Landscape* (Cambridge, 1988); for helpful discussion, see Jonathan Bate, *The Song of the Earth* (London, 2000).
61. I. Bernard Cohen, *Revolution in Science* (Cambridge, MA, 1985); Casey, *The Fate of Place*.
62. Denis E. Cosgrove, *Social Formation and Symbolic Landscape*, 2nd edn. (Madison, 1984), 13; see also W. J. T. Mitchell (ed.), *Landscape and Power*, 2nd edn. (Chicago, 2002); Malcolm Andrews, *Landscape and Western Art*

(Oxford, 1999). For a seminal discussion on landscape painting and poetry, see John Barrell, *The Dark Side of the Landscape* (Cambridge, 1980).

63. Colley, *Britons*; Murray Pittock has taken issue with Colley's emphasis on Protestantism as a single, unifying force in *Inventing and Resisting Britain* (Basingstoke, 1997).

64. Benedict Anderson, *Imagined Communities: Reflections on the Origins and Spread of Nationalism*, rev. edn. (London, 1991), 36.

65. Ann Jensen Adams, 'Competing Communities in the "Great Bog of Europe": Seventeenth-Century Dutch Landscape Painting', in Mitchell (ed.), *Landscape and Power*, 35–76.

66. Bate, *Song of the Earth*, 73.

67. Friedrich Schiller, *On the Naïve and Sentimental in Literature*, trans. Helen Watanabe-O'Kelly (Manchester, 1981), 31.

68. For analysis of Schiller's place in Romanticism, see Abrams, *Natural Supernaturalism*, 199–217.

69. 'A Hymn on the Seasons', ll. 37–8.

70. Joseph Warton, *An Essay on the Genius and Writings of Pope*, 4th edn. (London, 1782), ii. 185, cited by Malcolm Andrews, *The Search for the Picturesque* (Aldershot, 1989), 9.

71. Gilbert White, *The Natural History of Selborne* (1788–9), ed. Richard Mabey (Harmondsworth, 1977), 74.

72. Kavanagh, 'Parochialism and Provincialism', in *A Poet's Country*, ed. Quinn, 237.

73. White, *Selborne*, 33.

74. *Lyrical Ballads*, 325.

75. Cited by Joel Pace in 'Wordsworth and America: Reception and Reform', in Stephen Gill (ed.), *The Cambridge Companion to Wordsworth* (Cambridge, 2003), 230–45, at 235.

76. John Stuart Mill, *Autobiography* (London, 1924), 116.

77. Ibid. 125. See also Stephen Gill, *Wordsworth and the Victorians* (Oxford, 1998).

CHAPTER 3

1. 'Fears in Solitude', ll. 176–88, in *The Complete Poetical Works of Samuel Taylor Coleridge*, ed. E. H. Coleridge, 2 vols. (Oxford, 1912), i. 262. Edna Longley has discussed Edward Thomas's attraction to this poem during a moment of national crisis in 'Worn New: Edward Thomas and English Tradition', in *Poetry in the Wars*, 56.

2. 'To the Rev George Coleridge', ll. 17–18, in *Complete Poetical Works*, i. 174.

3. 'Frost at Midnight', ll. 52–4, in ibid. i. 242.

4. To John Thelwall, 14 Oct. 1797, in *The Collected Letters of Samuel Taylor Coleridge*, i. 349. For Coleridge's preoccupation with division and unity, see Seamus Perry, *Coleridge and the Uses of Division* (Oxford, 1999).

NOTES 313

5. Richard Price, *A Discourse on the Love of Country* (1789), 3rd edn.
(London, 1790), 2.

6. Burke, *Reflections on the Revolution in France*, 135.

7. Samuel Taylor Coleridge, *Lectures 1795 on Politics and Religion*, ed. Lewis
Patton and Peter Mann (Princeton and London, 1971), 163.

8. Ibid. 164.

9. William Wordsworth, *Guide to the Lakes* (1812), ed. Ernest de Selin-
court, with an introduction by Stephen Gill (London, 2004), 74. Words-
worth's *Guide*, originally published in Joseph Wilkinson's *Select Views
in Cumberland, Westmoreland, and Lancashire* (London, 1810), attracted a
wider audience when it was republished in *The River Duddon* volume in
1820.

10. Burke, *Reflections on the Revolution in France*, 120.

11. Kevin Whelan, *The Tree of Liberty* (Cork, 1996).

12. 'Place and Displacement', *Finders Keepers*, 114.

13. For Wordsworth's occlusion of politics and history, see Marjorie Levin-
son's seminal *Wordsworth's Great Period Poems*, 14–57; and, for counter-
argument, Charles Rzepka, 'Pictures of the Mind: Iron and Charcoal,
"Ouzy" Tides and "Vagrant Dwellers" at Tintern, 1798', *Studies in
Romanticism*, 42 (2003), 155–86.

14. Bate, *Song of the Earth*, 225.

15. *The Convention of Cintra*, in *Prose Works*, i. 328.

16. Ibid.

17. *Lyrical Ballads*, 746–7.

18. *The Prelude*, 1798–9, ii. 479. For a lucid account of the collapse of hope
in Britain in 1799–1800, see William Hague, *William Pitt the Younger*
(London, 2004), 447–61.

19. *Lyrical Ballads*, 746.

20. Ibid.

21. Ibid.

22. 'London, 1802', ll. 2–3, published with other 'Sonnets on Liberty', in
Poems, in Two Volumes. (All references to Wordsworth's sonnets are to
William Wordsworth, *Poems, in Two Volumes, and Other Poems, 1800–
1807*, ed. Jared Curtis (Ithaca, NY, and London, 1983)).

23. Gill, *Wordsworth: A Life*, 208–9.

24. To Sara Hutchinson, June 1802, in *Early Years*, 367.

25. 'Written in London, September 1802', l. 11.

26. John Milton, 'On the Lord General Fairfax at the siege of Colchester',
in John Milton, *Complete Shorter Poems*, ed. John Carey (London, 1971),
321.

27. 'The World is too much with us', l. 2.

28. 'There is a Knowledge which is Worse to Bear', ll. 11–14. See also
'London, 1802', 'Great Men have been among us', 'It is not to be
Thought of that the Flood'.

29. 'Calais, August 15th 1802' ('Festivals have I seen'), l. 4.
30. 'Calais, August 1802' ('Is it a reed that's shaken by the wind'), ll. 3–6.
31. To ?, Nov. 1802, in *Early Years*, 379.
32. *Lyrical Ballads*, 762; *Early Years*, 379.
33. *Early Years*, 379.
34. To John Wilson, 7 June 1802, in *Early Years*, 355.
35. 'Ode: There was a Time', ll. 7–9.
36. *A Letter to a Friend of Robert Burns* (1816), *Prose Works*, iii. 113.
37. To Sara Hutchinson, 14 June 1802, in *Early Years*, 367.
38. For details of the poetic dialogue, see Gene Ruoff, *Wordsworth and Coleridge: The Making of the Major Lyrics 1802–1804* (London, 1989); Lucy Newlyn, *Coleridge, Wordsworth and the Language of Allusion*, 2nd edn. (Oxford, 2001); Stephen Parrish (ed.), *Coleridge's* Dejection (Ithaca, NY, and London, 1988).
39. See Curtis's commentary on 'Resolution and Independence', in *Poems, in Two Volumes; The Complete Works of Thomas Chatterton*, ed. Donald S. Taylor, 2 vols. (Oxford, 1971), ii. 1114; John Carey suggests that the stanza, modified from Spenser, may have been Milton's invention, though Phineas Fletcher used the same form in a poem published in 1633 (Milton, *Complete Shorter Poems*, 102).
40. *William Wordsworth: Poems Selected by Seamus Heaney* (1988; London, 2001), p. ix; 'Place and Displacement', *Finders Keepers*, 112–15.
41. *William Wordsworth: Poems Selected by Seamus Heaney*, p. viii.
42. 'Crediting Poetry', 464.
43. To Sara Hutchinson, June 1802, in *Early Years*, 367.
44. 'Crediting Poetry', 464.
45. *Fenwick Notes*, 14.
46. *Lyrical Ballads*, 752.
47. Ibid. 751.
48. *The Works of Burns*, ed. James Currie, 2nd edn., 4 vols. (London, 1801). i. 325.
49. John Milton, 'Lycidas', l. 173, in *Complete Shorter Poems*.
50. *Last Poems, 1821–1850*, 475.
51. To Coleridge, 27 Feb. 1799, in *Early Years*, 256.
52. *Last Poems*, 475.
53. Lamb to Coleridge, 6 July 1796, in *The Letters of Charles Lamb*, ed. E. V. Lucas, 3 vols. (London, 1935), i. 37. On the fashion for Bürger's ballads in the 1790s, see Mary Jacobus, *Tradition and Experiment in Wordsworth's Lyrical Ballads, 1798* (Oxford, 1975), 217–24.
54. To Coleridge, 27 Feb. 1799, in *Early Years*, 255.
55. Ibid. 256.
56. 'Burns's Art Speech', in *Finders Keepers*, 357, 347.
57. Ibid. 359–60.
58. Ibid. 255.

59. Appendix on Poetic Diction, in *Lyrical Ballads*, 672.
60. 'Burns's Art Speech', *Finders Keepers*, 356.
61. Robert Burns, *Poems, Chiefly in the Scottish Dialect*, 2nd edn. (Edinburgh, 1787), preface; *Poems and Songs*, ed. Kinsley, iii. 971.
62. *Works of Burns*, ed. Currie, iv. 359–61. Kinsley includes the poem as 'Sketch', in *Poems and Songs*, i. 191–2, and confirms Currie's attribution; Andrew Noble and Patrick Scott Hogg restore the original title, 'Poem on Pastoral Poetry', in *The Canongate Burns*, ed. Andrew Noble and Patrick Scott Hogg (Edinburgh, 2001), 576–7; for further discussion, see also Andrew Noble, 'Wordsworth and Burns: The Anxiety of Being under the Influence', in Carol McGuirk (ed.), *Critical Essays on Robert Burns* (New York, 1998), 49–62.
63. Charles Martindale, 'Green Politics: The *Eclogues*', in Charles Martindale (ed.), *The Cambridge Companion to Virgil* (Cambridge, 1997), 107–24; Patterson, *Pastoral and Ideology*; Andrew Hadfield, *Literature, Politics and National Identity* (Cambridge, 1994), 170–201; Michelle O'Callaghan, *The 'Shepheards Nation': Jacobean Spenserians and Early Stuart Political Culture 1612–1625* (Oxford, 2000).
64. To Thomas Poole, 24 July 1800, in *Collected Letters of Samuel Taylor Coleridge*, i. 607. See also D. S. Roberts, 'Literature, Medical Science and Politics, 1795–1800: *Lyrical Ballads* and Currie's *Works of Robert Burns*', in C. C. Barfoot (ed.) *'A Natural Delineation of the Passions': The Historic Moment of Lyrical Ballads* (Amsterdam, 2001), 115–28.
65. As Nigel Leask has suggested in ' "The Shadow Line": James Currie's "Life of Burns" and British Romanticism', in Claire Lamont and Michael Rossington (eds.), *Romanticism's Debatable Lands* (Basingstoke, 2005), 64–79.
66. *Works of Burns*, ed. Currie, i. 97.
67. Ibid. i. 315–16.
68. Ibid. i. 29.
69. Ibid.
70. *Fenwick Notes*, 41.
71. Wordsworth, Annotations to *Paradise Lost*, iii. 543–54, in Joseph Wittreich (ed), *The Romantics on Milton* (Cleveland, OH, and London, 1970), 104.
72. Ibid.
73. *Biographia Literaria*, i. 81.

CHAPTER 4

1. Dorothy Wordsworth, 18 Sept. 1803, in *Recollections of a Tour Made in Scotland in 1803*, in *The Journals of Dorothy Wordsworth*, ed. Ernest de Selincourt, 2 vols. (London, 1941), i. 391.

2. Ibid. i. 406; to Lady Beaumont, 4 May 1805, in *Early Years*, 590. The comment was prompted by the publication of *The Lay of the Last Minstrel*, which includes a warm acknowledgement of Richard Polwhele's poem *Local Attachments*, first published in 1796.

3. Walter Scott, 'Essay on the Imitations of the Ancient Ballad', in *Minstrelsy of the Scottish Border*, ed. T. F. Henderson, rev. edn., 4 vols. (Edinburgh and London, 1902), iv. 41; J. G. Lockhart, *Memoir of the Life of Sir Walter Scott*, 7 vols. (Edinburgh, 1837–8), i. 352.

4. 'Essay on the Imitations of the Ancient Ballad', in *Minstrelsy*, iv. 25.

5. Of all Scott's works, 'The Eve of St John' was Hardy's favourite, and he was especially struck by the setting (*Life and Work of Thomas Hardy*, 250–1).

6. *Scott on Himself*, ed. David Hewitt (Edinburgh, 1981), 28.

7. Ibid. See also Edgar Johnson, *Sir Walter Scott: The Great Unknown*, 2 vols. (London, 1970), 54–5; Jane Millgate, *Walter Scott: The Making of the Novelist* (Edinburgh, 1984), 5–7.

8. Jacobus, *Tradition and Experiment in Wordsworth's* Lyrical Ballads.

9. Scott's response to *Ossian* can be seen in his review of Mackenzie's *Report of the Committee of the Highland Society . . . into the Authenticity of Ossian* in the *Edinburgh Review*, 6 (1805), 429–62, and *The Antiquary* (1816). His own work on German ballads and the *Minstrelsy* pre-dated the publication of the Highland Society's *Report* and Malcolm Laing's critical edition of *The Poems of Ossian* (1805), which both contributed to a major shift in opinions about the authenticity of Macpherson's work.

10. Lockhart, *Memoir*, i. 187.

11. *Scott on Himself*, ed. Hewitt, 1.

12. Scott, review of Cromek, *Reliques of Robert Burns*, *Quarterly Review*, 1 (1809), 19–36, in Donald Low (ed.), *Robert Burns: The Critical Heritage* (London, 1974), 196.

13. Lockhart, *Memoir*, i. 324.

14. 'Essay on Imitations of the Ancient Ballad', in *Minstrelsy*, i. 15.

15. Lockhart, *Memoir*, i. 346.

16. Ibid.

17. See *The Songs of Robert Burns*, ed. Donald Low (London, 1993); Kirsteen McCue, 'Burns's Songs and Poetic Craft', in Gerard Carruthers (ed.), *The Edinburgh Companion to Robert Burns* (Edinburgh, 2009), 74–85.

18. Scott, review of Cromek, in Low (ed.), *Burns: Critical Heritage*, 206.

19. R. H. Cromek, *Reliques of Robert Burns, Consisting Chiefly of Original Letters, Poems and Critical Observations on Scottish Songs* (London, 1808), 346–8.

20. Scott, review of Cromek, in Low (ed.), *Burns: Critical Heritage*, 205.

21. Ibid. 208.

22. *Minstrelsy*, i. 172.

23. *Poems and Songs of Burns*, i. 326. Kinsley includes Elizabeth Scott's verse epistle, which was first published in her collection of poems, *Alonza and Cora* (Edinburgh, 1801). Burns used to quote the same lines when asked about why he spoiled the purity of his verse by including Scots, as Coleridge recorded (*The Friend*, ed. Barbara Rooke, 2 vols. (Princeton, 1969), i. 293).
24. See Low (ed.), *Burns: Critical Heritage*, introduction.
25. *Poems and Songs of Burns*, iii. 972.
26. *Works of Burns*, ed. Currie, i. 313.
27. Ibid. i. 312; Blair, *Lectures on Rhetoric and Belles Lettres*, ii. 322.
28. Paul Mallet, *Northern Antiquities*, trans. Thomas Percy, 2 vols. (London, 1770), i. 385.
29. *Works of Burns*, ed. Currie, i. 321.
30. Ibid.
31. Ibid. i. 309.
32. Ibid. i. 159.
33. Ibid. i. 159–60.
34. In fact, several of the ballads probably originated in the north-east, another 'Border region', between the Highlands and the Lowlands; see David Buchan, *The Ballad and the Folk* (London, 1972), 28–34.
35. Raymond Williams, *The Country and the City* (London, 1973), 197.
36. Raymond Williams, *Politics and Letters* (London, 1979), 26. See also Williams's novels, *Border Country* (London, 1961) and *People of the Black Mountains* (London, 1989), and Dennis L. Dworkin and Leslie G. Roman (eds.), *Views beyond the Border Country* (New York and London, 1993).
37. *Politics and Letters*, 26.
38. Scott's attraction to medieval chivalry would later find literary expression in poems such as *Marmion* (1808) and novels such as *Ivanhoe* (1819) and in the architecture and furnishings of Abbotsford. For Scott's influence on Victorian culture, see Mark Girouard, *The Return to Camelot* (New Haven and London, 1981).
39. *Minstrelsy*, i. 175.
40. A. J. Youngson, *The Making of Classical Edinburgh* (Edinburgh, 1966); Ian Duncan, *Scott's Shadow* (Princeton, 2007).
41. *Minstrelsy*, i. 156.
42. Susan Oliver has traced Scott's 'conservative philosophy' in the *Minstrelsy*, in *Scott, Byron and the Politics of Cultural Encounter* (Basingstoke, 2005). See also David Harker, *Fakesong* (Milton Keynes, 1985), 48–9.
43. *Minstrelsy*, i. 175.
44. Ibid. i. 156.
45. Ibid. i. 116. Scott pays tribute to Burke at this point.
46. Ibid. i. 128.

47. Ibid.
48. Ibid. i. 167.
49. Ibid. i. 166.
50. Ibid. i. 165.
51. *Lyrical Ballads*, 753.
52. Lockhart, *Memoir*, i. 265.
53. Ibid. 265–6; W. S. Crockett, *The Scott Country*, 3rd edn. (London, 1905), 143–4.
54. *Minstrelsy*, ii. 282.
55. *Politics and Letters*, 26.
56. Neil Corcoran, 'On Seamus Heaney's Life', in *The Poetry of Seamus Heaney*, 236; cf. Scott's description of the Borderers as 'kind of outcasts' from both Scotland and England (*Minstrelsy*, i. 115).
57. 'Mossbawn', in *Finders Keepers*, 6.
58. Ibid.
59. *Minstrelsy*, iv. 89.
60. Seamus Heaney, introduction to *Sweeney Astray*.
61. 'Exposure', in *North*, 73.
62. Ibid.
63. See, e.g., Desmond Fennell's objections, *Whatever You Say, Say Nothing: Why Seamus Heaney is No. 1* (Dublin, 1991); Carson, 'Escaped from the Massacre?' For helpful analysis of different responses, see Brearton, *The Great War in Irish Poetry*, 217–50.
64. 'The First Flight', in *Station Island*, 102–3.
65. *Minstrelsy*, ii. 417–18. Scott also printed 'The Three Ravens' from Ritson's *Ancient Songs and Ballads* (1790), challenging his readers to see which was the more 'original'; see Oliver, *Scott, Byron and the Politics of Cultural Encounter*, 61–2; M. J. G. Hodgart, *The Ballads* (London, 1950), 41–5.
66. Thomas Blackwell, *An Enquiry into the Life and Writings of Homer* (London, 1735), 23.
67. 19 Sept. 1803, in *Journals*, i. 394.
68. *Journals*, i. 406.
69. *Minstrelsy*, i. 358.
70. *Journals*, i. 214.
71. The ballad 'Johnny Armstrong' is introduced by an extensive note which mentions the withered trees of Carlanrig (*Minstrelsy*, i. 330–62).
72. *Journals*, i. 405.
73. *Prelude*, xii. 9.
74. 'Crediting Poetry', 466–7.
75. 'Introduction to Canto First: To William Stewart Rose, Esq.', ll. 63–4, in *Marmion*, in *The Poetical Works of Sir Walter Scott*, ed. J. Logie Robertson (Oxford, 1904), 90.

76. 'Introduction to the Canto Third: To William Erskine, Esq.', ll. 168–75, in *Marmion*, in *Poetical Works*, ed. Robertson, 114. Lockhart included a substantial extract from this poem in his biography, observing that 'no poet has given to the world a picture of the dawning feelings of life and genius, at once so simple, so beautiful and so complete' (*Memoirs*, i. 110–11).
77. *Scott on Himself*, ed. Hewitt, 29.
78. Nicola Watson, *The Literary Tourist* (Basingstoke, 2007), 150–63.

CHAPTER 5

1. 24 Sept. 1803, in *Journals*, i. 408.
2. 18 Aug. 1803, in ibid. i. 200.
3. This stanza was written in 1803 but later revised for publication in 1842; *Last Poems*, 308.
4. *Journals*, i. 200.
5. Cf. *Journals*, i. 202.
6. 'Thoughts Suggested the Day Following, on the Banks of the Nith' was written in 1835 and published in *Poems, Chiefly of Early and Late Years* (London, 1842); *Last Poems*, 310–2. Wordsworth's title recalled Burns's *Poems, Chiefly in the Scottish Dialect*.
7. Liam McIlvanney, *Burns the Radical* (East Linton, 2002), 226–7. On the appeal of Burns's cottage for nineteenth-century visitors, see Nicholas Roe, 'Authenticating Burns', in Robert Crawford (ed.), *Robert Burns and Cultural Authority* (Edinburgh, 1997), 159–79; Nicola Watson, *The Literary Tourist* (Basingstoke, 2007).
8. To William Greenfield, Dec. 1786, in *The Letters of Robert Burns*, ed. J. de Lancey Ferguson, 2nd edn., ed. G. Ross Roy, 2 vols. (Oxford, 1988) i. 74.
9. To John Moore, 2 Aug. 1787, in *Letters*, i. 144.
10. In the same month that Burns composed 'There was a lad', he was toasted by the Grand Master of the Scottish Freemasons as 'Caledonia's Bard', as described by Robert Crawford in *The Bard: Robert Burns, a Biography* (London, 2009), 243–4.
11. David Daiches, *Robert Burns* (London, 1952), 251.
12. Catherine Carswell, *Robert Burns* (London, 1930), 63.
13. Introduction to *Robert Burns: Poems Selected by Don Paterson* (London, 2001), p. xii. Paterson makes an exception of 'Tam o' Shanter', which was published five years after the Kilmarnock edition.
14. Ibid., p. xii.
15. *Poems and Songs*, i. 137.
16. Preface, 1786, in *Poems and Songs*, iii. 971, 972.
17. To Moore, Aug. 1787, in *Letters*, i. 141.

18. 'The Vision', l. 23, in *Poems and Songs*, i. 103.
19. Ibid. 105.
20. Aug. 1785, in *Robert Burns's Commonplace Book*, ed. J. C. Ewing and D. Cook (Fontwell, 1965), 36. The note is included in *Poems and Songs*, iii. 1070–1, and was first published in 1808 in Cromek, *Reliques of Robert Burns*.
21. *Robert Burns's Commonplace Book*, 36; *Poems and Songs*, iii. 1070–1.
22. 'To W. S****n, Ochiltree', ll. 37–9, in *Poems and Songs*, i. 94.
23. *Don Juan*, i. 5.
24. Various letters between 1783 and 1786 are signed Robt Burness (*Letters*, i. 20–30). See also 'Elegy on the Death of Robert Ruisseaux', where 'burns' is translated into the French 'ruisseaux' or brooks (*Poems and Songs*, i. 321–2).
25. Allan H. Maclaine, *The Christis Kirk Tradition: Scots Poems of Folk Festivity* (Glasgow, 1996).
26. Douglas Dunn, 'Burns's Native Metric', in Crawford (ed.), *Robert Burns and Cultural Authority*, 68.
27. 'Epistle to J. L****k an old Scotch Bard', 9, in *Poems and Songs*, i. 85. McIlvanney, *Burns the Radical*, 119.
28. Ian Campbell, 'Burns's Poems and their Audience', in Donald Low (ed.), *Critical Essays on Robert Burns* (London, 1975).
29. 'Burns's Art Speech', in Crawford (ed.), *Robert Burns and Cultural Authority*, 225; Heaney republished a revised version of the essay in *Finders Keepers*.
30. 'Burns's Art Speech', 227–8.
31. Cf. Pope, *The Rape of the Lock*, i. 138, 'Puffs, Powders, Patches, Bibles, Billet-doux'.
32. Kinsley notes the allusion to *Dunciad*, i. 19–20, in *Poems and Songs*, iii. 1129.
33. *Poems and Songs*, i. 152.
34. For helpful commentary on key critical interpretations of Burns's religious satire, see *The Canongate Burns*, ed. Noble and Hogg, 41–3.
35. 'Epistle to a Young Friend', l. 67, in *Poems and Songs*, i. 250. In the Edinburgh edition, Burns included 'The Calf' immediately before 'Address to the Deil'. The volume also contained 'Address to the Unco Guid', whose similar title points to similar themes.
36. Murray Pittock, *Scottish and Irish Romanticism* (Oxford, 2008), 149.
37. *Paradise Lost*, i. 84; v. 658–9. For helpful discussion, see John Lennard, *Naming in Paradise* (Oxford, 1990).
38. *Paradise Lost*, i. 362–3.
39. Ibid. i. 375; i. 128.
40. The birds and beasts receive their names from Adam and simultaneously pay him 'fealty with low subjection' (*Paradise Lost*, viii. 343–5).

41. Walter McGinty, *Burns and Religion* (Aldershot, 2003), 81; To Mrs Dunlop, 21 June 1789, in *Letters*, i. 419.
42. To John Moore, Aug. 1787, in *Letters*, i. 136.
43. Ibid. 135.
44. Crawford suggests that the farmer's daughter mentioned to Gavin Hamilton in January 'may have been Margaret Chalmers' (*The Bard*, 249), a suggestion reinforced by Ross Roy's tentative identification of a letter written to 'My Dear Countrywoman' in the same month (*Letters*, i. 79, 81).
45. Aug. 1787, in *Letters*, i. 146.
46. To Robert Aiken, 16 Dec. 1786, in *Letters*, i. 73.
47. Ian McIntyre, *Dirt and Deity: A Life of Robert Burns* (London, 1995), 135.
48. *Poems and Songs*, i. 320–1.
49. To Greenfield, Dec. 1786, in *Letters*, i. 74.
50. To William Dunbar, 30 Apr. 1787, To George Lowrie, 5 Feb. 1787, in *Letters*, i. 89, 109.
51. To the Earl of Buchan, 7 Feb. 1787, in *Letters*, i. 92.
52. To Hugh Blair, 4 May 1787, in *Letters*, i. 110.
53. To John Ballantine, 14 Jan. 1787, in *Letters*, i. 82; To John Muir, Dec. 1786, in *Letters*, i. 72.
54. To William Chalmers, 27 Dec. 1786, in *Letters*, i. 76.
55. To Mrs Dunlop, Apr. 1787, in *Letters*, i. 108, quoting *Paradise Lost*, i. 250–1.
56. To William Nicol, 18 June 1787, in *Letters*, i. 123; for critical discussion, see Susan Manning, 'Burns and God', in Crawford (ed.), *Robert Burns and Cultural Authority*, 114.
57. To James Smith, 11 June 1787, in *Letters*, i. 121, quoting *Paradise Lost*, i. 250–3.
58. *Paradise Lost*, ix. 119.
59. To James Smith?, 30 June 1787, in *Letters*, i. 26.
60. *Paradise Lost*, iv. 73–5.
61. To John Ballantine, 14 Jan. 1787, in *Letters*, i. 82, quoting Robert Blair, 'The Grave' (London, 1743), l. 14.
62. To Mrs Dunlop, 25 Jan. 1790, in *Letters*, ii. 7; Thomas Crawford, *Burns: A Study of the Poems and Songs* (Edinburgh and London, 1960), 257.
63. To Mrs Dunlop, 22 Mar. 1787, in *Letters*, i. 101.
64. Note on 'There Said the Stripling', in *The Fenwick Notes*, 53; William Wordsworth, *Sonnet Series and Itinerant Poems*, ed. Geoffrey Jackson (Ithaca, NY, and London, 2004), 648.
65. *Fenwick Notes*, 53.
66. *Poems and Songs*, iii. 1241. Burns's note was published by Cromek in 1808. The poem was published in the *Scots Musical Museum*, Aug. 1792 along with a song to Jean.
67. Review of J. G. Lockhart, *The Life of Burns*, *Edinburgh Review*, 48 (Dec. 1828), 311–12.

68. *Poems and Songs*, i. 423.
69. Kinsley, 'A Classical Commonplace Derived from Persius, Prologue to the *Satires*, 1–3 (Dryden's translation, 1693)', in *Poems and Songs*, iii. 1278.
70. To Moore, Aug. 1797, in *Letters*, i. 140.
71. *Poems and Songs*, ii. 668. On 'the democracy of sex' in Burns's work, see Daiches, *Robert Burns*, 280; McIlvanney, *Burns the Radical*, 165–85.
72. To Peter [Patrick] Miller, 20 Oct. 1787, in *Letters*, i. 162.
73. 5 Feb. 1789, in *Letters*, i. 370.
74. *The River Duddon* (London, 1820), 39.
75. On the wider significance of rivers, see Lucy Lippard, *The Lure of the Local* (New York, 1997), 160–8.
76. To Johnson, 15 Nov. 1788, in *Letters*, i. 340.
77. Kinsley includes the text from the Edinburgh edition of 1793, with its new title, 'On the Late Captain Grose's Peregrinations thro' Scotland', in *Poems and Songs*, i. 494.
78. To Mrs Dunlop, 11 Apr. 1791, in *Letters*, ii. 83.
79. Crawford, *The Bard*, 316. Grose's *Classical Dictionary of the Vulgar Tongue* was published in 1785 and his *Provincial Glossary* in 1787. For discussion, see Julie Coleman, *A History of Cant and Slang Dictionaries*, ii. *1785–1858* (Oxford, 2004), 14–71.
80. The oral sources of 'Tam o'Shanter' were recounted to Grose in June 1790 (*Letters*, ii. 29–31). On the dialogue between the antiquarian attitudes and those of 'Hidden Scotland', see Pittock, *Scottish and Irish Romanticism*, 155–65.
81. To John Moore, 14 July 1790, in *Letters*, ii. 37.
82. 'Tam O'Shanter', ll. 83–4, 19–20; 'To the Rev. John M'Math', ll. 7–8, 34–36.
83. Crawford, *The Bard*, 328.
84. *Poems and Songs*, iii. 1364; To A. F. Tytler, Apr. 1791, in *Letters*, ii. 85.
85. See Kinsley's commentary, *Poems and Songs*, iii. 1350–4, and for more recent analysis of this aspect of the poem, Gerard Carruthers, *Robert Burns* (Tavistock, 2006), 86–94.
86. *Works of Burns*, ed. Currie, i. 325; Josiah Walker, 'An Account of the Life and Character of Robert Burns', in Low (ed.), *Critical Heritage*, 233.
87. To John Forbes Mitchell, 21 Apr. 1819, in *The Letters of William and Dorothy Wordsworth: The Middle Years, 1812–1820*, rev. edn., ed. Mary Moorman and Alan G. Hill (Oxford, 1970), 533.
88. On Burns's inspiration to writers in various regions, see McIlvanney, *Burns the Radical*, 220–40; Valentina Bold, *James Hogg: A Bard of Nature's Making* (Oxford, 2007), 41–83, 247–94; Fiona Stafford, 'Scottish Poetry and Regional Literary Expression', in John Richetti (ed.), *The Cambridge History of English Literature 1660–1780* (Cambridge, 2005), 340–62.

CHAPTER 6

1. J. G. Lockhart, *The Life of Robert Burns* (London, 1904), 235.
2. Lockhart, 'The Cockney School. IV', *Blackwood's Edinburgh Magazine*, 3 (1818), 519–24, repr. in G. M. Matthews (ed.), *John Keats: The Critical Heritage* (London, 1971), 97–8.
3. Ibid.
4. Marjorie Levinson, *Keats's Life of Allegory* (Oxford, 1988); Nicholas Roe, *John Keats and the Culture of Dissent* (Oxford, 1997); Jeffrey Cox, *Poetry and Politics in the Cockney School*.
5. Bernard Shaw, *Pygmalion*, ed. Dan H. Laurence and Nicholas Grene (London, 2003), 17.
6. John Keats, 'To Solitude', in *The Poems of John Keats*, ed. J. Stillinger (London, 1978), 41. All references in this chapter are to this edition.
7. 10 Mar. 1795, in *Collected Letters of Samuel Taylor Coleridge*, i. 82–3.
8. Ibid.
9. Roe, *John Keats and the Culture of Dissent*, 34–41.
10. Lucy Newlyn has explored the implications of Milton's lines for Romantic poets in ' "In City Pent": Echo and Allusion in Wordsworth, Coleridge and Lamb, 1797–1801', in *Coleridge, Wordsworth and the Language of Allusion*, 2nd edn. (Oxford, 2001), 205–26; see also Roe, *John Keats and the Culture of Dissent*, 194–201. Wordsworth's sonnets on London were published in *Poems, in Two Volumes* (1807), Part the Second, 'Sonnets Dedicated to Liberty', and had been republished in the recent *Poems* of 1815.
11. 'O! How I Love on a Fair Summer's Eve'.
12. *European Magazine* (Oct. 1815), 365.
13. As noted by Miriam Allott in John Keats, *The Complete Poems*, ed. M. Allott (London, 1970). For Keats's response to Poussin in 'Sleep and Poetry', see Ian Jack, *Keats and the Mirror of Art* (Oxford, 1967), 135–40.
14. To Benjamin Bailey, 8 Oct. 1817, in *The Letters of John Keats*, ed. Hyder E. Rollins, 2 vols. (Cambridge, MA, 1958). i. 170.
15. W. J. Bate, *John Keats* (Cambridge, MA, 1963), 191.
16. To Benjamin Bailey, 22 Nov. 1817, in *Letters of John Keats*, i. 185.
17. Ibid. 184.
18. 'To Reynolds', l. 66.; Jack, *Keats and the Mirror of Art*, 127–30; Grant F. Scott, *The Sculpted Word: Keats, Ekphrasis and the Visual Arts* (Hanover and London, 1994), 73–86.
19. Unsigned review of *Poems*, *The Champion*, 9 Mar. 1817, 78, in Matthews (ed.) *Keats: Critical Heritage*, 46.
20. To Taylor, 24 Apr. 1818, in *The Letters of John Keats*, i. 271.
21. Ibid.

22. Bate, *John Keats*, 146–8; for the contemporary contexts, see Scott, *The Sculpted Word*, 45–67; William St Clair, *Lord Elgin and the Marbles*, 3rd edn. (Oxford, 1998).
23. For the composition and reception of *Endymion*, see Andrew Motion, *John Keats* (London, 1997), 160–207. See also Cox, *Poetry and Politics in the Cockney School*; Matthews (ed.) *Keats: The Critical Heritage*, 75–148.
24. *Don Juan*, xi. 60; 'To B. R. Haydon, with a Sonnet written on Seeing the Elgin Marbles', l. 4.
25. To Reynolds, 27 Apr. 1818, in *Letters of John Keats*, i. 274.
26. To Reynolds, 3 May 1818, in *Letters of John Keats*, i. 278.
27. Ibid.
28. Ibid.
29. To Haydon, 10 Jan. 1818, in *Letters of John Keats*, i. 203; Preface to *The Excursion* (1814), 41.
30. To Reynolds, 3 May 1818, in *Letters of John Keats*, i. 278.
31. Ibid.
32. 'Cockney School. I', *Blackwood's Edinburgh Magazine*, 1 (1817), 39. See Roe, *John Keats and the Culture of Dissent*, 214–17, for discussion of the 'suburban school' and Keats.
33. *Lectures on the English Poets*, in *The Complete Works of Hazlitt*, ed. P. P. Howe, 21 vols. (London, 1930–4) v. 53.
34. Ibid. 128.
35. Ibid. 128–9.
36. Alexander Peterkin, *A Review of the Life of Robert Burns and of Various Criticisms of his Life and Character* (Edinburgh, 1815).
37. *European Magazine* (July 1815), 5.
38. Ibid.
39. *Complete Works of Hazlitt*, ed. Howe, v. 15–16.
40. To Bailey, 18 July 1818, in *Letters of John Keats*, i. 342.
41. Charles Brown's *Walks in the North*, published in the *Plymouth and Devonport Weekly Journal* (1840), reprinted by Rollins in *Letters of John Keats*, i. 427. For an attractive, illustrated account of their tour, see Carol Kyros Walker, *Walking North with Keats* (New Haven and London, 1992).
42. To Tom Keats, 27 June 1818, in *Letters of John Keats*, i. 301.
43. Ibid.
44. John Middleton Murry noted this connection in his pioneering chapter on 'Keats and Wordsworth', in *The Mystery of Keats* (London, 1949), 237.
45. To Reynolds, 13 July 1818, in *Letters of John Keats*, i. 323.
46. Ibid. 324.
47. Ibid. 325.
48. To Tom Keats, 9 June 1818, in *Letters of John Keats*, i. 320.
49. To Bailey, 8 Oct. 1817, in *Letters of John Keats*, i. 170.
50. 'Epistle to a Young Friend', ll. 77–80.

51. *The Mystery of Keats*, 238.
52. 'Praised be the Art', ll. 7–8, published in 1815.
53. Wordsworth, *Lyrical Ballads*, 753.
54. Review of *Poems*, 1817, *The Champion*, in Matthews (ed.) *Keats: The Critical Heritage*, 46.
55. To Tom Keats, 26 July 1818, in *Letters of John Keats*, i. 348–9.
56. Ibid.
57. To George Keats, 14–31 Oct. 1818, in *Letters of John Keats*, i. 394.
58. Ibid. 394, 404.
59. Ibid. 403.
60. To the George Keatses, 31 Dec. 1818, in *Letters of John Keats*, ii. 18.
61. Preface to *The Excursion*, 53–5.
62. To the George Keatses, 31 Dec. 1818, in *Letters of John Keats*, ii. 25.
63. Keats transcribed the passage in Jan. 1819 and sent it to his brother, George (*Letters of John Keats*, ii. 25).
64. To B. R. Haydon, 3 Oct. 1819, in *Letters of John Keats*, ii. 219.
65. To Fanny Keats, 12 Apr. 1819, in *Letters of John Keats*, ii. 52.
66. Ibid.
67. For Keats's reference to Druids and to Celtic influences more generally, see Christine Gallant, *Keats and Romantic Celticism* (Basingstoke, 2005).
68. *Complete Works of Hazlitt*, ed. Howe, v. 18.
69. To Reynolds, 21 Sept. 1819, in *Letters of John Keats*, ii. 167. See Bate, *John Keats*, and *The Burden of the Past and the English Poet* (London, 1971). Keats's approval or otherwise of the published 'Hyperion' remains somewhat unclear; see *Poems of John Keats*, 640.
70. 'If by Dull Rhymes our English must be Chained', l. 5.
71. 'He seems to us to write a line at random, and then he follows not the thought excited by this line, but that suggested by the rhyme' (Croker, review of *Endymion*, *Quarterly Review*, 19 (1818), in Matthews (ed.) *Keats: The Critical Heritage*, 112).
72. To George Keats, 3 May 1819, in *Letters of John Keats*, ii. 108.
73. To George and Tom Keats, 27 Dec. 1817, in *Letters of John Keats*, i. 193.
74. Ibid. 194; 'Ode on a Grecian Urn', ll. 44–5.
75. Philip Levine, 'Keats in Detroit', *New York Times* (29 Oct. 1995), 13, quoted by Greg Kucich, 'Keats in Transition: The Bicentenary and its Provocations', *Romanticism*, 2/1 (1996), 7.

CHAPTER 7

1. George Eliot, *The Mill on the Floss*, ed. Gordon S. Haight with an introduction by Dinah Birch (Oxford, 1996), 41–2.

2. To Wordsworth, 30 Jan. 1801, in *The Letters of Charles and Mary Lamb, Volume One, 1796–1801*, ed. Edwin W. Marrs Jr. (Ithaca, NY, and London, 1975), 267.

3. 'The Londoner', *Morning Post*, 1 Feb. 1802, in Charles Lamb, *Essays of Elia*, ed. Thomas Hutchinson (London, 1924), 50.

4. Lamb's account of Wordsworth's letter survives in a letter to Thomas Manning of 15 Feb. 1801, included in Wordsworth, *Early Years*, 316.

5. The races of mankind were routinely catalogued by natural historians of the period following the work of Linnaeus and Buffon. For Saree Makdisi, this passage suggests an imperial return of the repressed as Britain's capital is overrun by those it has exploited all over the world (*Romantic Imperialism: Universal Empire and the Culture of Modernity* (Cambridge, 1998)).

6. On the phenomenon of the London crowd, see Peter Ackroyd, *London: The Biography* (London, 2000), 389–406.

7. See Sekora, *Luxury*; Berg, *Luxury and Pleasure in Eighteenth-Century Britain*; Williams, *The Country and the City*.

8. Michel de Certeau, 'Walking in the City', in *The Certeau Reader*, ed. Graham Ward (Oxford, 2000), 102. See also Andrews, *Landscape and Western Art*, 77–85. The continuing desire to see the city whole is evident in the popularity of the panorama in the nineteenth century; see Christopher Prendergast, *Paris in the Nineteenth Century* (Oxford, 1995), 46–73.

9. Pope, *Windsor Forest*, 15. See also John Barrell, 'The Public Prospect and the Private View: The Politics of Taste in Eighteenth-Century Britain', in Simon Pugh (ed.), *Reading Landscape: Country–City–Capital* (Manchester, 1990).

10. Andrews, *Landscape and Western Art*, 21–2.

11. *The Prelude*, vii. 118–20.

12. 'The Londoner', 51.

13. Ibid.

14. Ibid. 51–2.

15. Lamb to Coleridge, 10 Dec. 1796; 'Imperfect Sympathies', 1821, in *Lamb as Critic*, ed. Roy Park (London, 1980), 190–1.

16. 'The Londoner', 52.

17. Ibid.

18. Ibid.

19. Coleridge, 'This Lime Tree Bower my Prison', ll. 28–30 in *Complete Poetical Works*, i. 179. Lamb objected more to being described as 'gentle-hearted' (*Letters*, i. 224); see Richard Holmes, *Coleridge: Early Visions* (London, 1989), 154.

20. 'The Londoner', 52.

21. For an important exception, see John Gay's *Trivia*, 1716, in Clare Brant and Susan E. Whyman (eds.), *Walking the Streets of Eighteenth-Century London* (Oxford, 2007).

22. For a useful introduction to the new print culture, see John Mullan and Christopher Reid (eds.), *Eighteenth-Century Popular Culture: A Selection* (Oxford, 2000).

23. Philip Carter, 'Faces and Crowds', in Brant and Whyman (eds.), *Walking the Streets*, 27–42.

24. No. 82, No. 568, Joseph Addison and Richard Steele, *The Spectator*, ed. Donald Bond, 5 vols. (Oxford, 1965), i. 350; iv. 539; nos. 82 and 568.

25. Ibid., No. 69, i. 295.

26. Ibid.

27. Ibid., No. 10, i. 45; Anderson, *Imagined Communities*, 35.

28. *Boswell's London Journal, 1762–1763*, ed. Frederick Pottle (London, 1950), 130. See also pp. 68, 153, 233, 270, for further examples.

29. Review of *Table Talk* (1821), in *Lamb as Critic*, ed. Park, 301.

30. Ibid.

31. Ibid.

32. 'The South Sea House' (1820), in *Essays of Elia*, 472.

33. Ibid. 474.

34. Charles Dickens, *Sketches by Boz and Other Early Essays 1833–1839* ed. Michael Slater (Columbus, OH, 1994), 72. See also Alan Robinson, *Imagining London, 1770–1900* (Basingstoke, 2004), 90–101.

35. *Sketches by Boz*, 73.

36. For discussion of allusions to ancient cities in modern urban writing, see Lynda Nead, *Victorian Babylon* (New Haven and London, 2000); Alexander Welsh, *The City of Dickens* (Oxford, 1971); Prendergast, *Paris*, 28.

37. *Sketches by Boz*, 76.

38. *Essays of Elia*, 780–5.

39. Charles Dickens, *Oliver Twist*, ed. Stephen Gill (Oxford, 1999), 196.

40. Ibid. 196–7.

41. Charles Dickens, *David Copperfield*, ed. Andrew Sanders (Oxford, 1997), 163. This section of *David Copperfield* reworks an earlier essay, 'The Streets', in *Sketches by Boz*, 54, and personal memories of his childhood; see John Forster, *Life of Dickens* (London, 1872–4), i. 23–6, and F. S. Schwarzbach, *Dickens and the City* (London, 1979), 26–7.

42. Cf. Williams, *The Country and the City*, 165.

43. To Charles James Fox, 14 Jan. 1801, in *Early Years*, 315; *Oliver Twist*, 3.

44. Bernard Mandeville, *The Fable of the Bees: Or Private Vices, Publick Benefits*, 5th edn. (London, 1728), 131; Smollett, *The Expedition of Humphry Clinker*, 119. Pierce Egan included a speech on 'the MIGHTY POWER of DRESS' by Mr Primefit of Regent St in his popular *Life in London* (London, 1822), 136.

45. *Dombey and Son*, ed. Alan Horsman (Oxford, 1974), 76.

46. John O. Jordan, 'The Purloined Handkerchief', repr. in the Norton Critical Edition of *Oliver Twist*, ed. Fred Kaplan (New York and London, 1993), 588.

47. Ibid. 590.
48. Eliot, *The Waste Land*, iii. 6, in *The Complete Poems and Plays of T. S. Eliot* (London, 1969), 67; James Joyce, *Ulysses* (Harmondsworth, 1969), 11; Monica Ali, *Brick Lane* (London, 2003), 98.
49. Charles Dickens, preface to the 1847 edition, in *The Pickwick Papers*, ed. Mark Wormald, rev. edn. (London, 2003), 760.
50. *David Copperfield*, 207.
51. Charles Dickens, *Great Expectations*, ed. Margaret Cardwell (Oxford, 1994), 217.
52. Leerssen, *Remembrance and Imagination*, 35–8; see Chapter 2 above.
53. *Oliver Twist*, 57. For extended analysis of Dickens's use of different kinds of speech, see G. L. Brook, *The Language of Dickens* (London, 1970).
54. Henry James, *A Small Boy and Others* (London, 1913), 316, 322; James Joyce, 'The Centenary of Charles Dickens', in *Occasional, Critical, and Political Writing*, ed. Kevin Barry (Oxford, 2000), 184. See also K. Lynch, *The Image of the City* (Cambridge, MA, 1985).
55. To John Forster, Oct. 1844, in *The Letters of Charles Dickens*, ed. Madeline House, Graham Storey, and Kathleen Tillotson, 12 vols. (Oxford, 1965–2002), iv. 200; see also Forster, *Life*, i. 333; Schwarzbach, *Dickens and the City*, 26–7.
56. G. K. Chesterton, *Charles Dickens* (London, 1906; repr. 1943), 120.
57. To John Forster, 29 Jan. 1854, in Dickens, *Letters*, viii, ed. Graham Storey, Kathleen Tillotson, and Angus Easson (Oxford, 1993), 260.
58. Joyce, 'The Centenary of Charles Dickens', 184.
59. Ibid. 185.
60. P. Waller (ed.), *The English Urban Landscape* (Oxford, 2000).
61. 'The Death of Edwin Waugh', *Pall Mall Gazette*, 1 May 1890; Edwin Waugh, *The Poems and Songs of Old Lancashire* (1859; repr. Manchester, 1992), 137; Samuel Laycock, *Collected Writings*, ed. G. Milner (Oldham and London, 1908). For further comment on Laycock, see Simon Armitage, *All Points North* (London, 1998), 4.
62. Francis D. Klingender, *Art and the Industrial Revolution*, rev. edn. (London, 1968). See also Margaret Drabble, *A Writer's Britain* (London, 1979), 195–205; David Dimbleby, *A Picture of Britain* (London, 2005), 124–41; Nicholas Taylor, 'The Awful Sublimity of the Victorian City', in H. J. Dyos and M. Wolff (eds.), *The Victorian City*, 2 vols. (London, 1973), ii. 431–47.
63. Elizabeth Gaskell, *Mary Barton*, ed. Stephen Gill (Harmondsworth, 1970), 41.
64. Asa Briggs, *Victorian Cities* (London, 1963), 89; G. F. Chadwick, 'The Face of the Industrial City', in Dyos and Wolff (eds.), *The Victorian City*, i. 247–56.
65. Gaskell to Mary Howitt, 18 Aug. 1838, in *The Letters of Mrs Gaskell*, ed. J. A. V. Chapple and Arthur Pollard (Manchester, 1966), 33; for Gaskell's

extensive debts to Wordsworth, see Gill, *Wordsworth and the Victorians*, 120.

66. Joyce told Grant Richards that no writer had 'yet presented Dublin to the world' (15 Oct. 1905, in *The Letters of James Joyce*, ed. Richard Ellmann, 2 vols. (London, 1966), ii. 122.

67. As Alasdair Gray makes Kenneth MacAlpin reflect: 'Imaginatively, Glasgow exists as a music-hall song and a few bad novels…That's all we've given to the world outside' (*Lanark* (Edinburgh, 1981), 243).

68. Ciaran Carson, 'Turn Again', in *Belfast Confetti* (Dublin, 1989).

69. Ciaran Carson, 'Patchwork', in *The Irish for No* (Dublin, 1987), 59.

70. Ciaran Carson, *The Star Factory* (London, 1997), 223.

71. Ibid. 222.

72. Ibid. 244.

73. Ibid. 224.

Bibliography

PRIMARY SOURCES

Addison, Joseph, and Steele, Richard, *The Spectator*, ed. Donald F. Bond, 5 vols. (Oxford, 1965).

Ali, Monica, *Brick Lane* (London, 2003).

Anderson, Robert, *Poems on Various Subjects* (Carlisle, 1798).

—— *The Poetical Works of Robert Anderson, Author of Cumberland Ballads*, 2 vols. (Carlisle, 1820).

Armitage, Simon, *All Points North* (London, 1998).

—— *Selected Poems* (London, 2001).

Arnold, Matthew, *Lectures and Essays in Criticism*, ed. R. H. Super (Michigan, 1962).

Austen, Jane, *The Novels of Jane Austen*, ed. R. W. Chapman, rev. Mary Lascelles, 5 vols. (Oxford, 1965–9).

Beattie, James, *Essays on Poetry and Music* (London, 1776).

—— *The Minstrel, or the Progress of Genius* (1770), with Memoirs of the Life of the Author by Alexander Chalmers (London, 1811).

Blackwell, Thomas, *An Enquiry into the Life and Writings of Homer* (London, 1735).

Blair, Hugh, *Lectures on Rhetoric and Belles Lettres*, 2 vols. (London, 1783).

Blake, William, *The Letters of William Blake*, ed. G. Keynes (London, 1968).

—— *The Complete Poetry and Prose of William Blake*, ed. David Erdman, rev. edn. (New York, 1988).

Bloomfield, Robert, *The Farmer's Boy* (London, 1800).

—— *Selected Poems*, ed. John Goodridge and John Lucas (Nottingham, 1998).

Boswell, James, *The Life of Samuel Johnson*, ed. G. Birkbeck Hill, rev. L. F. Powell, 6 vols. (Oxford, 1934–50).

—— *Boswell's London Journal, 1762–1763*, ed. Frederick Pottle (London, 1950).

Burke, Edmund, *Reflections on the Revolution in France*, ed. Conor Cruise O'Brien (Harmondsworth, 1968).

Burns, Robert, *Poems, Chiefly in the Scottish Dialect*, 2nd edn. (Edinburgh, 1787).

—— *The Works of Burns*, ed. James Currie, 2nd edn., 4 vols. (London, 1801).

—— *The Poems and Songs of Robert Burns*, ed. James Kinsley, 3 vols. (Oxford, 1968).

—— *Robert Burns's Commonplace Book*, ed. J. C. Ewing and D. Cook (Fontwell, 1965).

—— *The Letters of Robert Burns*, ed. J. de Lancey Ferguson, 2nd edn., ed. G. Ross Roy, 2 vols. (Oxford, 1988).

—— *The Songs of Robert Burns*, ed. Donald Low (London, 1993).

—— *The Canongate Burns*, ed. Andrew Noble and Patrick Scott Hogg (Edinburgh, 2001).

—— *Poems Selected by Don Paterson* (London, 2001).

Byron, Lord George Gordon, *Byron's Letters and Journals*, ed. Leslie A. Marchand, 13 vols. (London, 1973–94).

—— *Lord Byron: The Complete Poetical Works*, ed. Jerome J. McGann, 7 vols. (Oxford, 1980–93).

Calvino, Italo, *Invisible Cities*, trans. William Weaver (London, 1974).

Carlyle, Thomas, 'The Life of Robert Burns. By J. G. Lockhart', *Edinburgh Review*, 48 (1828), 267–312.

Carson, Ciaran, 'Escaped from the Massacre?' review of *North, The Honest Ulsterman*, 50 (1975), 183–6.

—— *The Irish for No* (Dublin, 1987).

—— *Belfast Confetti* (Dublin, 1989).

—— *The Star Factory* (London, 1997).

Chatterton, Thomas, *The Complete Works of Thomas Chatterton*, ed. Donald S. Taylor, 2 vols. (Oxford, 1971).

Clare, John, *Poems, Descriptive of Rural Life and Scenery* (London, 1820).

—— *The Village Minstrel* (London, 1821).

—— *The Shepherd's Calendar* (London, 1827).

—— *The Rural Muse: Poems* (London, 1835).

—— *The Later Poems of John Clare*, ed. Eric Robinson and David Powell, 2 vols. (Oxford, 1984).

—— *The Early Poems of John Clare*, ed. Eric Robinson and David Powell, 2 vols. (Oxford, 1989).

—— *Poems of the Middle Period*, ed. Eric Robinson, David Powell, and P. M. S. Dawson, 5 vols, (Oxford, 1996–2003).

—— *John Clare by Himself*, ed. Eric Robinson and David Powell (Ashington and Manchester, 1996).

Coleridge, Samuel Taylor, *The Complete Poetical Works*, ed. E. H. Coleridge, 2 vols. (Oxford, 1912).

—— *The Collected Letters of Samuel Taylor Coleridge*, ed. Earl Leslie Griggs, 6 vols. (Oxford, 1956–71).

—— *The Friend*, ed. Barbara Rooke, 2 vols. (Princeton, 1969).

—— *Lectures 1795 on Politics and Religion*, ed. Lewis Patton and Peter Mann (Princeton and London, 1971).

—— *Biographia Literaria*, ed. J. Engell and W. J. Bate, 2 vols. (Princeton and London, 1983).

Cowper, William, *The Poems of William Cowper*, i. *1748–1782*, ed. John D. Baird and Charles Ryskamp (Oxford, 1980).

Cowper, William, *The Letters and Prose Writings of William Cowper*, ed. J. King and C. Ryskamp, 5 vols. (Oxford, 1992).

Cromek, R. H., *Reliques of Robert Burns, Consisting Chiefly of Original Letters, Poems and Critical Observations on Scottish Songs* (London, 1808).

Denham, John, *Cooper's Hill* (London, 1642).

Dickens, Charles, *Sketches by Boz and Other Early Essays*, ed. Michael Slater (Columbus, OH, 1994).

—— *The Pickwick Papers*, ed. Mark Wormald, rev. edn. (London, 2003).

—— *Oliver Twist*, ed. Stephen Gill (Oxford, 1999).

—— *Dombey and Son*, ed. Alan Horsman (Oxford, 1974).

—— *David Copperfield*, ed. Andrew Sanders (Oxford, 1997).

—— *Bleak House*, ed. Stephen Gill (Oxford, 1996).

—— *Great Expectations*, ed. Margaret Cardwell (Oxford, 1994).

—— *The Letters of Charles Dickens*, ed. Madeline House, Graham Storey, and Kathleen Tillotson, 12 vols. (Oxford, 1965–2002).

Duck, Stephen, *Poems on Several Occasions* (London, 1736).

Edgeworth, Maria, *Castle Rackrent and Ennui*, ed. Marilyn Butler (London 1992).

Egan, Pierce, *Life in London* (London, 1822).

Eliot, George, *Scenes of Clerical Life*, ed. Thomas A. Noble (Oxford, 1985).

—— *Selected Critical Writings*, ed. Rosemary Ashton (Oxford, 1992).

—— *The Mill on the Floss*, ed. Gordon. S. Haight with an introduction by Dinah Birch (Oxford, 1996).

—— *Middlemarch*, ed. David Carroll (Oxford, 1998).

Eliot, T. S., *The Complete Poems and Plays of T. S. Eliot* (London, 1969).

Ferguson, Adam, *An Essay on the History of Civil Society*, ed. D. Forbes (Edinburgh, 1966).

Gaskell, Elizabeth, *Mary Barton*, ed. Stephen Gill (Harmondsworth, 1970).

—— *North and South*, ed. Angus Easson (Oxford, 2008).

—— *The Letters of Mrs Gaskell*, ed. J. A. V. Chapple and Arthur Pollard (Manchester, 1966).

Goldsmith, Oliver, *The Collected Works of Oliver Goldsmith*, ed. A. Friedman, 5 vols. (Oxford, 1966).

Gray, Thomas, *The Poems of Gray, Collins and Goldsmith*, ed. Roger Lonsdale (London, 1969).

Gray, Alasdair, *Lanark* (Edinburgh, 1981).

Grose, Francis, *A Classical Dictionary of the Vulgar Tongue* (London, 1785).

—— *The Antiquities of Scotland*, 2 vols. (London, 1791).

Hardy, Thomas, *The Wessex Edition of the Novels of Thomas Hardy*, rev. edn., 24 vols. (London, 1912–31).

—— *The Life and Work of Thomas Hardy*, ed. Michael Millgate (London, 1984).

Hazlitt, William, *The Complete Works of William Hazlitt*, ed. P. P. Howe, 21 vols. (London, 1930–4).

——Metropolitan Writings, ed. Gregory Dart (Manchester, 2005).

Heaney, Seamus, Death of a Naturalist (London, 1969).

——Wintering Out (London, 1972).

——North (London, 1975).

——Field Work (London, 1979).

——Preoccupations: Selected Prose 1968–78 (London, 1980).

——Sweeney Astray (London, 1983).

——Station Island (London, 1984).

——The Government of the Tongue (London, 1988).

——Seeing Things (London, 1991).

——The Redress of Poetry (London, 1995).

——The Spirit Level (London, 1996).

——Opened Ground: Poems 1966–1996 (London, 1998).

——Beowulf (London, 1999).

——Electric Light (London, 2001).

——Finders Keepers: Selected Prose 1971–2001 (London, 2002).

——District and Circle (London, 2006).

Hogg, James, The Shepherd's Calendar, ed. Douglas Mack (Edinburgh, 1995).

——Anecdotes of Scott, ed. Jill Rubenstein and Douglas Mack (Edinburgh, 1999).

——Winter Evening Tales, ed. Ian Duncan (Edinburgh, 2002).

——Altrive Tales, ed. Gillian Hughes (Edinburgh, 2003).

James, Henry, A Small Boy and Others (London, 1913).

Jeffrey, Francis, review of Robert Southey's Thalaba, Edinburgh Review, 1 (Oct. 1802), 63–83.

——review of William Wordsworth's Poems, in Two Volumes, Edinburgh Review, 11 (Oct. 1807), 214–31.

——review of R. Cromek's Reliques of Robert Burns, Edinburgh Review, 13 (Jan. 1809), 249–76.

——review of The Excursion, Edinburgh Review, 24 (Nov. 1814), 24–38.

Johnson, Samuel, The Yale Edition of the Works of Samuel Johnson, 18 vols. (New Haven and London, 1958–2005).

——The Lives of the English Poets, ed. Roger Lonsdale, 4 vols. (Oxford, 2006).

Jones, David, Epoch and Artist (London, 1959).

Joyce, James, Ulysses (Harmondsworth, 1969).

——Dubliners, ed. Terence Brown (Harmondsworth, 1992).

——A Portrait of the Artist as a Young Man, ed. Seamus Deane (Harmondsworth, 1992).

——The Letters of James Joyce, ed. Richard Ellmann, 2 vols. (London, 1966).

——Occasional, Critical, and Political Writing, ed. Kevin Barry (Oxford, 2000).

Kavanagh, Patrick, A Poet's Country, ed. Antoinette Quinn (Dublin, 2003).

Kavanagh, Patrick, *Collected Poems*, ed. Antoinette Quinn (London, 2005).
Keats, John, *The Letters of John Keats*, ed. Hyder E. Rollins, 2 vols. (Cambridge, MA, 1958).
—— *The Complete Poems*, ed. M. Allott (London, 1970).
—— *The Poems of John Keats*, ed. J. Stillinger (London, 1978).
Lamb, Charles, *Essays of Elia*, ed. Thomas Hutchinson (London, 1924).
—— *The Letters of Charles Lamb*, ed. E. V. Lucas, 3 vols. (London, 1935).
—— *The Letters of Charles and Mary Lamb, Volume One, 1796–1801*, ed. Edwin W. Marrs Jr. (Ithaca, NY, and London, 1975).
—— *Lamb as Critic*, ed. Roy Park (London, 1980).
Laycock, Samuel, *Collected Writings*, ed. G. Milner (Oldham and London, 1908).
Locke, John, *An Essay on Human Understanding*, ed. P. H. Nidditch (Oxford, 1975).
—— *Two Treatises of Government*, ed. Peter Laslett, 2nd edn. (Cambridge, 1967).
—— *Some Thoughts Concerning Education*, ed. J. W. and J. S. Yolton (Oxford, 1989).
Lockhart, J. G., 'Cockney School of Poetry, No. IV', *Blackwood's Edinburgh Magazine* (Aug. 1818), iii. 519–24; repr. in G. M. Matthews (ed.), *John Keats: The Critical Heritage* (London, 1971), 97–110.
—— *Memoir of the Life of Sir Walter Scott*, 7 vols. (Edinburgh, 1837–8).
—— *The Life of Robert Burns* (London, 1904).
Long, Richard, *Heaven and Earth* (London, 2009).
Mackay Brown, George, *For the Islands I Sing* (London, 1997).
Macpherson, James, *The Poems of Ossian*, ed. Howard Gaskill (Edinburgh, 1996).
Mallet, Paul, *Northern Antiquities*, trans. Thomas Percy, 2 vols. (London, 1770).
Mandeville, Bernard, *The Fable of the Bees: Or Private Vices, Publick Benefits*, 5th edn. (London, 1728).
Mill, John Stuart, *Autobiography* (London, 1924).
Milton, John, *Complete Shorter Poems*, ed. John Carey (London, 1971).
—— *The Complete Poems*, ed. J. Carey and A. Fowler, 2nd edn. (London, 1998).
Nash, Paul, *Poet and Painter: Letters between Gordon Bottomley and Paul Nash 1910–1946*, 2nd edn. (Bristol, 2000).
Peacock, Thomas Love, *The Halliford Edition of the Works of Thomas Love Peacock*, ed. H. F. Brett-Smith and C. E. Jones, 10 vols. (London, 1924–34).
Percy, Thomas, *Reliques of Ancient English Poetry*, 3 vols. (London, 1765).
Plato, *The Republic*, trans. H. D. P. Lee (Harmondsworth, 1955).
Polwhele, Richard, *The Influence of Local Attachment with Respect to Home* (London, 1796).

Pope, Alexander, *The Twickenham Edition of the Works of Alexander Pope*, gen. ed. John Butt, 11 vols. (London, 1938–68).

—— *The Poems of Alexander Pope*, ed. John Butt (London, 1963).

Price, Richard, *A Discourse on the Love of Country* (1789), 3rd edn. (London, 1790).

Ramsay, Allan, *Poems by Allan Ramsay and Robert Fergusson*, ed. A. M. Kinghorn and A. Law (Edinburgh and London, 1974).

Ray, J., *The Wisdom of God Manifest in the Works of Creation* (London, 1690).

Reynolds, Joshua, *Discourses on Art*, ed. Robert R. Wark (New Haven and London, 1997).

Schiller, Friedrich, *On the Naïve and Sentimental in Literature*, trans. Helen Watanabe O'Kelly (Manchester, 1981).

Scott, Walter, *Minstrelsy of the Scottish Border*, 2 vols. (Kelso, 1802).

—— *Minstrelsy of the Scottish Border*, ed. T. F. Henderson, 4 vols. (Edinburgh, 1902).

—— *The Lay of the Last Minstrel* (London, 1805).

—— review of *The Report of the Highland Society on Ossian*, *Edinburgh Review*, 6 (1805), 429–62.

—— *Marmion* (Edinburgh and London, 1808).

—— *The Waverley Novels*, 24 vols. (London, 1924).

—— *The Poetical Works of Sir Walter Scott*, ed. J. Logie Robertson (Oxford, 1904).

—— *Scott on Himself*, ed. David Hewitt (Edinburgh, 1981).

Shaw, Bernard, *Pygmalion*, ed. Dan H. Laurence and Nicholas Grene (London, 2003).

Smollett, Tobias, *The Expedition of Humphry Clinker*, ed. Angus Ross (Harmondsworth, 1967).

Spinoza, Benedict de, *On the Improvement of the Understanding, The Ethics, Correspondence*, trans. R. H. M. Elwes (New York, 1955).

Thomson, James, *The Seasons*, ed. James Sambrook (Oxford, 1981).

Waugh, Edwin, *The Poems and Songs of Old Lancashire* (1859; repr. Manchester, 1992).

White, Gilbert, *The Natural History of Selborne* (1788–9), ed. Richard Mabey (Harmondsworth, 1977).

Wordsworth, Dorothy, *The Journals of Dorothy Wordsworth*, ed. Ernest de Selincourt, 2 vols. (London, 1941).

—— *Recollections of a Tour Made in Scotland*, ed. Carol Kyros Walker (New Haven and London, 1997).

Wordsworth, William, *The Letters of William and Dorothy Wordsworth*, ed. Ernest de Selincourt; i. *The Early Years, 1797–1805*, rev. Chester L. Shaver (Oxford, 1967); *The Middle Years, 1806–11*, rev. Mary Moorman (Oxford, 1969); *The Middle Years, 1812–1820*, rev. edn., ed. Mary Moorman and Alan G. Hill (Oxford, 1970); *The Later Years 1821–1853*, rev. Alan G. Hill, 4 vols. (Oxford, 1978–88).

Wordsworth, William, *The River Duddon* (London, 1820).
—— *Poems, Chiefly of Early and Late Years* (London, 1842).
—— *The Fenwick Notes*, ed. Jared Curtis (Ithaca, NY, and London, 1971).
—— *The Prose Works of William Wordsworth*, ed. W. J. B. Owen and Jane Worthington Smyser, 3 vols. (Oxford, 1974).
—— *William Wordsworth: Poems Selected by Seamus Heaney* (1988; London, 2001).
—— *Guide to the Lakes*, ed. Ernest de Selincourt, with an introduction by Stephen Gill (London, 2004).
—— *The Cornell Edition of the Works of William Wordsworth*, gen. ed. Stephen Parrish, 22 vols. (Ithaca, NY, and London, 1975–2007). Volumes from which quotations in this book have been taken:
Home at Grasmere. Part First, Book First, of the Recluse, ed. Beth Darlington (Ithaca, NY, and London, 1977).
The Prelude, 1798–9, ed. Stephen Parrish (Ithaca, NY, and London, 1977).
Poems, in Two Volumes, and Other Poems, 1800–1807, ed. Jared Curtis (Ithaca, NY, and London, 1983), 128.
Shorter Poems, ed. Carl H. Ketcham (Ithaca, NY, and London, 1989).
The Thirteen-Book Prelude, ed. Mark L. Reed (Ithaca, NY, and London, 1991).
Lyrical Ballads, and Other Poems, 1797–1800, ed. James Butler and Karen Green (Ithaca, NY, and London, 1992).
Last Poems, 1821–1850, ed. Jared Curtis (Ithaca, NY, and London, 1999).
Sonnet Series and Itinerant Poems, ed. Geoffrey Jackson (Ithaca, NY, and London, 2004).
The Excursion, ed. James Butler and Sally Bushell (Ithaca, NY, and London, 2007).
Yearsley, Ann, *Poems, on Several Occasions* (London, 1785).
—— *Poems, on Various Subjects* (London, 1787).
Yeats, W. B., *The Poems*, ed. Daniel Albright (London, 1990).

SECONDARY SOURCES

Abrams, M. H., *The Mirror and the Lamp* (London, 1953).
—— *Natural Supernaturalism* (New York and London, 1971).
Ackroyd, Peter, *London: The Biography* (London, 2000).
Adams, Ann Jensen, 'Competing Communities in the "Great Bog of Europe": Seventeenth-Century Dutch Landscape Painting', in W. J. T. Mitchell (ed.), *Landscape and Power*, 2nd edn. (Chicago, 2002), 35–76.
Anderson, Benedict, *Imagined Communities: Reflections on the Origins and Spread of Nationalism*, rev. edn. (London, 1991).
Andrews, Malcolm, *The Search for the Picturesque* (Aldershot, 1989).
—— *Landscape and Western Art* (Oxford, 1999).

Anon, *Jane Austen Centenary* (Steventon, 1917).

Appleton, Jay, *The Experience of Land*scape (London and New York, 1975).

Aubin, R., *Topographical Poetry in XVIII-Century England* (New York, 1936).

Bachelard, Gaston, *The Poetics of Space*, trans. Maria Jolas (1964; London, 1994).

Barrell, J., *The Idea of Landscape and the Sense of Place* (Cambridge, 1972).

—— *The Dark Side of the Landscape* (Cambridge, 1980).

—— *The Political Theory of Painting* (New Haven and London, 1986).

Baron, Michael, *Language and Relationship in Wordsworth's Writing* (London and New York, 1995).

Barusch, Moshe, *Theories of Art: From Plato to Winckelmann* (New York and London, 2000).

Bate, Jonathan, *Shakespeare and the English Romantic Imagination* (Oxford, 1986).

—— *Romantic Ecology* (London and New York, 1991).

—— *The Song of the Earth* (London, 2000).

—— *John Clare: A Biography* (London, 2003).

Bate, W. J., *John Keats* (Cambridge, MA, 1963).

—— *The Burden of the Past and the English Poet* (London, 1971).

Berresford Ellis, Peter, *The Story of the Cornish Language* (Redruth, 1990).

Berg, Maxine, *Luxury and Pleasure in Eighteenth-Century Britain* (Oxford, 2007).

—— and Eger, Elizabeth (eds.), *Luxury in the Eighteenth Century* (Basingstoke, 2002).

Bold, Valentina, *James Hogg: A Bard of Nature's Making* (Oxford, 2007).

Bourassa, Steven C., *The Aesthetics of Landscape* (London and New York, 1991).

Bowness, A., and Brown, D., *St Ives, 1939–64* (London, 1985).

Brant, Clare, and Whyman, Susan E. (eds.), *Walking the Streets of Eighteenth-Century London* (Oxford, 2007).

Brewer, John, *The Pleasures of the Imagination: English Culture in the Eighteenth Century* (London, 1997).

Briggs, Asa, *Victorian Cities* (London, 1963).

Brearton, Fran, *The Great War in Irish Poetry* (Oxford, 2000).

Breward, C., Ehrman, E., and Evans, C. (eds.), *The London Look* (New Haven and London, 2004).

Brook, G. L., *The Language of Dickens* (London, 1970).

Buchan, David, *The Ballad and the Folk* (London, 1972).

Butler, J., 'Tourist or Native Son: Wordsworth's Homecomings of 1799–1800', *Nineteenth-Century Literature*, 51/1 (1996), 1–15.

Cardinal, Roger, *The Landscape Vision of Paul Nash* (London, 1989).

Carey, John, *What Good are the Arts?* (London, 2005).

Carruthers, Gerard, *Robert Burns* (Tavistock, 2006).

Carruthers, Gerard, (ed.), *The Edinburgh Companion to Robert Burns* (Edinburgh, 2009).

Carswell, Catherine, *Robert Burns* (London, 1930).

Casey, E., *The Fate of Place* (Berkeley and Los Angeles, 1997).

De Certeau, Michel, 'Walking in the City', in *The Certeau Reader*, ed. Graham Ward (Oxford, 2000), 101–18.

Chesterton, G. K., *Charles Dickens* (London, 1906; repr. 1943).

Christmas, William, *The Lab'ring Muses* (Newark and London, 2001).

Clive, John, *Scotch Reviewers: The Edinburgh Review, 1802–1815* (London, 1957).

Cohen, I. Bernard, *Revolution in Science* (Cambridge, MA, 1985).

Coleman, Julie, *A History of Cant and Slang Dictionaries*, ii. *1785–1858* (Oxford, 2004).

Colley, Linda, *Britons: Forging the Nation, 1707–1837* (New Haven and London, 1992).

Copley, S., and Whale, J. (eds.), *Beyond Romanticism: New Approaches to Texts and Contexts 1780–1832* (London, 1992).

Copley, S., and Garside, P. (eds.), *The Politics of the Picturesque* (Cambridge, 1994).

Corcoran, Neil, *The Poetry of Seamus Heaney* (London, 2002).

Cosgrove, Denis E., *Social Formation and Symbolic Landscape*, 2nd edn. (Madison and London, 1998).

——and Daniels, Stephen (eds.), *The Iconography of Landscape* (Cambridge, 1988).

Cox, Jeffrey, *Poetry and Politics in the Cockney School: Keats, Shelley, Hunt and their Circle* (Cambridge, 1998).

Crawford, Robert, *Devolving English Literature* (Oxford, 1992).

——*Identifying Poets* (Edinburgh, 1993).

——(ed.), *Robert Burns and Cultural Authority* (Edinburgh, 1997).

——(ed.), *The Scottish Invention of English Literature* (Cambridge, 1998).

——*The Modern Poet* (Oxford, 2002).

——*The Bard: Robert Burns, a Biography* (London, 2009).

Crawford, Thomas, *Burns: A Study of the Poems and Songs* (Edinburgh and London, 1960).

Cresswell, Tim, *Place: A Short Introduction* (Oxford, 2004).

Crockett, W. S., *The Scott Country*, 3rd edn. (London, 1905).

Crookshank, Ann, and the Knight of Glyn, *Ireland's Painters, 1600–1940* (New Haven and London, 2002).

Curran, Stuart, *Poetic Form and British Romanticism* (Oxford, 1986).

Curtis, Jared, *Wordsworth's Experiments with Tradition: The Lyric Poems of 1802* (Ithaca, NY, and London, 1971).

Daiches, David, *Robert Burns* (London, 1952).

Damrosch, L., 'Generality and Particularity', in *The Cambridge History of Literary Criticism*, iv, ed. H. Nisbet and Claude Rawson (Cambridge, 1997), 381–93.

Davis, Leith, *Acts of Union: Scotland and the Literary Negotiation of the British Nation 1707–1830* (Stanford, 1999).

Deane, Seamus ' "Unhappy and at Home": Interview with Seamus Heaney', *The Crane Bag*, 1/1 (Spring 1977), 61–7.

Demata, M., and Wu, D. (eds.), *British Romanticism and the Edinburgh Review* (Basingstoke, 2002).

Dimbleby, David, *A Picture of Britain* (London, 2005).

Dobson, Michael, *The Making of the National Poet* (Oxford, 1992).

Drabble, Margaret, *A Writer's Britain* (London, 1979).

Draper, R. P. (ed.), *The Literature of Region and Nation* (Basingstoke, 1989).

Duff, D., 'Paratextual Dilemmas: Wordsworth's "The Brothers" and the Problems of Generic Labelling', *Romanticism*, 6/2 (2000), 234–61.

——and Jones, C. (eds.), *Scotland, Ireland and the Romantic Aesthetic* (Lewisburg, 2007).

Duncan, Ian, *Scott's Shadow* (Princeton, 2007).

Dworkin, Dennis, L., and Roman, Leslie, G. (eds.), *Views beyond the Border Country* (New York and London, 1993).

Dyos, H. J., and Wolff, M. (eds.), *The Victorian City*, 2 vols. (London, 1973).

Egerton, Judy, *Wright of Derby* (London, 1997).

Erskine-Hill, Howard, *Poetry of Opposition and Revolution from Dryden to Wordsworth* (New York, 1996).

Fairer, David, *English Poetry in the Eighteenth Century* (London, 2003).

Farrer, Reginald, 'Jane Austen. Ob. July 18, 1817', *Quarterly Review*, 452 (1917), 1–30.

Fauvel, J., Flood, R., Shortland, M., and Wilson, R. (eds.), *Let Newton Be!* (Oxford, 1988).

Fennell, Desmond, *Whatever You Say, Say Nothing: Why Seamus Heaney is No. 1* (Dublin, 1991).

Ferguson, Frances, *Wordsworth: Language as Counter-Spirit* (New Haven, 1977).

Ferris, Ina, *The Romantic National Tale and the Question of Ireland* (Cambridge, 2002).

Forster, John, *Life of Dickens* (London, 1872–4).

Fulford, Tim, *Land, Liberty and Authority: Poetry, Criticism and Politics from Thomson to Wordsworth* (Cambridge, 1996).

Fussell, Paul, *The Great War and Modern Memory* (Oxford, 1975).

Gallant, C., *Keats and Romantic Celticism* (Basingstoke, 2005).

Gill, Stephen, *William Wordsworth: A Life* (Oxford, 1989).

—— *Wordsworth and the Victorians* (Oxford, 1998).

—— (ed.), *The Cambridge Companion to Wordsworth* (Cambridge, 2003).

—— 'Wordsworth and the River Duddon', *Essays in Criticism*, 57/1 (2007), 22–41.

Gilmour, Robin, 'Regional and Provincial in Victorian Literature', in R. P. Draper (ed.), *The Literature of Region and Nation* (Basingstoke, 1989), 51–60.

Girouard, Mark, *The Return to Camelot* (New Haven and London, 1981).

Goodridge, J., *Rural Life in Eighteenth-Century English Poetry* (Cambridge, 1995).

Griffin, Michael, 'Delicate Allegories, Deceitful Mazes: Goldsmith's Landscapes', *Eighteenth-Century Ireland*, 16 (2001), 104–17.

Groom, Nick, *The Making of Percy's Reliques* (Oxford, 1999).

Hadfield, Andrew, *Literature, Politics and National Identity* (Cambridge, 1994).

Hague, William, *William Pitt the Younger* (London, 2004).

Harker, D., *Fakesong* (Milton Keynes, 1985).

Hartman, G., *Wordsworth's Poetry 1787–1814* (New Haven and London, 1964).

Highet, G., *Poets in a Landscape* (London, 1957).

Hodgart, M. J. G., *The Ballads* (London, 1950).

Holmes, Richard, *Coleridge: Early Visions* (London, 1989).

Hooker, Jeremy, *Imagining Wales* (Cardiff, 2001).

Jacobus, Mary, *Tradition and Experiment in Wordsworth's* Lyrical Ballads, *1798* (Oxford, 1975).

Jack, Ian, *Keats and the Mirror of Art* (Oxford, 1967).

Johnson, C. R., *Provincial Poetry 1789–1839: British Verse Printed in the Provinces: The Romantic Background* (Otley, 1992).

Johnson, Edgar, *Sir Walter Scott: The Great Unknown*, 2 vols. (London, 1970).

Johnston, Dillon, 'Violence in Seamus Heaney's Poetry', in *The Cambridge Companion to Contemporary Irish Poetry*, ed. Matthew Campbell (Cambridge, 2003), 113–32.

Johnston, K., *The Hidden Wordsworth* (New York, 1998).

Jones, Catherine, *Literary Memory* (Lewisburg, PA, 2006).

Jones, Vivien, 'The Coquetry of Nature: Politics and the Picturesque in Women's Fiction', in Stephen Copley and Peter Garside (eds.) *The Politics of the Picturesque* (Cambridge, 1994), 120–44.

Jordan, John, O., 'The Purloined Handkerchief', repr. in the Norton Critical Edition of *Oliver Twist*, ed. Fred Kaplan (New York and London, 1993).

Kearney, Richard, *Postnationalist Ireland: Politics, Culture, Philosophy* (London and New York, 1997).

Kiberd, Declan, *Inventing Ireland* (London, 1995).

—— *Irish Classics* (Cambridge, 2000).

Klingender, Francis, D., *Art and the Industrial Revolution*, rev. edn. (London, 1968).

Kneale, J. Douglas, *Monumental Writing* (Lincoln, NA, and London, 1988).

Kucich, G., *Keats, Shelley and Romantic Spenserianism* (University Park, PA, 1991).

—— 'Keats in Transition: The Bicentenary and its Provocations', *Romanticism*, 2/1 (1996), 1–8.

Lamont, C., and Rossington, M. (eds.), *Romanticism's Debatable Lands* (Basingstoke, 2005).

Leask, Nigel, '"The Shadow Line": James Currie's "Life of Burns" and British Romanticism', in Claire Lamont and Michael Rossington (eds.), *Romanticism's Debatable Lands* (Basingstoke, 2005), 64–79.

——and Riach, Alan, *Stepping Westward: Inaugural Lectures* (Glasgow, 2008).

Leerssen, Joep, *Remembrance and Imagination: Patterns in the Historical and Literary Representations of Ireland in the Nineteenth Century* (Cork, 1996).

Lennard, John, *Naming in Paradise* (Oxford, 1990).

Levinson, Marjorie, *Wordsworth's Great Period Poems* (Cambridge, 1986).

——*Keats's Life of Allegory* (Oxford, 1988).

Lippard, Lucy, *The Lure of the Local* (New York, 1997).

Liu, Alan, *Wordsworth: The Sense of History* (Stanford, 1989).

Lloyd, David, *Anomalous States: Irish Writing and the Post-Colonial State* (Dublin, 1993).

Longley, Edna, *Poetry in the Wars* (Newcastle, 1986).

Low, Donald (ed.), *Robert Burns: The Critical Heritage* (London, 1974).

——(ed.), *Critical Essays on Robert Burns* (London, 1975).

Lynch, Kevin, *The Image of the City* (Cambridge, MA, 1985).

McCracken, David, *Wordsworth and the Lake District: A Guide to the Poems and their Places* (Oxford, 1985).

McGann, J., *The Romantic Ideology* (Chicago, 1983).

——*The Beauty of Inflections* (Oxford, 1988).

McGinty, Walter, *Burns and Religion* (Aldershot, 2003).

McGuirk, Carol, *Robert Burns and the Sentimental Era* (Athens, GA, 1985).

——(ed.), *Critical Essays on Robert Burns* (New York, 1998).

McIlvanney, Liam, *Burns the Radical* (East Linton, 2002).

McIntyre, Ian, *Dirt and Deity: A Life of Robert Burns* (London, 1995).

Maclaine, Allan H., *The Christis Kirk Tradition: Scots Poems of Folk Festivity* (Glasgow, 1996).

Makdisi, Saree, *Romantic Imperialism: Universal Empire and the Culture of Modernity* (Cambridge, 1998).

Martindale, Charles, 'Green Politics: The *Eclogues*', in Charles Martindale (ed.), *The Cambridge Companion to Virgil* (Cambridge, 1997), 107–24.

Matthews, G. M. (ed.), *John Keats: The Critical Heritage* (London, 1971).

Meek, Ronald, *Social Science and the Ignoble Savage* (Cambridge, 1976).

Millgate, Jane, *Walter Scott: The Making of the Novelist* (Edinburgh, 1984).

Mitchell, L., 'The *Edinburgh Review* and the Lake Poets 1802–1810', in *Essays Presented to C. M. Bowra* (Oxford, 1970), 24–38.

Mitchell, W. J. T. (ed.), *Landscape and Power*, 2nd edn. (Chicago, 2002).

Motion, Andrew, *John Keats* (London, 1997).

Mugglestone, Lynda, '*Talking Proper*' (Oxford, 1995).

Mullan, John, and Reid, Christopher (eds.), *Eighteenth-Century Popular Culture: A Selection* (Oxford, 2000).

Murry, John Middleton, *The Mystery of Keats* (London, 1949).

Nairn, Tom, *After Britain* (London, 2000).

Nead, Lynda, *Victorian Babylon* (New Haven and London, 2000).

Newlyn, Lucy, *Coleridge, Wordsworth and the Language of Allusion*, 2nd edn. (Oxford, 2001).

—— *'Paradise Lost' and the Romantic Reader* (Oxford, 1993).

Nicolson, M. H., *Mountain Gloom and Mountain Glory* (New York, 1959).

Nisbet, H., and Rawson, C. (eds.), *The Cambridge History of Literary Criticism*, iv. *The Eighteenth Century* (Cambridge, 1997).

Nussbaum, Felicity, *The Autobiographical Subject* (Baltimore, 1989).

—— 'Biography and Autobiography', in *The Cambridge History of Literary Criticism*, iv, ed. H. Nisbet and Claude Rawson (Cambridge, 1997), 302–11.

O'Brien, Eugene, *Seamus Heaney and the Place of Writing* (Gainesville, 2002),

O'Callaghan, Michelle, *The 'Shepheards Nation': Jacobean Spenserians and Early Stuart Political Culture 1612–1625* (Oxford, 2000).

O'Driscoll, Dennis, *Stepping Stones: Interviews with Seamus Heaney* (London, 2008).

Oliver, Susan, *Scott, Byron, and the Politics of Cultural Encounter* (Basingstoke, 2005).

Pace, Joel, 'Wordsworth and America: Reception and Reform', in Stephen Gill (ed.), *The Cambridge Companion to Wordsworth* (Cambridge, 2003), 230–45.

Pagden, Anthony, *European Encounters with the New World* (New Haven and London, 1993).

Parrish, Stephen (ed.), *Coleridge's Dejection* (Ithaca, NY, and London, 1988).

Patterson, Annabel, *Pastoral and Ideology: Virgil to Valéry* (Oxford, 1988).

Penny, Nicholas (ed.), *Reynolds* (London, 1986).

Perry, Seamus, *Coleridge and the Uses of Division* (Oxford, 1999).

Peterkin, Alexander, *A Review of the Life of Robert Burns and of Various Criticisms of his Life and Character* (Edinburgh, 1815).

Pittock, Murray, *Inventing and Resisting Britain* (Basingstoke, 1997).

—— *Poetry and Jacobite Politics in Eighteenth-Century Britain and Ireland* (Cambridge, 1994).

—— *Scottish and Irish Romanticism* (Oxford, 2008).

Porter, Roy, *London: A Social History* (London, 1994).

Prendergast, Christopher, *Paris in the Nineteenth Century* (Oxford, 1995).

Pugh, Simon (ed.), *Reading Landscape: Country–City–Capital* (Manchester, 1990).

Reed, Mark, *Wordsworth: The Chronology of the Early Years, 1787–1799* (Cambridge, MA, 1967).

Rennie, Neil, *Far-Fetched Facts* (Oxford, 1996).

Richetti, John (ed.), *The Cambridge History of English Literature, 1660–1780* (Cambridge, 2005).

Roberts, D., 'Literature, Medical Science and Politics, 1795–1800: *Lyrical Ballads* and Currie's *Works of Robert Burns*', in C. C. Barfoot (ed.), *'A Natural Delineation of the Passions': The Historical Moment of Lyrical Ballads* (Amsterdam, 2001), 115–28.

Robinson, Alan, *Imagining London, 1770–1900* (Basingstoke, 2004).

Roe, Nicholas, *Wordsworth and Coleridge: The Radical Years* (Oxford, 1988).

—— *John Keats and the Culture of Dissent* (Oxford, 1997).

—— 'Authenticating Burns', in Robert Crawford (ed.), *Robert Burns and Cultural Authority* (Edinburgh, 1997), 159–79.

—— *The Politics of Nature: William Wordsworth and Some Contemporaries* (Basingstoke, 2002).

—— *Fiery Heart: The First Life of Leigh Hunt* (London, 2005).

Rollins, Hyder, E., *The Keats Circle*, 2 vols. (Cambridge, MA, 1948).

Rose, Jonathan, *The Intellectual Life of the Working Classes* (New Haven and London, 2002).

Ruoff, Gene, *Wordsworth and Coleridge: The Making of the Major Lyrics 1802–1804* (London, 1989).

Rzepka, Charles, 'Pictures of the Mind: Iron and Charcoal, "Ouzy" Tides and "Vagrant Dwellers" at Tintern, 1798', *Studies in Romanticism*, 42 (2003), 155–86.

St Clair, William, *Lord Elgin and the Marbles*, 3rd edn. (Oxford, 1998).

—— *The Reading Nation in the Romantic Period* (Cambridge, 2004)

Samuel, Raphael, *Island Stories, Patriotism*, 2 vols. (London, 1996, 1998).

Schwarzbach, F. S., *Dickens and the City* (London, 1979).

Scott, Grant, F., *The Sculpted Word: Keats, Ekphrasis, and the Visual Arts* (Hanover and London, 1994).

Sekora, John, *Luxury: The Concept in Western Thought from Eden to Smollett* (Baltimore, 1977).

Smith, Anthony D., *Nationalism and Modernism* (London, 1998).

Smith, Bernard, *The European Vision and the South Pacific*, 2nd edn. (New Haven and London, 1985).

Smith, Olivia, *The Politics of Language 1791–1819* (Oxford, 1984).

Southam, Brian, *Jane Austen and the Navy* (London, 2000).

Sperry, Stuart, *Keats the Poet* (Princeton, 1973).

Stafford, Fiona, *The Sublime Savage* (Edinburgh, 1988).

—— *The Last of the Race* (Oxford, 1994).

—— *Starting Lines in Scottish, English and Irish Poetry* (Oxford, 2000).

—— 'Scottish Poetry and Regional Literary Expression', in John Richetti (ed.), *The Cambridge History of English Literature 1660–1780* (Cambridge, 2005), 340–62.

—— 'Inhabited Solitudes: Wordsworth in Scotland in 1803', in D. Duff and C. Jones (eds.), *Scotland, Ireland and the Romantic Aesthetic* (Lewisburg, 2007), 93–113.

Stafford, Fiona, 'Writing on the Borders', in Claire Lamont and Michael Ross-
ington (eds.), *Romanticism's Debatable Lands* (Basingstoke, 2005), 13–26.
—— ' "Plain Living and Ungarnish'd Stories":Wordsworth and the Survival
of Pastoral', *RES* NS59 (2008), 118–33.
Terry, Richard, *Poetry and the Making of the English Past* (Oxford, 2001).
Thomas, Keith, *Man and the Natural World* (Harmondsworth, 1984).
Thompson, T. W., *Wordsworth's Hawkshead*, ed. Robert Woof (London,
1970).
Toland, John, *The Life of Milton* (London, 1698).
Trezise, Simon, *The West Country as a Literary Invention* (Exeter, 2000).
Trumpener, Katie, *Bardic Nationalism: The Romantic Novel and the British
Empire* (Princeton, 1997).
Turner, J., *The Politics of Landscape* (Oxford, 1979).
Vendler, Helen, *The Odes of John Keats* (Cambridge, MA, and London,
1983).
—— *Seamus Heaney* (London, 1998).
Waldron, Mary, *Lactilla, Milkwoman of Clifton* (Athens, GA, and London,
1996).
Walker, Carol Kyros, *Walking North with Keats* (New Haven and London,
1992).
Wallace, David, *Premodern Places* (Oxford, 2004).
Waller, P. (ed.), *The English Urban Landscape* (Oxford, 2000).
Watson, George, 'From Hanover Street to the Garvaghey Road: Growing
Up in Portadown,' *Ideas*, 8/2 (2001), 24–35.
Watson, Nicola, *The Literary Tourist* (Basingstoke, 2007).
Weil, Simone, *The Need for Roots* (1949), trans. Arthur Wills (London,
2002).
Welsh, Alexander, *The City of Dickens* (Oxford, 1971).
Westfall, R., *Never at Rest: A Biography of Isaac Newton* (Cambridge, 1980).
Wilcox, Timothy, *Francis Towne* (London, 1997).
Williams, Raymond, *Border Country* (London, 1961).
—— *The Country and the City* (London, 1973).
—— *Politics and Letters* (London, 1979).
—— *People of the Black Mountains* (London, 1989).
Wilton, Andrew, *Turner Abroad* (London, 1982).
Whelan, Kevin, *The Tree of Liberty* (Cork, 1996).
Wittreich, Joseph (ed), *The Romantics on Milton* (Cleveland, OH, and
London, 1970).
Woof, Robert (ed.), *William Wordsworth: The Critical Heritage*, i. *1793–1820*
(London and New York, 2001).
Wu, Duncan, *Wordsworth's Reading*, 2 vols. (Oxford, 1993–5).
Youngson, A. J., *The Making of Classical Edinburgh 1750–1840* (Edinburgh,
1966).

Index